Screening the Mafia

Screening the Mafia

Masculinity, Ethnicity and Mobsters from *The Godfather* to *The Sopranos*

GEORGE S. LARKE-WALSH

McFarland & Company, Inc., Publishers

Jefferson, North Carolina, and London

LIBRARY OF CONGRESS CATALOGUING-IN-PUBLICATION DATA

Larke-Walsh, George S., 1965–
    Screening the mafia : masculinity, ethnicity and mobsters
from The Godfather to The Sopranos / by George S.
Larke-Walsh.
            p.   cm.
    Includes bibliographical references and index.

    ISBN 978-0-7864-4311-6
    softcover : 50# alkaline paper ∞

    1. Gangster films — United States — History and criticism.
2. Gangster television programs — United States — History and
criticism.   3. Mafia in motion pictures.   4. Masculinity in
motion pictures.   5. Ethnicity in motion pictures.   I. Title.
PN1995.9.G3L37   2010
791.43'655 — dc22   2010004215

British Library cataloguing data are available

Front cover: Paul Newman in *Road to Perdition*, 2002
(Dreamworks/Photofest)

Manufactured in the United States of America

McFarland & Company, Inc., Publishers
  Box 611, Jefferson, North Carolina 28640
  www.mcfarlandpub.com

Contents

Introduction

This book will explore gangster films from 1967, the year of *Bonnie and Clyde's* release, to the present day, focusing mainly on important films but also including the HBO TV series *The Sopranos* (1999–2007). The task may appear enormous, but the motivation for covering such an extensive period is to track trends and developments rather than focus on just one particular film, style or decade. Trends and developments in the gangster films of the classical era have received considerable critical attention, while more recent films have received less. These recent films merit close study, first for the ways in which they differ from those of the classical era, and second, and more specifically, for the ways in which they articulate a number of key concerns of recent decades. These concerns center on the relationship between masculinity and ethnicity, constituted especially through a developing mythology of the Mafia. I have marked my starting point as 1967, but it is more appropriately the release of Francis Ford Coppola's adaptation of Mario Puzo's *The Godfather* (1972) that heralded a new era in gangsters on film. This film has done more to influence the concept of the Mafia as it appears in modern American popular culture than any other. Consequently, *The Godfather* remains at the center of this book and influences all its analyses.

I have witnessed a tendency in academic writing to favor classical gangster films and the post-war noir films as they provide such a rich area of study. In many ways I agree with this view, but I believe that the postclassical films are worthy too. What causes friction in academic study is perhaps the fact that the later films are connected so much to popular culture and excessive violence. In other words, they are mentioned mainly as popular rather than critically acclaimed films (although of course the originals were popular and violent in their time and that was one cause of their demise). Furthermore, my chosen era of study is not as clearly defined as the classical period, which

1

can make it appear less dramatic. There are many inconsistencies in the ways films are marketed, reviewed and received. Therefore, it will be my task to impose some order onto the era so that we can identify patterns and tendencies. It is also my task to investigate this modern era of American filmmaking as one that has displayed an intense fascination with the Mafia. Therefore, the extra textual influences of such a fascination will be a significant part of my discussions.

The questions raised in this book can be summarized as follows: How did the gangster genre develop after 1967 and specifically from *The Godfather* to *The Sopranos*? How useful is it to regard such films as constituting a specific genre? In what ways do these films construct notions of masculinity and ethnicity through their articulation of Mafia myths, and how do these notions function within the films? Studies have already explored the films as white male fantasies and critiques of late capitalism; my study tracks the development of such charges and considers what readings these gangster films have generated and what points of tension can be discerned within these readings. My central argument is that gangster films of this period have been marketed and popularly accepted as a reflection of real Mafia activity in America. This association means that each film operates within that larger discussion and in the context of its place within genre — not just in its aesthetics or narrative structure, but it in its attention to Mafia activity. In short, since the 1960s gangster films have influenced popular perceptions of Mafia activity in America as much as, if not more than, any other social or political discourse. Therefore, the films are much more than just violent entertainment: they can be viewed as a continuous text that perpetuates Mafia mythologies. *The Godfather* has come to define, not only the genre, but also the mythology of the Mafia. I want to track that development from genre film to legend and assess the continued importance of mythologies at the intersection of popular culture and history.

While my analyses focus mainly on Hollywood films, it is obvious that the HBO series *The Sopranos* will be a prominent feature as well. In fact, while the last 40 years has been an exciting era for the gangster film, *The Sopranos* raises a further question: Has TV killed the gangster film? Reading the reviews, web forums and critical studies of *The Sopranos*, it has surprised me how much cultural discourse has shifted over the past 40 years. Now *The Godfather*, which originally received mixed reviews, is treated with reverence, and while the mythology of the Mafia should have been completely undermined by high-profile court cases and exposés of organizations and events, it remains as steady in mainstream popular culture as ever. The main difference between *The Sopranos* and the other examples in my discussion is that it is set in the present and not the past. It also, in my opinion, changed its character over the course of each series. What began as an intelligent parody of Mafia mythologies developed into a dark vision of mainstream male prejudices and desire. While the series has often been attacked for its defamatory presentation of Italian ethnicity, it has not been called to task about its vision of American masculine identities. It is suggested as a comment upon "social class, upward mobility, and all-American assimilation" (Caryn James, *The New York Times*, April 12, 2000), but as such it offers some pretty damning observations. Therefore, while *The Sopranos* is a crucial text in the study of the Mafia in popular culture, it will have to be approached differently than the films. I will focus on particular storylines and audience reactions (through internet forums) to discuss how the series fits into the larger discussion of gangster films and Mafia myths.

One of the primary differences between modern gangster films and the 1930s originals is the focus on groups rather than individuals. Gangster films of the classical era have been summarized as focusing on lone individuals (Warshow, 1948) within contemporary urban settings (McArthur, 1972). Some of the defining aspects of more recent gangster films are that they are often set in the past and express notions of the Mafia as an identifiable and traceable organization. Consequently, the issues I am concerned with will include the articulation of collective identities and how the positioning of narratives in the past allows for a romanticized and distanced view of events. Other issues coincide, such as how films represent family and ethnic traditions. *The Sopranos* is very different than *The Godfather*; in fact, it can be suggested as the biggest "debunking" of the Mafia mythology found in the films focused on in this book. However, contrary to some of the scholarly work on *The Sopranos* series, I will argue that the TV series operates within the same parameters as the films and only appears to mock them. Many of the themes found in the films and in *The Sopranos* are interconnected, and the mythology of the Mafia remains constant through each text. My overarching aim is to identify the ways such features are represented by tracing the ways in which the genre has shifted in response to cultural changes; this includes the Mafia myths that form the substructure of these films and the shifting conceptions of masculinity and ethnicity that have informed such changes.

Before proceeding, I feel it necessary to provide a brief explanation of the time period I am studying and a short theory and history lesson to contextualize the gangster image in earlier popular film. While *The Sopranos* dominates the millennium period, the films it draws upon are from very particular moments in cinema history. A reason for explaining the time period stems from the fact that American film history between the mid-sixties and the mid-seventies was an era of great changes, therefore an understanding of how I interpret those changes will help to illustrate my approach to the corresponding films. The term "postclassical" is worth a moment of discussion. Heavily value-laden, it has been a highly contested term. In brief, changes in the production and consumption trends of Hollywood films since the sixties have led to the general use of the term "postclassical" to differentiate post–1950s films from those of the earlier period. Postclassical cinema is a category associated with aesthetic and economic developments in film since 1948,[1] but has also been said specifically to allude to films of the 1967–1975 period, when the proliferation of independent filmmaking appeared to allow for more freedom in the range and treatment of themes and form.[2] Postclassical, as a category, has emerged from the suggestion that the structure of both film texts and the cinema industry has changed to a sufficient extent that it could be distinguished from the classical era. These changes can be traced from both a production point of view, through the falling away from a "pure" studio system and through textual shifts, towards looser or more hybrid generic forms. The corresponding trend to distinguish such cultural changes with the prefix "post," as for example with the term post-modernism, means that postclassical has emerged to represent the changes in cinema after, but in relation to, the classical era.[3]

To avoid complicating the issue further, but recognizing that a label is useful for referencing the distinction between now and then in film production, I shall use the term postclassical to identify trends in Hollywood filmmaking after 1967. However, the term has less currency in relation to later films, and so I will also use the term post–*Godfather*. The reason for this is because I feel that while *The Godfather* is an example of postclassical filmmaking, all subsequent gangster films are defined by their relation to *The Godfather* as much as if not more than in their relation to classical films. In short, I wish to demonstrate how the films of the last 40 years present coherences reminiscent of a "continuous text" that draws upon the classical period, but is mainly influenced by *The Godfather*. I have chosen 1967 as the start date for two reasons: firstly because it is the year *Bonnie and Clyde* was released and so offers a convenient starting point for discussions on the re-emergence of the gangster film, and secondly because it coincides with the date censorship finally evolved into a ratings system (1968). The decline of the Production Code during the 1950s and 1960s gradually freed filmmakers from aiming their products to all age groups simultaneously. It was now possible to differentiate products to target various audiences. Thus, family entertainment became separated from films aimed at teenagers and young adults. Violence and sex became more explicit because of the R (Restricted to over 16, later 17 years of age) and X (adult only, graphic content) ratings. This made it far easier for audiences to identify films that might suit them, and for studios to successfully market and distribute their films. This development is significant for the gangster film in that it allowed criminals back to the emotional center of the narrative, especially in the "Restricted" ratings. Consequently, this period of Hollywood history is a significant turning point in the development of the gangster film. Postclassical gangster films are representative of their era(s), in that they display some of the changes in production, structure and reception reflected in films of the period, especially with regard to genre.

As background to my analysis it is useful to note that recent studies of the gangster film in the classical era (Ruth, 1996; Munby, 1999)[4] and *The Sopranos* in the new millennium (Lavery, 2002 & 2006; Barreca, 2002) have shifted their attention from the product as text to the production and reception of cinema, TV and its cultural products. They no longer attempt to isolate meaning within a single component, such as the text or the director; they consider the intertextual, contradictory, yet mutually informing plethora of concerns cohabiting in cinema and TV as entertainment but also as industry. It is no longer sufficient to talk about the meaning of a film text, as if it were an autonomous construct, separate from commercial concerns or audiences' responses. However, attempting to consider all these can be a contradictory task. Commercial influences, such as marketing and distribution, often do not align with the director's view or that of the audiences. Therefore, such analyses can often be irresolute in their findings. Having said this, I do find myself in line with these recent developments, in that I do not intend to isolate singular meanings within postclassical gangster films, but to examine a variety of possibilities. In this sense, my approach is similar to that proposed by Christine Gledhill in her "Pleasurable Negotiations" (1988). She states,

> As a model of meaning production, negotiation conceives cultural exchange as the intersection of processes of production and reception, in which overlapping but non-matching determinations operate. Meaning is neither imposed, nor passively imbibed, but arises out of a struggle or negotiation between competing frames of reference, motivation and experience. This can be analysed at three different levels: institutions, texts and audiences — although distinctions between levels are ones of emphasis, rather than of rigid separation [169].

I will seek to trace the negotiation of meanings in postclassical gangster films, and I agree with Gledhill when she says, "While the majority of cultural products are polysemic, they are not open to any and every interpretation" (174). The usefulness of Gledhill's article to my study is that it recognizes the fact that texts can be read differently by different audiences, but that various patterns, or conventions, can still be traced within those texts. I will trace the conventions of postclassical gangster films, without claiming them as fixed or stable, by concentrating on narrative, genre and particular themes.

Discussions will address issues that constitute what Gledhill terms "the *conditions and possibilities of reading* [emphasis in original]" (174), by tracing the forms and some of the responses to postclassical gangster films in the chosen period of cinema history. Extra-textual influences, such as cultural discourses of Mafia myths, reviews and web forums, plus discourses of ethnicity and masculinity, can offer a traceable web of meanings surrounding gangster films. Narrative themes encourage different readings that are evidenced in reviews and other critical writings on the films, and thus enter the ever-increasing circulation of meaning. The intention is to trace some of these in order to provide an analysis of postclassical gangster films that is not conclusive, but will provide substantive solutions to the questions about the functions and forms of such a popular genre. I hope to answer or at least provide clues as to why *The Sopranos* is so popular and how it has possibly given the impression of "closing the door" on Mafia mythology.

*　　*　　*

Before I begin to discuss the last 40 years, I first want to look back at the classical gangster film. As my study builds upon work that has already been produced on the gangster in popular culture, I think it's appropriate to provide a brief overview of some of the articulations and functions of the gangster image in early twentieth-century American culture. This provides the cultural landscape from which postclassical gangster films have developed and so reveals the historical and theoretical context from which my own study has grown.

The Gangster in Early Twentieth-Century American Culture

The early 1920s had seen an explosion of crime in urban areas of America, resulting in debates similar to those that would occur in the fifties. The causes of crime and the resulting moral dilemmas were discussed in political and law enforcement domains and most importantly filtered through news reportage and entertainment media. D.E. Ruth, in his analysis of the cultural invention of the gangster, notes "This discussion [...] concerned much more than the causes of lawbreaking, for participants used the issue of criminality to grapple with some of the most troubling cultural dilemmas of their time" (Ruth, 1996: 11). However, the debate was *not* about the existence of a nationwide organized crime syndicate called the Mafia. The discussion was about the gangster, whom later critics accused of instigating organized crime in America, but who was initially identified as simply one who is a member of an organised gang of criminals. This term had evolved from the criminal gangs who had been operating in America's cities and had thus been part of literature, news and political debate since the early nineteenth century. These gangs had mostly operated within the confines of particularly poor districts, such as New York's Lower East Side, the Bowery, or Hell's Kitchen. Even though all these areas had high immigrant populations, gangsters were of a very mixed descent. They included Irish, Jewish, or other mainly European nationalities, and gangs tended to remain within their own neighborhoods.[5]

Many social and economic factors could be held responsible for the expansion of "gang-related" crime in America in the 1920s. The most obvious is the onset of prohibition: the period between 1920 and 1933 when the manufacture, sale and transportation of intoxicating liquors were banned in the U.S. This would partially explain why gangs became more prominent outside of the ghettos. The manufacture and distribution of illicit liquor was a lucrative business and thus made some gang members extremely rich. Meyer Lansky, Charles "Lucky" Luciano and Frank Costello in New York, and of course Al Capone in Chicago, all made their money during prohibition. Crime became far more visible, to the extent that by the end of the decade a journalist noted that whereas in the past, "All big cities had their underworld zones and underworld joints [...] the new underworld is here, there, everywhere" (Grey, 1929 cited in Ruth: 28).

Another valuable source of income for the gangster was the illegal numbers, or policy racket, also known as the Italian Lottery. Such enterprises demanded organization, but were extremely lucrative. Participants bet on a specific "previously agreed tabulation, such as the final digits of the United States Treasury cash balance" (Ianni: 93). Gambling rarely produced much widespread indignation from politicians or the public, as it was viewed as a relatively harmless vice. Consequently, it spread easily from its neighborhood origins to many city districts.[6]

The wealth gangsters accumulated bought political influence and immunity from prosecution. In Chicago newspapers from the mid-twenties onwards, a campaign against corruption and the public apathy that allowed such practices featured prominently in editorials: "Gangsters were no longer mere outlaws but 'superlaws,' unaccountable for their crimes. While other less-dangerous criminals were executed, gangsters were protected" (McDonough, 1989: 17). Some editorials were fairly precise in attributing blame for this corruption: "They escape by political arrangements, by jury bribing, by pardons, and by other means" (*Chicago Tribune*, 1924 cited in McDonough: 18). Thus, gangsters became some of the most powerful forces in urban areas. They provided illicit liquor and gambling to a complicit, if not openly accepting, market, and protected their interests by paying off corrupt local law enforcers and politicians: "The *Tribune* agreed that the alliance with crooked politicians allowed gangsters immunity, but it was the vast profits from bootlegging that gave organized crime the money to effect that alliance" (McDonough, 1989: 23). They were businessmen as much as criminals, and provided services that, due to unpopular laws, could not be provided by legitimate means.

Associations between business and crime dominate American cultural history. The spirit of free enterprise, depending on how it is interpreted, can be used to defend all kinds of business practices, especially from the point of view that success works to legitimate the means of achieving that success. Daniel Bell's seminal work, *Crime as an American Way of Life: The Queer Ladder of Social Mobility* (1953) asserts crime to be one of "the queer ladders of social mobility" in that success brings money, money pays politicians, and politicians defend their financial backers. Organized crime in the 1940s, according to Bell, attempted to legitimize itself and its connections with law enforcement by suggesting itself as protection against smaller, more vicious bands of criminals: "When the gambling raids started in Chicago the 'combine' protested that, in upsetting existing stable relations, the police were only opening the way for ambitious young punks and hoodlums to start trouble" (Bell, 1953: 130). This hierarchy of criminals could not have occurred if the original racketeers had not had lucrative business opportunities available to them in earlier decades.

According to Bell, it was successive government obsessions with excessively moral laws against liquor and gambling that allowed criminal gangs to achieve wealth and status. Duncan Webster (1988) also asserts a similarity between enterprise, crime and American identity in his discussions of various American literary works.[7] He posits the notion that business opportunities are akin to the perfect crime: "If they don't take the chance they are found guilty of being both unmanly and un–American" (Webster: 142). Therefore, borders between business and crime are often blurred in American ideologies. As Bell states, "The distinction between the 'good guys' and the 'bad guys,' so deep at the root of the reform impulse, bears little relation to the role of organized crime in American society" (Bell: 127). This blurred division between criminality and business, or identifiably good or bad guys in organized crime and ordinary society, is another aspect of criminal hierarchies that I will explore in more detail in my discussions of postclassical films. The comparison is useful in that the gangsters portrayed in the 1930s cycle of films were operating at the beginning of these enterprises and were therefore still at the bottom of the "queer ladder." The post-war gangster films, however, concentrated on their more business-like successors. The notion of a hierarchy of criminals, plus a business-like structure, as a means for organized crime to legitimize its existence and its operations, is one that influences many post-war fictional gangster narratives.

Aggressive capitalism is often regarded as another reason behind the growth of the gangster in American society. Frank Pearce observes big business in relation to the development of American social, political and economic structure in the early twentieth century. He notes that many business ideals are obsessed with controlling the market at all costs. He emphasizes the fact that "the capitalist is committed to profit and growth" (Pearce, 1973: 20). When his study sets out some of the capitalist's ideals, such as controlling competition, prices and consumers, dominating labor and effectively influencing the government (*ibid.*), it is easy to see the connection with gangster activity. Bootlegging and numbers rackets operate as capitalist enterprises. Gangsters guarantee their market by intimidating all competition. This controls both prices and customers, because they have no choices. In addition, the nature of the gangster business is in opposition to government legislature, but as stated earlier, it provides services that are not available by other means. The political climate and economy of the early twentieth century encouraged opportunism, but moralistic legislature made business and criminality close allies. Big business and the gangster rose together as products of the same ideals, in that they both operated on a purely self-centered profit-orientated basis, while the government struggled to decide just how much consumer freedom their citizens should have. Later analyses have also suggested this as a link to Sicilian Mafia styles and ideals (Albini, 1971; Cressey, 1969).[8] Albini considers the origins of the Mafia as a purely mercenary construct of patrons over various clients. These clients originally included the absentee landlords of estates in nineteenth century Sicily, plus bandits and peasants of the estates. The Mafia operated as a mediating force between all-out rebellion from the bandits and peasants and feudal dominance from the landlords. In essence, just as in America, the Mafia provided a much-needed service between two opposing forces. Crucially though, as in America, this arrangement ultimately profited the Mafia more than its clients.

The dilemma for politicians, law enforcers and the media was how to categorize this new phenomenon and therefore make sense of its arrival. The fact that "many Americans came to believe that rampant crime was a defining element of their society" (Ruth: 1) meant that specific reasons and solutions had to be found in order for ordinary, responsible Americans to feel physically and morally secure in urban areas. To this end, the figure of the gangster was constructed in factual and fictional mediums as both a product of American urban societies and yet somehow different from the responsible American. The gangster came to epitomize the wealthy opportunism and spirit of the modern age, while also shouldering the blame for all the corruption and debauchery with which this new wealth was often associated. Therefore, the specific origin of the gangster was not so important, as long as it was made clear that gangsters were different from "real" Americans. As

Ruth notes, the gangster was often displayed as a product of modern consumerism:

> As they dressed the criminal in fine clothing, adorned him with jewellery, and placed him in a luxurious nightclub, writers, filmmakers, and their audiences explored the abundance of goods that had transformed their society. Through the gangster image Americans previewed new paths to individual fulfilment apparently opened by a mass-consumption economy. At the same time they pondered how the new standards of consumerism affected older categories of social order, especially class and ethnicity. These were crucial cultural concerns, and the gangster offered not just illumination but guidance as well. The inventors of the public enemy used him to promote values about the urban consumer society he epitomized [Ruth: 64].

Ruth argues that the public became fascinated with the gangster from his very first appearance. He believes that this image of the gangster helped make America's newly prosperous and increasingly commodity-driven culture less frightening to the ordinary citizen. The gangster epitomized individual wealth and style through the accumulation of material goods. This, according to Ruth, provided Americans with a new sense of place and identity: as a consumer, rather than as a self-sufficient producer. Such a concern with appearance and consumption is something I will address in discussions of the post-classical gangster as a generic icon and an embodiment of a particular type of masculinity. Costume as a signifier of power, virility and belonging, as well as affluence, is an important feature of gangster films. It not only represents (and sometimes exaggerates) the wealth of American culture in a particular period, but also provides clues to an individual's credibility as a gangster type within genre conventions and Mafia myths, which are also partially dependent on ethnicity and corresponding masculine ideals.

Ruth's analysis suggests quite a positive use of the gangster image in American culture. The gangster novel and film as a popular format did not really emerge until the late twenties and thirties. This coincided with the end of prohibition and the beginning of the Depression era. Therefore, if we accept Ruth's assertion that the gangster epitomized commodity-driven culture, the expensively tailored gangster of Hollywood fame was providing its audience with an image that was increasingly out of their own grasp. This has significant implications for the gangster's appeal. Either, as Thomas Pauly suggests in his review of Ruth's book, "This well dressed gangster was more of a challenge to the operative assumptions of the era's commercial culture than Ruth allows" (Pauly, 1997: 781), or, as Smith (1975) states, he represents an outlaw hero of the depression era by actively and visually contradicting ordinary experience — which now consisted mainly of unemployment and general lack. The audience may have enjoyed witnessing examples of individual wealth and the accumulation of material goods, but this success could not be said to mirror most audiences' experiences in the early thirties. Jonathan Munby's analysis of *Little Caesar* argues that the immigrant experience especially, in America at this time involved

> alienation from both roots in the old world and the projected future in the new. *Little Caesar*, as an urban production coming in the wake of the Crash and designed for metropolitan audiences plugged straight into this realm of contradiction. The question it raised on behalf of the disenfranchised was "Why haven't we been granted access to power?" Rico plays out the role of the entrepreneur but is condemned to do so from the wrong side of the tracks [Munby, 1999: 50].

It is more appropriate to say that these gangster images were approached with the usual contradictory impulses, which is reminiscent of Robert Warshow's view of the gangster as a character who "appeals to that side of all of us which refuses to believe in the 'normal' possibilities of happiness and achievement" (Warshow, 1954: 454). The gangster could be said to epitomise individual enterprise, but also the corruption often involved in such ambitions. He could also be said to epitomize, through his eventual demise, the fragility of such affluence. Produced at a time when the early twentieth-century boom in industry was rapidly turning into bust, the gangster could be said to show the frailty of individual enterprise in the face of a fluctuating economy. Add to this his immigrant identity and the gangster is revealed as symptomatic of the social and economic barriers between *his kind* and the ideal of American identity.

What seems apparent is that by the time the gangster became a prominent figure in literature and film during the 1930s his ambition and consumer style was noted for its aggressive vulgarity rather than wealth and opportunism. This image of the gangster concentrated on his "otherness": his difference from ordinary, responsible Americans. While Munby argues that *Little Caesar* is a "critique of the corrosive features of modern capitalist society and its (lack of) social mores" (46), it is apparent that the gangster is the locus of such critiques. From his very inception, the American gangster in fact and fiction was positioned to simultaneously promote the consumer economy, aggressive capitalism and the pursuit of individual wealth, while also operating as a scapegoat for all the corrupt ideals these activities encouraged. Could it be argued that *The Sopranos* represents a conversation that has come full circle? It is certainly feasible to say that Tony Soprano for all his suburban attributes has more connection with Rico Bandello (*Little Caesar*) than any of the Corleones. Therefore, it could also be argued that the TV series offers the same critiques and scapegoats.

Fictional crime of the early twentieth century inevitably echoed the news stories of the time. The fictional gangster is said to have been born in novels such as D.H. Clarke's *Louis Beretti* (1929) and W.R. Burnett's *Little Caesar* (1929).[9] However, his image had been circulating in theater plays, newspapers, cartoons and comics for most of the early twentieth century.[10] The essential difference between the "ordinary" criminal and the gangster, noted earlier in Bell's description of the "queer ladder of social mobility," appeared to be the element of ambition. Prohibition offered an opportunity for the criminal to advance in society. Stealing was no longer simply a means of self-sufficiency, but an avenue to wealth, power and respect. Thus, as Ruth has previously noted, the narratives echoed the concerns of ordinary Americans in urban areas who could no longer simply work for themselves, but were encouraged to look to the acquisition of material goods for a sense of achievement. Clarke's hero, Louis Beretti, was a bootlegger, and "everyone who knew Louis treated him with the respect due a human being who could make his way in a tough environment" (Clarke, cited in Smith, 1975: 92). Burnett's gangster was Rico Bandello, "brave, shrewd, ambitious, impatient, and on occasion, short tempered" (Smith: 92). Bandello went on to become one archetypal image of the fictional gangster with the help of Edward G. Robinson's portrayal of him in Mervyn LeRoy's 1930 film, *Little Caesar*. However, the two were similar images. They were both products of their society, had material ambitions and lacked any introspective tendencies or family loyalties. The story of Tony Soprano of course is hinged on his attempts at introspection (as a result of debilitating anxiety attacks). This is what makes him a perfect parody of the early gangster archetype. He is a Rico Bandello with an unwelcome conscience.

For Smith, the fictional gangster was a depression-era hero, just as the cowboy was a hero of the frontier. This echoes Colin McArthur's (1972) view that the Western and gangster film "have a special relationship with American society. ... It could be said that they represent America talking to itself about, in the case of the Western, its agrarian past, and in the case of the gangster film/thriller, its urban technological present" (McArthur, 1972: 18). However, Smith also states that the popular fictional gangster was much more of an outlaw figure than a businessman: "They were not highly organized persons; they had instincts toward leadership and could therefore direct other men, but they did not operate from the safety of an organization and were not occupied in creating a structure that would survive them" (Smith: 98). This is an important distinction between the gangsters of the 1930s and the more business-like gangsters of the 1950s and beyond. I shall argue that the popular image of gangsters in the postclassical era focuses on their actions as part of a wider organization, or on-going business. For this reason, gangster films after the 1950s concentrate on the activities of the Mafia, rather than on gangsters as individuals. The gangster as businessman, according to Smith, arrives in the thirties in the detective thrillers of such writers as Dashiell Hammett and Raymond Chandler. None are "heroes"; all are secondary characters, "shadowy figures who participate only indirectly in the main action" (*ibid*: 99) and thus do not provide the same pleasures to the reader. These pleasures for the public are described as "a mirror of its own expectations" (*ibid*: 105). The public tended to reject images created from in-depth research and an attention to factual detail. According to Smith, the success of Burnett's book was a result of the fact that "he captured in vivid style a generally held public image of the Chicago gangster" (*ibid.*). Burnett, not a resident of the Chicago he writes about, claimed his book was influenced by the news, a police reporter he knew and a young Italian American he met who claimed mob connections. To accept this would be to suggest that archetypal fictional gangsters of this era were built upon a complex set of assumptions, hearsay and prejudices derived from newspapers, police reports and gossip. To a large extent this could be said to summarize the original gangster myths, which had evolved into Mafia myths by the 1950s.

In the 1930s, then, aggressive capitalism was regarded as inviting corruption and crime, while also providing prosperity for the American individual. The gangster was identified by law enforcement agencies as a primary beneficiary of this development — and thus given the label "public enemy," However, in fiction, even in the depression era, the American public appeared to be fascinated with the gangster. The fictional gangster epitomized the image of the traditional outlaw as much as a public enemy. Consequently, the attempt to alert the public to an enemy at large was diluted by the display of freedom and individual expression the gangster image provided. Hence, the Hollywood image of the gangster contradicts the true accounts, because it was the recognizable stereotypes that appeared to engage popular attention. Munby suggests that censorship of the gangster film developed from "the need to enforce a consensus on what is decent and compatible with some ruling definition of Americanness" (90). The Production Code, which essentially hampered or diverted the production of gangster films into other areas (such as outlaws, G-men and backroom syndicates,[11] from 1934 to the mid-sixties) was a significant extra-textual factor for the classical era. As stated earlier, it is crucial to an understanding of the postclassical gangster to emphasize the fact that *Bonnie and Clyde* also marks the decline of the Code. In one sense it marks a return to the environment that delivered *Little Caesar*, *Scarface* and *Public Enemy*, by allowing the gangster to return to center stage. However, thirty years had changed both the environment and the gangster, so that the films that I shall explore not only reference earlier ones, but reflect the developments in American culture and the film industry since that time.

* * *

We can see how the image of the gangster has always been prevalent and influential in American crime narratives. Since the relaxation of the

Production Code in favor of a commercial ratings system, the gangster has experienced a significant rebirth. My study tracks that rebirth and its function in late twentieth century American culture. Each chapter of this book will discuss the era as a whole. This is necessary, because it is the underlining premise of my study that all the films interconnect. Therefore, while I can track trends and developments, I cannot completely isolate one period from another.

Chapter 1 provides an overview of gangster films produced in Hollywood between 1967 and 2007. It begins in 1967 because that is the year in which *Bonnie and Clyde* was released and that marks the beginning of the era I have chosen to identify as postclassical. It should be noted that there are some films before this date that display aesthetic elements or themes that foreshadow later films, but for the purposes of providing a boundary, they will not be included fully within the discussions. The purpose of the overview is to provide a map of an expansive era of filmmaking. In order to do this, it is my intention to split the films into thematic categories and suggest the existence of production cycles. The categories are as follows: gangsters as outlaws, gangsters as Mafia or ongoing businesses, and gangsters as gangs or "wannabes." The term "wannabes" is used to suggest gangs that are on the fringes of or completely separate from the Mafia, but either consciously or unconsciously display similarities to the Mafia. This is not meant to suggest a typological approach to gangster films, because these categories are merely suggestive of trends, rather than fixed or complete definitions of what is or is not part of the gangster genre. They are being used simply to divide a very large collection of films into manageable groupings. This will make later discussions more coherent, for instance, one aspect of later analyses will be a focus on the Mafia ideal. This is traced mainly through the films identified in Chapter 1 as gangsters as Mafia, and is used to show how gangsters as gangs operate as "wannabes."

Secondly, I shall suggest the existence of production cycles during this era. These cycles bear a strong resemblance to the structure of genre cycles detailed by Thomas Schatz (1977) and John Cawelti (1978). However, their analyses suggested identifiable beginnings and endings to a particular genre through the expression of particular textual conventions. I am not attempting to do the same. The purpose of identifying cycles is to show how successful films influence later production and to show how cycles tend to begin with a critical and box office success and end with parodies. Again, these cycles are not fixed or complete, but do provide a map of the era that facilitates analysis. While contemporary scholarly work denigrates the use of genre cycles as old-fashioned, I note that many writings on the gangster film or TV series suggest such trends exist without explicitly saying so. It is fairly obvious that trends occur and so I will use them again to split the 40 years of production into more manageable pieces.

Chapter 2, "Theorizing the Gangster Genre," will address the issues of production cycles, aesthetic and thematic similarities through an analysis of how the gangster film has been theorized as a genre. The importance of genre in Hollywood cinema has not diminished since the decline of the studio system. It has remained part of the marketing strategy of producers and a guiding category for audiences and critics alike. However, the ever-present hybridity or interpenetration of genre categories means that deciding the genre to which a film belongs has become a complex matter, and also depends on why such classification is to be employed: as a marketing tool, for purposes of academic analysis, or to make a viewing decision. Genre is still the mainstay of discussions on the aesthetics of film,[12] but like narrative and other elements of film style, it is as much influenced by commercial factors as artistic ones. The intention is to trace some of the elements that inform genre, taking into consideration some textual and extra-textual considerations, including ways in which films have been categorized in reviews. This allows for postclassical gangster films to be afforded the same level of consideration as films of the classical era, but it is not my intention to replicate earlier approaches. This chapter will argue that to analyze effectively the uses of genre in postclassical cinema it is necessary to assess the context in which it operates as a marker: marketing, academia, reviews, etc. Only then can genre be effectively placed within the cultural discourses that surround a film. One issue raised within this chapter is the notion of genre as a continuous text (Leutrat, 1973). I will conclude that, while the structure and themes of gangster films are fluid, there remains a sense of intertextuality through which individual films refer to previous examples and to surrounding cultural discourses. These issues, combined with the question of why the gangster film re-emerges at the time it does and what the function of the genre might be, provide the framework for the discussion of Mafia myths in Chapter 3.

In the films I have chosen to study, I wish to foreground the connections between gangster characters and the Mafia. Therefore, Chapter 3 will address the development of Mafia myths in twentieth-century American culture. Developments of Mafia myths since the fifties, in cultural discourses such as journalism, political legislation and fiction, have focused on organized crime as an inter-connecting network. The corresponding increase in biographies and testimonies has encouraged a sense of collective history in gangster films that is more pronounced than in earlier films. This is not to say that previous gangster narratives lacked any sense of history, but this element is more pronounced in films after 1967. I will explore gangster films as articulations of Mafia myths, as well as examples of a fictional genre. One of the primary assertions is that postclassical gangster films do not simply refer to previous films. They draw upon many extra-textual influences that surround the production and consumption of film. Myth allows for the films to be read in different ways. The ever-shifting reference points and criteria by which Mafia activity is represented through myths allows for the Mafia group to be both romanticized and condemned without recourse to fact. This chapter will suggest that one of the functions of Mafia myths, with regard to cinema, is to articulate the complexity of modern American identities whose reference points are increasingly shown to be fluid and unstable.

A topic that informs all the discussions in this book is the reason the gangster film re-emerges in the late sixties. The influences of changes in film production due to the relaxation of censorship and the introduction of a ratings system has already been noted. The corresponding development in structural and thematic emphases pertaining to genre will be addressed in Chapter 2. In Chapter 3 it will be suggested that myths provide answers for cultural anxieties that have developed since the sixties. These cultural anxieties can be summarized in general as the crises in American masculine identity, brought about by such issues as the Vietnam war, civil rights movements, the "second wave" of feminism, and increasing distrust of government bodies.[13] I do not attempt to trace any specific discourses between these sociological and political issues and the structural and thematic construction of postclassical gangster films. However, events such as the Senate hearings[14] on the existence of the Mafia in the United States during the fifties and sixties did have an indirect influence on the content of later gangster films, because of the cultural myths that surrounded these events, as well as others.

*   *   *

America's involvement in a war usually encourages a sense of national unity. However, the involvement in the Vietnam war also revealed some of the underlying tensions in American society. These included gender and racial inequalities in society in general, and an increasing gap between big business and central government on the one side and the ordinary citizen on the other. The emergence of films about the Mafia reflects these issues in various ways: The Mafia as a criminal organization can be seen to operate in similar ways to big business and central government. Indeed, the Mafia can be blamed for the corruption prevalent in modern business and government departments. Conversely, the Mafia, as an organization that operates outside of the law, can be seen as offering an attractive alternative to the institutions of big business and central government. Therefore, the Mafia can be viewed as the reason for, a metaphor of, or an alternative to some of the political and sociological problems of American urban society in the sixties and beyond. These particular issues will be discussed in chapters 3 and 4.

The women's movement and civil rights protests of the sixties have had a profound effect on cultural debates surrounding gender and ethnic identity. These debates are also reflected in postclassical gangster films and will be discussed in Chapter 4. For instance, masculinity has developed as a topic for critical debate since the sixties, along with and in relation to femininity. Gangster films, with their tendency to focus on exclusively male environments, provide interesting popular culture case studies for such debates. Furthermore, the aftermath of the Civil Rights protests encouraged a great deal of critical interest in the representation of race in popular culture. The foregrounding of Italian ethnicity, which is fundamental to Mafia myths, is also prevalent in postclassical gangster films.

I am not suggesting that the gangster genre re-emerged in the late sixties as a *direct result* of the factors detailed above, but it is evident that these factors can be identified as *significant influences* on the emergence, structure, and themes, of postclassical gangster films. We can, for example, point to the political influence of the government's focus on organized criminal activity in America during the fifties and sixties. There are also contradictory desires evident in earlier gangster images in popular culture that are replayed by positioning the Mafia as both anti-heroes (for example, anti-establishment, anti-war) and also as the focus of blame for the increasing crises in American identity (for example in masculinity and ethnicity) and rising crime in the sixties. Postclassical gangster narratives, through their perpetuation of Mafia myths, reflect these political and cultural influences, while also providing a scapegoat for them. The discussion of Mafia myths will show how the primary reference points for gangster films are not purely filmic. This will lead into the final chapter through the view that Mafia myths also reflect crises in American identity, especially with regard to masculinity and ethnicity. Crises in masculine identity are inextricably linked with crises in American identity. This subject is well-served by Mafia narratives, because, as stated, they offer exclusive male environments and thus offer an ideal arena for playing out masculine fantasies and anxieties.

* * *

I shall suggest in the final chapter that gangsters articulate both non-homogenous and dominant white American identity. Furthermore, they display both a collective and an exclusive masculine identity. This chapter will discuss the impact of shifts in cultural discourses (relating to film) that focus on the construction of gender and ethnic identity. The intention is to examine some of the theoretical developments surrounding these topics, in conjunction with analyses of film gangsters, to show how cultural discourses influence cinema and vice versa. Masculinity and ethnicity have been chosen because they have always been common features in gangster narratives. Ever since Robert Warshow described the gangster's purpose as "an effort to assert himself as an individual" (Warshow, 1946: 88), then pinpointed this individuality as a cause of his death, theorists have been fascinated with the gangster as "a powerful individual" (Cawelti, 1978: 508). However, whereas these theorists focus on a lone individual in the world of crime, the later films lay more emphasis on groups of men.[15] It is my intention to show how postclassical gangster films articulate discourses of masculinity as collective identities. The emphasis in the films on family organisations, or shared cultural heritages (part of Mafia myths), articulates masculinity as complex identifications based on the interactions between a group of men. Films of this era are interested in the relationships between men as much as, if not more than, between men and women. The criminal group acts as an environment in which characters are nurtured, tested and constantly reassessed in relation to each other. This constant reassessment provides one of the reasons behind my view that postclassical gangster films articulate masculinity in contradictory ways. In summary, this chapter will show how the films reflect these different aspects of masculine gender personalities and how this can encourage contradictory readings of the films.

In conjunction with the discussion of masculinity, I shall argue that postclassical gangster films foreground particular ethnic identities to a greater extent than earlier examples of the genre. The decline of censorship in the film industry during the sixties allowed the gangster to regain the emotional center of crime narratives. Changes in social and political environment during and after the Civil Rights Movement of the 1960s have encouraged significant discussions on ethnicity in film. The development of Mafia myths since the 1950s, which identify Italian cultural heritage as the primary driving force behind organized criminal activity, means that the representation of ethnicity is an important element in postclassical gangster films. The gangster film has provided the model for other portrayals of non–WASP ethnicities, in particular the blaxploitation and gangsta films that draw heavily upon these generic conventions. While these films are not the focus of this book, I do recognize their cultural importance as another strand of discourse that emanates from within Mafia myths.

As with masculinity, ethnicity in postclassical gangster films is displayed as a collective identity based on a shared cultural heritage, definable characteristics and ideals. Such collectives are associated mainly with the Italian or Sicilian race, but are not confined to biological determinism. Cultural heritage is of more importance. Italian ethnicity in particular is portrayed as the ideal. This is partly due to the critical and commercial success of Italian American gangster films, such as *The Godfather* trilogy (1972, 1974, 1990), or *Goodfellas* (1990), from writers Mario Puzo and Nicholas Pileggi, directors Francis Ford Coppola and Martin Scorsese, and actors such as Al Pacino and Robert De Niro. Even though it is problematized in such films, Italian ethnicity remains at the romanticized center of Mafia myths and postclassical gangster films. My analysis will consider the function of such contradictory representations. I will conclude that Italian ethnicity, because it is a white ethnicity, allows for contradictory readings. Ethnic heritage can be interpreted as a way of distancing the criminal group from ordinary society, and also as a way of providing a seemingly stable source of identification for them.

Overall, my discussions will show how gangster films are categorized in various ways, especially in media reviews, but argue that categories are influenced by articulations of Mafia myths, masculinity and ethnicity. The boundaries of these categories fluctuate to include crime films, thrillers and melodramas, but within them they provide a sense of collective Mafia identity. This cannot be isolated as a product of film texts, production trends, or reviews, but exists within the discourses of all three, as an intertextual discourse around organized crime in American culture. The gangster and Mafia myths, as sites of both non-homogenous and dominant white American identity, plus both collective and exclusive masculinity, become sites for working through the anxieties surrounding American identity and the contradictions this implies. The film texts are thus contradictory and ambivalent, but also powerful repetitions of myths and genre. In other words, they encourage strong elements of identification for viewers, while also articulating elements of non-identification. As such, the films appear to be articulations of a continuous text that occurs through multiple reference points and discourses.

1

Gangster Films Since 1967: An Overview

This chapter provides an overview of gangster films from 1967 to 2007. The selection of films is not exhaustive, but is intended to show a cross-section of American film production that references Mafia activity during this period. It is not confined to studio releases, but includes some semi-independent productions (*Lucky Luciano* [1973], *Miller's Crossing*, [1990]), television films (*The Don Is Dead*, [1973], *Gotti* [1996]) and of course the TV series *The Sopranos* (1999–2007). For practical reasons, the selection foregrounds those films that focus on organized crime, because my study is concerned with the portrayal of crime as an ongoing business. This can include lone gangsters, or hit men (*Carlito's Way* [1993], *Leon* [1994] as well as those in identifiable criminal groups (*The Godfather* [1972], *Heat* [1995]). However, it does not include criminals involved in isolated crime sprees (*Badlands*, 1973, *Natural Born Killers*, 1994). This is because my study is primarily concerned with representation of crime as a continued way of life, or family tradition. I also do not focus on the rise of "black gangsta" films in the 1990s and beyond. This may appear as a questionable omission, but in my opinion the trajectory of those films from gangland to organized crime is a specific story in and of itself and so I shall leave that subject for further study elsewhere. In short, this book does not claim to provide an exhaustive list of gangster film production from the United States between 1967 and 2007. However, it does explore a substantial range of films in order to show the diversity of gangster-related narratives.

* * *

This chapter traces particular patterns of film production and discovers that it is possible to suggest four cycles within this era: The 1970s is the first, opening with *The Godfather* (1972) and receding after *Bugsy Malone* (1976); the 1980s begins with *Scarface* (1983) and ends with *Married to the Mob* (1988); the 1990s starts with *Goodfellas* (1990) and stops with *Analyze This* (1999); and the millennium is dominated by *The Sopranos* (1999–2007). This is useful in that it splits the era into more manageable sections; however, this process is not meant to represent a way of defining the postclassical gangster film. These cycles will be qualified by further categorizing films under certain trends. As stated in the introduction, gangster film will be categorized under three interconnecting headings, gangsters as outlaws, gangsters as Mafia families or ongoing businesses, and gangsters as gangs or "wannabes." From these cycles and trends key texts will be identified and discussed in more detail in the following chapters. It is important to note that while these cycles are textually defined and therefore resemble the models of generic evolution suggested by John Cawelti (1978) and Thomas Schatz (1981), the intention of this book is not to isolate the gangster genre within production patterns or text-based criteria. However, I do concur with Rick Altman (2000) in believing that "the constitution of film cycles and genres is a never-ceasing process" (64) determined through complex and constantly evolving criteria. With this in mind, the merits of such approaches will be discussed in this and the following chapter. The intention here is to isolate particular trends in gangster film production and especially the influence of three significant examples (*The Godfather, Scarface* and *Goodfellas*) in shaping particular changes in the structure and themes of gangster films during this era. In summary, the purpose of this chapter is to provide a contextual map of film production that identifies cycles, trends and influential films that will then inform the discussions in later chapters.

Cycles

Theorizing the gangster genre will be addressed in Chapter 2, but in order to contextualize my use of the term "cycles" in this chapter it is necessary to explain its origins within genre study. In the mid–1970s, genre criticism was beginning to consider the notion that a genre's framework was no more than "the basic underlying coordinates" (Sobchack, T, 1975: 103) which conveyed a familiarity to the audience. Thomas Sobchack asserted that an audience should never be surprised or confused by a genre film, suggesting that any surprises should be assessed as defects or flaws in the texts. Furthermore, Sobchack insisted that a film can only be part of a specific genre or "group" if it is an "imitation of that which came before." Thus, not all films fit into genres. This echoes Warshow's view that the gangster film in its purest form exists only in the short cycle of films in the early thirties. This is one of the clearest examples of how genre criticism has differed from other cultural discourses on genre. Richard Maltby (1995) states that the film industry, which has always publicized films using genre categories, claims that all films fit. Therefore, a situation wherein the industry publicizes a film as a gangster film and audiences predominantly refer to it as such, but genre criticism discounts it because it is not an "imitation of that which came before," raises questions of judgment. Whose is the more appropriate judgment: that of those who produce the films, that of those who consume them, or that of those who study them?

* * *

Thomas Schatz's (1977) analysis continues in the same vein as Sobchack by stating that genres operate as "related systems that exhibit fundamentally similar characteristics" (Schatz: 97). Such analyses presuppose a fixed system of meaning and recognition situated within the text. There is no provision within this framework for a genre's progression and ideological function in relation to cultural changes. It adheres to notions of authorship, which place the director at the helm of production, with the ability to either adhere to generic convention or to openly flout it. John Cawelti's article, "*Chinatown* and Generic Transformation in Recent American Films" (1978), is an example of the trend to explain genre development as a process of auteur-based manipulation. Cawelti used Roman Polanski's *Chinatown* (1974) to show how familiar structures in genre film are redefined through a frequently auteur based process he labels transformation. He identifies four different transformations of genre: the burlesque, the cultivation of nostalgia, the mode of demythologization and the affirmation of myth for its own sake.

　　Cawelti's concern with the mode of demythologization is the most interesting. He explains the process as a deliberate provocation from the director to invoke

> the basic characteristics of a traditional genre in order to bring its audience to see that genre as the embodiment of an inadequate and destructive myth [*ibid.*: 507].

For Cawelti, a film such as *Bonnie and Clyde* (1969) is a demythologization of the classic gangster film. The narrative emphasis places the central protagonists as "victims of society's bloodlust" (*ibid.*: 508), rather than as violent aggressors, thus inverting the "classic" justification of a gangster's death. The crux of Cawelti's argument, as with Warshow's, is that the classic form of their chosen genre was a uniquely "innocent" period of dialectic simplicity that contemporary films could no longer capture. New films can only ever imitate, parody, or disrupt the primary structure, but they are not seen to progress or evolve. It was this formalist constriction upon the genre form that exhausted genre theory by the end of the seventies but which I will argue still pervades many reviews and scholarly writings on genre today. Without recognition of the possible fluidity of genre development and interpretation, theorists hit an impasse wherein their allegiance to structural formalism appeared to deny any further progression.

One way in which genre studies tried to break this mold was to assess the evolution of genre: how they had progressed or been transformed in relation to historical changes in social attitudes and production concerns. Thomas Schatz (1981) charts the increasingly self-conscious construct of genre from classic structures, through "parody," to "contestation" and "deconstruction." He argues that genre evolves in a circular fashion into increasingly self-reflexive constructs of thematic evaluation. Unfortunately for Schatz and for genre studies, this formula still denies progression beyond the evolutionary cycle. Once genre has arrived at the deconstruction stage, the genre is at an end. From then on, the original structure can only be dissected and destroyed, which is an explanation, according to Schatz, of why certain genres fade. The gangster genre, as depicted in the films of the 1930s, no longer exists. From Schatz's viewpoint, it has completed its cycle, beginning with films like *Scarface* (1932) and ending with deconstructions, such as *Bonnie and Clyde* (1969) and *The Godfather* (1972).

*   *   *

This model of genre study suggests that the gangster genre no longer exists after *The Godfather*. It is evident that this is not true. However, it can be suggested that *The Godfather* both deconstructed the classical gangster genre while also opening a new cycle. Schatz's approach to the genre may appear short-sighted to us now with the benefit of historical hindsight, but the plethora of literature that surrounds *The Sopranos* echoes Schatz in the claims that the gangster film has nowhere left to go after HBO's deconstruction. When we look back, we can always see trends, cycles and turning points in film production, and so I shall use such mapping as my starting point. The merit of a cyclical approach to genre is that it provides a way of mapping film production into particular trends. However, as a solution to the development of the gangster genre since 1967 it is very restrictive in that it is primarily text-based and does not allow for fluidity or development in the genre form. This book is primarily concerned with the exciting possibilities that tracing such fluidity and development will uncover. Therefore, it is only concerned with cycles as a springboard to building a larger picture of gangster film production over the past forty years. This allows for significant films to be highlighted, so that later discussions can focus on the chosen details. It is necessary to be selective in order to provide in-depth analyses, but it is not the intention here to claim a fixed definition of what is and what is not a gangster film.

Influences

To begin the discussion of gangster films since 1967, it is useful first to provide a brief overview of some of the significant factors at play in the industry during the 1960s. This is a decade that saw significant changes in both the aesthetic and commercial development of Hollywood film. The 1960s saw an unprecedented slump in cinema attendance. There were many possible reasons for this: For instance, the popularity of television and the increasing mismatch between Hollywood's product and available audiences meant that Hollywood needed to rethink its product. It appeared that audiences no longer wanted to see previously popular formats: musicals, biblical epics and action films that were mainly aimed at an undifferentiated family audience. According to David A. Cook (1991), "By 1962, Hollywood's yearly box-office receipts had fallen to their lowest level in history" (1991: 919). In the coming year expensively produced box office flops such as *Cleopatra* (1963) did nothing to aid the industry. A surprise revival came with *The Sound of Music* (1965), but this only gave the industry false hope and encouraged more expensive musical blockbusters that failed to recoup their production costs: *Doctor Doolittle* (1969), *Hello Dolly!* (1969) and *Paint Your Wagon* (1970).

In contrast, European cinema was enjoying an economic boom. Young independent filmmakers, such as Jean-Luc Godard, François Truffaut, Michelangelo Antonioni and Federico Fellini proved that "art" cinema could also be profitable. These were also filmmakers who had been influenced by and contributed to Bazin's glorification of the auteur.[1] Films such as Godard's *À bout de souffle* (1960) disrupted classical narrative, while Antonioni's *Il deserto rosso* (1964) was a display of expressionistic color and images: Both are representative of the ultra-chic European new waves of filmmaking. Hollywood took notice, especially of the fact that these films were produced on minimal budgets when compared to American movies. Subsequently, the 1950s and 1960s saw a gradual rise in semi-independent productions in Hollywood that emulated European styles. This strategy was partly aimed at recouping some of the heavy losses incurred from failed blockbusters and partly at cashing in on the popularity of European styles.

Bonnie and Clyde (1967)

As stated in the introduction to this book, after thirty-four years in the shadows, it is appropriate that one of the films credited as reflecting the final end of Hays Code Censorship had outlaws as its heroes. *Bonnie and Clyde*

(1967) has been seen as a turning point in Hollywood filmmaking (Cook: 923). It was released one year before the ratings system came about — and possibly encouraged its hasty development. The film has been described as "a sophisticated blend of comedy, violence, romance and — symbolically, at least — politics, which borrowed freely from the techniques of the French New Wave" (*ibid.*). The film was financed by Warner Bros., but much has been made of the role its eventual star, Warren Beatty, had in raising finances and securing a screenwriter and director.[2] After Truffaut and then Godard passed, Arthur Penn was finally enlisted and the subsequent film was heralded as "a watershed picture."[3] Critical responses to the film were often emotional, as summarized by one of the writers, Robert Benton: "It was perceived to be a thumbing-your-nose attitude, a moral flipness, an arrogance, because nobody in this movie ever said, 'I'm sorry I killed somebody'" (cited in Biskind, 1999: 48).

Bonnie and Clyde was hailed as a return to gangster violence and anti-heroism on the cinema screen (French, 1968). The success of such a violent and essentially pro-criminal film not only accelerated the demise of censorship and encouraged a new film-rating system instead, but it also placed criminals at the emotional center of the narrative. It is important to remember, though, that *Bonnie and Clyde* was not unique in its focus on outlaws; depictions of sympathetic criminals on the run occurred throughout classical Hollywood, as films like *You Only Live Once* (1937), *Gun Crazy* (1949) and *They Live by Night* (1948) testify. What made *Bonnie and Clyde* a significant text for the 1960s was its mockery of law and order and its emulation of European film aesthetics. Previous films, such as those listed above, focused on sympathetic but desperate young criminals. *Bonnie and Clyde*'s criminals had fun and their activities were based on lifestyle choices rather than desperation. For this reason, *Bonnie and Clyde* is an important film for my study, because it marks the beginning of a new era for criminals on screen. However, the film belongs to a subgenre of outlaw films that feature romantic desperados, whose characters were influenced by the real-life legend John Dillinger.[4] Munby defines such characters as "the gangster as fugitive" (113). For me, *Bonnie and Clyde* fits into a trend I have identified as gangsters as outlaws. The film is important to my discussions insofar as it features characters and situations common to the gangster film. However, in terms of history and mythology, the film draws upon the legends of Western heroes, such as Billy the Kid and Jesse James, as well as depression era criminals such as John Dillinger and Machine Gun Kelly, rather than any urban gangsters or Mafia families, and it is thus outside the main focus of this book. This does not exclude it from the label "gangster," but it does show how the gangster as a cinematic figure can appear across many different genres and genre hybrids. This will be discussed further in Chapter 2.

* * *

Even though *Bonnie and Clyde* is not a key text for this book, it was a profoundly influential film. It resembles *À bout de souffle* (1960) in the way that it depicts criminals who are aware of their own media notoriety and also model themselves on media legends. This also reflects the legends surrounding the real Bonnie and Clyde, whose letters and poems written in response to reports of their crimes also appeared in the media. While Michel (Jean-Paul Belmondo) constructs his own persona based on his screen idol Humphrey Bogart, Bonnie Parker and Clyde Barrow (both real and fictional) fashion themselves on the exploits of the real John Dillinger, but also on cinematic representations of him.[5] Therefore, it can be argued that the films and their characters are self-conscious and narcissistic. They are aware of their influences and actively promote their own notoriety as particular types, at both film and character level. In terms of intertextual referencing, Warren Beatty's costume is reminiscent of that of Jean-Paul Belmondo in Jean Pierre Melville's *Le Doulos* (1962). This is further emphasized by the fact that the actors look quite similar: Beatty's fedora hat and the cut of his dark suit is the same as Belmondo's even though *Bonnie and Clyde* is set in the thirties and *Le Doulos* in the early sixties. These referential styles may suggest that it was more important for Beatty to look fashionable in his film than it was for him to reflect historical accuracy.[6] Such cross-cultural and intertextual referencing is important to my study because myths of the Mafia are constructed through visual tropes such as costume and character stereotypes. Jean-Pierre Melville's iconic gangsters of the 1950s and '60s paid homage to classical Hollywood, but the costume style was more urban chic than vulgar consumerism. Post-classical Hollywood gangster films also reference their classical origins, but they did so while being heavily influenced by European aesthetics and costume.

Other gangster films before and after the release of *Bonnie and Clyde* include *The Rise and Fall of Legs Diamond* (1960), a classic rise-and-fall narrative featuring a self-conscious anti-hero who is aware of his own notoriety,[7] and *The Saint Valentine's Day Massacre* (1967) which focuses on the bosses of organized crime. Yaquinto calls the latter a "tongue-in-cheek nostalgic gore fest" (Yaquinto, 1998: 92), but its documentary style has also been noted as a reference to French New Wave aesthetics (McCarty, 1993). Directed by Roger Corman, *The Saint Valentine's Day Massacre* followed on from his previous biopics *Machine Gun Kelly* (1958), based on the real-life outlaw who ran with Dillinger, and *I, Mobster* (1958), an urban gangster narrative. His later *Bloody Mama* (1970) features a young Robert De Niro and resembles *Bonnie and Clyde* in setting and style. It also references crime as media spectacle, as in the scene where locals turn up to cheer on both sides in the final shoot-out. Therefore, we can already identify a clear demarcation between outlaw films, such as *Machine Gun Kelly* and *Bloody Mama*, and the other, more urban and Mafia-orientated narratives. *I, Mobster, The Rise and Fall of Legs Diamond* and *The Saint Valentine's Day Massacre* foreshadow *The Godfather Part I and II* (1972 and 1974), insofar as they focus on the business dealings of the bosses (*Legs Diamond* and *Saint Valentine's Day Massacre*) and make reference to senate hearings on Mafia activities (*I, Mobster*). The TV series *The Untouchables* starring Robert Stack as Eliot Ness was also a prominent feature of the early sixties gangster style. This series ran from 1959 to 1963 and echoed many of the film noir depictions of syndicate crime. Not only was its cinematography reminiscent of the noir era, but its depiction of criminal bosses remained fixed in that era too.

1968–1972

The Brotherhood (1968) is reportedly the first Hollywood film to mention the Mafia by name.[8] It focuses on the callous, corporate nature of the Mafia. However, it also features a conflict between two brothers: Don Francesco (Kirk Douglas) and Vincent (Alex Cord). Vincent wishes to modernize the business, while Francesco wants to retain its traditional form. Mafia Dons order Vincent to kill his brother to ensure business progress. The relationship between the brothers, the inclusion of certain Mafia symbols — a canary is placed in the mouth of a dead informer, Vincent gives Francesco the "kiss of death" before he kills him — all anticipate the fixation with Mafia-lore found in *The Godfather*. Hence, it is clear that late sixties Hollywood production included a resurgence of interest in both the outlaw film and the urban gangster.

Between 1968 and 1972, however, gangster film production was fairly uneventful. Instead, it was the violent cop who took center stage, in films such as *Bullitt* (1968) and *Dirty Harry* (1971). This type of film has dominated the postclassical era as much as any other crime film. A trend in postclassical films is to perceive cop heroes as emotionally damaged men.[9] This is part of a general trend, apparent since the Noir films of the forties, which suggests that cops need to be as brutal as their opponents in order to function as the film's heroes. This is exemplified in some popular responses to *The Untouchables* (1987), wherein Eliot Ness (Kevin Costner) is viewed as too "squeaky clean" (*Newsweek*, June 22, 1987) to win a charisma battle with Robert De Niro's Al Capone. Ness is "heaved off the screen" (Yaquinto) by Capone's presence: "In the two nose-to-nose matchups between Ness and Capone, the inequity is downright embarrassing" (Yaquinto: 157). Up until 1997, *The Untouchables* was a rare postclassical example of a cop-versus-gangster narrative. On the whole, since the 1970s the violent cop narrative has developed alongside the gangster narrative. *Death Wish* or *Dirty Harry*[10] movies that showcase the violent cop/vigilante, in consequence, tend to downplay the criminal characters. Mainstream examples of charismatic villains and cops were not generally gangsters, but international terrorists that emulate the super-criminal characters of James Bond films,[11] such as those in the *Die Hard* and *Lethal Weapon*[12] films. The only examples of postclassical gangster films that give equal screen time to both the law and the gangsters were *Dillinger* (1973), *Heat* (1995) and *Donnie Brasco* (1997).[13] For the most part, violent cop narratives and gangster narratives co-existed in Hollywood, but rarely combined. Since 1997 the cop versus gangster theme has re-emerged in films such as *The Departed* (2005) and *American Gangster* (2007). This is significant and will be addressed later in this chapter.

The Godfather (1972)

In 1972 *The Godfather* was an international box-office record breaker.[14] For this reason alone, the film has had a profound effect on all gangster films made after this date. However, there are many other reasons this film is significant. It is evident that *Bonnie and Clyde* is an important precursor to *The Godfather*, but it was not essentially about gangsters or the Mafia, but about outlaws and lovers. *The Godfather* draws upon a wider history of films, including the "syndicate" crime films (McArthur 1971, Yaquinto, 1998) of the fifties and sixties. Films such as *On the Waterfront* (1956), *Murder Inc.* (1960) and *Underworld USA* (1960) alluded to the Mafia as an often invisible, but powerful force that rules or more often ruins the main protagonist's life. A trend had developed from the films of the late forties and fifties that portrayed the Mafia as mainly absent groups controlling events from the shadows of the narrative: for example *The Killers* (1946), *Kiss of Death* (1947), *The Big Heat* (1953) and *Asphalt Jungle* (1950). These films showcased monstrous gangster henchmen, such as Tommy Udo (Richard Widmark in *Kiss of Death*) and Vince Stone (Lee Marvin in *The Big Heat*). Such characters, along with Cody Jarrett (James Cagney in *White Heat*, 1949) epitomized Hollywood's post-war preoccupation with masculine psychology in relation to violent cop narratives. In many of these films, the honest but emotionally damaged hero was pitted against the psychopathic gangster, who represented the invisible but ever-present criminal syndicate, and also invariably destroyed the hero by the end of the film.[15] These films have been seen as pessimistic indictments of a negative post-war American psyche (Yaquinto and McArthur, 1972, Krutnik, 1991). However, they also foreground the syndicate, or Mafia, as an all-powerful and organized business, and thus act as a precursor to *The*

Godfather.[16] *The Brotherhood* (1968) also provides a link back to the syndicate films in that the Mafia is portrayed as a faceless power that decides the fate of the brothers. It features family loyalties between gangsters, but again sympathizes with the lower echelons. *The Godfather* refers to these syndicate films, but also breaks from their conventions by unveiling the previously shadowy bosses. The only earlier film to do this is Roger Corman's *The Saint Valentine's Day Massacre* (1967), where the narrative focuses on the business operations of the Mafia bosses and depicts criminal organizations as comfortable bedfellows of more "legitimate" American business. Vera Dika has noted that *The Godfather* presents us with a Mafia made up of "upper classes" (Dika, 2000: 95). It is a film about the bosses of a Mafia family that is already in authority, not on the henchmen or a rise to fame of a lowly gangster. What is different about *The Godfather* is that *all* its main protagonists are members of the Mafia.[17] It isn't a film about the effects of the Mafia on an ex-convict or a private investigator, as in *The Outfit* (1973) or *The Big Heat*. It is a film about life in the Mafia — the loyalties, arguments, marriages and killings. The fact that these elements might make the film seem romantic, Manichean, or overly sentimental are separate, though valid arguments, which will be discussed later. The defining element that distinguishes this film from earlier examples is the fact that it opens the secret workings of the upper echelons of the Mafia and portrays these men as the film's heroes. In this film there are no buffers or intermediaries[18]; there are no narrative devices to separate viewers from this world.

The Godfather, like *Bonnie and Clyde* makes reference to and breaks from cinema history. *The Godfather* references the previously shadowy bosses found in syndicate films, but it is not structurally unique in the same way as *Bonnie and Clyde,* as its narrative is linear and not evidently self-conscious. However, the film does pay homage to the French New Wave in very discreet aesthetic ways. The opening reverse zoom shot that introduces Don Corleone (Marlon Brando) resembles the opening shot of Jean-Pierre Melville's *Le Samurai* (1967) as it introduces Jeff Costello (Alain Delon). The cold, business-like manner of Jeff Costello is also similar to Michael Corleone's persona (Al Pacino) later in the film. Michael even wears a fedora and trench coat[19] in the latter part of the film. Primarily, it is *The Godfather*'s sense of nostalgia that makes it significant in Hollywood gangster history, but also connects it to the French New Wave. Classic gangster films have a sense of immediacy and a progressive nature. The narratives are about ambition and growth. The protagonists are looking forward, precisely because they lack a sense of history or tradition (Warshow, 1948). However, the films of the French New Wave, *Bonnie and Clyde* and *The Godfather* evoke past times and romanticize them, either through costume and characters (*Le Doulos* 1962, *À bout*

de souffle 1959, *Bonnie and Clyde*) or through historical settings and morali-
ties (*The Saint Valentine's Day Massacre, The Brotherhood, The Godfather*).
Success or ambition in *The Godfather* is founded in resisting progress;
for example, the Don is against the new drug trade, but also Michael's assim-

Vito Corleone (Marlon Brando, standing) and Michael Corleone (Al Pacino).
The Godfather © 1972, Paramount.

ilation into mainstream America is rejected in favor of saving the traditional family way of life. Therefore, *The Godfather* is a romantic film, in that it prioritizes the past. *Le Doulos* and *À bout de souffle* are also romantic, but in a different way. They evoke both the costume and masculine anxieties featured in noir films of the forties, but only as a self-conscious aesthetic romanticism, based on the look and themes of a past cinematic era. While the gangster films of the French New Wave and postclassical cinema often focus on the past, they do so in very different ways.

1972–1973

Spin-offs from the commercial success of *The Godfather* include *Honor Thy Father* (1973), *Crazy Joe* (1973) and *The Don Is Dead* (1973). All of these focus on families, business and betrayals. However, due to TV production restrictions, *Honor Thy Father*, a TV film based on Gay Talese's bestselling book on the rise and fall of the real-life Bonnano family, mainly prioritizes the emotional side of Mafia life, while *The Don Is Dead* glories in set-piece brutality. *Crazy Joe*, a biopic of Joseph Gallo, uses a semi-documentary style and focuses on the main protagonist's preoccupation with Hollywood gangsters. *The Valachi Papers* (1972) adapted Peter Maas' best-selling book of Joe Valachi's real-life testimony[20] to the screen. This book had clearly influenced Puzo's *The Godfather*, especially in the capo-regime structure of the crime family. The film adaptation is a low-budget, documentary-style piece, in which the subject matter foregrounds the internal workings of the Mafia in the same way as others of this period.

Dillinger (1973), a biopic of John Dillinger's life and death, is reminiscent of *Bonnie and Clyde*, mainly due to its rural setting and the historical associations between the two stories. It also resembles the violent cop narrative in that it gives equal screen-time to Melvyn Purvis (Ben Johnson), the FBI agent tracking, as it does to Dillinger (Warren Oates). Purvis' quest to hunt down all of Dillinger's gang is shown as an obsession, but so is the fight for the media spotlight. Purvis laments the tendency for newspapers to headline Dillinger's activities more than the FBI's, but he also confesses the extent to which the FBI breaks laws in order to eradicate these criminals. The film is an interesting precursor to *The Untouchables*, but Purvis is more Harry Callahan (Clint Eastwood in *Dirty Harry*) than Eliot Ness.

Francesco Rosi's *Lucky Luciano* (1973) is also a biopic and offers many documentary style scenes of the United Nations International Conference on Drug Traffic (1952), which foreshadow the Kefauver scenes in *The Godfather Part II* (1974).[21] At times this film feels more like a public information broadcast than a film, in that many scenes are set and scripted to discuss the political reasons behind Luciano's criminal success. However, stylized, slow-motion death scenes that show bodies literally dancing in the gun-fire are reminiscent of *Bonnie and Clyde*. The soft chiaroscuro lighting in many of the intimate scenes draws heavily on the aesthetics of *The Godfather*.

The early seventies also saw a wave of films categorized as blaxploitation, many of which utilized crime narratives, such as *Shaft* (1971), *Superfly* (1972) *Black Belt Jones* (1973), *Cleopatra Jones* (1973), *Coffy* (1973) and *Foxy Brown* (1974). *Black Caesar* aka *The Godfather of Harlem* (1973) is a straightforward gangster film. Its rise and fall narrative is classical, but its uncompromising brutality is more representative of the postclassical era. McCarty notes that it was financed specifically as a black version of the original *Little Caesar* (80). It features characters outside the Mafia image of gangsters, rural or urban, and is structurally reminiscent of the 1930s films.

In summary, the gangster films of the early seventies divide into three trends: rural outlaws (*Bloody Mama, Dillinger*), Mafia businesses (*The Godfather, Honor Thy Father, Crazy Joe, The Don Is Dead and Lucky Luciano*) and blaxploitation films (*Superfly* and *Black Caesar*). Biographical narratives and semi-documentary aesthetics feature prominently, as does an emphasis on period detail. The latter is important, as most films concentrate on historical rather than contemporary narratives. *Black Caesar* is unique in that it refers directly back to the classical gangster films and their role as social problem narratives. The focus on true stories or biographies is not a new element of gangster films, as references to factual events have always been significant.[22] The publicized senate hearings in the 1950s influenced many of the films of the 1960s and beyond. The films of the classical era were influenced by the real-life man-hunts for John Dillinger and Bonnie and Clyde, whereas the films of the 1960s and beyond combine these elements with political debates and media interest in senate hearings on organized crime, as well as an increase in gangster biography literature. Therefore, the increase in documentary-style filmmaking, or the prioritizing of factual events, is not just an aesthetic trend, but a result of public discourses on the subject of organized crime and the possible existence of an international Mafia network.

Mean Streets (1973) and *The Godfather Part II* (1974)

Two more films of the seventies that are influential for later trends in film production are Francis Coppola's *The Godfather Part II* (1974) and Martin Scorsese's *Mean Streets* (1973). Coppola's sequel to *The Godfather* continued the story of the Corleone family. One of the main attractions, or distractions, of the film is the fact that its narrative straddles the time period depicted in Part I showing Vito's young life intercut with Michael's continuing story. It is well documented that Coppola deliberately chose to break the linear narrative in order to "show that as the young Vito Corleone is building this thing out of America, his son is presiding over its destruction" (Coppola cited in Chown: 103). However, this choice of structure was to cause the most controversy among reviewers.[23] The film also included senate hearings similar to those found in *I, Mobster*, *The Valachi Papers* and *Lucky Luciano*. The narrative is woven around factual events, such as American corporate investment in Cuba and the ensuing revolution. However, events are romanticized in that they function as backdrops to the family's growing sense of omnipotence and the international power of organized crime. At one point in the narrative Hyman Roth (Lee Strasberg) declares, "We're bigger than U.S. Steel," and later Michael states, "If history has taught us anything, it is that you can kill anyone." The film's romanticism then is centered on the fact that, although Michael may be losing his soul, the mob remains an invincible power. *The Godfather Part II*, like the syndicate films before it, shows how the Mafia as an organization is bigger and exists beyond a single participant.

Mean Streets (1973) and *The Godfather* have both been described as "the two most important gangster films of the seventies" (Hardy: 331). It is also suggested that the original idea for *Mean Streets* was based on contempt for Puzo's *The Godfather*, "then a bestseller, which Scorsese knew bore no relation to the truth. He would tell it how it was" (Biskind: 229). Biskind's claim cannot be taken as any more than recorded gossip. However, it is noted that Scorsese views *The Godfather* as a little romanticized (Smith, 1990; Christie, 1990).[24]

Mean Streets is very different from *The Godfather* in terms of style. It refers much more to the documentary style of the French New Wave, or Italian Neo-realism, in that it concentrates on the incidental activities of a group of fairly ordinary New Yorkers, rather than the grand romanticism of Coppola's bosses. Scorsese's characters are street guys rather than Mafiosi. Only Charlie (Harvey Keitel) expresses an interest in a Mafia career. The characters and narrative of *Mean Streets* are part of the trend of gangs, or wannabes, because they inhabit the margins of Mafia activity rather than the center. The narrative concentrates on the individuals' admiration for, or emulation of gangster activity, rather than their role within a Mafia hierarchy. The similarities between *Mean Streets* and *The Godfather* begin and end in the fact that the allusions to Mafia activity occur within the tight-knit Italian community of New York. The figure of Charlie's Uncle Giovanni (Cesare Danova) could, metaphorically and intertextually, be linked to the Mafia families portrayed in *The Godfather*, in that he operates within the same fictional structure, albeit lower down in the hierarchy. Gavin Millar suggests,

[It] "echoes the grander Mafia higher up the social scale" (*The Listener* April 11, 1974). Vincent Canby (*New York Times*) describes Uncle Giovanni as an "old world gangster, full of cold resolve and ponderous advice" (October 3, 1973). In this way, he resembles the many advisers to Michael Corleone in *The Godfather*, including his father Vito Corleone (Marlon Brando), Clemenza (Richard Castellano) and Tessio (Abe Vigoda). In essence, the link between *The Godfather* and *Mean Streets* is found within the mythologies of Mafia activities and presence, rather than in any narrative connections.

1974–1982

From 1974 to 1976 it is difficult to find coherent links across films. They all appear to be projects that tried to cash in on a renewed interest in gangster films. Steve Carver's *Big Bad Mama* (1974) and *Capone* (1975) are direct remakes of Roger Corman's originals *Bloody Mama* (1970) and *The Saint Valentine's Day Massacre* (1967) respectively. Sydney Pollack's *The Yakuza* (1974) is a Robert Mitchum vehicle that explores the link between American and Japanese organized crime, but takes its format from the cop-revenge films. Meanwhile, the only bio-pic of any note is *Lepke* (1975), which concentrates on the Jewish gangster Louis Lepke Buchalter. This film pays homage to the syndicate films as well as *The Godfather* in terms of its content and style. *Monthly Film Bulletin* suggested that it "produces a very stiff and po-faced melange of gangster clichés" (Glaessner, 1975: 83). However, it is a hitherto rare excursion into the Jewish Mafia, continued later by *Once Upon a Time in America* (1983) and *Billy Bathgate* (1991).

Alan Parker's *Bugsy Malone* (1976) could be said to truly underscore the renewed popularity of gangster films. However, even though it could be argued that films such as *The Godfather* encouraged the market for a film such as this, *Bugsy Malone* echoes the styles and iconography of the 1930s classics rather than films such as *The Godfather*. *Bugsy Malone* is aimed at the family audience. It utilizes the settings, costumes and characters of the classic gangster film and turns it into a family comedy with custard pies and pedal cars. *Bugsy Malone*, as a parody, appears to end a cycle of gangster films, as production is low-key between 1976 and 1983. There are many possible reasons for this. One may be that the immediate post–Watergate and Vietnam atmosphere was not conducive for films with criminals at the emotional center. Perhaps it was thought that American audiences were not so interested in watching that side of their national character on screen, damaged as it was by the revelations of corruption in real life. It is evident that, as result of a number of different factors, the gangster film receded into the background until the early eighties, when it returned with vigor.

Scarface (1983)

Scarface is the most prominent film to emerge at the beginning of the next cycle of gangster films.[25] This cycle includes films that suggest themselves as reactions to the films of the seventies, especially *The Godfather*, but also as precursors to the more aesthetically and thematically self-conscious films of the nineties. Therefore the films of this cycle are eclectic, but reflect the changing thematic and aesthetic emphases in production.

Brian De Palma is another of the Italian American directors to emerge in the seventies. Before *Scarface* he was best known for his horror and slasher films, especially *Carrie* (1976) and *Dressed to Kill* (1980). His work has not attracted the critical acclaim that Scorsese and Coppola have received, but nonetheless his remake of the classic gangster film is a landmark, if nothing else for its excesses in graphic violence and materialist hedonism. De Palma's trademark is his allusion to previous films or filmmakers. For *Scarface*, De Palma updates the original 1930s Capone-like gangster Tony Camonte for a new audience. Al Pacino plays a Cuban, Tony Montana, who claims political asylum in the United States of the mid-seventies.[26] The film receives little or no notice in critical histories of the genre. McCarty states, "Like most De Palma movies, *Scarface* starts out looking as if it might amount to something, just to become a send-up of itself" (McCarty, 1993: 69).[27] Scripted by Oliver Stone, the narrative is a blatant reaction to seventies excess. The racketeering commodity is drugs, money is flaunted, loyalties are virtually nonexistent and the ensuing violence is immense. Dismissed by most critics as an attempt to "exploit the knee-jerk excess of the era and the genre" (Yaquinto: 149), *Scarface* remains a cult classic[28] and therefore important from an audience point of view. There are many ways in which its style foreshadows the later films by Scorsese, in that it concentrates on the excessive nature of gangsters through costume, ambitions and violence, which was also dominant in the classical examples. *Scarface* can be positioned primarily within the trend for gangs and wannabes. It follows the classical gangster narrative structure, in that it focuses on the rise and fall of an individual. It also includes many scenes that demonstrate the popular appeal and function of the classical gangster in American society, such as when, during a drunken restaurant outburst, Montana harangues the WASP diners: "You need people like me so you can point your fucking finger and say, 'That's the bad guy!'" The film bears no resemblance to the romanticism of *The Godfather*, nor the realism of *Mean Streets*. It is, however, a pivotal film that marks the end of both the romanticism and the realism of the seventies films and foreshadows the pre-occupation with excessive style, multiple ethnicities and the harsher brutalities that emerged in the nineties.

Once Upon a Time in America (1984)

In contrast to *Scarface*, Sergio Leone's epic, *Once Upon a Time in America*, has been deemed "a masterpiece" (Hardy, 1998) in some genre histories, on a par with *The Godfather* (McCarty, Yaquinto).[29] Like the *Godfather* trilogy it spans the twentieth century, this time focusing on a small band of Jewish gangsters, none of whom are blood relations. It is, in this sense, an epic narrative. Even though it is similar in style to *The Godfather*, this film fits into the trend of gangs and wannabes, simply because it is not focused on the Mafia, but on a gang of thieves. However, the film's aesthetics have encouraged many comparisons to *The Godfather*. Hardy suggests that Scorsese's and Coppola's films are based on nostalgia, while Leone's focuses on memory (Hardy: 405). This is due to the film's rather complicated narrative combining subjective flashbacks and subplots. The narrative is reflective insofar as the characters are shown to simultaneously regret previous actions while also yearning for those earlier "happier" times. Having said this, the film is similar in style to *The Godfather*, in that it romanticizes the sights and sounds of a bygone era. Themes also focus on the loss of loyalties and trust, and the ability of big business to hide its past.[30] In this sense, the film is definitely nostalgic because, while the actions of the young boys are self-serving rather than protective as in *The Godfather*, the sanitized New York setting is idealized as a young criminal's playground. Furthermore, as with Al Pacino in *Scarface*, the inclusion of Robert De Niro as the main character, "Noodles," invokes obvious comparisons to the young Vito Corleone in *The Godfather Part II* and continues a growing tendency for prominent gangster roles to be played by either De Niro or Pacino. *Once Upon a Time in America* encourages interesting reactions, such as from the *New York Times*, who declared that it "looks and sounds more authentically Italian" (June 1, 1984), even though its subject matter is Jewish. This reaction is probably due to Sergio Leone's and Robert De Niro's involvement. Such a description suggests that the film encourages comparisons to *The Godfather*. The themes also successfully combine gangs, wannabes and Mafia trends within one narrative, thus providing an interesting development of themes from the 1970s' films.

1985–1990

Other eighties films of note include Coppola's *The Cotton Club* (1984), intended as a historical account of black cabarets in the Harlem renaissance era of the twenties and thirties. The film is basically a set of love stories. However, either due to Coppola's involvement, or narrative weaknesses, discussions of the film (Hardy, McCarty) tend to focus on gangster characters, such as Dutch Schutlz (James Remar) and Bumpy Rhodes (Larry Fishburne) even though they do not dominate the narrative. De Palma's *The Untouchables* (1987) merges the gangster film with the Western: "I never saw it as a gangster movie. I saw it more like a *Magnificent Seven*" (De Palma, cited in Yaquinto: 156). The film bears little resemblance to any other gangster film of this era, but this may be primarily because it concentrates on the police force and not on the gangsters. However, as stated earlier, it begs attention mainly because its criminal figure, Al Capone (Robert De Niro), gained the most prominence in film publicity[31] and, it is suggested (Yaquinto, McCarty), exudes the most charisma on-screen. The film's supposed hero and star, Eliot Ness (Kevin Costner), is not charismatic enough to compete against De Niro's Capone, and thus the film never manages to become the "face-off" it aspires to be (Yaquinto). Even though De Niro's Capone is a simplistically brutal gangster figure, he still encourages audience sympathies after Malone's death as there is no equally charismatic alternative.

Michael Cimino's *The Sicilian* (1987) suffers a similar fate. An adaptation of a Mario Puzo novel, *The Sicilian* combines the gangster as outlaw with a Robin Hood–style narrative based on the true story of Salvatore Guiliano in 1940s Sicily. It is only the Puzo connection that links this film to other Hollywood gangster films discussed here. Interestingly, Puzo included Michael Corleone's visit to Sicily (featured in *The Godfather Part I*) in the novel, therefore consciously linking the narrative to *The Godfather*.[32] However, this element was dropped from the film; otherwise it would have provided an interesting point of connection.

1980s Comedies

De Palma's *Wise Guys* (1986), Jeff Kanew's *Tough Guys* (1986) and Jonathan Demme's *Married to the Mob* (1988) are black comedies. The beauty parlor scenes in *Married to the Mob* that show the wives gossiping about cosmetics while their husbands are out killing, foreshadow similar scenes in Scorsese's *Goodfellas*. *Wise Guys* and *Tough Guys* parody the theme of aging Mafiosi operating in a world that no longer appreciates their rules and traditions. Thus they reflect the nostalgic themes of many Mafia films that romanticize the old traditions, such as *The Godfather Part I and II*— and foreshadow the romanticism of aging gangster Lefty Ruggiero (Al Pacino) in *Donnie Brasco* (1997). *The Freshman* (1990) and *Sister Act* (1992) are interesting comedies, not least in that the former has Marlon Brando recreate his Don Corleone and the latter sees Harvey Keitel (Charlie in *Mean Streets*) as the silk-suited mob boyfriend of Whoopi Goldberg. Both comedies succeed through star personalities rather than script or particular themes. However, *The Freshman* is a commentary on *The Godfather*, insofar as it sees film stu-

David "Noodles" Aaronson (Robert De Niro, seated) and Max Bercovicz (James Woods) *Once Upon a Time in America* © 1984, Ladd/Embassy International.

dent Clark Kellogg (Matthew Broderick) experiencing events that mirror those of the classic film.[33] The emergence of these comedies at the end of the eighties, as with *Bugsy Malone* in the seventies, shows how the gangster image is ingrained in popular culture, for only instantly recognizable scenarios parody well. However, this time the reference points are not in the classic 1930s, but in the iconography and personae of *The Godfather*. *Scarface* refers back to the classic gangster films of the thirties, but also operates as a cynical antidote to the romanticism of *The Godfather* films. Other films of the decade refer directly to *The Godfather*, such as *Once Upon a Time in America*, *Prizzi's Honor*, *The Sicilian* and *The Freshman*. As such, the cycle of gangster films of the eighties reflects an increasing eclecticism in their references to the classical films, European influences and now also Hollywood films of the seventies.

The Godfather Part III (1990)

Sixteen years after the original, *The Godfather Part III* was finally released in 1990. This is a key film, in that it extends the focus on Michael and provides a sense of completion in terms of his story. Some found its grandiose style a fitting tribute, "A grand guignolesque morality tale" (*Evening Standard* February 2, 1991). David Ray Papke summarizes the mixed reaction to *Part III* in a way that reminds us that these films can appeal on many different levels. He notes that, even though it may be regarded as an inferior film to the previous two, *Part III* still has its uses: "Michael as the Mafia as America is a corrupt bully who now wants to be granted dignity and honor" (Papke: 16). He also notes, "A viewer coming cold to *The Godfather Part III* might not enjoy or admire it, but anyone familiar and enamoured with the films that preceded it cannot resist this completion of a cinematic epic" (*ibid.*: 17). This suggests that *The Godfather* trilogy has taken on the mantle of soap opera, wherein the fate of "known" characters is the underlying appeal.[34] *The Godfather* is deemed a classic for various reasons. Pauline Kael suggests it as "the greatest gangster movie ever made in America" (cited in *Independent on Sunday*, July 7, 1996), as do reviewers of the re-mastered screen release in *The Guardian*, July 4, 1996 and *Daily Telegraph*, July 5, 1996. It is also valorized for the photography, voted as No. 2 in the "Best Shot Films 1950–1997" in *American Cinematographer* (1999). Furthermore, nearly all reviews of *Part III* made reference to the "majesty" of Coppola's original (*Guardian*, March 3, 1991, *Times*, March 7, 1991, *New Statesman and Society*, March 8, 1991, *Spectator*, March 16, 1991). In addition, film histories (McCarty, 1993; Hardy, 1998; Yaquinto, 1998) all note *Part I* and *II's* influential stature: "Coppola took a tired cinematic genre [...] and pushed it in an epic new direction" (McCarty: 187). Popular responses to *The Godfather Part III* reflect the notion that, by the nineties, *The Godfather* had become firmly established as a classic film. Certainly, *Part III* has some great melodramatic moments, especially Michael's confession to Cardinal Lamberto (Raf Vallone) or Connie's (Talia Shire) zealous desire to now defend the family she once denounced. The weakness came in the form of the next generation. The film tried to open new stories as the old ones closed and it felt contrived, like two films sewn together.

It is a shame that reviewers focus on the bad elements though, as there are many majestic moments. Michael states his sadness at the corruption in big business and its effects even on the Vatican; "the higher I go, the crookeder it becomes." The interweaving of real events within the Corleone story keeps the focus, as Papke noted, on Michael as Mafia as America. Corporate business practice, always a source of anxiety in American film, is now connected with religion and undermines the sanctity of personal identity that is achieved through faith. If you cannot trust the church, then what is left? Faith in yourself and your family, is what Coppola was hoping to state, but the film instead mainly shows us how much has been lost. The future generation does not offer much and so it is not surprising that *Part IV* has not been encouraged.

Goodfellas (1990)

In the same year as *The Godfather Part III*, Scorsese directed *Goodfellas*, the Coen Brothers, *Miller's Crossing* and Abel Ferrara, *King of New York*. Of these, *Goodfellas* has received the most critical attention, perhaps because of its high-profile director and box-office success. Based on Nicholas Pileggi's biography, *The Wise Guy* (1985), the film chronicles the life of Henry Hill, who fulfilled his childhood dream to be a gangster, but later informed on his boss, Paul Vario, and friend, Jimmie Burke (re-named Paulie Cicero and Jimmy Conway in the film). It has been suggested that Scorsese's film manages to show the "excitement, the terror and the seediness of lawless life" (Hardy: 447). Scorsese calls it "staged-documentary" (Yaquinto; Smith, 1990) in that the film's style suggests documentary style film-making, while simultaneously employing more classical Hollywood cinematic narrative devices. For example, while lengthy shots and improvised dialogue are often used, many scenes are also minutely choreographed. The long tracking shot through the club that introduces the Mafia family has the simultaneous feel of providing an informal insight, while also displaying such formal choreography. Such styles have been viewed as a welcome alternative to the "grand opera" of Coppola's films (Smith, Yaquinto, McCarty), in that it offers a less romantic view of Mafia life: "They don't live the ethnic holism of the Corleones, with their sturdy links to Sicilian traditions. Instead, these hoods reflect the breakdown of the family order and the infiltration of yuppie nihilism" (Yaquinto: 169). However, Jimmy Conway (Robert De Niro) is still mentioned as a romantic figure; he's "the polished front man for the story's deeper cesspool" (Yaquinto: 171). None of the others, especially the narrator, Henry Hill (Ray Liotta), are sympathetic characters. Henry is merely the eyes through which we view the gangster world, but we are not encouraged to care about him. This has led some critics (for example, Stanbrook in *The New States-man* January 24, 1991, Lane in *Independent on Sunday*, October 28, 1990) to suggest that *Goodfellas'* popularity is due to its style more than its content. This film effectively combines the gangsters as gangs and wannabes with the gangsters as Mafia more than any other film of the chosen forty-year era and is the most dominant precursor of *The Sopranos*. Like the TV series, its style and characters are eclectic. The film resembles the realist style of *Mean Streets* at times, which then conjures up memories of the French New Wave, but its characters are too flamboyant to be considered sincerely realist. Alan Stanbrook, in *The New Statesman*, suggests, "all its surface glitter, there is something rancid about Scorsese's film" January 24, 1991). This bluntly states what other critics have mainly hinted at: the film is "simultaneously fascinating and repellent" (Kael, *Variety*, September 10, 1990). I will argue that the same could easily be said about *The Sopranos* and indeed has been said about *The Godfather* too. The difference is that the characters in *The Godfather* believe in themselves, whereas most of those in *The Sopranos* and *Goodfellas* are playing out myths that no longer appear immutable. Their world is dying, or is already dead and therefore their actions are at odds with the realities of the environments they inhabit. I will discuss this more in Chapter 3, but for now it's important to remember that *Goodfellas* appeared at the beginning of and has had a profound influence on a busy decade for gangster films. In short, the nineties saw an emphasis on violence and costume as crucial signifiers of the Mafia, alongside, but not necessarily concurrent with, claims to factual authenticity.

New Groups, Old Stories

King of New York (1990) signals a shift away from an exclusively Italian American Mafia and towards an emphasis on present-day America. The film reflects the trend of gangs and wannabes, but it also features crime as an ongoing business with Frank White (Christopher Walken) as the white[35] boss of an African American criminal family. This puts the emphasis on business rather than ethnic solidarity, and also comments on the drug trade. Trade is shown here to be run by white business men with ethnic groups as their primary market. Frank White's well-tailored suits also mark him out as different from his more casually-clothed gang. He looks like a Mafia man while they look like members of a street gang. Furthermore, he is offered as the only fully-rounded, sympathetic character. He deals in drugs, but also donates large amounts of money to local charities. Drug dealing is shown as "a necessary means by which he can hold the social fabric together" (Hardy: 451), rather than simply an exploitative crime. However, by sympathizing with him, audiences are also in danger of condoning Eurocentric ethnic hierarchies. *King of New York* is a film that focuses on the pursuit of money. White feels that profit, which provides drugs and women for his gang, is the only way to ensure allegiance. This is similar to *Goodfellas*, which had the pursuit of profit as the primary motivators for Hill, Conway and DeVito to keep their allegiances to the mob. Their payments to Pauly were to ensure their safety in the neighborhood, rather than to show respect to the boss. In consequence, these films suggest that profit is more important than ethnic allegiance. It is difficult to pinpoint specific influences on *King of New York*, because it does

Tommy DeVito (Joe Pesci, 2nd from left) and Jimmy Conway (Robert De Niro, beneath light) other actors unidentified. *Goodfellas* © 1990, Warner Bros.

not readily resemble any others. It has its strongest links with *Scarface*, but it displays its material excesses in a more business-like manner. *New Jack City* (1991) echoes the style of *King of New York*, although here, the cinematic influence is explicit in that African American gangster Nino Brown (Wesley Snipes) dreams of being Tony Montana (*Scarface*). Allusions to the blaxploitation films of the seventies can be traced through ethnicity, Brown's excessive interest in his appearance, and the emphasis on music. However, Nino Brown is more concerned with emulating other cinematic gangsters, than asserting his own ethnic heritage and thus further emphasizes the film's place in the gangs and wannabes trend. *King of New York* and *New Jack City*, along with aspects of *Goodfellas*, represent the beginning of new waves of gangs and wannabe films. These foreground the visual style of gangsters, through costume and gestures as the main signifiers of gangster identity, rather than allusions to Sicilian heritage or Mafia myths.

More easily identifiable gangsters are found in *Bugsy* (1991), *Billy Bathgate* (1991) and *Carlito's Way* (1993). Both *Bugsy* and *Billy Bathgate* are biopics. *Bugsy* is based on Bugsy Siegel, the man who founded Las Vegas.[36] *Billy Bathgate* is mainly fictitious but involves historical figures such as Dutch Schultz, Lucky Luciano and Otto Berman. *Bugsy* is a classic rise-and-fall narrative of one man's flawed ambition, while *Billy Bathgate* has similarities to *Goodfellas* in that the main character, Billy, is an awestruck observer of Mafia activities in a similar vein to Henry Hill. *Carlito's Way* teams Al Pacino with director Brian De Palma again, only this time the gangster is Puerto Rican. Older and wiser than Tony Montana (*Scarface*), Carlito Brigante has done his time in prison and now wants to lead a reformed life — similar perhaps to the aged Michael Corleone (*The Godfather Part III*). However, the gangster world keeps pulling him back in. Loyalty to his corrupt lawyer, Kleinfeld (Sean Penn), implicates Carlito in a mob murder and hastens his demise. However, it is the examination of hero-worship that makes this film interesting. Carlito finds it difficult to escape his former life because his reputation inspires many young criminals. This makes him notorious, but also a target. The young Benny Blanco (John Leguizamo), a "would-be" gangster, earns his stripes by shooting Carlito at Grand Central station. In this way *Carlito's Way* echoes the themes of classical gangster films such as *Public Enemy* (1932) or *The Rise and Fall of Legs Diamond* (1960) through hits that focus on the Darwinian nature of the gangster world. A gangster's death is most likely to occur at the hands of a rival and his demise serves as a warning to all young would-be gangsters. However, in *Carlito's Way* there is no moral message for the young criminals. The film heaps all the sympathy onto Carlito by giving him almost uninterrupted point of view and voice-over narration. Therefore, the film is more about bitter fate, in a similar vein to the film noir classics

Out of the Past (1947) and *Kiss of Death* (1947). The primary focus of the narrative is Carlito's inability to escape his past.

Miller's Crossing (1990)

Miller's Crossing (1990) adapted the literary world of Dashiell Hammett to the screen. It has received less critical acclaim than *Goodfellas*, but its style foreshadows the coming decade in similar ways. Influenced by hard-boiled detective novels such as *Red Harvest* and *The Glass Key*,[37] *Miller's Crossing* combines the pessimism of film noir with the style and intrigue of Mafia rivalries. The film is preoccupied with its aesthetic style, from the sepia-toned photography and Tom Reagan's (Gabriel Byrne) dreams about his hat, to Leo O'Bannion's (Albert Finney) single-handed extermination of would-be assassins at his home. The participants are caricatures from Hollywood history: the cold and indifferent hero (Reagan), the semi-psychotic Mafia chief Johnny Casper (Jon Polito), the double-crossing small-time crook Bernie Bernbaum (John Turturro), and the amoral mistress Verna (Marcia Gay Harden). The settings and costume are from the 1920s, but the themes combine 1940s film noir with postclassical self-awareness. It fits mainly into the gangsters as Mafia trend in that it relies on audiences' cinematic and/or cultural knowledge of Mafia mythologies to appreciate its irony. Later films, such as *L.A. Confidential* (1995), *Bound* (1995), *Get Shorty* (1996) and *Last Man Standing* (1996), all use a similar style of character short cuts to parody the Mafia. In fact, Chili Palmer (John Travolta) in *Get Shorty* resembles Tom Reagan in many ways. They are both deeply involved, yet emotionally detached from the events that surround them. In all of these films, the Mafia is represented by middle-aged Italians, with more brute force at their disposal than brains.

Other gangster films of the early nineties include Phil Joanou's *State of Grace* (1990), which like *Miller's Crossing* pits an Irish-American crime family against the traditional and more capable Italian Americans. Like *New Jack City* and *Carlito's Way*, *State of Grace* represents Italian American gangsters as authoritative and brutal adversaries to other ethnic groups: African Americans, Puerto Ricans, or even the Irish. This is a further example of how the Italian Mafia inhabits Hollywood history as the epitome of organized crime.

In summary, the first two years of the nineties saw the release of a number of gangster films, perhaps due to the commercial success of *The Godfather Part III* and *Goodfellas*. Two trends can be identified in the subsequent films. Firstly, there is a focus on gangs and wannabes, contemporary settings, and non–Italian ethnicities in non–Italian films such as *King of New York*, *State of Grace* and *New Jack City*. Secondly, we can see a return to historical subjects and/or biopics in *Bugsy, Miller's Crossing* and *Billy Bathgate. Good-fellas* combines the two trends in that it combines an outsider's perspective through Henry Hill, while simultaneously romanticizing Mafia mythologies. Furthermore, it is also significant to note that reviews of nearly all of these films include references to a tendency for style to dominate over content:[38] "Stylish, but empty" (*King of New York* in *Daily Telegraph,* June 20, 1991), "High gloss escapism" (*New Jack City* in *Times,* August 29, 1991), "A smooth movie" (*Bugsy* in *Scotsman Weekend,* March 28, 1992), "Style calls the shots" (*Miller's Crossing* in *Scotsman Weekend,* February 23, 1991) and "Beautiful photography, but lacks depth" (*Billy Bathgate* in *Times,* January 9, 1992). These are all tendencies that characterize the gangster films of the nineties and suggest a new emphasis on visual signifiers of the gangster, or Mafia, in film.

Quentin Tarantino

Two films epitomize the extent to which ethnicity and historical authenticity are becoming less defined or traceable, and film style is taking precedence over narrative. These are *Reservoir Dogs* (1992) and *Pulp Fiction* (1994). Quentin Tarantino, a star-director, regards his films as eclectic constructions of various styles, in that settings costumes and characters are hybrid concoctions from various aspects of American cultural history.[39] This is just one of the reasons *Reservoir Dogs,* essentially a heist film, has often also been referred to as a gangster film[40]; this is partly because of the costume and tentative loyalties between some of the team. In fact, the costume is reminiscent of the sixties brat pack heist film, *Ocean's Eleven* (1960), which featured a similar black-suited gang. Furthermore, *Pulp Fiction* (1994) parodies the gangster stereotype in two philosophizing but essentially dumb henchmen anchoring an episodic narrative of crime and violence. These characters are reminiscent of Momo and Ernest in François Truffaut's *Shoot the Pianist* (1960). Both of Tarantino's films have little to *say* about the mythology of the Mafia, but they do employ the costume and gestures of gangster stereotypes, along with many other cinematic allusions. There is no sense of the ethnic unity, or factual authenticity detailed in Mafia-orientated gangster films.[41] However, characters do connect across narratives. Tarantino is quoted as saying, "To me, they're all living inside of this one universe" (Smith, 1994: 41), which is reminiscent of the inter-textual referencing in films such as *The Godfather, Mean Streets* and *Goodfellas. Reservoir Dogs* reflects the gangs and wannabes trend, while *Pulp Fiction* alludes more to Mafia. Both refer to mythologies of organized crime through costume, gestures and actions, and the commercial success of the films has made them influential.

New Syndicates

The Grifters (1990), *Hoffa* (1992), *The Firm* (1993), *True Romance* (1993) *Leon/The Professional* (1994), *Bound* (1995) and *Get Shorty* (1996) see the Mafia moving back into the shadowy syndicate mold and providing the motivations that guide the narratives' main characters. For instance, the primary characters of these films are not always Mafia members, but their stories involve contact with the Mafia. *Hoffa* is about union strikes, *The Firm* is about crooked lawyers, *Leon/The Professional* is an assassin and *True Romance* is about young lovers on a crime spree. However, all three narratives use Mafia activity as the motivation for the actions of the main characters. These films are interesting for my discussion because, again, the Mafia is always Italian and often employs recognizable actors, bringing connections to previous films: Paul Sorvino in *The Firm* and Danny Aiello in *Leon/The Professional*. *Mad Dog and Glory* (1992) and *A Bronx Tale* (1993) have Robert De Niro playing against type as the straight man against stereotypical gangsters (Bill Murray in *Mad Dog and Glory*, Chazz Palminteri in *A Bronx Tale*). Christopher Walken resurfaces to parody a gangster stereotype in *True Romance* (1993), but later heads a family in *The Funeral* (1996).

The Funeral (1996) and *Donnie Brasco* (1997)

Abel Ferrara's *The Funeral* concentrates on Italian American cultural heritage within one family and the political environment of 1930s America. The protagonists are three brothers who operate an extortion racket at the time of the union battles, also depicted in the earlier film, *Hoffa*. The film examines the possible psychosis that pervades a Mafia family, whose history is built on violence and paranoia. The film develops an increasingly claustrophobic tension that is influenced by the Mafia stereotypes portrayed by Christopher Walken, Chris Penn and Vincent Gallo. As the *Sunday Telegraph* asserts, "You know these guys are capable of *anything*" (April 4, 1997), a knowledge that is based on previous gangster films as much as this specific narrative. I find this to be one of the more interesting gangster films of the 1990s mainly because it uses Mafia stereotypes in a brutal but intelligent way. It will be an important example in my later analyses. The characters in *The Funeral* are motivated by superstition and fear to act in the way they do. This is a fate mirrored in a later film, *Donnie Brasco* (1997).

Donnie Brasco is based on a biography. Joe Pistone (Johnny Depp), an FBI agent, infiltrates the Mafia, under the pseudonym Donnie Brasco, by befriending a small-time hood, Lefty Ruggiero (Al Pacino). The tired and disillusioned figure of Lefty dominates the film. The pathos surrounding the character is far greater than was evidenced in Pacino's previous gangster film, *Carlito's Way*. Lefty has never been anyone's hero, and this is shown as the reason for his weakness in his relationship with Donnie. The film expertly dissects the intricate hierarchy of Italian American Mafia relationships. The notion of the morality of traditional bosses in *The Godfather* appears naive after the brutality of *Goodfellas* and sympathy is now focused on the vulnerability of the little-men, rather than the angst of the upper echelons. Furthermore, the style is reminiscent of *Goodfellas,* in that many scenes are constructed as "staged documentary," as if monitored by FBI cameras. However, as with *The Godfather* or *The Funeral* the film's emphasis is on emotions as much as action. The characters may not be likeable, but they have well-rounded personalities and are not simply caricatures. The *Village Voice* describes Lefty as a "loveable goombah" (March 4, 1997). *Donnie Brasco* marks a significant shift in narrative focus from violence and style to psychological angst — a fitting precursor to the TV Series *The Sopranos.*

Another similar film from this era is *Gotti* (1996). Based on the life of John Gotti, the media obsessed head of the Bonnano crime family in New York, the film portrays Gotti (Armand Assante) as a personable man. This film is also intriguing because it focuses on a real life Mafia boss who was himself obsessed with Hollywood gangsters. John Gotti was a media hero at the same time he was on trial for murder. His public persona is one of the best examples of how Mafia mythology is an eclectic mix of media hype, real-life crime and pop culture history. It is hard to say how much the public persona of John Bonnano is based on a socially inherited Mafia character or a Hollywood-influenced stereotype. In turn, the film's narrative is loaded with explanations about Mafia hierarchy, procedures and history. Therefore, the film references *The Godfather* and predicts *The Sopranos* in that it is a clear example of the desire to link Mafia fiction with factual U.S. cultural and political history.

Casino (1995)

Casino (1995) takes us back to Las Vegas, and in the same style as *Bugsy* (1991) shows us the ambition of one man to rule the city. However, this time we're back in the early seventies. Mafia bosses are consigned to caricature vignettes in back rooms, making this film similar in focus to the syndicate-styled *Hoffa*, *The Grifters* and *The Firm.* The narration is delivered in voice-over by Sam "Ace" Rothstein (Robert De Niro) and (posthumously) by Nicky Santoro (Joe Pesci). What Sam wants more than anything is control over his share of the business empire in Vegas. However, the Mafia bosses are shown to be small-minded and untrusting of Sam's Jewish heritage, preferring to have the psychotic Nicky oversee Sam rather than allowing him free rein. As in

Bugsy, Scorsese shows the pursuit of profit by the bosses as the poison in the well of the Vegas dream. Many of the characters resemble the cast of *Goodfellas*. Pesci's character is an overt exaggeration of the previous psycho Tommy DeVito, and Sam is cooler but no less paranoid a front man than Jimmy Conway. As with the reviews of early nineties gangster films, style is noted as more dominant than narrative. *The Guardian* suggests "There are bits of almost every movie Scorsese has made blurred in it" (February 23, 1996). However, most reviews agree that it is mainly a re-working of the characters in *Goodfellas*: "Mere cartoon versions," according to the *Daily Mail* (February 23, 1996). The Mafia bosses remain in the shadows, as in the syndicate movies, and mostly the film concentrates on the cold brutality of these men. As in *The Godfather*, these bosses do not flaunt their wealth, but rather than romanticize this, *Casino* presents this trait as simply another part of the bosses' selfish control over the lower ranks. The bosses are shown as racist (against Sam) and out of touch with the business world (they do not care how the money is made, as long as they get their regular payments).

In summary, after 1991 films can be split into another two trends. Firstly, the Mafia itself recedes into the background, but the Italian stereotype is re-asserted. Back room bosses deliver the orders for the main protagonists to act upon (*The Grifters, Hoffa, Leon, Get Shorty*), or provide the danger for the main protagonist to overcome (*The Firm, True Romance, Bound*). Other films feature a return to more emotionally laden themes (*Carlito's Way, The Funeral, Donnie Brasco*), where the main gangster character is the focus for audience sympathies. The end of the nineties sees yet another resurgence of comedies in *Grosse Pointe Blank* (1997), *Analyze This* (1999), *Mickey Blue Eyes* (1999) and *Mafia!* (1999). All but *Grosse Pointe Blank* feature Italian American Mafia stereotypes and contemporary settings. *Mafia!* is a direct parody of the *Godfather* trilogy and *Casino*, while *Analyze This* and *Mickey Blue Eyes* combine the excessive style and brutality of *Goodfellas*, with Michael Felgate (Hugh Grant, *Mickey Blue Eyes*) romanticizing the gangster life in similar ways to Henry Hill. Martin Blank (John Cusack, *Grosse Pointe Blank*) parodies the "lone-wolf" hit man by suffering a personality crisis while fighting against an attempt to recruit him into a hit man trade union. The film also makes many references to this type of criminality as merely a career choice, foreshadowing the themes in such films as *Heat*. Similar to Martin Blank, Paul Vitti (Robert De Niro, *Analyze This*) is a mob boss with stress problems. De Niro's star persona obviously references previous roles, such as Jimmy Conway in *Goodfellas*, but *Analyze This* also parodies eighties and nineties Hollywood and its pre-occupation with damaged masculinities by de-mythologizing the usually exaggerated masculinity of an Italian Mafia boss. This theme is translated directly from the film into the television series *The Sopranos*, which effectively draws upon the same cinematic Mafia history, but is delivered in a TV soap opera format. I'll discuss the series in a moment.

*   *   *

Before I move on to *The Sopranos* and beyond I will take a moment to mention a relevant variation on gang films that developed in the 1990s, starting with *Colors* (1989), developed in *New Jack City* and epitomized in *Boyz n the Hood* (1991), *Menace II Society* (1993) and *Clockers* (1995). Reminiscent of black culture as portrayed in the blaxploitation films of the seventies, plus rags-to-riches and drug culture films, such as *Scarface* (1983), these films present a realistic view of life on the streets for young African Americans.[42] Protagonists are involved in, or at least surrounded by, gang rivalries, drugs, crime and violence. Rap music has brought the term "black gangsta" into mainstream culture and the loyalty oaths and vendettas enacted by some gangs resemble some of the mythologies of the Mafia. Therefore, these films can be associated with the gangs and wannabe characters discussed earlier. Most of these films suggest that inner city depravities and racial bigotry lie behind the rise in gang warfare. This links the gangs to the Italian and Irish immigrant experience in the early twentieth century. However, modern African American and Latin American gangs, represented as exploiting the drug habits of their own people (as the earlier immigrants exploited the gambling habits of theirs), fight only each other and thus actively participate in their own segregation from mainstream society. It is interesting to note that black assimilation is appearing in the world of pop music, where Rap, previously the voice of the dis-enfranchised, is now part of the mainstream. Therefore, it could be argued that images of black gangstas are assimilating into American popular culture in similar ways to early images of gangsters. For this reason, Munby (1999) suggests that black gang films are the nearest contemporary equivalents to the classical gangster films.

*   *   *

Black gangstas aren't the only multi-cultural examples of the gangster genre. It should also be noted that even though this book concentrates on Hollywood Gangsters, other cinemas have contributed to the style and character of Hollywood films. I have researched among others Russian, Italian, Japanese and British Mafia and gangland films. There are enough interesting examples to fill a lifetime of books. Each continent has its own history, myths and generic conventions. I do not have time to provide any kind of comprehensive overview. I would like to highlight post-sixties British films, such as *Get Carter* (1971), *The Long Good Friday* (1980) and *The Krays* (1990) and their focus on London gangland crime. They have tended to provide relatively unsentimental portrayals of organized crime. *The Long Good Friday* provided a cold antidote to *The Godfather Part I*, long before *Goodfellas*.[43] *The Krays* (1990), like many Hollywood films of the nineties, focuses on the ways in which the twins constructed their personae: "Clothes are important. They make you what you are [...] glamour is fear. If people are afraid of you, you can do anything" (Gary Kemp as Ronald Kray in *The Krays*, cited in McCarty: 205). These sentiments have continued through the millennium. Neo-noirs such as *Sexy Beast* (2001) and *Layer Cake* (2005), and gangland films such as *Charlie* (2004) *Love, Honor and Obey* (2006) and *The Business* (2006) keep the British gangland mythologies healthy at the box office. These myths also echo in the style-conscious feel of Hong Kong films, such as *A Better Tomorrow* (1987), *City on Fire* (1987) and *The Killer* (1989), or Japanese films, such as *Sonatine* (1993). Hong Kong films tend to be stylized and violent representations of contract killers and gangsters. The maintenance of a particular persona is a prominent feature of these films, as is the nemesis theme between a cop and his hunted criminal. Exchanges between Hong Kong, Japanese, or British films and Hollywood will not be examined in this book, as the focus is on the development of gangster films within America only, but the discussion of male melodrama in Chapter 4 will make reference to work on Hong Kong film.

Millennium Gangsters

Since *The Sopranos* has cornered the Mafia-as-emotional-soap-opera narrative, Hollywood has re-developed the face-off between cop and criminal in Scorsese's *The Departed* (2006) and Ridley Scott's *American Gangster* (2007). Both films rely on star power and stock scenes as shorthand for Mafia character. Frank Costello (Jack Nicholson) is a mix of Italian and Irish Mafia lore. He quotes the ever present mantra in Scorsese's Mafia world: "When I was your age they would say we can become cops or criminals," a development of the gangster or priest dichotomy. He also provides a neat reference to Mafia as a "dying breed." In answer to the news that someone's mother is dying he straightens his tie and states, "We all are — act accordingly." This is a performative gesture of identity that references the Mafia mythology of both dignity and fate: act your role until the bitter end. Costello meets his end like Tommy DeVito, or Lefty Ruggiero — dressed and ready for the occasion.

American Gangster refers directly to *The Godfather Parts I and II*. When Frank's (Denzel Washington) wife is threatened in an assassination attempt, he does a passing imitation of Michael Corleone's "study speech" to Frank Pentangelo. Michael's anger at having his family targeted in an assassination attempt is evident in his disgusted speech to Pentangelo: "In my home ... in my bedroom ... where my wife sleeps ... where my children come and play with their toys" (*The Godfather Part II*). Frank's imitation is brief— he explains his distress to Dominic Cattano (Armand Assante) in a similar study setting: "They tried to kill my wife! Who are they huh? ... Maybe it was one of your people." While *American Gangster* is meant to be based on a true story and *The Godfather* is pure fiction, the language and stock scenes reference the same mythology. The film further solidifies its attachment to generic convention when Frank's prophetic warning to his kid brother — "the loudest one in the room is the weakest"— pre-empts the beginning of his own downfall: He wears his wife's fur coat to a boxing match, thus drawing attention to himself and alerting the waiting cop, Richie Roberts (Russell Crowe), to his identity and prominence in the criminal underworld. The use this fatal flaw motif further reduces the film to a construction of set sequences. As suggested by the *Evening Standard* (March 13, 2008) *American Gangster* "rehashes the *French Connection* and *Goodfellas* clichés." *The New York Times* (December 7, 2007) notes how the characters are reduced to genre staples; "Denzel Washington wears the black hat, Russell Crowe wears the white."

Both *Gangs of New York* (2002) and *Road to Perdition* (2002) are father-son narratives that use gangland and Mafia activity as their backdrops. Set in the 1930s, *Road to Perdition* is a somber film full of "heavy trench coats, classic cars and cavernous wood-paneled offices" (*The Herald News* July 11, 2002), but as most reviews agree, the success of the film is achieved through aesthetics rather than narrative (*Times-Courier* July 27, 2002, *Newsday* July 12, 2002). The inclusion of Capone's crew and a ghoulish hit man Harlan Maguire (Jude law) reinforce Mafia stereotypes, but with muddled ethnicities, some Italian and some Irish. The film is part of a trend, as found in *Miller's Crossing* and *Last Man Standing*, which references the style and genre conventions of classical gangster film. *Gangs of New York* is set in 1863. It is an interesting period piece as the original book prefigures the rise of gangland activities in North America during the late nineteenth and early twentieth century immigration years. At best, the film re-enacts the petty turf wars of urban gangs and thus references the power of immigrant gangs to hold sway over certain areas. In this sense, the film suggests the history before Vito's story in *The Godfather Part II*, but with Irish gangs instead of Italian. On a surface narrative level however, the film is about revenge: The son returns to gain justice for his slain father. None of the detail that is painstakingly woven into the period setting and costumes is directed into the narrative. The film is brutal in its violence, beautiful in its cinematography, but it carries no resonance in the gangster genre. In the main, cinematic Mafia have been ominously quiet since the millennium.

The Sopranos 1999–2007

Maybe *The Sopranos* has "whacked" the cinema gangster, or perhaps, as Glen Creeber suggests, the cinematic gangster declined a while ago from "cinematic epic to standard Video or television fare" (Creeber, 2002: 125), and *The Sopranos* is "an attempt to look back longingly to a genre that was once perhaps more morally stable and secure than it can ever be today" (*ibid.*). His argument is that cinema has been too heavily influenced by TV aesthetics and this has resulted in the demise of Mafia grandeur on screen. While it is true that the Mafia in cinema has been quiet in the new millennium, his argument focuses almost entirely on Tarantino's films as the cause, which as I already mentioned do prioritize style over content. However, they are not the only examples of the gangster genre in the nineties, even though they do highlight a significant trend. I think that the cinematic grandeur of *The Godfather* has always been understood as unique and that there's more at work in post–*Godfather* films than a battle between TV and cinema. This will become apparent as the book proceeds. Right now, let's take a brief look at the style and structure of *The Sopranos*.

To summarize a TV series that spans six seasons in eight years of production to a set of styles and tendencies is obviously difficult. What began as a parody, the suburban gangster with a mid-life crisis, grew into a more complex study of modern American life. While *The Godfather* remains the most commonly quoted reference point for the characters in the series, the later episodes are able to reference their own "classic moments." For instance, while Pussy's murder was originally a reference to Luca Brazi "swimming with the fishes" (*The Godfather*) by season six, the reference to Pussy's death stands alone. The show is generally accepted as one of the most successful TV series of recent years. It has held court while Hollywood gangsters have been notably absent. Therefore, it is not surprising that it gives the impression of wiping gangsters from the big screen to the small. Creeber again suggests that Tony Soprano is a "cinematic-sized gangster trapped in TV land: Frustrated by the constant need to express his feelings, this Mafia boss is not simply resisting the contemporary preoccupation with self-analysis but also struggling to adapt to television's obsession with the private and personal dynamics of human experience" (127). I find this a truly entertaining approach to the series and it certainly accounts for the format that simultaneously idolizes the cinematic grandeur while prioritizing self-involved melodrama. However, it is Tony Soprano's identity as Mafia boss as American male that results in some of this series' most uncomfortable themes.

The series continues the 1990s tendency to prioritize real-life stories. George de Stefano notes how David Chase draws on actual events for his storylines. The opening storyline for the fifth season involves two gangsters recently released from prison, Feech La Manna (Robert Loggia) and Tony Blundetto (Steve Buscemi). This storyline, according to Stefano, came straight from an article in the Newark *Star-Ledger* about the RICO[44] trials of the 1980s (161) and how the men imprisoned then would now be eligible for parole. The series also concentrates on traditional Mafia business practices, internal hierarchies, economic structures, as well as offering perceptions of gender, racial and sexual prejudices. The series simultaneously promotes realism and genre conventions. It not only presents Mafia as an ongoing business, but also gangs as wannabes. They want to be the old style gangsters, but that time has gone. In the later series, the family witnesses the steady decline of family businesses to corporations local stores sold to "Jamba Juice." Hence, the series, like many postclassical gangster films, is focused heavily on nostalgia. Silvio Dante (Steve Van Zandt), probably the most constant of Mafia figures in the series, is the main repository of Mafia lore. It is significant then that he is the only character who is not self-obsessed and does not self-destruct. I would argue that he is the only one who truly views himself within the context of Mafia history (albeit the mythology). The others all want to control history, or rise above it. The series is a suitable ending to my study, because it answers the nostalgia of *The Godfather*. It is hard to compare across mediums, but *The Sopranos* is a hugely significant cultural text and thus stamps a significant footprint on the continuation of Mafia mythologies on screen.

Conclusions

To return to the initial discussion of genre cycles, it is evident that the gangster genre does not fade away after the films Cawelti and Schatz describe as deconstructions, *Bonnie and Clyde* and *The Godfather*. However, Schatz's model is still useful because films from 1967 onwards are noted as self-reflexive in terms of cinema, and also cultural histories. Furthermore, films continue as cycles within each particular decade, beginning with pivotal films such as *The Godfather* (1972), *Scarface* (1983) and *Goodfellas* (1990), and ending in *Bugsy Malone* (1976), *Married to the Mob* (1988), *Analyze This*, or *Mickey Blue Eyes* (1999) and finally *The Sopranos* (1997–2007). These cycles in some ways reflect Schatz's model of the classical era, but also differ from it. For instance, films in the early seventies reflect previous European films and styles, plus the styles of Hollywood films. *The Godfather* is different to earlier gangster films mainly because it deals with the Mafia community, rather than an individual. Some films that follow *The Godfather* reflect this new approach and offer biopics and romantic fictionalizations of Mafia communities. There is then a parody, *Bugsy Malone*, and the gangster film fades away for a while. However, not all films follow *The Godfather* model. *Mean Streets*, *The Outfit* and in fact the parody refer back to the 1930s films.

* * *

Similarly, in the 1980s, *Scarface* offers a re-working of the original film, but with the graphic violence and excessive materialism of modern America. Later films also focus upon material excess and lead to the parody *Married to the Mob*. However, other films, such as *The Untouchables* and *The Sicilian*, romanticize the gangster and prioritize the history of organized crime or ethnic loyalties. In the nineties, *Goodfellas* mixes self-conscious style with realistic brutality to show the work-a-day existence over three decades of Italian Mafia business. Later films also expose the fragility of Mafia existence from an outsider's point of view and lead to the parodies *Analyze This* and *Mickey Blue Eyes*. However, the nineties also employ Italian Mafia stereotypes in marginal roles (*The Firm*, *Leon*), black gangstas (*New Jack City*, *Pulp Fiction*) and WASP gangsters (*King of New York*, *Reservoir Dogs*). *The Sopranos* dominates the post-millennium era and is a cycle all on its own. It develops from parody to darkness to romanticism and it certainly stands alone as the modern face of screen Mafia while the cinema remains quiet.

There are many reasons the Mafia remains quiet in cinema. Italian American directors have moved on to different subjects. The cop-versus-gangster narrative has made a return, as has the superhero narrative. Both of these move Mafia from center stage to the dark shadows. The Italian Mafia has become a stereotype that is instantly recognizable in marginal roles; they are very useful in providing instant terror or intrigue to a mainstream crime narrative. This is evident in the screen adaptations of John Grisham's novels, such as *The Firm* and *The Client* (1994), and is as prevalent in post–*Soprano* crime narratives. *In the Electric Mist* (2009) uses the popular stereotype to identify Julie "Baby Feet" Balboni (John Goodman). His narrative purpose is instantly recognizable, not as the primary criminal, but as the reason the criminal exists. Balboni's business practices provide a haven for the film's serial killer (an ex-cop turned security manager). As such, the Mafia becomes shorthand for, or at least a driving force behind, all criminal activity. It does appear that at present the Mafia has receded from the center of narratives and instead appears through stereotypes that present them as a simplistic and much-maligned force; they are instantly recognizable though through name, stature and attitude. In the next two chapters I seek to show how this has occurred through the gradual development of genre and Mafia myths.

In conclusion, it is possible to trace cycles of production through aesthetic styles, but this does not account for the fluidity of themes and structures within these films. The films display levels of self-referentiality and intertextuality, which undermine any analysis that adheres only to production or text-based evidence. Furthermore, Schatz's model requires a classic structure to which all others refer. This cannot occur, even in the classical era, because films always refer to previous styles, cinematic or otherwise (literary, factual events and cultural myths).[45] What is identifiable is that cycles of films occur over the four decades since 1967, and each time the reference points become wider, thus allowing for more wide-ranging examples of films that can be categorized as part of a gangster genre. This is also traceable in the classical era; for example, film noir includes some examples that can also be categorized as syndicate films.[46] However, postclassical films have the added input of more expansive mythologies of crime, which will be discussed in Chapter 3, together with critical credibility and commercial successes, star directors and actors, which will be discussed in Chapter 2. These have all added to an ever-increasing cultural interest in Mafia activity in popular culture.

Gangster films, then, can be split into four cycles that move from influential films to parodies, one in each decade. Within those cycles, the three trends of gangster films, which have been labeled gangsters as outlaws, gangsters as Mafia families or ongoing businesses, and gangsters as gangs and wannabes, thrived. To summarize the entire era, some of the significant factors that distinguish postclassical gangster films from their predecessors are as follows. Firstly, the tendency is to focus on the Mafia as an organization rather than the gangster as a lone individual. The syndicate, or invisible organization that featured in the fifties and sixties, is unveiled in films such as *The Godfather* and *Goodfellas,* so that issues of community and specific ethnic traditions are as important as the criminal business. In essence, the Mafia that once inhabited the margins of society,[47] or Hollywood narratives, has now moved into the center. James Cagney and Edward G. Robinson portrayed transient figures, only tasting success for a brief moment. Postclassical gangster heroes include these character types, but also successful bosses. Furthermore, as central protagonists, their sense of morality, although criminal, is presented as an unavoidable and binding element of their world. Ethnic heritage is now at the forefront of film narratives, with the Italian American Mafia dominating mainstream examples of organized crime.

Reference points and trends in gangster films of the nineties are eclectic in the extreme, incorporating classical Hollywood, European influences and Hollywood films of the seventies and eighties. The distinct trends of gangs and wannabes against gangsters as Mafia are still identifiable, although cross-references are also more apparent. One of the reasons for this change is the propensity for gangsters to be identified by costumes or gestures that allude to gangster stereotypes, an element often referred to in reviews as the style of organized crime. Supposed authenticity and biographical research is still prioritized in the publicity and reviews of a core of films (*Goodfellas, Bugsy, Casino, Gotti* and *Donnie Brasco*), but others self-consciously draw upon the mythologies to supply short-hand characters (*Miller's Crossing, Reservoir Dogs, Pulp Fiction, Leon, The Firm, Hoffa,* et al.). The trend in gangs and wannabes has focused increasingly on African Americans, while one or two films have offered new twists on old themes (*Carlito's Way* and *The Funeral*).

In general, classical Hollywood gangster films did not focus on themes of history and community, insofar as the narratives tended to focus on the future and individual ambition. History and tradition, both cinematic and cultural, to the point where an individual can be forced to sacrifice personal ambition for the security of the community (e.g. *The Godfather* and *Gotti*), are important themes in postclassical gangster films. Furthermore, Mafia mythologies are larger than one family, or one film. Therefore, we can identify community and a sense of history as crucial elements of postclassical gangster films. *The Godfather* progresses this type of cinematic allusion by alluding to the history of the Italian American Mafia in real life as well as film. Later films, such as *Goodfellas* and *Pulp Fiction*, have returned to the French New Wave's attention to costume and gestures. Therefore, this subject will be discussed in Chapter 2, as a key to generic identity.

* * *

Having provided an overview of the key films of the chosen era, in the next chapter I will build on this analysis by developing the discussion of genre. The intention is to provide an overview of how the gangster genre has been discussed in the past and how new genre theories have developed to embrace more discursive approaches. By showing how genre is evoked through narrative, iconography, publicity, newspaper reviews and academic writing, in the next chapter examines the discursive nature of genre. The intention is to make a contribution to the continuing debates within genre study, as well as exploring the question of how it is that so many different films, especially in the nineties, came to be associated with the gangster genre.

2

Theorizing the Gangster Genre

There is always a concern when studying film as part of a genre that it is somehow reductive, limiting the analysis rather than opening it out. However, the gangster genre is an ever-present label in discourses in and around Hollywood cinema. Film marketing, reviews and academic scholarship all refer to the gangster genre as knowable and culturally understood. On the other hand, genre theorists often ignore the gangster genre (or fold it into a discussion on crime films in general). Perhaps it is because the gangster genre appears so easily understood that it receives so little special attention. In my view, the gangster genre has been overlooked in recent serious genre studies, and while I do not want to limit my discussion to what does or does not constitute a genre, I do think an understanding of how genre is spoken of in and around film is a necessary part of my analyses.

Recent scholarly work (Jancovich and Geraghty 2008) berates genre analyses for creating canons and identifying key films and thus neglecting others. This is a valid point especially in respect to the creation of value-based canons. However in practice, especially with the gangster film, key texts do occur at least as common reference points in marketing, reviews and other related discourses to which later ones openly refer and are compared. Nothing makes this more apparent than *The Sopranos'* love affair with *The Godfather* and *The Godfather Part II*, which the TV series values above all other films. David Pattie (2003) notes how the Soprano family displays utter disdain for the Scorsese films, but reverence for *The Godfather*. He notes how the series quotes *The Godfather* as "not simply a film; it is an original myth, both for the series and the community it reflects" (140). In contrast, "Tony and his crew do not love *Goodfellas*; in fact, they rarely mention it" (141). Pattie suggests that this is because Scorsese's work reflects their own positions too closely and undermines the grandeur of the Mafia mythology they worship. This is one cause to be sure, but their reverence also quite simply reflects a natural inclination to identify favorites, or prioritize some narratives over others. One of the unique qualities of gangster films is the way in which film texts openly reference each other. This goes beyond the postmodern trend for cinematic allusion or self-referential knowingness. It is part of the Mafia meta-text that exists within American popular culture. *The Sopranos* obviously is both "like" *Goodfellas* and "in love" with *The Godfather* because it is of the same genre and draws from the same myths. However, *The Sopranos'* reverence for the latter film dominates because of its notoriety as a key genre text. In this sense, *The Godfather* is not only a key text in the gangster genre through iconography, narrative or themes, it is a key text because of the effect it has had on viewers, reviewers, scholars and subsequent films and TV shows. In view of this, I want to use an extended discussion of genre theory to map out patterns of discourses across the cycles of gangster films identified in Chapter 1 to show how the gangster genre is formed partly through intertextual discourse. I believe that genre is as a fluid concept, but one which still includes certain tendencies and responses.

The intentions of this chapter are constituted by three interconnecting discussions. Firstly, it provides an overview of the way in which the gangster film has previously been discussed as a genre. This focuses primarily on producers and classic texts, as these elements have tended to dominate genre theory. Secondly, it discusses the role of genre theories more generally, with a view to providing an initial context for the case studies. This discussion considers some of the cultural shifts in genre theory that have focused on fluidity, hybridity and the importance of reception. Thirdly, this chapter assesses postclassical gangster films in response to previous writings on the gangster film and recent genre theories. Topics discussed in this chapter include textual analyses of narrative and iconography, and extratextual analyses of authorship, stars and film reviews. This chapter will show how both textual and extratextual information combine to provide a discursive network of gangster images and how these operate as signifiers of the gangster genre.

Discussions of genre predate cinema. Andrew Tudor has noted: "It is very difficult to identify even a tenuous school of thought on the subject" (Tudor, 1973: 3). However, for nearly four decades a particular debate has been circulating within film theory: what is the process through which films are categorized into particular genres? For instance, is it a textual issue, a property of the text, which it is the business of viewers and critics to determine? Is it a marketing issue, a matter determined in the processes of production? Or is it a cultural issue, a matter of the wider social issues which circulate around texts? The approach to this question has taken various routes, most of which have understandably echoed the theoretical discourses of the period. Genre theory has variously focused on the producers, the text and the consumers in an attempt to determine how categorization works.

Classical Theories: Classic Texts

Warren Buckland (1998) has outlined two approaches to genre: descriptive and functional. The descriptive approach is concerned with identifying the structural elements, such as narrative, setting and costume, which could be said to distinguish a particular genre. For example, Colin McArthur (1971) identifies particular styles of clothes, guns, cars and urban settings across many crime films. Similarly, Robert Warshow (1946) had already identified a particular "rise and fall" trajectory in classic crime narratives and a central protagonist who was both hero and villain personified: a "tragic hero." Warshow identified the gangster genre as a "complete and self-contained drama" (Warshow, 1954: 466), quite simply "a story of enterprise and success ending in precipitate failure" (*ibid.*: 453). The functional approach leads on from such descriptions to explore the themes and pleasures of a particular genre. The gangster film, according to Warshow, encourages an audience to glory in the gangster's acts of violence, but this appeal is encouraged by his "weakness as much as his power and freedom" (*ibid.*: 454). The gangster's eventual demise is shown to be a direct result of his over-indulgent lifestyle, not a restrictive justice or social system. As with the Westerner, another stalwart figure of genre criticism, Warshow describes the gangster as an exciting hero, but in contrast to the Westerner's ability to display justifications for his acts of violence, the gangster relishes an "irresponsible freedom" (*ibid.*: 465). Categorizing his life as uncontrollably dangerous legitimizes his destruction. The function of the gangster genre is to provide a fantasy of excess: "He appeals to that side of all of us which refuses to believe in the 'normal' possibilities of happiness and achievement" (*ibid.*: 454), but it also ultimately releases the audience from that fantasy, which the gangster "shows to be dangerous" (*ibid.*).

Both descriptive and functional approaches tend to produce a fairly restrictive framework. Very few films fulfill the selected criteria completely. Warshow concentrated on only three gangster films, *Little Caesar* (1930), *Public Enemy* (1931) and *Scarface* (1932). Subsequently, from his description, they became the quintessential examples of the genre. They are labeled as the "classic form" to which all others refer. This is representative of the fact that his descriptive approach to genre focused on narrative structures. Warshow's account of the rise-and-fall narrative (1946) as part of the "typical" gangster film, and demonstrated in the three classic examples, apparently closed the book on the subject: the genre had a specific meaning, which was manifest within the rise and fall narrative. By 1954, Warshow wrote, "The gangster movie [...] no longer exists in its 'classical' form" (*ibid.*: 453). This statement is not surprising as his criteria called for all gangster films to have virtually the same narrative and the production code had as much to do with that demise as anything else. Warshow's analyses are useful in two ways. Firstly, along with Andre Bazin and Lawrence Alloway, he was a pioneer of genre study. All three began writing in the 1950s and 1960s and all maintained that genres "carried an intrinsic meaning or significance" (Hutchings, in Hollows and Jancovich, 1995: 61). Warshow's analyses are also important in that they are the first academic writings to conceive of the gangster film as a unique form: distinct from other crime films. Secondly, his work offered a "sense of the cultural and historical specificity" (*ibid.*: 63) of the films, in that he regarded the gangster as a critique of, or an expression of ambivalence towards, American values. He also broached issues of production and of audience expectation:

> The gangster film is simply one example of the movies' constant tendency to create fixed dramatic patterns that can be repeated indefinitely with a reasonable expectation of profit [...] It is only in an ultimate sense that the type appeals to its audience's experience of reality; much more immediately, it appeals to previous experience of the type itself; it creates its own field of reference [Warshow, 1948: 85].

Warshow recognized the fact that genre films are an industry staple and audiences are aware of particular narrative conventions in relation to them. However, his writings maintain the view that the intrinsic meaning or significance of the genre is to be found *within* particular texts, rather than in audiences' experiences of the texts.

Genre criticism as a specific subject area grew in popularity by the late 1960s and began to challenge narrative-based identification of genres. Structuralism appealed to genre theorists because it allowed for discrepancies within, and the evolution of, genre texts. This was because methods of analysis concentrated on the relationship between elements in a particular signifying process, or communication, rather than simply the elements themselves. Considerations of narrative, myth and structural iconography are the dominant features of early 1970s genre criticism. The focus was on a search for a specific element, or relationships between elements, that can isolate one genre from another, and according to which all films can then be safely classified. Notions of authorship still featured prominently in film studies at this time and genre criticism reflected this fact, by incorporating notions of iconography and myth along with directorial decisions.

*   *   *

Notions of iconography and myth are important terms for this book, in that I shall trace how postclassical gangster films operate as carriers of myth, using variations on iconography and convention. Furthermore, the following chapter will examine how Mafia myths also inform the structure and credibility of postclassical gangster films. Lawrence Alloway was one of the first to introduce to the analysis of cinema the notion of iconography, whereby certain visual motifs are identified as characteristic of particular genres. Like Warshow, Alloway prioritized the text as the site of meaning, decrying auteur theory by stating that "typical patterns of recurrence and change in popular films can be traced better in terms of iconography than in terms of individual creativity" [Alloway, 1971: 41]. He was quickly joined by critics such as Jim Kitses (1969), whose analysis of the Western (*Horizons West*) and Colin McArthur (1971), whose work on the gangster film (*Underworld USA*), appear to agree that an iconographic analysis could lead to a more coherent form of genre definition. Adhering closely to the text, both studies concentrate on the composite form of narrative themes and visual styles. The results include Kitses' now famous "wilderness vs. civilization" table of oppositional elements[1] and McArthur's iconographic description of common gangster motifs: "The peculiar squareness of their hated and coated figures is an extension of their physical presence, a visual shorthand for their violent potential" (McArthur, 1971: 26). The importance of iconography became apparent when it was discovered that certain elements were able to signify a particular genre when viewed beyond their filmic context (e.g. the Stetson as an icon of the western). It is through a familiarity with narrative and contextual themes, according to theorists such as Kitses, that such identifications occur. It is not the item alone that signifies the genre, but its function as part of the associated pattern of that genre. This theory relies upon structural consistencies in genre repetition and therefore continues to construct a formalist rubric for genre determination. Where Kitses and McArthur agree most is on the premise that genre is made up of recurrent patterns of narrative, thematic and iconographic motifs that combine to form an overall signification pattern, or definable style.

The comforting familiarity of genre allows not only the form, but individual images to take on special importance as icons or symbols: the Stetson hat in any image context cannot be disassociated from its signification as an icon of the West. Vivian Sobchack (1977) states that particular icons possess an emotional weight that carries beyond their filmic context. In view of the inherent contextuality of all images and discourses, it is perhaps more accurate to suggest, as Lévi-Strauss does, that the icon would not exist without its contextual foundation as part of a pattern: "If there is meaning to be found in mythology, this cannot reside in the isolated elements which enter into the composition of a myth, but only in the way the elements are combined" (Lévi-Strauss, 1966: 105). If we attach special affection to certain icons of the gangster genre (for example, the tommy gun, or silk suits) it is only because of their contextual relationship to other elements in the films. The ritualistic form of genre is founded upon the way these combinations are repeated in such a way as to give each element a sense of autonomous significance. In this way, Leutrat's (1973) definition of genre as a "continuous," or meta-text is useful. He states, "The only way a genre model or genre rules can be said to exist is as [...] a memorial metatext and on that level alone. It is because viewers/readers operate with sets of expectations and levels of predictability that it is possible to perceive instances of variation, repetition, rectification and modification. In this way, genre can be considered as one single continuous text" (Neale, 1980: 51). In other words, as myth, the form must both evolve and reify itself to each new generation of viewers/readers within practically the same framework in order to retain its significance, but sustain popularity. This could go part way to explaining how gangster films evolve while remaining so familiar. I will return to the discussion of iconography and myth in a moment to assess the extent to which both have evolved in the postclassical period. However, before this can be achieved effectively, let's look at the narrative structures in our chosen gangster films.

Narrative Structure

For Warshow, the gangster's story was one of "enterprise and success ending in precipitate failure" (Warshow, 1954: 453). No other structural definition has been offered in writings on the gangster film to contradict the "rise and fall" narrative that he posits. It could be suggested that *The Godfather Parts I* and *II*, if added together, fit this narrative model. However, Michael is not killed, imprisoned, or bankrupt at the end of the narrative. Instead, his failure is implied by the loss of his family and is thus emotional rather than physical. Rise-and-fall narratives still occur: *Bonnie and Clyde*, *Scarface*, *Goodfellas*, *New Jack City*, *Bugsy*, *Casino* and *American Gangster* have uncomplicated rise-and-fall narratives. The protagonists die by the end, except Jimmy Conway, Henry Hill (*Goodfellas*), Sam Rothstein (*Casino*) and Frank Lucas (*American Gangster*), who all lose their freedom or power instead. The narrative structure of *Once Upon a Time in America* makes a rise-and-fall trajectory difficult to isolate. Noodles' downfall occurs half-way through the narrative when he betrays his friends to the law. By the end of the narrative, Max is presumed dead, but Noodles is now relieved of his guilt. The structure of the narrative is such that intermittent flashbacks portray Noodles' memories, and thus any cause-and-effect trajectory is dominated by the more prominent narrative of deception and revelation. In my view, while the rise-and-fall narrative can still be traced through many of these films, it is not the core of the genre's narrative structure.

It could be suggested that postclassical films refer to the rise and fall structure, but simply re-negotiate the trajectory. *The Godfather Part I* depicts the success of the family, while *Part II* displays both the rise and the beginning of the fall. *Once Upon a Time in America* still portrays the rise and fall of the gang, albeit within a parallel mystery narrative. Many films begin at the point of success and track the downfall; for example, *The Brotherhood*, *Miller's Crossing*, *State of Grace*, *King of New York*, *Carlito's Way*, *The Funeral* and *Donnie Brasco*. There are also those that do not adhere to these structures: for example, *Mean Streets*, *Gloria*, *Prizzi's Honor*, *The Untouchables*, *The Godfather Part III*, *Reservoir Dogs*, *Mad Dog and Glory*, *Pulp Fiction* and *Analyze This*. Some of these are arguably genre hybrids whose connections to the gangster genre are less likely to be based on narrative structure, but some, such as *Mean Streets* and *The Godfather Part III*, have narrative elements that resemble the rise-and-fall trajectory but in different ways. Structurally *The Godfather Part III* resembles *Part I*, in that power is passed on from the father figure to the son, while in *Mean Streets* a group of friends inhabit the peripheries of organized crime and are affected by its presence. They do not rise within the organisation, although Charlie is shown to be ambitious in this way. As such, both films feature characters that rise-and-fall, but it is not the main structuring element of their narratives.

The Sopranos refers to the rise-and-fall structure when Christopher Molisanti (Michael Imperioli) is attempting to write his own gangster film scripts during seasons 1 and seasons 6. However, it is also evident that Christopher's story is the one that most resembles the classic rise-and-fall trajectory over the six seasons. He is ambitious and gains responsibility within the family. He craves more, even considering usurping his Uncle Tony. However, in the end his fatal flaw of drug addiction makes him a liability for the family, and his death is not a real surprise. Tony's story is an adaptation of the rise-and-fall trajectory in that he takes over the business and maintains it against all odds over six seasons. The finale pays homage to this most classic of genre conventions by setting up a scenario for Tony's demise (with plenty of allusions to the classic diner scene in *The Godfather*) but it refuses to follow through. This is a fitting way for the series to end, because throughout the writers have simultaneously acknowledged and undermined genre conventions. The fade-to-black as the diner door opens (admitting either Meadow or Tony's killer) provides the possibility for either the soap opera or the gangster ending and leaves it to audiences to decide which one they want. It is evident that a TV series must offer a more complicated web of stories, but not all gangster films can employ the same narrative trajectory either.

*   *   *

Warshow's analysis also concluded that gangster films display a narrative of "enterprise and success" (*ibid.*). This is appropriate to most of the films identified above and especially the TV series, if we interpret enterprise and success to represent organized crime as a business. This is one of the themes that distinguish postclassical gangster films from earlier examples,[2] but again not *all* those identified as gangster films display it. Gangster films all feature some element of organised or ongoing business alongside the enterprises of the main protagonists. This may simply be a sense of history that the current criminal group aspires to, as in *New Jack City*, or it may be an ongoing business that the main protagonist is employed by, as in *Leon/The Professional* (1994). The important factor here is that enterprise is contextualized within a larger criminal organization that is identified within the narrative, rather than being an extratextual influence interpreted by viewers, such as previous films, mythologies and other cultural associations. Therefore, the narrative presents other Mafia members, meetings, deals, or confrontations that show the wider criminal world in which the main protagonists operate: for example, meetings with Charlie's Uncle Giovanni (Cesare Danova in *Mean Streets*), Tony (Danny Aiello in *The Professional*), or confrontations with other drug dealing gangs in *New Jack City*. The level of success achieved in such enterprises is not consistent across films. Vincent Canby (*New York Times*) describes Charlie (*Mean Streets*) as a "trainee executive in the syndicate" (October 3, 1973). His success as a trainee is limited because of his loyalty to friends, such as Johnny Boy (Robert De Niro), who disregard the rules of the Mafia. Lefty Ruggiero's (*Donnie Brasco*) success resides only in the fact that he has survived twenty years in the business. *Reservoir Dogs* focuses on the mistakes made by a gang of criminals, not only in the featured heist, but in dialogue about past exploits. Therefore, success cannot be said to characterize all postclassical gangster films, even when interpreted as a business analogy. In short, narrative alone, or a singular overriding theme (Warshow), is not enough to account for the diversity of gangster films, especially in the postclassical era. However, it is still possible to trace instances of rise-and-fall narratives within the collection of films and so it is still an identifiable trend.

Theoretical Challenges: Cultural Shifts

A reassessment of the nature of genres is conducted in Steve Neale's *Genre* (1980). He suggests that they possess a dialectic function, as "systems of orientations, expectations and conventions that circulate between industry, text and subject" (Neale: 19). His view is that the elements that constitute a genre are part of a discursive process which is constantly "modifying, transforming and restructuring" (*ibid.*) itself in line with the influences and expectations of the industry, text and subject. He argues that far too much emphasis has been placed upon icons in films, stating that the repetition of signifiers is subject to modifications, in that it "always involves an element of difference" (*ibid.*: 50). In other words, the repeated appearance of items such as the Stetson hat does not possess exactly the same significance each time. The nature and function of iconography has to take account of difference and variation as well as repetition. Neale does not diminish the role of iconography; he simply argues against restricting signifiers to one meaning.

In this way, he suggests that genres are capable of both evolution *and* self-referentiality. This is an important issue in that iconography remains a crucial aspect of signification in the gangster film and the recognition of both its familiarity and its ability to evolve is something I will engage with in a moment. By releasing genre theory from its roots in textual and auteur analysis, Neale sees Hollywood cinema as a more fluid environment capable of "both regulation and variety" (*ibid.*: 51). These suggestions have enabled the arena of genre studies to develop a less rigid schema for the analysis of its subject.

It was 1991 before Steve Neale's essay, "Questions of Genre," came along to seriously reopen the genre debate. This essay defines genre less as a construct of icons, narrative patterns and film styles, and more as an "attitude" that surrounds the production and consumption of the individual film. A genre is a mosaic of concerns that includes all the structural elements, but also shifts between audience or individual perceptions, marketing and an ambiguous sense of "style." Neale's interpretation of genre as a process, which he began in 1980, is now expanded into three interactive levels: expectation, the generic corpus and the rules or norms that govern both. Thus, Neale assimilates the notion of cinematic genre with the literary convention of "canon," wherein each example does not exist on its own, but is assessed in relation to a general hierarchy of proposed concerns and other examples.[3] Consequently, Neale's work searches for criteria by which the construction of genre could be assessed, suggesting such avenues as everyday discourse, newspaper reviews and studio publicity. While he maintains both a textual and context based approach, he argues that genres cannot be simply ideological vehicles or "collective cultural expressions" (Williams, 1984, quoted in Neale, 1991: 178). On a structural level he states, "Genres can each involve a 'dominant' aesthetic device" (Neale: 179), and even though this dominant may not be an exclusive element, it can still help to underpin a particular genre's form.

Iconography and Conventions

Alloway and McArthur both suggest that iconography, along with narrative and thematic patterns, can identify a particular genre. Leutrat views genre as a continuous, or meta-text, in that signifiers of the genre such as iconography constantly evolve through repetition within the same framework. In this book, I will include convention alongside iconography, as it is not only visual motifs that suggest genre. Particular dialogue and plot scenarios are repeated across many examples and thus can be identified as conventions of the gangster film, and thus also influence genre recognition. Therefore, we can extend previous arguments to suggest that iconography and conventions encourage genre recognition across different frameworks. In other words, iconography and conventions can suggest a particular genre within any film. Subsequently, iconography can no longer be accepted as a cause-effect approach, wherein certain iconography (hats, coats, or urban settings) signify certain themes, but must be viewed as more open and discursive. Alloway *et al.* were searching for defining elements, whereas it is more appropriate to suggest that certain iconography and conventions conjure particular generic references that influence genre recognition. One example would be *Mean Streets*, in that the inclusion of Uncle Giovanni, with his formal suits and heavy jewelry, can be identified as referencing the iconography of the gangster genre. Furthermore, the link between Italian American men and crime can be seen as a convention of gangster films, achieved and developed through the repetition of such gangster activity in Hollywood movies. In consequence, films that portray Italian American families often also include allusions to gangster activity: for example, *A Brooklyn State of Mind* (1996), which is essentially a romance, includes references to Mafia traditions employed in the Italian American family, even though most are not shown to be criminally active. Danny Parente (Danny Aiello) is a similar character to Uncle Giovanni (*Mean Streets*). He signifies Mafia traditions within the local Italian American community through his activities as much as visual appearance. Dressed mostly in ordinary looking suits, making him look like a regular business man — not unlike the appearance of Vito Corleone — his presence amongst the neighborhood is as a man to whom all families and businesses defer seemingly out of respect. He is often viewed at the head of family tables talking about the honor of family, or patronizing local businesses and expressing his belief in the importance of keeping such places open and profitable. Therefore, his persona is similar to Vito Corleone, a patriarchal figure whose protection of Italian traditions and morals is a binding force for the local community. The narrative then proceeds to unveil Parente's criminal past and in consequence destroys the community's respect for him, thus revealing the contradictory impulses of Mafia patriarchy in the Italian American community.[4] This is similar to the actions of the funeral director Bonasara (Salvatore Corsitto) who appeals for the Don's help during the opening scenes of *The Godfather*, but is then distressed at the outside world discovering his association with such a man. The gangster element is sub-text in *A Brooklyn State of Mind*, rather than the main narrative, but the iconography and conventions exist and encourage responses to the film that include references to the gangster genre. Reviews compared it unfavorably to other gangster films: Variety called it "Dramatically functional, but [the film] has little to add to the well-trodden genre" (cited in *Halliwell's Film and TV Guide*, 1999), which is slightly unfair, as the film's narrative is not focused on gangster activity. The iconography of the film also includes two actors, Abe Vigoda and Morgana King, best known as Tessio and Mama Corleone in *The Godfather* which probably further encouraged reviewers to search for evidence of Mafia associations within the narrative.

An important example of iconography influencing genre recognition is that of *Bonnie and Clyde*. As stated in Chapter 1, labeling it a gangster film is justifiable, in that the fugitives are criminals. However, their actions are similar to mythologies surrounding John Dillinger, as well as the obvious references to the real-life Bonnie and Clyde. It is the narrative structure (enterprise and failure), as well as the iconography of cars, guns and costume that alludes to the gangster in this film. Clyde wears the kind of fedora hat, suit and spats that are associated with gangsters of the 1930s, especially *Little Caesar* and *Scarface*. The best example of the gangster iconography in *Bonnie and Clyde* are the photographs taken by the gang that show Bonnie and Clyde holding guns and posing by one of their cars. The costume, guns and car are iconographic of classic gangster films, most notably *Scarface*, as Clyde's costume and the couples child-like enthusiasm with guns resembles that of Tony Camonte (Paul Muni). Such similarities are not surprising as both films are set in the 1930s, but also because the real-life Bonnie and Clyde were said to model their looks and demeanor on the screen gangsters of the time. *Bonnie and Clyde* may have a rise-and-fall narrative, but the couple's crimes are not organized as part of a larger criminal scheme, thus also eliminating them from the business-enterprise schema often associated with gangster films. It is a crime spree rather than an organized, ongoing business. Later films that are directly influenced by *Bonnie and Clyde* include *Badlands*, *True Romance*, *Kalifornia* and *Natural Born Killers*. None of these films, except some elements of *True Romance* (discussed later), feature organized crime as an ongoing business.

Examples of convention influencing genre recognition include *Reservoir Dogs* and *Heat*. Essentially heist films, these allude to other gangster films in very specific ways. Both display the conventions of crime as part of an organized, ongoing business. Both include communities of men. The criminal group in *Reservoir Dogs* has been constructed for this one job only and they hide their true identities behind pseudonyms, such as Mr. White, or Mr. Blue. Consequently, any inference of history or loyalty is undermined from the beginning by the fact that the men are strangers to each other. In contrast *Heat* features a gang who have worked together for years and are wary of any newcomers. Their fears are proved correct when newcomer Waingro (Kevin Gage) turns a heist into a murder spree and threatens the security of the gang. This is also relevant for the criminal group in *Reservoir Dogs*, which sees Mr. Blue (Michael Madsen) turn the diamond robbery into a savage shoot-out. Both films emphasize the need for trust and professionalism from each individual within a group, and in consequence, the potential risks involved in working with strangers. This suggests that their gang functions as a type of family, in that they have a history together, specific loyalties and rules. Such films allude to the Mafia community. However, the gang's loyalties are based only on mutual profit, rather than any allusions to ethnic ties. One of the ways *Heat* resembles a gangster film is through its references to profit as a binding force for the Mafia, which have become a significant thematic element of postclassical gangster films. This is especially noticeable since *Goodfellas*, but also features in *Once Upon a Time in America* and is reminiscent of many earlier heist films.[5] In this sense, a criminal gang is a business enterprise, constructed to make profits for all, and being a gangster is a job, rather than a complete way of life. In contrast, films such as the *Godfather* trilogy, *The Funeral*, *Donnie Brasco* and to a much lesser extent *The Sopranos* catalogue the lives of Mafiosi, whose entire histories and identities are based on organized crime. In these cases, organized crime is not just a job, but a complete way of life.

It is a distinct theme of films such as *Reservoir Dogs* and *Heat* that these men may have, or desire, lives outside of their criminal activities. J.A. Lindstrom (2000) notes, "*Heat* directly addresses questions of the relation between one's work, commitment to a profession, and quality of life" (Lindstrom: 22). It is suggested in this article that both the cops and criminals are merely employees within their chosen profession, and thus sympathy is divided equally between them in the narrative. This is highlighted in the pivotal café scene, wherein both Vincent Hanna (Al Pacino) and Neil McCauly (Robert De Niro) state they are simply working in the jobs that they do best. It has also been suggested that *Goodfellas* reveals the corporate nature of Mafia life. Philip French suggests that "the characters are viewed as working men, not as tragic heroes" (*The Observer*, October 28, 1990). This is also relevant for *Once Upon a Time in America*, as it becomes apparent that Max has betrayed his fellow criminals for the price of individual business success. However, in this case the strength of loyalty is later revived. Max employs Noodles to kill him as an act of retribution for his sins. The overall theme in this case suggests that profit cannot substitute for friendship. The convention of crime as business, and thus, criminal gangs bound together through working practices, can work as a signifier of gangster films, but a lack of Mafia codes of honor is often the cause of the gang's destruction. By a process of complicated associations, this encourages very different crime films to be recognised as gangster films mainly through convention.

To continue the discussion of crime as a business and associated iconography, it is interesting to note the extent to which costume signifies Mafia, or organized crime. A suited criminal suggests crime as a business, which in turn suggests organized crime and the Mafia. The sunglasses, black suits, black ties, black shoes and white shirts worn in *Reservoir Dogs* are a uniform. The intention is to mask any individuality that may lead to eyewitness identification of the robbers, but the uniform also associates the group with gangster iconography. The suit, mainly in a crime-based narrative, is an iconographic signifier of the gangster film. Therefore, the slow-motion shots of the gang isolated against the backdrop of orange brickwork and single blue truck that accompanies the title music not only foregrounds the stark nature of their costume, but also encourages a connection with the gangster film. Similarly, the black suits of Vincent Vega (John Travolta) and Jules Winnfield (Samuel L. Jackson), the two henchmen in *Pulp Fiction*, identify them as gangsters. However, this is a self-conscious identification, as the men have to make the effort to "get into character" before embarking on a violent job. The suits worn by the gang during the bank heist in *Heat* are iconographic in similar ways. Neil McCauley wears a suit throughout the film and this not only suggests him as professional, but also consequently encourages an association with the image of the successful gangster. So on the level of costume alone films such as *Reservoir Dogs*, *Pulp Fiction* and *Heat* can function as gangster films.

The notion that costume defines a gangster character in postclassical film is discussed by Stella Bruzzi (1997) and is epitomized in a scene from *Goodfellas*, in which the young Henry Hill arrives home to show his mother his first silk suit. Her despairing reaction is, "My God, you look like a gangster." As previously stated, costume has long been an important signifier in the identification of a gangster, and thus the gangster genre (McArthur). In the early seventies, as violent cop and outlaw films featured more contemporary, and casual clothing,[6] the immaculate suits featured in *The Godfather* and *Mean Streets* (especially Uncle Giovanni) continued to emphasize a visual association between tailored suits and organised crime established in the classic films. This also continues the iconographic association of a particular costume and gangster identity. Costume as an extension of a character's identity, or masculinity, is parodied in *Miller's Crossing*, where Tom Regan (Gabriel Byrne) has nightmares about chasing his hat, which has blown off in the wind. It has been suggested that the hat signifies masculinity (Bruzzi)[7] or control. This is similar to Jeff Costello (Alain Delon in *Le Samurai*), who never removes his hat outside of his apartment, even when it would help him to escape detection during flight from the police. Bruzzi suggests that the image of the classic gangster is something both the French New Wave and postclassical Hollywood examples seek to emulate. She describes the main protagonist of *Le Samurai* thus: "Jeff Costello serves as the epigrammatic distillation of the cinema gangster myth, a figure whose identity is signalled only by his superficial adherence to an imaginary, fictional and ultimately destructive ideal" (Bruzzi: 80). Bruzzi argues that the modern gangster uses costume to signify his status as gangster, but that this status is based on an unachievable ideal. Bruzzi's assertion is useful to my discussion because it highlights how the image of the gangsters can be referenced through the use of costume. It is evident that costume is an important signifier of organized crime.

Traditionally, in gangster films of the classical era, particular kinds of suits were associated with criminality. The expensive, elaborate suits of gangsters contrasted with the more understated attire of detectives or the ordinary citizen.[8] However, increasingly throughout classical Hollywood, and also significantly since the French New Wave, any suited criminal has come to signify the gangster within crime films. Suits are no longer standard masculine costume in society, and so the wearing of a suit has developed different cultural significances: as a signifier of formality, business, or organized crime. Lefty Ruggiero dresses up to go to work (*Donnie Brasco*), as do Tony Soprano and his crew. The tailored suit is the uniform of the Mafia and embodies all the conventions of generic iconography. Both *Reservoir Dogs* and *Pulp Fiction* contribute little to the mythology of the Mafia; they simply emulate the costume and gestures of the Hollywood Gangster stereotype. Mafia is here signified by a uniform worn by paid killers. As Bruzzi suggests, the style-consciousness of the postclassical gangsters is reminiscent of the French New Wave criminals. However, costume does not only signify the self-reflexivity of the postclassical gangster persona; it also operates as a genre signifier, a signifier that is traceable across films and encourages the reading of some crime films, as stated earlier, as gangster films, mainly because of such iconographic inclusions.

* * *

The emulation and importance of gangster style and costume is exaggerated in *New Jack City*. Nino's body is made a spectacle through frequent

Sam "Ace" Rothstein (Robert De Niro, left) and Nicky Santoro (Joe Pesci). *Casino* © 1995, Universal.

displays of his muscled torso. A prime example of this occurs during a scene in which Nino is entertaining his closest friend Gee Money (Allen Payne) at home. Nino is dressed in electric blue silk pajamas, the shirt open to the waist. As Nino proclaims his wish to "have it all," just like Tony Montana in *Scarface*, his well-toned torso is emphasized against the big TV screen in the room. This is unique, in that usually a gangster's bare body is not shown on screen. One reason for Nino's display must lie in the perpetuation of cultural associations concerning African American men and exaggerated sexuality. The scene is not only for the purposes of displaying Nino's ambition, but is also a flirtation between him and Gee Money's girlfriend, Uniqua (Tracy Camilla Johns). Soon after they are shown making love, which is another unusual visual inclusion in gangster films (another rare example occurs in *Carlito's Way*). In fact, pre–*Sopranos*, explicit sex is curiously absent from gangster narratives. I will address this phenomenon in Chapter 4, but suffice to say, pre–*Soprano* genre conventions tended to align overt sexual activity with weakness. Sexual activity signifies the beginning of Nino's downfall, thus suggesting overt sexuality as part of his fatal flaw. Nino is a gangster, in that he emulates the costume and fraternity of Hollywood Mafia, but his character is an ethnic stereotype, similar in its crudeness to *Scarface* (1932, 1983). In consequence, Nino Brown's preoccupation with his own physique and sexual prowess, and his emulation of gangster gestures and costume, marks him as simultaneously a signifier of the gangster genre and distinct from it. This is because, even though gangsters are associated with ethnicity, Nino's blackness is distinct from the general conceptualization of mainly Italian American ethnicity that has been prioritized in the postclassical era. This kind of contradictory visual signification, wherein characters display a gangster persona without the historical associations with organized crime, is dominant within the films I categorized as "gangsters as gangs and wannabes." This category can also be used for *Reservoir Dogs, Pulp Fiction, Heat* and *American Gangster,* as the effect of costume as a signifier of the gangster contributes to their categorization as gangster films.

Dialogue, Gestures and Violence

Other elements such as gestures, dialogue and violence are also important signifiers of genre. These are elements of style, rather than costume, or setting and thus are more readily recognisable as conventions of the genre, rather than iconographic, although gestures and violence are visual and so can relate to both. One of the ways that genre can be shown as a fluid concept, but operating as a system of familiarities, is to catalogue patterns of conventions across a history of films. Traceable styles in dialogue, gestures and violence will complete my examination of textual iconography and conventions and will also begin to examine notions of authenticity in postclassical gangster films. It is useful to examine how certain mannerisms and catch phrases have developed over the post–*Godfather* era, because many of them can be associated with issues of authenticity, both historical and corresponding to Mafia myths. The Capo-regime structure of the Corleone crime family in *The Godfather* came with very little explanation within the text. However, the inclusion of such intimate allusions to Mafia structures in *The Godfather Parts I* and *II* was a major influence on later representations of Mafia families and dialogue.[9] The word "respect" was used by Don Corleone to express his sense of honor and the loyalty he expected of others. In *Goodfellas*, Tommy De Vito (Joe Pesci) notes that "respect" is something you show to "Made Men,"[10] for example, by giving some of the profits from a theft to boss man Paulie (Paul Sorvino). This is similar to Fanucci's (Gaston Moschin) discussion with the young Vito Corleone in *The Godfather Part II*, wherein Vito was advised to show his "respect" by letting Fanucci "wet his beak" (take some of Vito's wages). Lefty Ruggiero (*Donnie Brasco*) reminds the young Donnie that showing "respect" to gangsters will help him stay alive longer. Carlito Brigante (*Carlito's Way*) laments that young gangsters no longer have any "respect," suggesting that they no longer abide by the traditional rules of the Mafia.

In black gangster films such as *New Jack City* or *American Gangster,* "respect" is used as a greeting, to show one's allegiance to other brothers, but also to assert "respect" for their ethnic identity. Therefore, 'respect' is a term used to display an awareness of the rules and loyalties of Mafia traditions, or the loss of them, as in *Carlito's Way.* As with all dialogue, one single definition is not achievable, nor is the case that all of these usages derive from *The Godfather.* The use of the word between criminals in Hollywood film evokes the loyalty and traditions of organized crime, and *The Godfather* is a major influence on this type of dialogue. Further evocations of the term are sourced in mythologies of the Mafia, not in cinematic history. For example, dialogue is often described by screenwriters and directors as authentic,[11] but it is virtually impossible to authenticate the dialogue of a secret society for two reasons: firstly, because it has never been proven that testimonies, such as Joe Valachi's, were totally truthful, especially at the level of everyday activities; and secondly, it is evident that after a whole century of Hollywood film it is likely that many real-life Mafia members may have adopted some of the dialogue witnessed on screen. Al Capone enjoyed Hollywood gangster films,[12] and John Gotti is also a fan.[13] De Stefano's account of the criminal dialogue in *The Sopranos* draws heavily on the memoirs of Joseph D. Pistone (the real-life Donnie Brasco) to confirm the TV series' verisimilitude. The fact is, all "true accounts" are filtered through multiple texts and conscious or unconscious desires to perpetuate myths or self-promotion. Films such as *The Godfather, Goodfellas, Donnie Brasco* and *The Sopranos* that either assert their factual roots, or display similarities to biographical accounts, offer intriguing insights into the structure, dialogue and general demeanor of Mafia and its members. However, these insights cannot be said to authenticate Hollywood narratives, or make the films realist. They develop mythologies of the Mafia, influence the aesthetic styles of Mafia stereotypes and further encourage the identification of genre conventions.

Gestures are also extremely important to representations of the Mafia and are especially noticeable in coherent patterns in films of the nineties. As iconography, the visual gestures of James Cagney in the 1930s have long been the epitome of gangster demeanor. It is important to note that these were representative of Cagney's persona as much as displays of a gangster character type. However, the shoulder shrug, reminiscent of Tommy Powers in *Public Enemy,* is especially noticeable in Tommy De Vito (*Goodfellas*), Nino Brown

(*New Jack City*), Vincent (*Pulp Fiction*), Johnny Tempio (*The Funeral*), Lefty Ruggiero (*Donnie Brasco*) and Silvio Dante (*The Sopranos*). It is often used by less-powerful gangsters in order to express strength, or power. It is like a nervous tic or part of a boxer's warm-up pose, used to assert some kind of bravado brought on by a lack of "respect" from others. This is especially noticeable with Lefty, who tends to use the shrug to intimidate Donnie, or criminals he perceives as lower than himself in the criminal hierarchy. During the first encounter between Lefty and Donnie, Lefty reacts to Donnie's attempt to leave with a combination of movements to emphasize his words — "Hey, whaddya think you're doin'?" — followed by a thump on the arm (reminiscent of one of James Cagney's most common gestures), an exaggerated shrug of the shoulders, a weight shift on his feet and a sharp sniff of the nose. The display, similar to that of a boxer getting ready to strike, is common among gangsters as a sign of violent potential. The most stereotypical character in *The Sopranos* has to be Silvio Dante, but all of the main characters to some extent follow these familiar gestural patterns. Other gestures, such as coin flipping, are associated with particular characters such as Rinaldo (George Raft in *Scarface*), whose mannerisms were later associated with the real-life Bugsy Siegel. Therefore Warren Beatty, who repeats the action throughout *Bugsy,* is reproducing an iconographic gesture that is particular to a certain character.[14] It is also interesting to note that Vincent (John Travolta in *Pulp Fiction*) copies Michel (Jean-Paul Belmondo in *À bout de souffle*) in his gesture of running his thumb across his lips, which in turn was a tribute to Humphrey Bogart.

Finally, the "kiss of death," still confined only to Italian or Italian American Mafia films, began as the most "troubling aspect" of *The Brotherhood,* because publicity posters featuring this image suggested it as a "fag film" (*Variety,* 1968: 6). This was later overwritten by two instances in *The Godfather Part II,* wherein Michael kisses Fredo on the lips to signal the severity of Fredo's treachery. This first occurs during the New Year's party in Cuba. Michael grasps Fredo on either side of his face, kisses him and then holds his brother's face close to his own when he declares, "I know it was you Fredo. You broke my heart. You broke my heart." Therefore, the gesture combines love and violence, occurring as it does amid the celebrations and the beginning of the Cuban revolution. The combination of celebration and tragedy is emphasized by the streamers and confetti that continue to rain down on their heads as the brothers stare at each other. It is an emotive display of Michael's anger and despair at Fredo's betrayal, plus Fredo's realization of the consequences of his actions. Fredo quickly flees his brother's grasp and goes into hiding. The second kiss, during their mother's funeral, seals Fredo's fate. Michael kisses and embraces his brother by his mother's coffin. The scene ends with Fredo seated, but clasping his brother just above the waist. Michael returns the embrace, but stares over his brother's head. The point of view shot shows Al Neri (Richard Bright) nod his understanding of Michael's actions. Now that their mother is dead, Michael's kiss has communicated the order for Fredo's death. Since that time, kissing on the cheek has become accepted as a sign of loyalty in Mafia films, but a kiss on lips is a message of death from one Mafioso to another. Such physical gestures are still used sparingly in gangster films and I believe that it may still be due to general anxieties associated with sexuality and masculine identity. In general, the more "Italian" the film, the less anxiety it appears to attract, but it is obviously not as simple as that. Consequently, I shall discuss their importance in more detail in Chapter 3 and 4. For now, gestures are traceable and are identifiable as signifiers of gangster characters. For this reason alone they can be associated with the recognition of genre.

*   *   *

Some of the most prevalent gestures in gangster films are the various displays of violence. This aspect of gangster films will also inform discussions on myths, masculinity and ethnicity, but it is important to note the significance violence has in the recognition of genre. In 1968 Philip French noted that there were no longer any disclaimers at the beginning or end of crime films.[15] The transference from the all-encompassing Production Code to the ratings system meant that more explicit sex and violence could be shown within certain films without the need for explicit scenes of moral awareness within the script to counteract the criminal activity.[16] Violence has always been an integral part of any gangster film. On-screen publicity for *Public Enemy* includes promises of "machine gunning through the decade of death." As already noted in my Introduction, the demise of the Production Code brought criminals back to the center of gangster narratives, but it also allowed for more explicit violence.

Initial reviews of *The Godfather* focused on its violent content. *The Daily Mirror* August 22, 1971 stated, "It is vicious, it is brutal and I doubt whether such casual and unremitting slaughter has ever been matched in a single motion picture." *The Sun* offered: "Never since Goebbels has the propaganda of violence been so beautifully put together" August 22, 1972). Nazi analogies did not end there; *The Scotsman* August 23, 1972) suggested that the film's attempts to promote Don Corleone as a "really lovely man" were akin to Nazi propaganda, noting the garden scene as "like Hitler playing with his grandson." These reviews focused on the association of violence with power. The film was suggested as propaganda, because the Corleones' loving family life was seen as a mask for the despicable brutality that lay beneath their prosperity. Violence in *The Godfather* is pre-meditated, or ordered to the point that critics have suggested that the Corleones are "controllers" of their surrounding society (Ryan & Kellner, 1990, Casillo, 1990). In contrast, reviews of *Bonnie and Clyde* have emphasised the extent to which the violence appears as "un-premeditated" (French, 1968: 3) and "non-professional" (*Monthly Film Bulletin*, v34 n.405, 1967). French suggests that this is one of the disturbing elements of *Bonnie and Clyde*, because in organized crime (he cites *The Saint Valentine's Day Massacre*, 1967), "Violence is directed towards specific ends [...] *Bonnie and Clyde* is quite the reverse — a form of gesture" (French: 3). French suggests that the violence in *Bonnie and Clyde* is more anarchic because of its lack of direction. Discussions of violence in gangster films always attract contradictory responses. It is as valid for reviewers to abhor the pre-meditated and controlled violence in *The Godfather* as it is for others to fear the anarchic less-organized displays in *Bonnie and Clyde*. There is a tendency to accept the violence of the Mafia more than outlaws because it confines its actions to a specific world. In contrast, the violence in such as *Bonnie and Clyde* does not show specific parameters; it is not confined only to other gangsters or law enforcers. This blurs the distinction between criminal and ordinary society, and therefore their violence can be viewed as more of a threat to the general public.

Post-*Godfather* films attracted responses that emphasized their association with violence. *Mean Streets* was perceived as "mercilessly [...] accurate" (*Daily Telegraph*, April 5, 1974), *The Untouchables* as "the most violent film of the year" (*Today*, September 11, 1987), *Goodfellas* as showing the "ruthless reality of life inside the Mob" (*Mail on Sunday*, October 28, 1990) and *King of New York* as "violent, foul-mouthed and truly nasty" (*Time Out*, June 19, 1991). *New Jack City* was attacked for inciting violence in its audiences (*Times*, March 18, 1991 and *Variety*, March 18, 1991). *Miller's Crossing* attracted acclaim as "a thinking man's bloodletting" (*Mail on Sunday*, February 17, 1991), but was also seen as "darkly violent" (*Guardian*, October 18, 1990). *The Funeral* was described as "regularly over-the-top in its depravity and realness" (*Village Voice*, November 5, 1996) while *Donnie Brasco* was applauded for the way the "violence makes you sickened — you get involved, deeply involved" (*Asian Age*, March 4, 1997). Interestingly, the ultra-violent *Departed* encouraged this almost apologetic response: "It's supposedly terrible to celebrate violence, but it makes for great cinema when done right" (John Kass, *The Chicago Tribune* October 8, 2006). Such differing reactions are significant in that the violence is either deplored, or admired, but is also often related to "realism" within the film. It is interesting that *New Jack* City is accused of inciting riots in cinemas, as no other gangster film has ever been accused of this. This can be attributed to social generalizations about black ethnicity in American soci-

Michael Corleone (Al Pacino, standing) and Fredo Corleone (John Cazale). *The Godfather* © 1972, Paramount.

ety, which I will address in more detail within Chapter 4. In terms of genre, violence is significant in that reviewers are often concerned with the context in which it is displayed within the narrative.

It is evident that violence in any film will attract differing reactions from viewers. As the focus here is on organised crime, and thus organized violence, it is useful to provide a brief comparison of violence in two commercially successful but very different gangster movies: *The Godfather Part I* and *Scarface*. This will help to pinpoint some of the criteria that influence reviewers' responses to representations of violence. Just as Warshow claimed that the gangster denies "the concept of success [...] by caricaturing it" (Warshow, 1954: 454), it is evident that Tony Montana (*Scarface*) parodies the orderly accumulation of power and wealth as represented by the Corleone family. Montana hurtles headlong into criminal deals without a hint of caution or self-conscious limitation. His meteoric rise and flaunting of wealth display none of the calculated caution observed by the Corleone family who, even when established, live in a limited economic environment, with no real evidence of lavish indulgence. In summary, the formal structure of the Corleones' world, displayed in the tightly choreographed *mise-en-scène*, suggests an aura of stability, which in turn emphasizes their position as controllers of their surroundings. Ryan and Kellner suggest the "frame compositions display a high level of organisation and symmetry of disposition" (67), emphasizing social stability maintained essentially by "strong leaders and firm order" (*ibid.*), and preventing the "chaos of nature" from encroaching upon familial order. In comparison the less refined cinematography of *Scarface* suggests a less ordered environment, subject to unforeseeable situations that may challenge the protagonist's control. Looser compositions and less formal editing (fewer form cuts and dissolves), harsher lighting and non-symmetrical character placement emphasize this informal construction and offers a very different conception of control, especially in the portrayal of violence.

Violence in *The Godfather* has been described as "ordered": "making it seem part of nature and intimating that such horror and brutality are part of the fated order of things" (*Ibid.*: 68).[17] Scenes such as Michael's assassination of Captain McClusky (Sterling Hayden) and Sollozzo (Al Lettieri), planned in minute detail beforehand, or the horse's head that materializes in a movie producer's (John Marley, as Jack Woltz) bed without any warning, provide instances of violence that reflect the Corleones' complete understanding of both their environment and their power within it. In contrast, Montana's shoot-out with Colombian drug dealers in a Miami hotel room during his first deal and his later killing of Sosa's (Paul Shenar) henchmen appear to undermine any attempts at planning. His backup arrives late in the original drug deal, while an innocent woman and child are threatened during the assassination attempt on a senator.

In *The Godfather* acts of violence, especially the climactic assassination of the heads of the five families, are another example of "firm order" (*ibid.*: 67). The sequence works to encourage both exultation in the violence and admiration for Michael's leadership qualities. However, Michael's appearance in the church suggests his divine, yet detached control over the family business. He no longer needs to physically participate in the protection of his family. His new role as dictator, giving unquestionable orders for others to carry out, releases him from the emotional, physical and personally dangerous role of the gangster as killer. In contrast, Montana's personal involvement in killings, with the insistence that he should "look them in the eyes," suggests brutality of a more direct kind. However, Sosa's proposed "remote control" assassination of a U.S. Senator sees Montana's initial enthusiasm undermined by the accidental inclusion of the Senator's wife and children. In comparison to *The Godfather* sequence, planning is shown to be subject to the unforeseeable intervention of nature. Even though the Senator has been watched meticulously in order to establish his routine, on the day of action his routine changes. Unnerved by events, the gangsters argue over the choices before them. Montana is forced to assess his commitment to "remote control killings." He concludes that they are inhuman, because the killers do not possess honor enough to look their victims in the eye. He kills Sosa's henchman for refusing to halt the assassination plan, thus making himself an enemy of Sosa. This instance suggests that Montana has misjudged the brutality of his environment and is reacting to it rather than controlling it. The style of violence is a crucial part of the representation of the gangsters' worlds and the conception of power in the two films. Viewers' responses are influenced by the textual styles, in that a high level of control (but no less violence) appears to attract less criticism.

Scarface and *The Godfather* provide different styles of violence, but the films are united in one crucial factor, and that is the exclusivity of their working environment. Ordinary people are unlikely to get caught in the crossfire of gangster violence on screen. This generic convention is epitomized in dialogue from *Reservoir Dogs*, where Mr. Pink (Steve Buscemi) is asked if he had killed anyone during the heist; "No," he states, "just cops, no real people." The notion of acceptable and non-acceptable killings is crucial to understanding the generic conventions influencing Tony Montana's decision to kill his associates rather than innocent women and children. Similarly, "no women, no kids" is Leon's (*Leon/The Professional*) only moral dictum. Such ethics do not cancel out the brutality of violence in the films, but they do provide a sense of awareness that violence is part of their working environment, not a "social gesture" as suggested in *Bonnie and Clyde*. It is interesting to note that such ethics are parodied in *Miller's Crossing*, where Caspar's (Jon Polito) indignation at the lack of respect shown by his criminal associates to the rules of the Mafia is undermined by his brutal behavior towards his own wife and children. The blurring of boundaries in such films as *Miller's Crossing* or *The Funeral*, where the farcical nature of violence to revenge violence is explored in detail, is an interesting development of generic convention. Consequently,

I will return to discuss the tendency for some films to focus on the moral emptiness of Mafia ethics in Chapter 4.

As previously stated, violence for millennium gangsters has tended to involve very clear references to previous films. The attempt on Frank Lucas' life (*American Gangster*) is a generic drive-by assassination attempt and leads to his appeal for ethics akin to *The Godfather Part II*. *The Sopranos* is full of violent episodes that make reference to previous gangster films. Christopher shoots a bakery clerk in the foot like Tommy DeVito shoots Spider in *Goodfellas*. Sal "Big Pussy" Bonspensiero is killed on a boat and "sleeps with the fishes" like Luca Brazi in *The Godfather*. Adriana Le Cerva is led into the woods like Bernie Bernbaum in *Miller's Crossing*. The body count in the TV series is excessive, which is not surprising seeing as the narrative has to entertain through six seasons. However, most violence adheres to generic norms and is mainly confined to those active in the organization.[18]

The question of whether violence in gangster films has steadily increased is impossible to gauge, as each film attracts attention for different reasons. *Scarface* attracted numerous comments on its violence and bad language.[19] However, *Goodfellas*, noted as having more bad language and comparable violence (*Daily Telegraph*, February 1, 1997), did not attract as much criticism on that basis. This may be due to Scorsese's critical reputation as a director who portrays the truth.[20] In comparison, De Palma is often referred to as a director of "slasher movies" in reviews of *Scarface* (*Observer*, September 18, 1983 and *Time*, November 7, 1983),[21] but also in critical histories.[22] It may also be due to the fact that by the nineties, violence is more accepted or expected in gangster films. However, it is not possible to categorically assess the reason for these differences in reviewer reactions. Annette Hill suggests that violent films such as *Reservoir Dogs* "attract a specific kind of publicity which draws consumers to view them in order to satisfy a cultural curiosity" (Hill, 1997: 177).[23] For instance, the press reaction to *Scarface* led *The Sun* to speculate that "the controversy is making it one of the biggest hits of the year" (*December* 12, 1983). This suggests violent content can be used strategically by marketing departments or companies to attract controversy and thus audiences. Certainly scandals, such as the British banning of the video release of *Reservoir Dogs* and *Natural Born Killers*[24] in the early nineties, encouraged wider publicity and possibly heightened sales when they finally were released.

Recognizing violence as a generic aspect of gangster films partly hinges on the extent to which a reviewer, censor or viewer can accept the depiction of violence in an individual film as part of the narrative. It is significant that, as well as receiving a lot of negative press about its content, *Reservoir Dogs* also provoked some questioning of the ethos of the whole ratings system. For instance, Alan Quinn argues that *Reservoir Dogs* is "not as violent as *Last of the Mohicans* that gained only a 12 Certificate" (*Independent on Sunday*, January 10, 1993). Similarly, Neil Asherson suggests, "*Home Alone* is more disturbing than Tarantino [... in that the film, specifically aimed at children] constantly suggests that if you smash an iron bar across someone's skull [..] he will stagger away more or less intact" (*Independent on Sunday*, October 30, 1994). Therefore, when reviewers describe *Scarface* as "animalistic" (*New York*, February 19, 1993), *Reservoir Dogs* as "a shocker and a dazzler" (*Daily Mail*, January 3, 1993), or that "the most frightening thing about *The Godfather* is the pleasure with which one follows the Corleones" (*New Society*, September 21, 1972), these are evidently personal reactions to the contextualizing of violence. It is my view that what draws people to defend violence in gangster films is the convention of confining violence to identifiable participants: other criminals and law enforcers. This keeps it within an identifiable and exclusive universe, apart from ordinary society. This is in contrast to other crime films (even those with marginal Mafia characters), such as cop mysteries, serial killer, kidnap, or even heist films that often include more arbitrary violence and portray criminals who are a more obvious threat to mainstream society.

The idea that violence is an integral part of the gangster world is predetermined by cinematic and cultural history. It is this pre-determination that can make violence in a gangster film appear non-threatening, in that the violence is expected and therefore unsurprising. As Tillman states, "Murder in the family is a tragedy; killing someone else, the family business" (Tillman: 33). In this respect violence is just another aspect of Mafia ethics; it comes with the territory. However, the way in which an individual gangster or the narrative as a whole deals with or reacts to such violence is different within each film and attracts differing reactions. Adverse reactions to *Reservoir Dogs* and *Pulp Fiction* stem from the fact that they combine humor with violence. The films are not seen to be taking the issues of Mafia business seriously and so any acceptance of the violence depends on whether a viewer reacts to the film as a *parody* of gangster crime or a *glorification* of it. Violence is an integral part of any gangster narrative and is therefore part of narrative conventions that make up the gangster genre. As with other gestures and forms of dialogue, violence can be linked to historical authenticity and can also be deplored as gratuitous spectacle. However, as stated above, the ways in which violence is used to show the strength, weaknesses, or brutality of gangster life and ethics differs in each film. Consequently, it is the inherent familiarity of elements such as gestures, dialogue and even violence that function as genre signifiers and allow for a more fluid conceptualization of genre as discussed by Neale in the eighties. His fluid approach to iconography is therefore still useful in principle, but it is necessary to include the input of conventions and some extratextual factors to fully appreciate the intricacies of such familiarities in postclassical gangster films.

In Chapter 1 it was shown that generic cycles of the gangster film can be traced since *The Godfather,* but the reference points employed are wider than simply the classic gangster texts. Post-*Godfather* gangster films do not always adhere to a rise-and-fall narrative. However, there is a general tendency to represent crime as a business. Conventions and iconography including dialogue, gestures and violence present perceptions of a Mafia world that is distinct and traceable across a range of films. Responses to the films have begun to understand them in relation to a type of generic authenticity. Neale (1991) would regard this as generic verisimilitude: systems that provide spectators with "a way of working out why particular events and actions are taking place, why characters are dressed the way they are, why they look, speak and behave the way they do and so on" (46). Neale also utilizes Tzvetan Todorov's (1981) view that verisimilitude is both generic (textual) and subject to scattered discourses (social and cultural). Therefore, notions of authenticity are implicated in the gangster film for example, through "drawing on and quoting 'authentic' (and authenticating) discourses, artefacts and texts" (47). *The Godfather* and beyond do this by drawing on notions of Mafia myths, which include ideas of historical and ethnic "authenticity." These myths have developed a significant cultural currency since the 1950s.

The extent to which generic knowledge becomes a form of cultural knowledge and a component of public opinion (48) is something that Neale refers to, but does not fully explore. Certain images take on particular generic resonances (as discussed with reference to costume and gestures earlier), but such images do not result in the constitution of a generic corpus.[25] They encourage recognition of the ways in which genre and cultural verisimilitude interact. The next section of this chapter traces some of these interactions in all postclassical gangster films. These interactions are not confined to structural and industry elements, but also include extratextual discourses on authors and stars.

Authorship as a Signifier of Genre

Critical interest in narrative conventions and genre in the fifties and sixties coincided with discussions of authorship. Bazin's pioneering studies of what he termed the Hollywood aesthetic[26] later developed into the *politique des auteurs,*[27] which details the capacity for some directors to achieve "authorship," or convey a "personal vision" within their films.[28] Certain directors, according to Bazin, did so by utilizing the somewhat restrictive formalities of classical cinema in such a way as to produce a distinctive and personal appropriation of them. Bazin's theory, later adopted by the critics of the *Cahiers du Cinéma*, some of whom in turn became the leaders of the French New Wave (*Nouvelle Vague*), effectively elevated some filmmakers and their work to the status of artists and art. As suggested in Chapter 1, the young directors of the French New Wave have influenced postclassical Hollywood gangster films. It is also evident that the attendant interest in directors as authors has influenced critical debates on cinema since that time. However, whereas the critics of the *Cahiers du Cinéma* saw genre as a restrictive form that auteurs seek to transcend, later theorists such as Jim Kitses (1969) and Robin Wood (1977)[29] view genre as a significant source that an auteur may draw upon, in that genre is meaningful in its own right. Howard Hawks, Fritz Lang and John Ford are some of the directors identified as auteurs in classical Hollywood by critics of the *Cahiers du Cinéma*, but also Kitses and Wood. Hawks directed *Scarface* (1932), one of the films Warshow describes as the gangster genre in its pure form. However, whereas John Ford can be associated primarily with the Western, or Fritz Lang with psychological thrillers, there is no specific attachment between a single director or group of directors and the gangster film in classical Hollywood cinema. Consequently, notions of authorship and genre did not have a significant impact on debates about the gangster genre: Warshow's works on narrative remain as some of the most influential writings on the classical Hollywood gangster film.

In contrast to the classical era, postclassical gangster films can be clearly associated with certain directors. Francis Ford Coppola and Martin Scorsese are the two most prominent directors to be associated with the gangster film since the sixties, and it is very probable that their status as star directors has helped to give gangster films their critical and commercial prestige. Much has been written about the life and works of both directors.[30] It is not appropriate to examine all these writings here, as this book does not wish to examine the postclassical gangster film against classical definitions of authorship. It is more interested in the ways certain directors have achieved a level of critical and celebrity status that promotes them as the "stars" of their films as much as any leading actors. This stardom not only affects notions of authorship, but it also influences perceptions of genre. Coppola and Scorsese are among the most prominent candidates for the label 'new Hollywood auteur."

The works of Robert Kolker (1980) and Michael Pye and Lynda Myles (1979) detail the early careers of Francis Ford Coppola, Martin Scorsese, Robert Altman and George Lucas. These "movie brats" (Pye and Myles) were identified as a new generation of filmmakers who, educated in film schools or the movie industry, employed narrative and editing techniques that differed quite prominently from those of the classical era. Such elements of style included non-linear narratives, improvised dialogue, incoherent or ambiguous endings, jump cuts, disruption of the 180-degree rule, and the use of new technologies. Tasker suggests that "the work of such men can be understood as either the emergence of an American Art cinema, or as indicating the incorporation of techniques and themes associated with European art cinema into American structures and modes of production" (221). For the purposes of this book, the most crucial aspect of these developments is that the work of these directors attracted critical acclaim, which in turn elevated the critical status of the gangster film.

An important offspring of auteur theory is the recognition that certain directors function as important promotional or intellectual currency for a film. Filmmakers such as Coppola, Scorsese and Lucas can sell a film, or give it critical credence as much, if not more, than the stars involved. Timothy Corrigan's work "The Commerce of Auteurism" explains the nature of modern auteur filmmakers in detail:

> Auteurs have become increasingly situated along an extratextual path in which their commercial status as auteurs is their chief function as auteurs: the auteur-star is meaningful primarily as a promotion or recovery of a movie or group of movies, frequently regardless of the filmic text itself [Corrigan, 1991: 105].

Corrigan links this shift to the commercial interest in actors and filmmakers as "cult personalities" that developed in the early 1970s. This interest is evidenced in the inclusion of biographical details of stars in publicity campaigns, or foregrounding the actors' preparation and skill. The result was to increase the critical value of certain actors and/or filmmakers, which can have the effect of boosting box office success.[31] An interest in stars has been in evidence since the early days of Hollywood cinema, but stars such as Marlon Brando in the 1950s brought a new development into the extratextual currency of stardom — a "serious" or critical depth to the actor's role. This critical depth has gradually become more widespread in the cinema industry, and in the early 1970s, the emergence of the young "movie brat" directors, with their attention to innovations in film style and their knowledge of cinema history, encouraged their inclusion, as self-conscious authors, in the extratextual currency surrounding a film.

For instance, Francis Ford Coppola's persona as a star filmmaker, whose single-minded pursuit of perfection at any cost brought about constant conflicts between him and the Paramount Studio executives during the production of *The Godfather*, is documented by Biskind (1998), Lewis (1995), Lebo (1997) and Cowie (1997). Cowie documents Coppola's insistence on such issues as building a "loyal team of technicians" (1997: 18), honing the screenplay and fighting for his preferred locations. Publicity for both Coppola and Scorsese films[32] feature the director's name above the film title and often in comparable font and size. Scorsese's films demonstrate an obsession with New York City. This focus is given extra critical weight by the publication of interviews, biographies and associated critical literature that detail Scorsese's upbringing in Little Italy, New York, his obsession with film history, and his attention towards realism within his work.[33] These examples show the extent to which the directors' attract critical attention as auteurs and as detailed observers of their chosen subjects, especially Italian American districts and history.

Since the *politique des auteurs*, some filmmakers have been regarded as significant components in the production of a film's meaning.[34] A filmmaker's reputation, personality, or critical value exists outside of any one particular film text and thus, as Corrigan explains, can influence popular perceptions of their films:

> An auteur film today seems to aspire more and more to a critical tautology, capable of being understood and consumed without being seen [...] it can communicate a great deal for a large number of audiences who know the maker's reputation but have never seen the films themselves [Corrigan: 106].

Therefore, it is evident that auteurism in modern cinema signifies more than simple "authorship," or personal vision within a film text. It is part of a continual discourse about film that, as Dudley Andrew has noted, places the auteur "inside a system that is larger than he" (Andrew, 1993: 81). The filmmaker cannot be identified as the repository of the film's meaning, as Bazin suggested, but discourses surrounding the film maker can influence receptions of the film. This is especially relevant to the marketing and reception of Quentin Tarantino's films, wherein the director is the primary promoter of his films explicitly presented as a bricolage of borrowed styles and influences.[35] Reception is not only guided by the promotion of Tarantino's personal vision, but the extent to which the promotion of his films suggests a collection of conscious references to popular culture. This encourages reviewers and audiences to make their own connections based both on Tarantino's interviews and their own cultural heritage. Thus, Tarantino is not the repository of meaning, but merely another component through which meaning is filtered.

The widespread interest in authorship is evident in the extent to which writings on *The Godfather* focus on Coppola's vision (Farber, 1972; Kolker, 1980; Cowie, Lebo, Clarens, 1997), while most examinations of Scorsese's films focus on interviews with the director (Thompson and Christie, 1993, 1996; Friedman, 1997) . One reason for this approach to the films originates in the production and marketing strategies of this period of Hollywood history. The most significant change is to be found in the financing of film projects. Films are now produced as "packages," in that although studios still finance their own films, staff are hired on mainly single-project contracts. This means that each film takes on the feel of an independent project, backed financially by the studio, but headed creatively by a team of producers, scriptwriters and most significantly the director. The director often becomes the creative focal point of the completed film,[36] by featuring in the advertisements and other publicity materials. This is further encouraged by the celebrity persona of directors such as Scorsese and Tarantino, who appear happy to be interviewed at length about their films, influences and directorial styles.[37] In the process, Tarantino and Scorsese become the marketing focus, or stars of the film, in that it is their name that headlines the posters and screen advertising, and their persona that is used in publicity to attract audiences and critical endorsements. In these cases, the director is an extratextual star of the film, because his or her persona in publicity material, interviews and advertising co-exists with the performances of the actors.

An example of this is found in reviews of *Reservoir Dogs* and *Pulp Fiction*. The emphasis is on how Tarantino plans and executes camera angles, distances and lighting, encourages character performance, and chooses the final takes and edits the finished product (*Film Comment*, 1994). He also appears in his films, as does Scorsese.[38] Tarantino makes reference to the director's role as a "helmsman," who has a "firm control of the material" (Smith, 1994: 40), thus suggesting a view of himself as the creative controller of the finished film. This view of the director as creative controller is also reflected in interviews with Coppola, Scorsese and Leone.[39] In contrast, interviews with Brian De Palma are scarce within reviews, but his status as the creative focal point of the films is still evident.[40] The tendency for directors to be one of the focuses of publicity and to help encourage critical endorsement for films is a significant trend of postclassical cinema. Thus, it is not unique to gangster films. However, a significant number of gangster films of the postclassical era are "helmed" by critically acclaimed directors and this has influenced popular responses to them.[41] Tarantino and Scorsese feature as the marketing focus, or the star director of their films, in that it is their persona that is used to publicize the film and attract audiences.

Scorsese has always been happy to associate himself with the gangster film. When asked about his reasons for making *Goodfellas* (1990), he proclaims, "It was a project I could fall into" (Yaquinto: 169). Amy Taubin suggests that Scorsese "enjoys the wiseguys for their energy and single-mindedness, however murderous" (Taubin, in Brunette, 1999: 141). This is in contrast to Coppola, who has always appeared ambivalent towards his most successful source material: "I like the Italian part [...] but I always sort of resented that it took up so much of my life, and that it's about shooting people" (Coppola cited in Yaquinto: 168). It is also interesting to note that pivotal gangster films after

The Godfather were directed by already established directors, such as Brian De Palma, Sergio Leone, Martin Scorsese and Abel Ferrara. All of these directors are Italian, or Italian Americans. Part of their credibility as gangster film directors derives from their ethnic identities. The predominance of Italian directors has links with a general trend for presenting such films as factually authentic. Articles about Martin Scorsese often focus on his personal experiences growing up in New York's Little Italy: "*Mean Streets* may not be pretty, but — according to its maker — it is true to ghetto life. The character of Charlie, with his priest-spawned feelings of guilt, is based partly on Scorsese himself and partly on a close friend who still lives in Little Italy" (Flatley, in Brunette, 1999: 4). When Mike Newell directed *Donnie Brasco*, many articles focused on the fact that he was English, "and one name that would *never* spring to mind" (*Total Film*, 1997), or the amount of research he had to do to "go where Scorsese and Coppola had gone before" (*Guardian*, May 2, 1997). Newell maintains that watching every mob movie ever made was not enough ("I needed to get close to these people" [*ibid.*],) going on to recount the highlights of two months of conversations with Mafia members. In this sense, the importance of insider information and ethnic credibility on the part of the director is an important part of publicity for such films. This is part of a much wider perception that the authenticity of postclassical gangster films is critically significant.

It is important to note that much of the critical work and reviews that are referred to in my discussions have focused on interviews with directors and that these directors are significant in the extratextual currency of the films. The importance of the director as a participant in Mafia mythologies or as a marketing asset cannot be ignored and for this reason, the decline in Italian American directors focusing on Mafia narratives has to be one of the reasons the Mafia has declined in cinema since the nineties. The Mafia has receded into the backroom shadows while cops and superheroes have taken center stage. It is not necessarily TV that has killed the gangster, but perhaps, a disinterest in the subject from the directors who helped to create its dominance. This is not to say that directors hold the key to all the trends in filmmaking; they are simply one aspect of the discourses surrounding postclassical gangster films. However, in an era where the director has been lauded as the creative center of film, the concept of genre is bound to be influenced by the discourses surrounding their perceived critical identity.

Stars

The more fluid approaches to the study of genre that emerged from the mid-seventies coincided with an interest in star studies (Dyer, 1979; King,

1986; Stacey, 1994). The role of stars as signifiers of certain character types can be associated with conventions and iconography, in that the looks, gestures and dialogue of actors such as James Cagney have influenced many later gangster characters. Richard Dyer especially maintains that stars possess a cultural currency that extends beyond single films, which in turn affects responses to film. Thus, the inclusion of James Cagney in a crime film may influence the responses to that film and suggest that it be read as part of the gangster genre. I agree that certain star images can be associated with particular genres, but as Dyer and others agree they do more than simply signify genre.

The extratextual currency of stardom is something that Corrigan regards as a significant element of postclassical Hollywood. Dyer's work on stars directs attention away from "real" individuals to the ways in which star images articulate notions of myth and ideology.[42] He argues that stars do not embody one image, but a "structured polysemy" of images: a finite collection of meanings and images developed over time (Dyer: 63). In this sense, Dyer is not searching for the meaning of a particular star for an individual audience member at a particular point in time and place[43]; instead he is charting what he terms the multiplicity of meanings that a star image produces or reflects.[44] Using Dyer's model, the star image of Al Pacino includes the following elements: a quiet brooding reserve, tempered with an ability for explosive intensity; loyalty to, yet patriarchal domination of women; and a New York/ Italian American ethnicity. He is other-worldly, not only through stardom, but because his most successful roles have been as gangsters, figures similarly separated from ordinary society. His media image has developed over the years, from "prodigal son" (*The Godfather* and *The Godfather Part II, Dog Day Afternoon*[45]) to "worldly father-figure." This latter image is most notably displayed in *Donnie Brasco, Heat,* and *The Insider* (1999).[46] Alongside these two distinct roles, there is his image as a romantic hero, plus his critical status as a method actor, who takes his art very seriously.[47] A large proportion of Pacino's critical and commercially successful roles have involved violent action: the *Godfather* trilogy, *Dog Day Afternoon, Scarface, Sea of Love* (1989), *Carlito's Way, Heat, Donnie Brasco.*[48]

However, more importantly a significant number of these and other films focus on male groups and the loss of, or nostalgia for, past times. Susannah Radstone (1995) describes Pacino's role in *Sea of Love* as "a man whose authority is on the wane" (148), encouraging audiences to sympathize with his newfound vulnerability, which in turn encourages a nostalgia for his lost authority. This character type permeates many of Pacino's later roles, most notably *The Godfather Part III, Carlito's Way* and *Donnie Brasco,* but also *Scent of a Woman* (1992),[49] *The Insider, Any Given Sunday* (1999),[50] *Insomnia* (2002), *Angels in America* (2003) and *Two for the Money* (2005). It is not sufficient to say that

Pacino has become a father figure. Roles such as these focus just as much on his past glories, real or imagined (as in *Donnie Brasco*), as they do on his contemporary vulnerability through illness and old age (*Godfather Part III*), desire to change (*Carlito's Way*), or emotional anxieties (*Donnie Brasco*). Therefore, it is notable that a significant part of Pacino's star image, especially by the nineties and beyond, is maintained by characters who refer to the past as much as the present, in that an understanding or sympathy for their present condition relies on knowledge of their past within the text. For instance, audiences are encouraged to sympathize with Carlito Brigante's (*Carlito's Way*) desire to renounce his gangster life, not because he is no longer capable of it (the pool room shoot-out belies this), but because he no longer needs to prove himself in this way. His strength is shown through his ability to reject violence, while still enacting it. He represents a nobility that is built upon and constantly refers back to past glories.[51] This type of reflective process is something that has led me to believe that star images, such as Al Pacino's and Robert De Niro's, operate as elements of iconography in post-classical gangster films, in that they are visual signifiers of the genre. Their established association with the gangster genre encourages audiences to sympathize with characters in particular ways,[52] but also to categorize films as being in the gangster genre due to the visual presence of particular stars.

Pacino and De Niro have been involved in popular gangster films since their careers began. Al Pacino has appeared as Michael Corleone (*The Godfather Parts I, II* and *III*), Tony Montana (*Scarface*), Carlito Brigante (*Carlito's Way*) and Lefty Ruggiero (*Donnie Brasco*). Robert De Niro has played Vito Corleone (*The Godfather Part II*), David "Noodles" Aaronson (*Once Upon a Time in America*), Al Capone (*The Untouchables*) Jimmy Conway (*Goodfellas*), Sam "Ace" Rothstein (*Casino*) and Paul Vitti (*Analyze This*). The involvement of these two stars in a crime film is likely to encourage allusions to previous roles. In *Heat*, Pacino plays a cop, while De Niro is the criminal.[53] As stated earlier, the criminal gang in this film displays allegiances to one another through dialogue and gestures. There are no ethnic ties, but they operate as a business with connections to an underworld network of buyers for their goods, and also as sellers of information and back-up. The film alludes to crime as a business operation. Within the group Neil McCauly (De Niro) is immaculately dressed in expensive suits, discussed earlier as an iconographic signifier of the gangster. The style is not gaudy, to simply indicate criminal wealth as suggested by the classic gangster films (or insta-gangsters of other crime narratives); it is expensive and understated to accentuate his control and dedication to his work. The gangster image that De Niro invokes here is similar to that of the young Vito Corleone or Jimmy Conway. Both of these characters were "gentleman" gangsters, in that their abilities were always understated, but their business acumen and control of situations was definite. Consequently, when De Niro appears on screen as Neil McCauley, his star persona references previous roles. These are significant to audiences only in so far as they are aware of these previous roles. However, reviewers, who generally have a strong sense of cinema history, will also encourage such associations. Similarly, Pacino, who had starred in the *Godfather* trilogy, *Scarface* and *Carlito's Way* before *Heat* was released, also possesses a star persona that references these gangster roles, together with issues of Italian American ethnicity and the intimacy of male friendship. These two stars bring the memories of previous roles with them and thus encourage certain generic associations. It is also important to note that Robert DeNiro, Al Pacino, and Marlon Brando in his time are all noted as the best actors of their generation and the leading players in method acting. This is significant because their appearance in particular films then not only influences genre associations but also raises the film's critical credibility.

Involving star images in the iconography of a genre is problematic in some ways, because it suggests an ability to identify a star's image at a particular moment in time within a particular role. However, that is not the full answer since these star images help to encourage a coherent network of discourses across very different gangster films in the postclassical era simply through association. For instance, it is most likely that Sam Rothstein (*Casino*) will conjure memories of Jimmy Conway, Al Capone, Noodles and Vito Corleone for audiences who have seen these earlier roles. This occurs, if by no other means, through De Niro's looks, mannerisms and speech, which no amount of method acting can mask. The same thing applies to Al Pacino's roles, and thus each gangster film reflects others simply through the inclusion of certain actors.[54] Therefore, the continual appearance of particular stars in films becomes a major factor in the recognition of genre as a coherent form. Furthermore, this promotes the sense that gangster films are discursive, in that they make reference to previous films within themselves. This assumption is crucial to an understanding of Mafia myths and therefore I will return to discuss it in greater detail during Chapter 3.

Recent Developments in Genre Theory

Genre criticism in the 1990s and beyond has gradually begun to take account of the ambiguous nature of genre classification in the production and consumption of film texts. Even a text-based analysis that leaves little room for audience discourse is likely to suggest that a particular film covers more than one genre. Genre hybridity is one way critics have attempted to address overlaps between categories. For example, *The Godfather* may be a gangster-melodrama in that it addresses domestic and emotional themes as well as crimes and violence. Jim Collins (1993) considers hybridity to be a recent (1980–90s) development. However, this notion can only be accepted if you also agree with the belief in a classic period from which such hybrid referentiality can stem. Paradoxically, this aligns Collins with earlier genre critics as it relies on a classical form to which all later films refer. However, his assertion of genres as eclectic structures does work to encourage a more fluid approach to genre boundaries.

Even though Collins, in my view, mistakenly perceives hybridity as a relatively new occurrence in film, his observations on the mediated nature of contemporary cultural existences go part way to recognizing the sophisticated web of meanings that surround any image:

> The real now comes to us always already 'imaged' in any number of ways, the 'depth and latitude' of contemporary cinema depending on the negotiation of the thickness of representation [252–3].

Hybridity is not only a result of narrative complexities, but also of the complex organization of categorization. Different viewers and critics see different themes; therefore to value one interpretation above another is an aesthetically hierarchal practice. Genre then becomes merely a short hand to identifying the various themes in a text. For instance, Ellen Willis (2003) summarizes *The Sopranos* as "a hybrid genre of post–*Godfather*, decline of the mob movie and soap opera with plenty of sex, violence, domestic melodrama, and comic irony" (Willis: 2). This not only reveals the ever present desire to categorize a text — even a TV series — but it also shows how *Godfather* has become a recognizable pseudonym for gangster genre.

In the late 1990s Rick Altman (1999) and Steve Neale (2000) have offered two further approaches that attempt to encapsulate the discursive nature of genre. Altman's semantic/syntactic/pragmatic approach takes its lead from social linguistics and the work of Metz and Bazin. He is interested in genre as a particular type of media language: one that involves elements (semantics), grammar or patterns (syntax), and uses (pragmatics). The crux of Altman's approach is that it allows for interconnections or discourses across patterns of elements within one particular film and patterns of elements across different films. What this means is that genre is a constantly shifting, but essentially recognizable construction of patterns of significant elements. His emphasis is on the semantics and syntax of a genre itself as it develops through time, as much as it is interested in a particular example of a genre. He notes that it is important "to look at patterns of generic change — genre origins, genre redefinition and genre repurposing — along with the more traditional topics of genre stability and structure" (Altman: 208). Furthermore, he asserts that pragmatics, or in this case the uses to which a genre is put, are also a fundamental part of genre construction and definition:

> Always assuming multiple users of various sorts — not only various spectator groups, but producers, distributors, exhibitors, cultural agencies, and many others as well — pragmatics recognizes that some familiar patterns, such as genres, owe their very existence to that multiplicity [*ibid.*: 210].

Altman proposes an approach that:

- Addresses the fact that every text has multiple users.
- Considers why different users develop different readings.
- Theorizes the relationship among those readers and
- Actively considers the effect of multiple conflicting uses on the production, labelling and display of films and genres alike. (*ibid.*: 214).

Thus, in Altman's view, genre exists as an ever-changing complex of cycles and development in a constantly evolving circulation of meaning. This gives the impression of constantly shifting sands. In fact, Steve Neale suggests that the blurred frontiers between semantics and syntax are the main problem when applying Altman's concepts (Neale, 2000: 216). However, if a genre analysis is attempting to refer back to a desire for one definition, then Altman's approach is problematic; but if an analysis is willing to accept a traceable but intricate network of meanings that matches the kind of discussions one finds on internet forums, then Altman does provide a starting point. In summary, Altman appears to be happy with viewing genre as an ever-changing kaleidoscope of patterns. His approach has a romantic feel, in that he accepts the input of commercial factors but prefers to concentrate on the multiplicity of pleasures and uses audiences may experience. The cycles and trends identified in Chapter 1 can provide the starting point for such an analysis as this. It provides a map of film production, which can be developed to embrace an assessment of the elements and patterns of elements within texts and the pleasures these encourage. Thus, Altman's model is useful in that it encourages an acceptance of the fluidity of genre, but also suggests the traceability of dominant elements within and across the texts.

Neale's latest work attempts to integrate both ends of the production/ reception process. He embraces the fact that genres have multiple users and multiple uses, but he also focuses on how Hollywood (as a specific arena of film production) plans, finances and markets genres. In terms of textual practices, Neale both summarizes and extends his previous work on genre as a process[55] within the following three propositions:

> The repertoire of generic conventions available at any one point in time is always *in* play rather than simply being *re*played, even in the most repetitive of films, genres and cycles. [...] Any generic repertoire always exceeds, and thus can never be exhausted by, any single film. [...] Generic repertoires

> themselves can be at least partly compatible. [...] In this way hybrid films,
> cycles and genres are formed [219].

These propositions emphasize the notion that genre is a fluid concept, not defined by one single trait, but by many. Furthermore, these traits are not fixed, or bound to one particular genre. Neale cites Bordwell and Thompson (1979) in stating that genres can "cross-breed" (97). This notion of genre as a process is useful for this book, because it does not insist on the isolation of specific traits within a specific genre. This allows for a freer discussion of films as part of a genre by tracing particular traits without having to regard those traits as definitive.

Neale does not wish to restrict his study to the textual analysis of genres. He recognizes the power of the reader/viewer in the uses of texts, and is especially appreciative of the work of T. Roberts (1990).[56] Roberts suggests that not only do readers have different responses to a particular genre, from exclusivist to fan to occasional and "allergic," but "within every reading/viewing there lies an intricate pattern of addictions, preferences, random interests, avoidances and allergies which is never quite the same as the pattern in any other reader[or viewer]" (Roberts, cited in Neale: 226). Therefore it is evident that tracing the reception of genres is going to be problematic, because texts are experienced differently by each individual and by the same individual at different times and in different contexts. Evidently, the most that can be achieved is tracing the multiplicity of readings. In this sense, thus far, Neale's work resembles Altman's approach to genre.

Neale goes on to add a re-evaluation of the studio era of Hollywood filmmaking.[57] He lists the films for 1934 as they were reviewed in *Variety*, and then assesses the generic value of the descriptions. From this he asserts that genres are arbitrary and fluid. He explains that genres are simply tag-lines used in co-existent ways by both producers and users to convey a sense of what each film contains. These tags are not constant, in that they change depending on who is articulating the definition, to what purpose and when. Thus, as stated earlier, a melodrama in the 1930s may be re-categorized as an action film by the 1990s. Similarly, a comedy film for Warner Productions in the 1930s may be a Cagney film for a *Variety* reviewer and a romance for a viewer. Neale asserts that the function of this kind of approach is to move the emphasis away from individual genres and on to patterns of genres that dominate particular seasons or decades. There is no need to account for hybridization, or to trace dominant devices. There is also no need to be selective in the choice of films, which is something that both Neale and Maltby have noted as a weakness in most genre analyses. In view of this, it would appear that Neale is calling for an end to the search for genre classification and for "a cross-generic and multi-cyclic approach; for an approach which pays heed to local and minor genres and trends" (254).

Neale's call is justifiable in view of the limitations of any approach that searches for ultimate definitions, but it also tends to imply that all categories are equally valid, and thus denies the purpose of genre for both industry and audiences as a way of recognizing particular films. Neale's approach is fairly close to Altman's in that it is interested in tracing patterns in the production and consumption of genres, rather than identifying singular definitions within particular genre texts. However, analyzing production trends on their own will not provide much insight into the enduring popularity of particular types of film, apart from proving that they still exist. For my purposes, it is more useful to combine Altman's semantic/syntactic/pragmatic approach with the more ideological and industry-based approach from Neale in order to trace patterns in production, texts and the readings they encourage. Both Neale and Altman recognize the fluidity of genre classification as well as the significance of genres as cultural signifiers (tag lines) for producers and receivers alike. This book operates on the premise that gangster films are worthy of attention, perhaps not as uniquely definable genre, but at least as traceable patterns of genre conventions. Therefore, Altman's approach is useful as it considers a genre as traceable, as long as the parameters of construction and usage remain fluid. Neale's approach foregrounds the importance of production strategies, marketing and stars in encouraging the variety of genre classifications that have occurred. However, he suggests that an attention to one genre may be reductive. While this book only concentrates on gangster films, it is not in an attempt to impose a definitive classification upon them. Focusing attention onto one genre, as long as it is attentive to issues of hybridization and cultural shift, can be productive in tracing the shifting configurations of issues that the genre has been preoccupied with. For the gangster film, such issues include notions of Americanness primarily articulated through displays of masculinity and ethnicity. As such, this initial analysis of genre has been be used to develop the map of cycles identified in Chapter 1 into more fluid patterns of structures and themes involving processes of self-referentiality and intertextuality. As stated in the Introduction, the structure of this book is similar to recent writings on the classical gangster film, but not with the same end in view. The application of genre theories trace some of the elements that inform the type, taking into consideration some textual and extra textual considerations, including ways in which films have been categorized in reviews and internet forums. This allows for postclassical gangster films to be afforded the same level of consideration as the films from the classical era.

Audiences

Audience participation in the construction of meaning has not had a prominent role in studies of genre. Theorists such as Neale have tended to isolate consumption as a subject position determined on the whole by the text. Studies of real film audiences[58] have not focused on genre categorization. However, recent work on the gangster genre by such as Munby and Ruth do interpret the films as part of wider cultural discourses. For example, Ruth's work concentrates on the image of Al Capone in real life as well as on the screen, thus providing a wider perspective on the cultural impact of his persona as well as images of the gangster in general. Munby explores the social contexts of film production, including marketing strategies, censorship and box office trends. Both analyses broaden the field of film study and are part of a more general shift towards the ideas and concerns of cultural studies theorists and their focus on the role of media in everyday life.[59]

Richard Maltby's work on genre[60] combines an ideological approach with an analysis of the extra textual influence of production codes and studio marketing discourses. His view is that "because different audiences will use a genre in different ways at different times, its boundaries can never be rigidly defined, and at the same time it is susceptible to extensive subdivision" (1995: 108). Different discourses interact to the extent that a single film may encompass many narrative themes, styles and thus genre labels. Maltby cites the different uses of the term melodrama, which the industry in the 1920s used to describe adventure or action films. Shifts in cultural discourses, not least those surrounding genre criticism, have subsequently redefined melodrama as mainly a woman's film, or "weepie." Maltby asserts that this underscores the arbitrary nature of genre classification. To take another example, in Robert Sklar's *City Boys: Cagney, Bogart, Garfield* (1992), it is noted that *Public Enemy* (1931) was initially promoted as a social conscience film. Darryl F. Zanuck argued that one of its themes would be "the necessity of improving the environment and living conditions in the lower regions" (Sklar, 1992: 31). While Sklar does not concentrate particularly on audience responses, or the advertising of particular films, he includes a quotation from a contemporary review of *Public Enemy* that is useful to note: "The audiences yesterday laughed frequently and with gusto as the swaggering Matt and Tom went through their paces, and this rather took the edge off the brutal picture the producers appeared to be trying to serve up" (*New York Times*, cited in Sklar: 32). Sklar suggests that the audience reaction was due to the familiarity of these figures in surrounding neighborhoods. This, of course, is an assumption, but the review does supply evidence that the film was thoroughly entertaining to audiences and that the "tragic hero," as Warshow later described Tom Powers, was also for them a comic character.

In view of the fact that audiences, critics and all forms of publicity can embrace very different interpretations of films, it is appropriate to note, as Maltby does, that the boundaries of a genre dissolve not only to admit new movies, but also to incorporate the surrounding discourses of advertising, marketing, publicity, press and other media reviewing, reporting and gossip, and the "word of mouth" opinions of other viewers [113].

Thus, it is imperative that the cycles of films I identified in Chapter 1 are not seen as complete models of the development of the postclassical gangster film. By the time of the release of *The Godfather* (1972), surrounding discourses not only included the history of the gangster film, but also the history of gangsters in other media: for example, news reporting, fiction and political propaganda. Furthermore, the idea of genre itself was a powerful factor in assessing a new film's credibility. Gary Arnold in *The Washington Post* described *The Godfather* as "a new classic in a classic American film genre" (cited in Cowie, 1997: 69). It would appear that Arnold is valuing the film within contemporary genre criticism, which had decided that the classic form was confined to three 1930s films. Vincent Canby, in *The New York Times*, described it as "one of the most brutal and moving chronicles of American life" (cited in Cowie: 68), thus suggesting its importance as a possible encapsulation of American social identity. Canby appears to be raising the film to epic proportions. Alternatively, he is suggesting it be viewed as a social conscience film, one that perhaps offers a realistic portrayal of the American psyche. George De Stefano (2006) notes that the film "presented us with a paradox: the most vividly realistic and lovingly detailed depiction of Italian American life in the history of the movies [but] framed through the singular experience of an atypical group" (106).

Lynne Tillman (1992) lists the themes in *The Godfather* that appeal to her the most as loyalty, fathers and family. She tells us she is "seduced by appeals to undying loyalty [...] a wish for some ultimate authority to relieve [her] of the burden of conscience [and] the desire for an unshakeable tradition to which [she] would belong without question" (Tillman, 1992: 33). She relates these themes back to her own emotions about family: "my family romance in its family romance" (*ibid.*), thus suggesting that the film be viewed as a melodrama. As stated before, melodrama is an ambiguous term with various definitions. I am using it to define those gangster films that foreground the emotional existence of its main characters, such as *The Godfather Trilogy* and *Donnie Brasco*. These films focus on the Mafia as a family organization (not necessarily blood-related) and suggest the lives of gangsters as brutal but tragic, thus promoting their stories romantically. It is this element of *The Godfather* that appears to appeal to Tillman. The integration of generic terms is appropriate, because it shows how a film can articulate personal desires and fears in accordance with a particular viewer, over and above specific genre conventions or notions of familiarity within a particular cinema history.

Internet discussion forums can be a useful indicator of audience responses to genre. However, of course one has to factor in the recognition that most people who post on film forums are more than "casual film viewers." They will probably have watched any chosen film several times and have a desire to comment upon it. As such, I have included a very brief snapshot of some of comments here only as an indicator of discursive practices beyond the industry, rather than as a definitive study of film audiences. Websites such as the Internet Movie Database (imdb.com) have discussion forums for every film. While most discussions focus on favorite characters, quotes and moments in the films, other discussions compare films and attempt to rate their qualities. It is evident that *The Godfather* remains as popular as ever. One thread on imdb.com is entitled 'Ten Reasons why this is the best movie ever made." The discussion has had many participants and while not all agree on the film's superiority, those that argue against it are often in favor of *The Godfather Part II* as the alternative choice. Reelreviews.com and mafiaflix.com both rank *The Godfather* number 1 in their top films list. IMDB has it at number two in their "Top 250." Amazon.com's "Listmania" has many gangster film lists with *The Godfather* at the top. *Goodfellas* tends to be the most popular second film, and in fact the *Goodfellas* discussion thread on imdb.com as of June 9, 2009, has 429 replies to the thread "*Goodfellas* or *Godfather*?" The total so far is 167 to 159 in favor of *Goodfellas*. While many discussions do focus on likes and dislikes, this is not necessarily the only topic they explore.

Discussion of genre tends to occur in comparison threads. For instance, *The Godfather* board has a thread comparing *The Godfather* to *Once Upon a Time in America*. Most entries focus on particular likes and dislikes especially with regard to the more complicated narrative structure in the latter. However, there is no question that the films are perceived as similar gangster films, which is interesting because the narratives and characters are so very different. In contrast, a thread on the *King of New York* board entitled "Any Goodfellas fans like this film?" has a reply that states, "Maybe if you didn't label it a mob/gangster film. This film is totally different." *Miller's Crossing* has a thread entitled "this is a film noir right?" Replies include, "Not really," "It has neo-noir elements," and it is "influenced by pre-noir gangster movies." One in-depth reply suggests it is "a neo-noir and presents one of the more interesting amoral protagonists of the genre. It can also be a gangster flick, but that is quite secondary" (posted by paradx). One thread asks "*Miller's Crossing* or *State of Grace*?" A reply suggests, "they're nothing alike — except that both fall under the Irish-American mob category" (posted by SeanJoyce). Sopranoland.com has a discussion thread, "what is your favorite mob-related movie?" A reply states, "I wouldn't classify [*Scarface*] as a mob movie. That was more of a drug lord movie to me. Tony Montana only makes one reference to the mob in the whole movie" (posted by Iammizzbeehavin). Genre is used as a labeling tool, but the definitions of genre are obviously vague as this is not the focus of fan discussion. "Favorite gangster films" lists on imdb.com and amazon.com include a wide range of films. *The Usual Suspects* (1994) appears quite often, as does *Jackie Brown* (1997), *A History of Violence* (2005) and most recently *The Dark Knight* (2008). Jonathan Drewes, the creator of contractflicks.com, makes the following comments about the Top Ten Gangster Films listed on reelreviews.com. He notes that *Dark Knight, A History of Violence* and *Jackie Brown* are more crime films than Mafia. Furthermore, he states that *Analyze This* should be categorized as a comedy before a true mob/mafia movie. Web lists and discussion forums are not that different to most academic writing on genre; it is more common for writers to focus on what makes a film *different* than what makes it the same as others. Therefore, it is appropriate to remember that genre is not only something that "we know when we see it," but it's also something that "we know when we don't see it." This knowledge is going to be slightly different for every single viewer.

Discussion boards devote a lot of time to personal judgments. A film is often berated for being too "boring," "slow" (*The Godfather*) or "sappy" (*Carlito's Way*). These are then counteracted with replies of "masterpiece" (*Godfather*) and "underrated" and "more my feel" (*Carlito's Way*). Reasons for liking or disliking films will vary wildly of course: A *Goodfellas* fan on imdb.com (Neil4Real) suggests it is a better film than *The Godfather* because the latter is slow and boring with "not enough action," whereas *Goodfellas* is fast, and "so much happens." Attention to realism or true life events often surfaces in a discussion about a film's credibility as a gangster film. An argument that *Donnie Brasco* is an "overrated film" on imdb.com is countered by a reply that reminds us it is a "true story," which I believe is presented as a reason why it cannot be discounted as an important gangster film. *Goodfellas* is often noted as "realistic" (imdb.com) or "accurate" (sopranoland.com). Furthermore, while *The Godfather* is often chastised for being too "romantic" or "tame," this is countered by a reminder that it references many real events. It would appear that a link with real life events is most often prized as a marker of generic credibility. In contrast, narrative familiarity does not attract praise. *Carlito's Way* is berated for being "a little obvious and recycled." It offers nothing new to an "old story." This possibly suggests that genre is valued for the way it offers new visions of old stories, rather than replaying them. It is hard to know exactly how much familiarity and difference films require in order to be true to form while still offering something new, but it is evident that it is an important factor for audiences.

One way audiences adapt genre is to talk of alternative plotlines and endings, or to compare characters across films. A large number of threads on sites such as imdb.com and sopranoland.com discuss possible interpretations of *The Sopranos'* ending, or design additional plotlines for after that end episode. Chaselounge.net has a message board called "The movie never ends" dedicated to "fan fiction, proposed future storylines and speculation on what would or should happen to various characters after the finale." Most use generic conventions to form their narrative structure, in that there is a general acceptance that Tony must die or suffer for his crimes. However, the most fundamental desire is for the story to live on. There are also multiple discussion threads on various forums focusing on alternative plots for characters killed in earlier series. Reception theory has long asserted that creating alternative narratives is a dominant aspect of fandom. Fan fiction is a huge modern phenomenon that is now bleeding into the mainstream. At a basic level it provides glimpses of what aspects of the film or TV series fans find important. It reveals clues as to the popularity of characters, but also the popularity of events and cause-effect logistics. One thread on imdb.com discusses *The Godfather* and is titled, "I hated when Sonny died." The basis is a discussion of the popular appeal of both the Sonny Corleone character and James Caan's star persona, but replies also offer alternative plotlines. For instance, Sonny would survive the shooting and become the Don for a while. He would "inevitably get killed later though." His survival would only ever be temporary, because generic convention requires that his character type invites violence.

One extra aspect of "Sonny surviving" is revealed in the same post when the writer (Christine Frankenstein) suggests that such a plot shift would allow Michael to remain married to Appollonia, "an obedient Italian wife," and therefore the family would be safer and stronger. This is not an isolated suggestion. Another thread titled "If Appollonia had never been killed" also states that she would have been a better wife. She would have produced sons that would be loyal to the Mafia business and it would mean "none of Kay's stupid moral nonsense getting in Michael's way" (posted by Hermit C-1). Such a plotline blames Kay for much of Michael's problems and completely ignores the many plotlines that focused on Vito as well as Michael voicing their desire to have their sons go beyond the family business. However, that is the intrigue and revelation of such alternative plotlines. They do not have to adhere to the cause-effect logic of the original film. The alternative plot often reveals as much about the world view of the writer as it does about the appeal of the characters involved.

Alternative plotlines may appear separate to discussions of genre, but the practice often adheres to many of the conventions of genre. There is a desire to see characters live on, but this desire is usually tempered by the recognition that the cinema world they live in has specific rules. As such, alternative plotlines are just another discursive practice through which gangster film is recognized and explored by modern audiences.

All discussion forums have threads with interesting input, but they are also frustrating because there is often not enough information. Films are rated and compared, but because most replies are short there is little evidence to back up the personal opinion. For instance, when dtatroom suggests *Donnie Brasco* is "one of the best ever gangster movies (though a different type from the others)," we do not know in what ways it is different. As with all audience research, the researcher needs to be an active participant in the discussion in order to ask further questions, but then there is always the tendency to guide the discussion rather than simply facilitating it. Internet forums are snapshots of audience responses and as such they are extremely important indicators of film reception, but it must also be noted that they provide only partial answers.

Reviews

To complete this discussion of gangster films as a genre I will consider the reviewing process in relation to categorizing postclassical gangster films. Again, this is not to suggest that reviews can in some way provide conclusive proof for or against a film's inclusion within a genre. It is to show how reviews reflect the discursive nature of genre. I have separated this discussion from that of audience discussion in internet forums because reviews tend to be more formal even though they often cover similar topics. Reviews pick up on patterns and promote gangster films as part of a continuous genre narrative. Comparing and contrasting films of a similar kind in order to make sense of them is a fundamental part of film reviews. In this sense, they are quite similar to internet forums. However, most of the reviews I will focus on are from the pre-internet press and are therefore much more static in their discussion as opposed to the ever evolving forum threads that occur today. Traditional film reviews form an important extratextual influence on the development of genre and their inclusion here will extend the analysis again away from production and towards the critical reception of film. I have collected a cross-section of reviews from daily newspapers and magazines both in print and on-line from the U.K. and U.S.A. They are not meant to be exhaustive and only represent a sampling. The discussion will show how commercial success has influenced later production and how reference points constantly develop and shift to provide accepted discourses on gangsters that allude to a sense of historical and ethnic authenticity. It is evident that since *The Sopranos* became successful, on-line discussion forums and fan websites have also become a resource for critical reviews and so I will include some of their input where appropriate.

The commercial and critical success of *The Godfather* obviously encouraged later productions. Such factors are significant in defining the genre cycles identified earlier. Commercial influences are not something that Schatz and Cawelti note in their assessment of genre cycles, but these issues have since been examined in the work of Maltby and Neale. The biopics released in 1973 no doubt received financial backing based on the subject's seeming popularity. *Scarface* reawakened the gangster genre in the eighties. Similarly, Wolf Schneider (1990) notes that the increased presence of gangster films in 1990 "was conceived as a result of *The Untouchables'* substantial box office gross of $80 million three years ago" (4). The resulting commercial success of *Goodfellas* (1990) can be suggested to have sparked an increase in gangster films throughout the nineties. This demonstrates the extent to which responses to genre films correspond to box office trends and commercial leads in production. *The Godfather* is generally accepted as one of the biggest-selling films of all time. By the end of its first year of release *Variety* (May 9, 1973) noted it was "the top-grossing film of the last five years." Success has reached far beyond the American market and it has been suggested that "the international grosses exceeded anything in Hollywood history" (Cowie: 73). As such, the film stands as one of the first major blockbusters of the postclassical era. The high production costs, pre-release media hype and eventual box office success signify the film's status as a blockbuster. However, it remains slightly different to later blockbusters such as *Jaws* (1975), *Star Wars* (1977) or *Batman* (1995).[61] First, it did not fully exploit its potential for commercial merchandising. Second, the film gained as much critical praise as it did commercial success. *The Godfather* combines two responses together: critical acceptance along with commercial popularity. This is one of the important elements that isolate the film from its predecessors.

The thirties classics *Scarface*, *Public Enemy* and *Little Caesar* were all low-budget crime movies when released and were treated as such by the press. By the time that *The Godfather* was released, film study was an established academic discipline. Not only was Coppola schooled in it, so were many reviewers. This may account for much of the increased critical attention. The combination of commercial success and critical acclaim has influenced a trend of increasing critical respect for the gangster film. While some reviewers may balk at the violence or the romanticism of gangster films, the general trend is to treat them with deference. Some of this deference is a result of the commercial and critical status of particular directors, but also the promotion, through the commercial success of such films as *The Godfather* and *Goodfellas*, of Mafia mythologies in general.

To begin, it is interesting to note reactions to *Bonnie and Clyde*. The film's initial press reviews do not mention gangsters or genre traditions at all.

Therefore, it is evident that genre labels were applied later on. Initial reviews focus on the main characters as "naïve and feckless youngsters" (*Morning Star*, September 9, 1967, *Sunday Express*, September 10, 1967), "wayward kids" (*Saturday Review*, August 5, 1967), or "lovers and killers" (*The Sun*, September 5, 1967). The closest reviewers come to gangster imagery is "young hoodlums" (*Observer*, September 10, 1967) and describing Clyde Barrow as a "Robin Hood figure" (*Time*, August 5, 1967; *Daily Telegraph*, September 8, 1967). Discussions of narrative suggest it as "a love story" (*Queen's Journal*, November 24, 1967) and a "tragedy" (*Saturday Review*, August 5, 1967). It is only when we move on to the more academic journals that genre is mentioned. However, the film's uniqueness is also foregrounded here. Bonnie and Clyde are gangsters, but "non-professional" (*Monthly Film Bulletin*, v34 n.405, 1967). It is a gangster film, but "romantic imagination distinguishes it" (*Film Quarterly*, v21 n.2, 1967). Reactions to this film emphasised a similarity to the innovation found in European film, allusions to classic film styles (the banjo music, similar to the style of *The Keystone Cops*) and the "re-creation" (*Sight and Sound*, v37 n.1, 1968) of Bonnie and Clyde outlaw myths. Thus, the film was regarded as a testament to youth culture themes, such as an anti-authority, anti-establishment stance and sexual freedom. These responses underline the differences between *Bonnie and Clyde* and later gangster films of the post-classical period.

The *Brotherhood* is described as a "Mafia drama" (*Variety*, November 20, 1968), or a "tale of Mafia-ridden brotherly love and conflict" (*Monthly Film Bulletin*, v35 n.419, 1968). The story is described as

> a fairly familiar one of the conflict between the "traditional ways" and the "new breed"— it might have been set in the medical profession or on a ranch, (as indeed it was used as one of the themes in *Hud*) [*sic*], it just happens to use the backdrop of gangsterism [*Films and Filming*, v15 n.5, 1969: 43].

The Brotherhood is seen to display the classical themes of loyalty and betrayal, together with the more recent theme of transition from old traditions to new Mafia. Another aspect of *The Brotherhood* which drew attention was the publicity still of the "kiss of death." *Variety* suggests that this advertising does the film a "disservice" (November 20, 1968).[62] Such assertions, as stated in the discussion on gestures, show the extent to which the later popularity of *The Godfather* encouraged an acceptance of such Italian Mafia gestures and dialogue. Such displays have come to be popularly admired rather than feared. Pre-*Godfather* reviews of *Bonnie and Clyde* and *The Brotherhood* concentrate on the universal nature of the themes displayed, rather than making any recourse to genre.

The Godfather still receives a huge amount of attention in the popular press, especially as a benchmark to which later films refer. Coppola describes it as "an authentic ... film about gangsters who were Italian, how they lived, how they behaved, the way they treated their families, celebrated their rituals" (Coppola cited in Yaquinto, 1998: 125). He is often cited as associating the Corleone family with the trappings of monarchy, the main theme being "power and the succession of power" (cited in Yaquinto: 124 & Cowie: 15). In this, he attempts to appease those who may accuse him of perpetuating an assumption that all Italian Americans are gangsters, while maintaining that many of the themes in the film are universal. The main significance of *The Godfather* in relation to subsequent gangster films and the critical attention paid to them is the fact that it appears to satisfy reviewers, both at an emotional and an intellectual level. It is as justifiable for Penelope Houston to proclaim that the film is a "fairytale of princes and castles" (*New Statesman,* September 1, 1972) as it is for Philip Strick (*Monthly Film Bulletin,* v39, n.464, 1972) or Christopher Hudson (*The Spectator,* August 26, 1972) to see it as an analogy for "contemporary private enterprise." It allows for Michael Wood (*New Society,* September 21, 1972), Richard Roud (*The Guardian,* April 16, 1972) and Donald Zec (*Daily Mirror,* August 22, 1972) to emphasize the biblical proportions of a film "where epic and simplified heroes act out large and noble destinies" (Wood). Lastly, and perhaps most importantly, it allows critics almost unanimously to proclaim that *The Godfather* refers to its cinematic heritage while simultaneously transcending it. It is both mainstream and revolutionary, or as Thomas Wiseman states, "the significant twist to the old story is that now the Don, the supercriminal, is made to speak for the counter culture"(*Guardian,* May 31, 1972).

Reviews of *Mean Streets* focus on its authenticity (*Financial Times,* April 5, 1974, *Daily Telegraph,* April 5, 1974). The main characters are described as operating on "the criminal fringes" (*The Listener,* April 11, 1974), or the "seamy side of Mafia street" (*Daily Mirror,* April 5, 1974). Furthermore, they are characterized as "an ethnic and amoral bunch" (*New Statesman,* April 12, 1974) and a "closed circle" (*Time,* November 5, 1973). In short, the film attracted none of the romantic accolades of *The Godfather.* This may be attributed to the difference in the films' original publicity budgets, since later reviews deemed *Mean Streets* "a Mafia classic" (*Times,* February 20, 1993). It is not surprising to note that *The Godfather* dominated press reviews of gangster films in the seventies. Indeed, it appears to have re-established the genre in the hearts and minds of reviewers.

Reviews from the eighties and early nineties appear to concentrate more heavily on genre to describe films than those of the seventies did. This may be due to a desire for easily identifiable "tag-lines" for films, or to the fact that the popularity of gangster themes and images in film have become more widespread. The following overview of press reviews shows how genre is used to justify, criticize and most importantly distinguish films from earlier examples.

As stated earlier, *Scarface* received many negative reviews at the time of its release: it was seen as "a bitter comedy" (*Time*, December 5, 1983), that "lacks gangster conspiracies to enjoy" (*New Yorker*, December 26, 1983) and as delivering "crime without a point" (*Sunday Telegraph*, February 5, 1984). *Once Upon a Time in America* is clearly more satisfactory, identified as "an amalgam of *The Godfather* and *Angels with Dirty Faces*" (*Observer*, October 7, 1984), thus suggesting that the film be seen as a re-assessment of classical and postclassical themes, but most probably alluding to *The Godfather*'s epic length and the representation of the dead end kids in *Angels with Dirty Faces*. It is aligned with other gangster films, as a "melodrama of loyalty and betrayal" (*Times*, May 22, 1984), but it is also distinguished as "essentially a mystery story" (*Spectator*, October 13, 1984). *The Untouchables* is described as allowing "the good guys to get the last word" (*Daily Telegraph*, September 18, 1987), but as "untouched by reality" (*Times*, September 12, 1987) and operating as "flamboyantly acceptable entertainment" (*Mail on Sunday*, September 20, 1987). These films are being measured against both *The Godfather*, as the most recent benchmark, and the classical gangster films as the originals. In contrast, *Goodfellas* was said to have "arguably hi-jacked the genre by simply telling the truth" (*Western Mail*, October 26, 1990). Its authenticity was founded within Scorsese's ethnic identity and the screenplay's basis in a biography, *Wiseguy* (Nicholas Pileggi, 1984). Most reviews compare the film to *The Godfather*, as "the most accurate description of the Godsons rather than the Godfathers of the Mob" (*Guardian*, October 25, 1990). The characters are acknowledged as "lyrical, sensual and stylized in the way they have been filmed" (*Daily Mail*, October 3, 1990, *Sunday Telegraph*, October 28, 1990), but also as "un-romantic" (*Sunday Telegraph*, October 28, 1990; *Mail on Sunday*, October 28, 1990). This latter description marks the film as different to *The Godfather*, in that *Goodfellas* concentrates mainly on the street guys, rather than the bosses and is less romantic in its portrayal of the Mafia as a whole. This is something that I will be address further in Chapter's 3 and 4.

Reviews of *State of Grace* assert that it "brings the genre up to date [...] and shows there's plenty of life in the genre" (*Daily Mail*, June 14, 1991). This suggests to me an acceptance that *The Godfather* no longer dictates the standard and that the genre evolves or shifts in emphasis over time. The film is distinguished from others as a "realistic gang war saga" (*Village Voice*, September 18, 1990), or as a "precinct melodrama about tribal loyalties" (*Evening Standard*, June 13, 1991). *King of New York* was not received with the same understanding: "After Scorsese's 'epic scale,' Coppola's 'Mafia Opus' and Coen's 'ironic homage,' Ferrara takes us back to body count basics" (*City*

Limits, June 20, 1991). It was
viewed as a "gory excursion into
gangsterdom" (*Daily Telegraph*,
June 20, 1991), and as "stylish, but
empty" (*Times*, June 20, 1991).
This is similar to reviews of *Bugsy*,
although not because of the violence. *Bugsy* was said to exude
"glamorous sleaze" (*Evening Standard*, December 19, 1991) and to
display a "lavish surface" (*New
Yorker*, December 30, 1991). However, this also included the charge
of "witless beautification" (*City
Limits*, March 19, 1992). *New Jack
City* was hailed as "black imitations of gangster life" (*Evening
Standard*, August 29, 1991) and it
was admonished as preferring
"style over content" (*Independent*,
August 29, 1991), wherein "realism plays no part in this high gloss
escapism" (*Times*, August 29, 1991).
These reactions signal a growing
concern in film reviews of the

Michael Corleone (Al Pacino). *The Godfather Part III* © 1990, Zoetrope/Para-
mount.

early nineties about the dominance of style over content. It is suggested that
Bugsy needed "less smooch and more nitty gritty" (*New Statesman*, March 20,
1992), underlining the continued valorisation of authenticity in postclassical
gangster films. Having said this, *Billy Bathgate*, an unashamedly fictional work
on the Mafia, was said to "lack the gleeful high style of *Miller's Crossing*"
(*Times*, January 9, 1992), but it was also distinguished as "not just another
gangster movie, but something with time for character study" (*Daily Mail*,
January 10, 1992). This indicates that gangster films were beginning to be
associated with over-used style clichés and stereotypes.

These concerns about style and cliché mainly revolve around issues of
ethnicity and masculinity. Reviews that identify films, such as *New Jack City*,
as "black imitations of gangster life" (*Evening Standard*, August 29, 1991), or,
identify ethnicity as the root of criminal behaviour[63] go on to claim the films
as empty parodies of the genre, or dangerous influences for audiences. In
responses to representations of masculinity, suggestions that "Tarantino's version of masculinity is deeply regressive [...] paranoid, homophobic — women

get no more than 30 seconds screen time, people of colour get zero" (*Reservoir Dogs* reviewed in *Sight and Sound*, 1992) are in opposition to reviews of *The Godfather* that note the "frightening," yet "alluring" (*New Society*, September 21, 1972) masculinity on display. This may be because of the development in attitudes towards representations of masculinity on screen between 1972 and 1992, but it may also be due to concerns of style over content in *Reservoir Dogs*. Therefore, the motivation for aggressive masculine behavior may be clearer and more justified in the narrative of *The Godfather* than it is in *Reservoir Dogs*. It is important to note that it is not just an issue of factual authenticity that attracts concern. Some films, noted as authentic, also attract attention concerning the ideals of Mafia and issues surrounding the representation of masculinity. For instance, "if you're not with the Mob, you're not living" (*New Statesman*, January 24, 1991) is perceived as the dangerous claim of *Goodfellas*. The characters in *Donnie Brasco* are viewed as "Sadfellas — not wise guys" (*Daily Telegraph*, May 2, 1997). Furthermore, "Death is sudden and nasty, but fear is constant and nastier" (*Financial Times*, April 17, 1997) for characters in *The Funeral*. It is evident that authenticity is an important element of postclassical gangster films, as it provides motivation for both the fear of and sympathy for characters. These discussions will be addressed in more detail in Chapter 4.

* * *

It would appear from popular reviews that the epitome of style over content arrived in the form of *Reservoir Dogs*, *Pulp Fiction* and *Casino*. *Reservoir Dogs* is viewed as "self consciously hip" (*Village Voice*, October 27, 1992), "stylish, violent and empty" (*Today*, January 8, 1993) and "a smarty arty splatter movie [which operates under] a double standard, presenting gore and claiming it as intellectual" (*Sunday Times*, January 10, 1993). *Pulp Fiction* attracts criticisms such as "style wins over substance" (*Guardian*, 23/5/94). Intellectuals are blamed for defending Tarantino and instructing "us to enjoy the mindless and banal and consider it art" (*Daily Mail*, October 22, 1994). Scorsese, who normally attracts critical praise, received very little for *Casino*: "Realism fails him. There's too much gloss" (*Independent*, November 16, 1995); it is "too similar to *Goodfellas*, never takes a risk" (*Village Voice*, November 28, 1995, *Sunday Express*, February 25, 1996 & *Independent*, February 22, 1996). There are no allusions to genre in the reviews, except for the *Goodfellas* template (*Sunday Times*, February 25, 1996). Hence, this period of gangster film production attracted criticism as empty, exaggerated and more concerned with the looks and gestures (mainly violent) of gangster images, rather than any recourse to authenticity of fact or Mafia mythologies.

Carlito's Way, released between Tarantino's *Reservoir Dogs* and *Pulp Fiction*, was not always reviewed as a gangster film; it was described instead as a film noir (*What's On in London*, January 5, 1994; *Independent on Sunday*, January 9, 1994), or a thriller (*Mail on Sunday*, January 9, 1994). Furthermore, its style was described as "wistful" (*Independent on Sunday*, 9/1/94), or as "a mixture of seediness and nobility" (*Mail on Sunday*, January 9, 1994). It is not clear whether these descriptions merely reflect an antipathy towards the contemporary stylish trends in postclassical gangster films, or whether there is really something specifically unique about this film compared to those that surround it. When *Carlito's Way* is compared to a gangster film, it is viewed as "a tribute to Warner Crime Movies of the thirties" (*Sunday Express*, January 1, 1994), which in a way unusual for this decade ignores the influence of postclassical films. However, it does link back to De Palma's previous film, *Scarface*, which also paid homage to the classical form. Thematically, it is more similar to the romanticized tragedy of *The Godfather* rather than later gangster films and foreshadows the return of such brutal but romantic narratives found in *The Funeral* and *Donnie Brasco*.

Both postclassical influences and the significance of the gangster film as a genre were restored in reviews of *The Funeral*. It is linked with *King of New York* in "re-wiring the gangster film as a cold exposé of race, class and the economy" (*Independent*, April 3, 1997), which is interesting, as initial reviews found *King of New York* "empty." The film is also compared to *Mean Streets* (*Observer Review*, April 20, 1997), as they are both about sin and redemption. *Donnie Brasco* is viewed as "more ruthless than *Goodfellas* (*Guardian*, April 4, 1997). This is because it is "a slow mob film that can make you cry " (*Asian Age*, March 4, 1997), and a "mob informant melodrama" (*Village Voice*, March 4, 1997). Its authenticity is felt to be founded in a biography of an FBI agent, Joe Pistone.[64] It is suggested that the film "is not a Mafia movie" (*Financial Times*, May 1, 1997), because it contains none of the standard scenes of "balletic street gunnings and spaghetti eating." Thus, it would seem that throughout the nineties the genre expands in its repertoire, but reviewers still refer to stereotypes and conventions to assess the anomalies, which suggests that these images are ingrained in popular culture and provide commonly accepted signposts for understanding gangster narratives.

Therefore when *The Sopranos* begins its journey in 1999, it is not surprising that reviewers make reference to genre in their initial assessments. Caryn James notes that it is "shaped by mob movies" and therefore "takes off with the speed of an inside joke" (*New York Times*, January 8, 1999). Allan Johnson suggests *The Sopranos* as a "throwback to the gangsters of Edward G. Robinson and James Cagney, combined with the complexities of Michael Corleone" (*Chicago Tribune*, June 6, 1999). Paul Hoggart calls it a "peculiar hybrid of *Goodfellas* and *All in the Family*" (*The Times*, October 13, 2000). Simi Horwitz suggests it as "Don Corleone in a Woody Allen script" (*Washington*

Post, March 14, 1999). Most are at pains to note how the violence is tempered with family drama. Paul Hoggart suggests, "The racketeers are engaging, homely, even loveable in a cranky, psychotic sort of way" (*The Times*, October 13, 2000). At this early stage only Simi Horwitz signaled a link between mobster imagery and conservative American values (*Washington Post*, March 14, 1999), most felt that the humor in the series deflected most of the less palatable politics, although Caryn James notes that the series "depends on the trick of letting us see Tony's worst qualities and getting us to identify with him anyway" (*New York Times*, March 25, 1999). By 2002, Tony is an "everyman" and it is lamented, "If only more things in life were as dependable as the greatness of *The Sopranos*" (Tom Shales, *Washington Post*, September 15, 2002). By 2004 it is a unique cultural event that has English professors as well as web-based conspiracy theorists debating its cultural value (Libby Copeland, *Washington Post*, June 5, 2004) and by the end it is " a landmark in television drama" (*Washington Post*, April 8, 2007) that doesn't have to abide by the conventions of movie mob stories, but in its final episode made reference to many of them (Tom Shales, *Washington Post*, June 11, 2007). So, while *The Sopranos* had plenty of time to provide more complex studies of American culture and its fascination with the Mafia, it was bound to reference them as it is the universal approach to understanding the subject. The TV series is much more than genre and I will discuss its themes in the next chapters, but its attention to genre conventions as a defining structure is unquestionable.

In summary, reviews of postclassical gangster films appear to be concerned with two main issues: authenticity and violence. *The Godfather, Mean Streets, Once Upon a Time in America, Goodfellas, State of Grace, Carlito's Way, The Funeral* and *Donnie Brasco* are reviewed as authentic either in mythologizing or presenting a realistic observance of Mafia activity, especially when they also include elements of romance or what reviewers and I have termed melodrama. All of these films encourage sympathy for the protagonist. This reflects Schneider's overview of the genre: "Without the pathos, none of it matters very much" (Schneider: 4). *Scarface, Goodfellas, Miller's Crossing, King of New York, New Jack City, Bugsy, Reservoir Dogs* and *Pulp Fiction* are noted for their style, whether as parodies or as glorifications of Mafia images. *The Sopranos* achieves both melodrama and parody and as such appears to exhaust the genre. However, as it is set in the present and remains loyal to the memory of earlier Mafia mythology, it is hard to see how it has undermined the genre.

* * *

Finally, as discussed earlier, all the films are violent and those reviewers who accept the violence also assert the authenticity of the film in terms of historical accuracy or mythologies. This does not alter the fact that a few reviewers considered films such as *The Godfather* to represent "the propaganda of violence" (*Sun*, August 22, 1972), but this reviewer also suggested that the Old Testament morality gives "easy conscience to IRA gunmen, dope peddlers and bent cops" (*ibid.*). Thus, this reviewer's distaste is not a result of any factual authenticity in the text, but is an expression of his or her views on criminality in general.

In terms of genre, reviewers identify narrative conventions that make reference to films of the past. As such, gangster films appear to operate as a unique genre mainly because of the subject matter of organized crime. However, as discussed within this chapter, other factors such as costume, dialogue, gestures, violence, star personae and historical settings can also encourage allusions to the genre. Reviews or even internet forums cannot be accepted as substitutes for audience reception, but they do provide a catalogue of contemporary responses to films, which helps to contextualize some of the debates on violence and also to trace the patterns of familiarities across postclassical gangster films. This highlights the discursive nature of genre in that reviewers and discussion forums constantly refer backwards and sideways to other films and extratextual events in their assessment of the reviewed film.

Conclusions

To summarize, genre criticism has drawn upon structuralist methods of analysis, wherein the recurrent structures distill social rather than individual meanings. In this way, film genres act as a modern equivalent of folklore or mythology. As an extension to textual formalism, genre criticism has also embraced auteur theory, by suggesting that genres have basic underlying coordinates which can then be utilized and developed by particular directors. Since the deconstruction of textual formalism and the implosion of meaning in post-structuralist, postmodern discourses, the determinacy of genre categorization has dissolved. Discussions of the complexities of textual and extratextual discourses that surround the production and consumption of film have progressed the already prevalent notion that there is "no original, no real, or right text, but only variants" (Clover, 1993, cited in Maltby: 118).

The experience of watching film in the 21st century includes multi-media advertising (TV, internet, magazines, posters and occasionally associated merchandise). Defining which genre a particular film represents or is alluding to invariably includes contradictions, hybridities and a never-ending system of justifications. Definition can not be explored from purely one angle, as it is constructed by so many. The gangster film, for example, is an ambiguous construct of styles and attitudes. Generic verisimilitude can go some way towards explaining the expectations and hypotheses surrounding gangster films in terms of texts and reviews, but it has to accept that these discourses are constantly evolving. When reviewing this chapter myself I am always uncomfortable with the inherent contradictions a discussion of film as genre encourages. There is always a desire to define even though that definition is easily undermined. The gangster film exists as a genre but it cannot be isolated in its structure, its iconography, its development, or in its meanings. We know it when we see it, in costume dialogue setting or mood, but that knowledge is different for every viewer at different moments in history.

* * *

Genre is a fluid concept of film categorization that cannot be isolated within the individual machinations of production, text or reception. The purpose of this chapter was to examine some of the influences that contribute to film categorization. Perceptions of ethnicity and historical events concerning Mafia activity are major factors in attracting critical acceptance of a particular film within the referents of genre. Commercial successes can occur for films that allude to images of the Mafia, but these examples tend to raise concerns about the genre and its possible developments. It is my view that the films that concentrate on or resemble the Italian American Mafia community obtain the most critical credibility.

As genre categorization is fluid, any single central theme or structural consistency in the gangster film is unknowable, or at least cannot be satisfactorily identified. This corresponds to notions of myth, as discussed in the introduction to this book. Therefore, it is necessary for me to ask, in what ways do gangster films operate as myth? Furthermore, it can be argued that certain genres come to the fore at certain periods of ideological stress; for instance the cop series of the seventies, as mentioned in Chapter 1, occur at the time of law and order anxieties. Therefore, another question that needs to be addressed in the following chapter is this: why does the gangster film re-emerge so prominently in the late sixties? To answer these questions it is necessary to move on to examine the notion of Mafia myths and their influence on the structure and critical credibility of postclassical gangster films.

3

Mafia Myths

Mafia myths are central to the form that post-war and especially post-classical gangster films have taken. They have generated some of the most important elements to distinguish these films from the classic films of the 1930s. Myths surrounding the gangsters of the 1930s tended to focus on individual outlaws. Myths of the post-war period and beyond have concentrated on criminal organizations, or Mafia, and this has had a profound effect upon the structure and development of gangster films. This chapter will focus on the history of the term Mafia, rather than the gangster, tracing the myths that surround concepts of criminal organizations. The purpose is to examine further the proposition that gangster films operate as a continuous text (Leutrat) and that this process is influenced by textual and extra textual factors. The most important extra textual influences on postclassical gangster films are those drawn from Mafia myths.

Myths are essentially fictional, in that the content of mythology remains unproven. Myth is distinct from legend, in that the latter implies a nucleus of fact, whereas myth can be purely fictional. However, this does not mean that myths have no relationship to reality. As stated in Chapter 2, the Western has taken on the mantle of myth because it presents the realities of America's birth as an independent nation within a stable conceptual structure. Gangsters and the Mafia in popular culture embody mythology because they are based on characters and organizations that exist in history, but whose stories have been fictionalized.

* * *

Claude Lévi-Strauss (1966) argues that myths are systems of references made up of cultural contrasts, a whole system of references which operates by means of a pair of cultural contrasts: between the general and the particular on the one hand and nature and culture on the other [Lévi-Strauss, 1966: 105 quoted in Schatz, 1977: 97].

He later states, "The purpose of myth is to provide a logical model capable of over-coming [such] contradictions" (1968: 45). Myths are ways of making sense of or resolving tensions in human understanding. Later, Lévi-Strauss suggests that the function of myth is that it "gives man, very importantly, the illusion that he can understand the universe and that he does understand the universe; it is, of course, only an illusion" (1978: 17). Roland Barthes (1973) clarifies this by explaining myth through semiology: "Myth is a system of communication, it is a message [...] a mode of signification" (117). Therefore, myth is a form of discourse, in that it is one way in which a culture makes sense of an unstable concept through more stable narratives; both the unstable concepts and the more stable narratives are constantly evolving and being replayed and thus are discursive. Barthes also states, "The knowledge contained in a mythical concept is confused, made of yielding, shapeless associations" (129). In consequence, it is fruitless to try to pin a myth down to a single stable and unitary meaning. Myth is a cultural practice and so, as Michel Foucault has taught us, such practices are more interesting for their discursive shifts as for the binary oppositions they exemplify. The key is to trace instances of its existence and from that observe its properties and functions. This chapter traces particular definitions of the Mafia in twentieth century American cultural discourse to show how myths have developed and then assess how these have influenced postclassical gangster films. It is important to note that Mafia myths have not suddenly emerged in the fifties; they can be traced in the classical films as well, but the direction that myths have taken are distinct from those in earlier films.

While a discussion of the various definitions of Mafia are crucial in providing the context for my argument, this chapter is mainly concerned with the impact these myths have had on Hollywood filmmaking. To this end I have identified four elements that distinguish the Mafia myths of the fifties and beyond from the gangster myths of the earlier period. Firstly, there is the direct identification of Sicilian culture as the backbone of Mafia activity. Secondly, there is the focus on the extended family, not necessarily blood related, but bound by loyalties, marriage and *compareggio*.[1] Thirdly, there is the corporate approach to crime, as the sole source of income to support the family. Fourthly, there is the honor code of *omertà*[2] that not only protects the family against scrutiny and prosecution but also reflects the honor and pride of individual Mafiosi. Add to this the critical and commercial influence of *The Godfather*, a film that embodies all of these myths and we can start to see how Mafia myths have become so pervasive in Hollywood film. Mafia myths have become familiar to the extent that images of the Italian or Sicilian Mafia can be isolated as the ideal, to which all other images of organized crime refer. To show this, the following discussion provides examples of the appearance of Mafia myths in films, traces the origins of some allusions to factual events and begins to discuss the development of images of ethnicity. In consequence, the blurring of boundaries between fact and fiction, and the tendency for film narratives to allude to previous films, combine to produce the effect of a continuous narrative running throughout postclassical gangster films.

Mafia myths as continuous narratives running throughout films help to locate films as part of a coherent genre. Mafia myths do not require fixed narrative structures or themes; they form the historical background to films and encourage audience recognition of activities and loyalties. In essence, Mafia myths help to account for the fluidity of the gangster genre, while also helping it appear cohesive. This contradictory process is noticeable because Mafia myths are part of cultural discourses and are therefore constantly evolving. They appear cohesive and yet are constantly changing. The three cycles of film production identified in Chapter 1 are also connected by Mafia myths, in that each cycle represents new developments in the myth. *Scarface* is different from *The Godfather* and yet can be connected to it through Mafia myths. Similarly, *Goodfellas* and *The Sopranos* appear to de-mythologize the Mafia, and thus appear distinct from *The Godfather* and *Scarface*, but an examination of their use of Mafia myths shows the extent to which they operate within the same parameters and can be seen to offer the same conclusions. *The Sopranos* is a valiant attempt to lay bare the myths while also showing the extent to which the Mafia character depends upon them. However, the entire structure of *The Sopranos* is nostalgic. More than most of the films it relies on the myth to justify its existence.

Mafia myths are an extra-textual and intertextual phenomenon that permeate the films, but are not solely defined by them. It can be argued that in recent years, the concept of Mafia as a myth has been undermined by the proliferation of evidence about its very real existence. High profile court cases, FBI surveillance and exposé-style testimonies and books have all dissected the concept of Mafia in the United States to the extent that it should appear not only as knowable to the general public, but might also be viewed as pathetic. Mafia men are repeatedly revealed as simply small-time criminals who operate in an organized community. In court cases and exposés they are not presented as noble anti-heroes, loyal to family and codes of honor (especially as most high-profile revelations have broken such codes). In fact, most exposés focus on the ordinariness of Mafia men. Henry Hill and Joe Pistone both attempted to show the Mafia as groups of small-time crooks earning money for the bosses. However, such negativity does not seem to dampen the mythology. While it could be argued that many films since *The Godfather* have tried to expose the Mafia as cruel and unrefined, the mythology of *omertà*, honor and family loyalties has remained as a dominant ideal.

The Mafia ideal is still often reflected in real life events. For instance, John Gotti became a media celebrity during his lengthy court trials. In his article "The Last Mafia Icon," Allan May notes how, during Gotti's trial in 1990, prison guards gave him "V.I.P. treatment." The actors Tony LaBianco and Ray Sharkey were in attendance, possibly researching for future film roles. Also, when the verdict of not guilty was announced, "On Mulberry Street, [it] was greeted with cheers and celebratory fireworks. In Ozone Park, red and yellow balloons awaited Gotti's return" (trutv.com). A recent online article for *The Times* is headlined, "Fury as Mafia Godfathers Idolized on Facebook" (timesonline December 31, 2008). It describes how Salvatore Riina, currently serving twelve life sentences in Italy, has a Facebook fansite with over 2,000 subscribers who leave him messages of support. Maria Falcone, the sister of murdered anti–Mafia judge Giovanni Falcone, is quoted as saying "Unfortunately, evil still fascinates our young people." With more immediate and open access to worldwide events and people, fascination with Mafia activity remains. Access to factual information about their crimes, death or imprisonment does not seem to diminish their romantic appeal. On the contrary, it is often changes in Mafia practices and a more aggressive legal system that has been blamed for some of the disintegration of the Mafia, especially in America, and this promotes feelings of romantic nostalgia for the Mafia as a "disappearing tribe" — a part of a particular American way of life.

Strengthened legislation in the early 1970s has led to more aggressive investigations into organized criminal activity. This in turn has dismantled many Mafia families and unveiled their organizations for public scrutiny. De Stefano suggests that *omertà* is harder to maintain since "the RICO statute made it easier for the feds to bust up entire mob families and put their members in prison for decades" (156).[3] He suggests that, while *omertà* is still recognized as a crucial oath, "Wiseguys are increasingly forsaking silence in exchange for shorter sentences" (*ibid.*). De Stefano reflects on the fact that *The Godfather* remains the ideal because it focuses on an era of criminal organization that was not subject to such legal and media scrutiny. In essence, while it is obvious *The Godfather* is not based on a true story, it offers a picture of organized crime that is attractive and has a tenuous relationship to the reality of its time. *The Godfather* is an idealistic narrative because it presents the last period in American history when society recognized the "honorable" criminal, in the tradition perhaps of the Westerner or the extreme entrepreneur. In short, while they may be associated with violence, or corruption, they are also applauded for their attention to specific codes of honor and loyalty—codes that have always existed in discourses of American national identity.

The History of Mafia Myths

Before I can properly assess the ideals presented in *The Godfather*, it is necessary to show how Mafia myths have emerged. To do that I will provide a brief history of organized criminal groups beginning with the most generally used label of Mafia. The term Mafia appears in dictionaries under specific definitions, such as *the* Mafia defined as "a Sicilian secret criminal society" (Websters, 1989).[4] The term also denotes "any group considered to resemble *the* Mafia" (Collins, 1990), such as *La Cosa Nostra*, or the general term *organized crime*. It is evident that while the existences of international secret criminal organizations are widely accepted in Western Culture, the specifics are sometimes unclear. The term Mafia is often used to define similar groups of perhaps differing origin or ethnicity, but most probably adhering to a similar, essentially criminal purpose. This evidence suggests that the label Mafia has been or is used to define much more than any one criminal organization. However, this evidence is further complicated by the fact that, although the term is used variously, it still retains a direct attachment to Italian heritage. If it is used to define a particular criminal organization or crime wave in a particular country, such as "the Russian Mafia," the label linguistically connects that organization to the Sicilian original. Russia is then said to have one or more organized criminal groups that are considered to resemble *the* Mafia, which, as already noted, is said to have originated in Sicily. In short, such definitions tend to isolate the origins of Mafia within Italian/Sicilian history, while the generic use of the term Mafia to define any criminal group also contributes to an inconsistent yet world-wide definition of secret criminal organizations.

Nancy E. Marion (2008) states that, while Mafia, La Cosa Nostra and Organized Crime are all labels that tend to be used interchangeably, they are in fact three distinct concepts (3). In reality, the term Mafia originated in Sicily and is primarily meant to describe a type of criminal behavior. La Cosa Nostra, roughly translated as "this thing of ours," relates to the Italian criminal organizations that evolved in America.[5] The Sicilian Mafia had the most influence on the development of La Cosa Nostra, but it is not the only criminal organization in Italy. Camorra is the organization associated with Naples, while 'Ndranhgheta developed in Southern Calabria. Furthermore, it is recognized that not all organized criminal activity in America is connected to the Italian community. Some of the original immigrant groups involved in organized crime included the Irish and Jews. The term Organized Crime came into use in American legal discourses after World War II and was meant to describe all organized criminal activity regardless of ethnicity. The fact that these terms are regularly used interchangeably has only helped to blur the specific character of each separate one. It is evident that there are many different types and origins to organized crime; however, popular discourses have tended to prioritize the term Mafia and in many cases expand its Sicilian origins to represent Italian criminal culture as a whole. In consequence, Mafia and Italian heritage have come to represent the essential definition of organized criminal activity, the standard against which all others are compared.

I am going to explore Mafia myths as they exist in American culture because this will show why Hollywood film defines Mafia in the ways it does. To provide an introduction to Mafia myths it is necessary to delve further into the origins of the label "Mafia" and its use in European and American history. This history is important because, although the label of Mafia was not used in American cultural discourses on organized crime during the first half of the twentieth century, many mythical elements were established before and during this period. In consequence, I shall be prioritizing the Sicilian concept of Mafia, but in doing so I hope to show just how that has developed into the "Mafia ideal." Fascination with the Mafia has taken many forms and has many different motivations. For the purpose of studying Hollywood cinema it is only really necessary to concentrate on the beliefs and concerns of North American culture since the mid–nineteenth century. However, as we are dealing with a specifically transatlantic phenomenon, I think it is important to explore the European origins of many terms and beliefs, as well as many late twentieth-century evolutions.

Any explanation of the evolution of Mafia myths in American culture is hampered by the fact that there are various myths and these have been circulating in varied domains. There is the American political perspective, by which is meant the publicized concerns and beliefs of Congress. There is also the sociological consideration of immigrant assimilation in American society since the early twentieth century, which has included ethnographic studies of immigrant poverty in urban areas. The cultural histories of some European homelands are also used in immigrant biographies and ethnographic studies to explain behavior and beliefs. Furthermore, there is the law-enforcement perspective that is concerned with specific crime waves in America's recent history. And finally, there is the all-encompassing domain of the media text that has not only reported on all these perspectives, but has also provided commercial and cultural products featuring criminals in organized groups in literature, film and television.

Mafia myths have an extremely varied pedigree. They encompass many different elements that have collectively come to inhabit, or help define, the term Mafia. To begin with, the term Mafia was not used publicly or in a documented form to define a criminal organization until 1950.[6] Allusions to such an organization had occurred before that, as in the series of articles in *Collier's* in 1939, which suggested that the Mafia governed all other criminal groups or mobs in the underworld.[7] However, these were isolated occurrences that could not have made a significant impact upon contemporary cultural beliefs. Just over a decade later, in 1951, the Senate Crime Investigating Committee under the chairmanship of Senator Estes Kefauver issued a statement that categorically expressed its belief in a nation-wide criminal organization called the Mafia. It has been suggested (Moore, 1974) that the label "Mafia" was adopted at this point as a useful term to define all that is claimed about criminal organizations from all of the previously stated domains: "It is a credible enough conception to assure the average American of the 'Mafia's' existence yet intangible enough to allow each individual his own interpretation of it" (Albini, 1971: 83). Therefore, the fifties saw the emergence of new cultural discourses on organized crime, albeit developed from earlier concerns, but now grouped under a specific label — Mafia. These discourses, especially those surrounding the Senate hearings of the 1950s, have had a profound influence on Hollywood film-making.

Evidence that might indicate the existence of the Mafia in America has always been inconclusive. While much more is known now about the operations of criminal groups, especially in the prohibition era, the evidence is still contradictory or incomplete. Since the 1970s there has been a proliferation of legal documents, biographies and testimonies leading to a popular belief in the Mafia as an identifiable force in American society. However, there are two important factors to consider. Firstly, many of the publications defining the Mafia are heavily influenced by media speculation and fictive accounts of crime. Secondly, prior to the 1970s there was very strong scepticism about the existence of organized crime in America. Some cultural criminologists (Albini, 1971; Smith, 1975) firmly believed that criminal organizations were isolated gangs and dismissed the idea of a national syndicate. Some believed in its existence (Cressey, 1969; Ianni, 1972). Still, the social function of criminal groups came under scrutiny and most analyses pointed to the spirit or belief systems of the Sicilian people as a defining force in organized criminal activity.

One of the defining elements of Mafia mythology involves the behavior or attitude of *omertà*. It has always been used as one of the primary excuses for any lack of concrete evidence concerning the structure or activities of Mafia families. *Omertà* is now a widely understood word in American popular culture; it means that all operations or beliefs of an Italian family (criminal or otherwise) are not to be spoken of to any outside group. For the Mafia family, the fact that this code is protected by a threat of death against any who disobey means that investigation into the operations of a suspected Mafia family are unlikely to find any overt cooperation. It is a popular belief that when immigrants such as the Sicilians entered America their belief systems did not immediately dissipate (Smith, Ianni). In fact, their commitment to family or immediate community was integral to American populist ideals of the time. Early twentieth century American ideology held a contradictory commitment to both assimilation and populism. This meant that while the overarching goal was conformity and homogeneity, any agreement on homogeneity was confused by a populist constitution: individualism, or at least the rights of the individual, existed as the ideological underpinnings of American society. Duncan Webster (1988) argues, "Immigrants from Europe and elsewhere were seen as a threat until they were brought within the acceptable definitions of 'Americanness' or excluded from it entirely" (Webster: 44). Furthermore, "In the United States rights belonged to the individual rather than to social or ethnic groups" (*ibid.*: 46). Consequently, rather than quashing traditional or ethnic beliefs and values, commitment to "Americanness" resembled Sicilian beliefs in that it prioritized individual rights over the state, government and consequently, law enforcement. For Sicilian or Italian communities to distrust the law was not out of place in America; it paralleled American populist ideals.

For those who believe in the existence of the Mafia, *omertà* is used to explain why they do not have access to any concrete proof. However, those opposed to such theories believe that *omertà* is simply another facet of an overblown myth. In essence, this denies the possibility of proving or disproving the existence of the Mafia and thus leaves myths as the key repository of evidence. Political debates about the Mafia as a nationwide criminal organization only really became prominent in the 1950s. Until that time organized crime had existed under many different labels, such as gangs and teamsters, and was concerned with illegal operations such as beer bootlegging during prohibition and Union activity during the depression. Specific areas, such as New York's Lower East Side, were isolated as ganglands. Criminal operations were linked to certain immigrant groups and were thought to die out as that group became more assimilated into American society.

The first real evidence of organization beyond specific gangs or families emerged in the 1930s during the "Castellammerese War."[8] The war resulted in five families (all of Italian descent)[9] agreeing to operate together in a nationwide network of criminal activity. In 1931 Lucky Luciano became the "boss of bosses" in this organization and created what he called "the Commission"; a committee of bosses that presided over all the families. This is popularly thought to be the official birth of La Cosa Nostra. While the Commission

and its five families were all Italian, they cooperated with others, especially
Jewish groups, and thus operated on a national level. The Commission met
at various times during the next ten years, and while law enforcement agencies were aware of these meetings they were unable to prove their purpose.

In 1950 Democratic Senator Estes Kefauver created a committee with
the express purpose of proving the existence of a national organized crime
network in America. His motivation appeared to be primarily political: "If
he could exploit the crime issue without offending the national administration, [he] might well open up political opportunities for himself" (Moore,
1974: 47). His contemporary and competitor, Republican Joseph R.
McCarthy, was also hungry for recognition. While McCarthy set his sights
on eradicating Communism, Kefauver responded to the post-war crime scare
by offering a high profile exposé of criminal organizations: "Talk of nation-
wide crime syndicates and of the rediscovered Mafia served the functions of
scapegoating for the antilegalization forces and of titillating an increasing
number of newspaper readers (*ibid.*: 41). "Antilegalization forces" were concerned with the growing number of interstate gambling networks, which
some politicians were in favor of legalizing for their tax revenues. Many campaigners opposed to the legalization of such operations; began to demand a
crackdown on illicit gambling networks and the criminal groups that controlled them. Public campaigners, such as mayors and senators, were encouraged to act by eager crime journalists from all over America in the late 1940s
and early 1950s. These journalists ran features and editorials on gambling
rackets in papers such as *The Chicago Tribune, Miami's News, The Brooklyn
Eagle* and *The San Francisco News.* An extremely active anti-crime movement
of the late 1940s in turn encouraged political reaction.[10] In essence, the Kefauver Committee set out to prove whether an organized criminal network
existed, and if so, to expose it and its structure once and for all.

In fact, the committee failed to do this. Instead, what did occur was possibly the last thing that Kefauver would have wanted. The committee failed
to conclusively prove the existence of a national organized criminal network
with a central headquarters and criminal director, but it did open up a whole
new fascination with the history and romance of organized crime on the part
of the national media and public. The romance was encouraged by the fact
that Kefauver failed to prove anything, but nevertheless pursued the premise that it existed. This meant that cultural discourses were at liberty to draw
a myriad of reasons as to why politicians should do this. Romantic notions
could suggest that the Mafia were too clever and the code of *omertà* too strong
to allow them to be caught. The fact that the committee was convinced
enough to mount the investigation added fuel to the myths that were already
circulating. The inconclusive findings merely opened the door to more rumor,

as there were no conclusive facts to stifle speculation. William H. Moore's analysis of the committee's proceedings concluded:

> Inadequate evidence and the necessity to reach some conclusion rushed the committee into fuzzy ill-founded statements that brought the senators sensational headlines but left an ugly popular misunderstanding in the country [114].

The Narcotics Bureau had supplied the committee with a list of eight hundred criminals they considered active, not only in narcotics but in other areas as well, such as gambling, money lending and extortion. Kefauver publicly interrogated many of these including Joseph Profaci, the alleged boss of Brooklyn, and Frank Costello of New York, but failed to establish a proven link between these or others in different states. Tony Gizzo of Kansas City admitted to having a wide range of associates that included Profaci and Costello, as well as notorious figures on the West Coast and Florida, but he denied any business dealings.[11] The fact that the committee identified so many characters, all seemingly operating in similar ways and with respect to each other, gave credence to the notion of a nation-wide conspiracy. The committee consistently referred to the Mafia as a feasible organization. They interrogated each witness over their association with the Mafia: all the witnesses not only denied their involvement, but also claimed ignorance of the term. However, the fact that most of the witnesses were of Italian descent and that the Mafia was believed to have evolved from Sicily, added fuel to the initial premise and led the committee to make the following statement in 1951: "There is a Nation-wide crime syndicate known as the Mafia, whose tentacles are found in many large cities. It has international ramifications which appear most clearly in connection with the narcotics traffic."[12]

It would seem that the principal excuse for the lack of clarity has been secrecy, or *omertà* (Smith, 1975; Moore). The Kefauver Committee made no progress with their witnesses, but their constant reference to the Mafia meant that this lack of cooperation could be linked to the Mafia's central code of honor. According to Moore, the Committee did not help clarify matters by interpreting some witnesses' responses as influenced by *omertà* and issuing statements about this reaction, rather than providing concrete evidence.

Later in the 1950s a group of nearly seventy individuals gathered at the house of Joseph Barbara in the upstate New York village of Apalachin. On this now-famous November night in 1957 the police raided Barbara's home to discover such figures as Joseph Profaci, Frank Costello and Joseph Bonnano[13] among the influential guests. Arrests and convictions were made, but later overturned. The real impact was in the amount of publicity, editorial comment and political debate this raid inspired. The Apalachin incident, as it became known, attracted "repercussions until 1960 in Congress and the courts" (Smith: 202). It drew attention to the interstate crime network suspected by Kefauver, and inspired many debates on the reasons behind the meeting.

Smith maintains that the vast majority of these editorials, or exposé-orientated news reports, "were written originally either as anecdotal accounts of crime or as exhortations to the faithful" (*ibid.*: 200), but they provided plenty of scope for comment. A decade later, in 1967, the criminologist D.R. Cressey, who fiercely believed in the existence of a national criminal syndicate, defended the importance of the incident. He states, "No one has been able to prove the nature of the conspiracy involved, but no one believes that the men all just happened to drop in on the host at the same time" (Cressey, 1969[1]: 870). Despite the lack of standing convictions, the meeting was a disaster for La Cosa Nostra. It brought the issue of organized crime back into the media spotlight and encouraged political leaders to pour more money into finding ways to fight it.[14]

Exposé-orientated biographies have offered many interesting interpretations of the meeting. Francis Ianni's (1972) work claimed insider information and asserted, "Of the more than sixty *Mafia* [*sic*] bosses identified as participants at the famous Apalachin meeting [...] almost half were related by blood or marriage, and many of the others were related by *compareggio*" (Ianni: 168). Gay Talese in *Honor Thy Father* (1971) suggests that the purpose of the meeting was "to discuss pressing problems in the underworld — the tendency for some members to become involved in narcotics [and ...] the unresolved issues following the murder of Albert Anastasia" (Talese, 1971: 64). It is evident that this incident was crucial in fueling fascination with the Mafia, but it did very little to establish a coherent sense of what the Mafia actually was and where it came from. Smith concludes that "consistency and precision have seldom concerned those who have applied the 'Mafia' label, and under the circumstances in which it has been used, its bearers have had little reason to issue clarifications or to demand corrections" (Smith: 199).[15]

As we have seen, Kefauver's motivation for setting up the Senate hearings was political and his findings were based on information obtained from a law-enforcement point of view. His ambition was to prove the existence of a national crime syndicate in a court of law, and so accuracy in using the term "Mafia" was not a primary concern. In actual fact, according to Moore, Kefauver did at one point assert that the criminal organization in America was controlled by Charles "Lucky" Luciano in Sicily, and thus Mafia would be an appropriate label. However, Smith's frustration, as indicated above, is drawn from the fact that the use of the term in response to the Kefauver Committee and the Apalachin incident was wholly inconsistent across Congress, the courts and the media. Consequently, the term Mafia has been used to label an extremely wide range of illegal activities involving a correspondingly wide range of ethnic groups and classes.

In the 1960s interest in the Mafia was given three very influential boosts. Firstly, there was Joe Valachi's testimony to the McClellan Committee in 1963, which first saw the term "Cosa Nostra" used as an alternative to Mafia. Valachi's testimony included details about many top level meetings, business dealings and killings in the Mafia. More importantly, he described the structure and named all the titles and ranks, as well as names of many top-level Mafia bosses. His testimony has been discredited by some academics and later "Mafia autobiographies,"[16] especially in terms of his knowledge of specific events. However, the publicity that his testimony received, shown on live TV, coupled with the publication of his story by Peter Maas[17] and even a film of the events,[18] meant that his testimony has to be accepted as an influential piece, no matter how flawed.

Secondly, the President's Crime Commission in 1967 set out once again to answer the question, *Is there a Mafia?* This time they employed criminologists, such as D.R. Cressey, to assess the evidence. Cressey's conclusions, which categorically assert the existence of a nation-wide criminal organization, also maintain that this organization is based on the Sicilian Mafia: "The structure of the Sicilian Mafia resembles that of ancient feudal kingdoms [...] The structure of the American confederation of crime resembles feudalism also, as it resembles the structure of the Sicilian Mafia" (Cressey: 868). Cressey uses Valachi's *Capo-regime* structure of the crime family,[19] and the Kefauver Committee's statements as evidence for his claims. In doing so, for Smith, "He retreated to old questions for which new evidence simply recapitulated old answers and reinforced old stereotypes" (Smith: 200). This indicates that nearly two decades after the Kefauver committee failed to establish any evidence of an organized criminal organization, government funded commissions were still investigating the possibility. Attendant media interest also kept the subject in the public arena.

Thirdly, Mario Puzo's 1969 book, *The Godfather*, was thus published at a time when the fascination with Mafia myths was still prominent in news stories and government initiatives. Puzo's *The Godfather*, although primarily a work of fiction, unashamedly takes its form from Valachi's testimony and many of the events that he described. Its immense popularity,[20] followed by the equally successful film in 1972,[21] has meant that it has become one of the most influential descriptions of the American Mafia family. Though fictional, it appeared to give the definitive answer to many of the rumors circulating in popular discourses. As Smith concludes, "The search for reality was thus dominated by established conventions" (*ibid.*). Puzo's story recapitulated Cressey's, Kefauver's and Valachi's statements and thus appeared to confirm them.

The main sources that have been used in this chapter so far were produced at around the same time these debates occurred. Therefore we have a multitude of opinions and conclusions that have all been influenced by the events of the fifties and sixties and published between 1969 and 1975. This is a period of American history that saw increasing public cynicism leveled towards Government bodies. Anti-government feelings had escalated during the Civil Rights campaigns of the sixties and through the Vietnam War, finally finding apparent confirmation during the Watergate Scandal (1972–74). Interest in the Mafia suggests on the one hand a desire for something to blame for the disintegration of legal systems, or corruption in big businesses and government. However, it also suggests a desire for anti-establishment heroes, or outlaws. Figures that operate outside of conventional society are not subject to the bureaucracy that had become increasingly evident in traditional legal institutions. The Mafia suggested a simpler, perhaps even more ethical system when compared to the faceless corporations and institutions of modern American society.

*   *   *

Consequently, all the books that have been discussed here describe the history of the Mafia, but are influenced by contemporary debates, which in the case of the Mafia were couched in the form of a question: *Is there a nationwide criminal syndicate?* Kefauver, Cressey and Valachi's testimonies answer "yes," but they also state that it was based upon the Sicilian Mafia and thus implicitly suggest that Sicilians (if not Italians in general) were the primary leaders. Albini and Smith argue that these assertions cannot be proven and suggest that, although criminal groups do exist, they are disparate and declining organizations without a recognizable national network. The confusion lies in the fact that all these analyses focus on the question of the network, rather than the groups themselves. In doing so, they perpetuate myths of the Mafia by failing to prove anything on either side, while simultaneously keeping debate going. In short, they are reminiscent of many conspiracy theories that have entered popular discourse since the Cold War and beyond. In effect, Mafia myths continue by escaping through the holes in investigations. The people who want to believe in them, such as politicians for scapegoating crime problems or the media for good stories, can argue their case just as effectively as those who believe them to be unsubstantiated myths.[22] As Albini writes, "In few other subjects or areas can one find a more confused or less scholarly approach to a topic" (Albini: 86). Furthermore, the fact that Mafia myths have proven a fascinating topic across many areas of American culture means that consensus is virtually impossible, but speculation and the exploitation of sensationalist storylines is bound to continue.

* * *

Mafia myths since the 1970s have changed significantly. This is because of the proliferation of information regarding organized crime, but it is also because of the high-profile prosecutions of key criminal figures, such as the Strawman Cases (1978–1983) that focused on Kansas City and Cleveland families; the Pizza Connection case (1979–1987) that exposed the Bonnano/Gambino family in New York; the Commission Case (1986) that jailed eight high profile bosses in 1986 mainly using wire tap evidence; and of course the case against John Gotti that ended in his imprisonment in 1992. Most of these prosecutions occurred because of one of the most important legislative changes since the 1950s: the "Organized Crime Control Act of 1970" (also known as the Racketeering Influenced and Corrupt Organizations Act, or RICO). As stated earlier, this bill strengthened the government's ability to prosecute members of criminal organizations. In the past individual criminals had to be prosecuted based on a physical connection to a crime. Therefore it was almost impossible to prosecute bosses, who gave orders but rarely participated physically in criminal activity. RICO made "being a member of a criminal organization" a crime. Bosses could be prosecuted for their involvement in planning or even discussing a crime. Furthermore, jail sentences for crimes associated with Mafia activity were raised significantly. Individuals faced twenty years in prison for each offense plus seizure of all their assets. RICO is thought to be one of the primary reasons behind the change and steady decline of the Mafia in America. With tougher sentencing, law enforcement agencies found it easier to encourage individuals to inform on their associates. This also led to the high-profile court cases against previously protected bosses. All of these events brought saturated media coverage, books and films.

* * *

As well as the accounts discussed above, there has been an increase in biographical accounts or ethnographic studies of Mafia families since the late sixties. Ianni's history of the Lupollo family, a fictional name for an allegedly real Mafia family, provides a very generous account of family relationships, business and the evolution of their concerns and beliefs. Joseph Bonnano's autobiography (1983) and Gay Talese's 1971 account of the Bonnano family history are just two examples of the very popular format of Mafia biographies. In the nineties there have been biographies about the Gambino Family and John Gotti, while many other "inside stories" purport to offer the facts on the real Mafia.[23] More recent Hollywood films, perhaps influenced by *The Godfather*, are close adaptations of criminal biographies as opposed to simple allusions to factual events. Martin

Scorsese's *Goodfellas* (1990) is based on the true story of Mafia informant Henry Hill, while Mike Newell's *Donnie Brasco* (1996) is the screen adaptation of ex–FBI agent Joe Pistone's memoirs about his undercover infiltration of a New York mob. The exposé-oriented media of books and film appear to cater to a lucrative market and of course such publications also help to perpetuate Mafia myths. *The Sopranos* has added the most to Mafia myths by constantly alluding to real events and seamlessly folding them into fictional lives. Johnnie Sacramoni (Vincent Curatola) not only resembles John Gotti physically and career-wise, but the TV series also has him convicted, jailed and die of cancer in a barely disguised homage to the New York boss. What such allusions do is provide a seamless connection between fact and fiction. Hence, it is always difficult to be certain where one ends and the other begins.

*   *   *

Since the 1950s, components of Mafia myths included four key elements: firstly, that the origins of the Mafia are primarily located in Italian, or Sicilian culture and history. Secondly, that its structure is that of an extended family, in that although not all members are of the same blood lineage, allegiance to the organization is as strong as Sicilian family loyalty. Thirdly, the extended family structure allows for the organization to operate in a business-like manner; its primary motivation is to make money. Lastly, its airtight secrecy, *omertà*, protects the organization from outside scrutiny and prosecution, apart from certain leaks that have fueled the myths and led to the downfall of some families. However, these are not the only myths that have surrounded criminal gangs. The myths of the fifties and beyond were built upon an older set of components: a set that informed and were epitomized by the classic gangster films of the 1930s. These were very different ideas, concerned with the individual criminal rather than the family, opportunism rather than organization, and immigrants in general rather than specifically Italians. However, they provided the bedrock for later myths.

The allusion to factual events is not a new development in gangster films. From the earliest examples, such as *The Musketeers of Pig Alley* (1912) and *Outside the Law* (1921), gangster films declared their realism. McCarty notes how D.W. Griffith in *Musketeers of Pig Alley*

> simply capitalized on all the notoriety and public attention — as many other filmmakers have since done — by adapting his story right from the headlines. For added realism, he then shot much of the film in the same New York city locales where those headlines were being made. Biograph publicity handouts sensationally maintained that Griffith had even employed real gangsters in small parts to lend the film even more authenticity [McCarty: 3].

Onscreen advertising for *Outside the Law* made claims to a factual status: "Amazing in its realism [...] the one true story of the underworld kings."[24]

Thus, it is not allusions to, or the function of factual events that distinguish postclassical films from those before, it is the type of factual event that has changed. The function of all such allusions is to assert the realism of a particular film's narrative, characters, costume, dialogue and so on. The type of factual event referred to in the classical era begins with the activities of money-lenders, extortionists, bootleg racketeers, and progresses to money-laundering, shadowy organizations that rule over smaller criminal gangs, also gambling and prostitution racketeers in the syndicate films.

Allusions to actual events changed significantly after the televised senate hearings of the fifties and sixties. Two of the most important events, the Kefauver Committee Hearings (1951–52) and the McClellan Committee Hearings (1963) provided in-depth examinations of the supposed structures and internal workings of the Mafia. The Kefauver Committee suggested that the Mafia was an on-going national criminal networks, with a vast membership, but Sicilian-based heritage and many interconnected "families." Joe Valachi's testimony to the McClellan Committee included details of initiation ceremonies, the modes by which messages and orders were passed from the bosses to lower ranks, the structure and rules of hierarchy and styles of execution.[25] These events drew attention, not only to the criminal actions, but to the structure and beliefs of the Mafia as it is thought to exist in American society. Films, books, court cases and biographies since the 1950s have all contributed further to the mythology. Now Mafia activity is mainly linked to drug-trafficking, money lending, trash-hauling, prostitution, and gambling. Criminal families are more ethnically diverse, but the Italian ideal remains the essential definition. Perhaps most importantly in these later discourses, the character of the Mafia takes its cues as much from Hollywood as anywhere else. Therefore, the irony is twofold: while Hollywood has always claimed to reflect reality, it is evident that the modern reality of the Mafia reflects Hollywood. Mafia myths then are a product of both real history and popular culture. It is impossible to split fact from fiction.

Mafia Myths in Film

To begin the discussion on how Mafia myths have influenced film and vice versa, I shall run through the four key elements that have defined the modern gangster film: Sicilian/Italian heritage, structure, business and *omertà*. Within each one, I shall focus how each film asserts its association to "real events," or insider knowledge. Consequently, I will be able show how Mafia myths have developed into a sense of a Mafia "ideal" in films and from this I will be able to use the film examples to discuss the functions of such Mafia myths in popular culture more broadly.

Sicilian Culture and Heritage

There are varying, contradictory descriptions of the Mafia in Sicilian society. Albini, Smith and Hess (1998) suggest, "*Mafia* in Sicily is generic to the nature and development of Sicilian society itself" (Albini: 89). They view Mafiosi as self-serving criminals making money from the weaker members of their communities. Ianni states that the term is also used as an adjective to describe "a state of mind, a sense of pride, a philosophy of life and a style of behaviour" (Ianni: 24), as well as a noun to identify an organization.

Mafia first appeared in Italian writings in the nineteenth century, though there appears to be no firm account of its linguistic origin. It has been suggested that the term is an acronym formed from various revolutionary cries against the ruling French in the thirteenth century.[26] Alternatively, it may have been derived from the Arabic word *marfa*, which translates as "place of refuge" (Ianni: 25, Albini: 92) and is thus linked to early Sicilian Mafia hideouts in the hillsides, away from colonial oppression. However, the Sicilian language contains many colonial influences and since the word is not found in written form before the nineteenth century, its prior history is bound to be the subject of hearsay and conjecture.

Mafia as a state of mind, or what Ianni terms "the spirit of *mafia*" (25) has been called "the quintessence of south Italian culture — family and honor, in juxtaposition to a weak state, require that every man seek protection for himself and his loved ones in his own way" (*Ibid.*). This connects with the turbulent nature of southern Italy's social history. The southern parts of Italy do not appear to have embraced capitalism with the same enthusiasm as the north. The south has been described as "semi-feudal" (*ibid.*: 16) in nature, with the acquisition of power and respect rather than the acquisition of wealth the primary goal of its inhabitants. Their colonial history has encouraged "a defensive reaction — a psychological means of resisting and combating the various governments which ruled his land" (Albini: 109).

* * *

Various other criminal groups, such as the *Onorata Societa* and the *Camorra* that operated in early nineteenth century Calabria and Naples respectively, have been seen as contemporaries of the original Sicilian Mafia. Their influence is said to have benefited from the fact that these areas of Italy lacked any strong local government. These criminal organizations offered a simplistic but apparently effective form of government based upon a "vigilante spirit of swift and direct justice" (Ianni: 26). These criminal bands were linked to ideas of "brotherhood," Masonic codes of honor and a devotion to justice as manifested in the term *vendetta*.[27] Historical and literary interpretations of these organizations oscillate between adoration of their revolutionary spirit and disgust at their self-serving criminal principles. This contradictory response has been mirrored throughout late-twentieth century popular culture. The Mafia is presented simultaneously as a romantic and a despicable organization and it is this binary interpretation that still informs Hollywood cinema. However, as with any binary opposition, interpretations depend very much on the accumulation of those oppositions, and so it is important to show how gangster films combine the positive and negative attributes of Mafia myths within their parameters. In history and in modern culture it would depend on which account the reader, or viewer, chooses to accept as to whether these bands were seen as benevolent, or simply criminal organizations. The belief that criminal bands did and still do exist in Sicily, operating under unique values, has provided the framework for nearly two centuries of both literary and political debate.

* * *

Sicilian heritage and corporate-style criminal activity do not undermine the fact that the Mafia is simultaneously romanticized and condemned. *Goodfellas* was identified as the beginning of the third cycle of gangster film production in Chapter 1. It has been viewed as a relatively realistic portrayal of Mafia life (*Guardian*, October 25, 1990; *Daily Mail*, October 26, 1990, *Western Mail*, October 27, 1990), although realism, in this case, owes more to generic verisimilitude than historical fact.[28] In short, films that are reviewed as realistic tend to assert the brutal self-serving nature of the Mafia (*Goodfellas, State of Grace, Donnie Brasco, The Sopranos*), while those dubbed romantic focus on family loyalties and traditions (*Godfather* trilogy, *Carlito's Way, Analyze This*).[29] Under this rubric, *Goodfellas* has been seen as a condemnation of Mafia mythologies, while in comparison, *The Godfather* trilogy romanticizes them. From my discussions of genre in Chapter 2, it is evident that, although the films are different, it is problematic to simply contrast them in this way. As previously noted, *The Godfather* was condemned for its brutality at the time of its release (see for example, *Daily Mirror*, August 22, 1972; *Guardian*, August 22, 1972; *The Sun*, August 22, 1972; *Scotsman*, August 23, 1972), as much as it has been applauded both then and since (see for example, *New Society*, September 21, 1972; *The Guardian*, June 20, 1996). What is interesting is the ways in which the complexities of gangster narratives, especially with regard to mythologies, are reflected in the differing responses of reviewers and critics. *The Guardian, Daily Mail* and *Western Mail* give the impression that a condemnation of Mafia activity somehow releases the film from the realm of mythology and pushes it into that of realism.[30] However, as already noted, Albini's assertion that the Mafia are self-serving mercenaries is as important to mythologies as Ianni's belief in family loyalty. Films reflect elements from mythologies that may appear contradictory, but mythologies allow for such discrepancies. *Gotti* reflects the *Godfather*'s mythical version of the Mafia ideal, but is mingled with *Goodfellas*-style brutality. This is epitomized in a conversation between John Gotti (Armand Assante) and Neil Dellacroce (Anthony Quinn). Gotti has killed a "made man" from a rival family. The bosses call for Gotti to be killed in return, according to the rules or ethics of Sicilian Mafia. Neil successfully pleads for Gotti's life by identifying him as like a son, thus reflecting the family element of Mafia myths by implicitly suggesting Gotti's life is saved by such loyalties. However, Neil warns Gotti that if the bosses had said "you gotta go, I would have come here today with these two zips and you would go[...]. You break the rules and this whole goddamn thing of ours cracks and crumbles." Unlike Scorsese's films, but in a similar way to Coppola's, *Gotti* suggests that the rules are there for protection rather than constriction. Therefore Mafia mythologies can deflect any inconsistencies and contradictions within post-classical gangster films by encompassing very different representations of characters and activities and encouraging very different audience responses.

Casino develops Scorsese's earlier representations of bosses by representing the Mafia old guard as financial leeches upon the working guys as out-of-touch, overly controlling patriarchs who would kill a man for adultery, or for verbally disrespecting a made man. This develops earlier narratives, such as *Mean Streets*, where Charlie is advised to choose his friends wisely by Uncle Giovanni: "An honorable man has honorable friends" (Cesare Danova). The narrative then focuses on Charlie's conflict between loyalty to his "dishonorable" friends and aspirations for Mafia membership. In *Goodfellas*, Pauly Cicero (Paul Sorvino) explains that he cannot allow Henry to get divorced, as family is sacrosanct in Mafia life: "You gotta go back, it's the only way. You gotta keep up appearances." Similarly, in *Casino*, Remo Gaggi (Pasquale Cajano) asks Frank Marino (Frank Vincent) about Nicky Santoro's (Joe Pesci) affair with Ginger (Sharon Stone) as he is warned of its effect on business. Frankie's narration tells us, "What could I say? I knew if I gave them the wrong answer, I mean, Nicky, Ginger, Ace, all of 'em could wind up getting killed. Because there's one thing about these old timers, they don't like to see any fucking around with other guys' wives. It's bad for business." In this case, Sicilian Mafia ideals are shown to be profit-orientated, emphasizing the business element of the Mafia myths rather than the purely ethical, and suggesting that they are often used to bully the lower ranks into toeing the line. However, neither Nicky's, nor Ace's actions encourage audience sympathies, because they are so callously self-serving. Therefore, the bosses' fear of disorderly conduct is a justified reaction to the younger generation's inability to abide by traditional Mafia ideals.

In short, Scorsese's films often focus on the Mafia as a patriarchal construct, simultaneously protecting but also constraining a younger generation of Italian Americans, or gangster wannabes. Reviews have suggested that his films provide an "antidote to *The Godfather*'s mythic version of the Mafia" (Smith, 1990: 68). However, it is also important to remember that myths are always developing and so *Goodfellas* simply offers a new version of older myths. This does not mean to say that Scorsese's antidote eclipses previous myths. In fact, the individualism portrayed in his characters not only destroys the Mafia families, but in doing so justifies the bosses' seemingly old-fashioned rules and thus, reinforces the myths found in *The Godfather*. In short, *Goodfellas* develops the myths, but it does not eclipse previous examples. Therefore, the films can be understood as part of a continuous narrative that is constantly evolving. My argument that films refer mainly to Mafia myths even when they state an association with facts means that contradictory representations can be easily accommodated.

Interviews with the director and many reviews appear to suggest that the intention of *Goodfellas* is to de-mythologize the Mafia. Martin Scorsese states that his intention was to make the film "as close to truth as a fiction film, a dramatization, can get" (Scorsese, cited in review, *Film Quarterly*, 1991). McCarty suggests that the "blood and ritual" that rules the portrayed Mafia society is "amoral" (McCarty: 204). Other reviews suggest that the film "arguably hijacks the genre by simply telling the truth" (*Western Mail*, October 27, 1990) and that it is "un-romantic" (*Sunday Telegraph*, October 28, 1990; *Mail on Sunday*, October 28, 1990). Perhaps, most importantly, *Premiere* quotes the real Henry Hill, who claims, "That's really the way it was. It's all true" (December 1990: 148). However, *Goodfellas* does not de-mythologize the Mafia. It is evident, as with the case of *The Godfather Part II*, that it contributes to the mythologies of the Mafia and romanticizes their activities in similar ways. It makes allusions to factual events, such as the Lufthansa heist at JFK Airport in 1978 and, unlike *The Godfather*, the whole story is based directly on a biography, so it foregrounds the illusion of fact rather than myth. In addition, the film is a dramatization that frequently focuses on the privileges of being a wise guy: from jumping the bread queue at the bakeries and skipping school to unlimited credit and the best seats in clubs. Furthermore, the brutality of Mafia business is shown at street level: Tommy, Jimmy and Henry are brutal men. However, the point that undermines the "un-romantic" quality of this film is the fact that Paulie is portrayed as an old-school patriarch,[31] who doesn't like Tommy's behavior, advises Henry against dealing drugs and only deserts Henry when he discovers his involvement in cocaine smuggling. Therefore, the destruction of the family does not occur because the traditions of Mafia honor are revealed as amoral, but from the actions of a bad seed, Tommy, and two outsiders, Jimmy and Henry.

Jimmy and Henry are portrayed as lacking an understanding of Sicilian heritage and the need for unity in a family, while Tommy is portrayed as emotionally unstable, even psychotic, through his irrational displays of violence. He acts on impulse in a similar way to Sonny Corleone in *The Godfather*. Thus, *Goodfellas* shows the Mafia under pressure from non–Italian criminals who do not abide by the same strict codes of honour and deal in areas of criminal activity traditionally avoided, such as drugs. The film does not undermine the romanticism of *The Godfather*, as it romanticizes the bosses in a similar way. It does show the perils of a consumer society that promotes individualism and a Mafia that allows non–Italian members too far into its structure, so that their attention to personal gain infects and destroys a family. In this sense, *Goodfellas* displays a deterministic view of ethnic identity, suggesting that only Italians who understand and respect their heritage can understand the importance of Mafia honor. This reflects the scenes explored in *The Godfather Part II* and perpetuates mythologies of Italian superiority in organized crime.

*   *   *

Goodfellas is a dramatization of Henry's romanticized notion of life as a wise guy. The style of the narrative, which gives Henry and his wife Karen voice-over narrations and starts the film with Henry as an outside voyeur, watching and desiring to be part of the gangster life played out in front of him, suggests that Henry is a constant observer rather than a wholehearted participant in the Mafia life. In addition, the ending, which has Henry talk directly to the camera, links to the beginning to make the intervening narrative a visualization of Henry's desires and ideals. Henry tells us what he knows about Mafia life, his impressions of its heritage and rules. As such, the narrative is mainly a one-sided view from an outsider. Henry's ideals are obviously based around making lots of money and doing whatever he wants. He is reprimanded by Paulie for not respecting his wife and children, and defiantly ignores Paulie's fears of the drug trade. In conclusion, *Goodfellas* mixes fact with fiction to portray Mafia life through the eyes of an outsider. Henry still laments the fact that he has lost his lifestyle at the end of the film, but he does not seem to accept any of the blame for his own downfall. Far from de-mythologizing the Mafia, *Goodfellas* adds fuel to the existing discourses. It alludes to factual events and is based on a true-life biography, but it structures its narrative in such a way as to emphasize a mediated viewpoint. The film contributes to Mafia mythologies and does not effectively undermine the superiority and romanticism of the conceptions of the Italian Mafia.

Left to right: Jimmy Conway (Robert De Niro), Henry Hill (Ray Liotta) and Paul Cicero (Paul Sorvino). *Goodfellas* ©1990, Warner Bros.

The Sopranos has plenty of time to oscillate between myth, critical realism and parody in its six seasons. The entire premise of the show is based on Mafia myths, in that it focuses on the infiltration of popular concepts of Mafia into mainstream American life and identity. The fact that Tony Soprano lives in the wealthy suburbs and not in the city makes him both an image of the American Dream while also one of its fears. His twin roles as "everyman" and "bogeyman" allow for Mafia mythology to be constantly exploited both positively and negatively. The series is able to spend a few episodes softening him and peeling away his Mafia façade, before plunging the viewer back into the violent stereotype. Of course, Season One's episode "College" incorporates the two sides of his character perfectly: Tony is both a loving father taking his daughter to view college campuses, and also a Mafia boss who will take violent vengeance on an FBI informant he spots on the way. The series has more narrative depth than many films can encapsulate in their running time, but this does not mean that it debunks the mythology. De Stefano reminds us that "ultimately the show *is* a gangster story, one that honors the genre's conventions even as it departs from and comments on them" (161). The characters are motivated by mafia myths, as David Pattie has also noted

> Most of the references to Mafia movies are best understood, not as examples of postmodern self-referentiality *per se*, but as a symbolic framework within which Tony, Paulie, Christopher, Silvio and most of the other Mafia characters in *The Sopranos* attempt to find a meaning and justification for their lives [137].

This argument is part of a much larger discussion that suggests modern society defines itself through pop culture discourses. Mafia myths are a lively part of such a discussion, but its links with ethnic identity are also a crucial aspect of the TV characters' identities.

Family Loyalties

To return to the "spirit of Mafia" for a moment, it is much easier to concentrate on the principles of Sicilian culture that have defined the label rather than to argue over the organization's existence. In the late nineteenth century, when people in the north of Italy owned wealthy estates situated in the south, most critics agree that Mafia-style organizations evolved from the private armies employed by landowners to protect their properties and wealth from other bandits and unruly peasants (Albini, Ianni, Smith, Hess). A member of the Mafia was a mercenary figure who acted as a marshal for the landowners. However, this contract did not make the Mafia simply a tool of its employers. The Mafia juggled many associations with landowners and bandits alike. They balanced the absent landlord's interests against those of the community and, of course, themselves. The Mafia can be seen as providing a buffer between all-out rebellion and feudal dominance. Albini insists that this is essentially a patron-and-client relationship. The Mafia member acts as patron to a varied array of clients: "His strength depends upon the extent and kinds of patrons and clients that he has at his disposal" (Albini: 136). Albini views the mercenary nature as callous, self-serving anarchy, while Ianni argues that it is built upon respect and power: "Southern Italy has always been a land of anarchists, but not of anarchy, for the rule of law is replaced by a familial social order invisibly and spontaneously regulated" (Ianni: 19). Ianni's more generous account of the Mafia is built upon co-operative notions of familial pride and responsibility to each other: "The southern Italian treats government at any level with scepticism and diffidence. He surrenders everything to the family" (*ibid.*). Ianni maintains the Sicilian belief that wealth comes as a result of respect, rather than the general capitalist belief, that respect comes as a result of wealth. In this view, the Mafia is seen as a traditional extended family striving by whatever means necessary to gain power and respect in their community. Albini and Smith regard this view as pure romanticism. Consequently, as these histories have shown, the Mafia has always been both romanticized and condemned.

So far, the Sicilian Mafia can be summarized in at least two ways. It is, as Ianni describes, "a familial social order" unique to southern Italy: a belief system that concentrates on the needs and power of the family and all close associates by marriage, or *compareggio*,[32] before any outside force or law. Conversely, if it exists at all, which Albini, Smith and Hess insist is unlikely, it is simply a network of extortionists and killers who have no value system above personal profit.[33] It is interesting to note that all of the histories discussed here were written during the post–Kefauver resurgence of Mafia myths.[34] The opposing beliefs of the critical histories parallel the opposing conclusions the Kefauver Senate committee published concerning the existence of Mafia organizations. This further emphasizes the mythical nature of all Mafia histories. It is impossible to discover facts, and the myths are far stronger. The type of organization Ianni describes is more a way of life or belief system than a specific group with identifiable rules and structure. The gangs and individual bandits Albini, Smith and Hess describe are disparate criminals with no allegiances or rules at all. Thus, all histories are constructed upon hearsay and speculation and are consequently influenced by the particular beliefs of the teller. My discussion is not concerned with the true history of the Mafia; truth is the natural enemy of myths. (If the truth about Mafia history was known and accepted, the fascination would be over). My concern is with how these different histories and beliefs have helped to construct myths, which make stories of the Mafia popular and intriguing in American culture.

In America, definitions of the Mafia have always suffered from contradictions. Ianni maintains that, as a belief system, Mafia arrived in the hearts and minds of many Sicilian immigrants. These individuals subsequently discovered American society to be as hostile and alien to them as any colonial power in their home country, and thus approached life there with the Mafia spirit. In contrast, political groups, such as the Kefauver Committee, suggested that the Mafia infiltrated America as a working organization. They also stated that the head office, or top bosses, remained in Sicily, while its members sent them profits stolen from America's booming economy. Smith and Albini deny both of these claims in favor of identifying the Mafia as a small criminal element that continues to exist in immigrant, mainly urban and poor areas of America. This element, they say, feeds on the weaknesses of its surrounding community, such as gambling and unemployment, and thus gives an impression of power. In summary, all of these explanations have strong and weak points. Ianni's romanticism denies the brutality and essentially self-serving nature of some of the Mafia's operations. The Kefauver Committee, as we shall see later, was blinkered by its insistence on a nationwide cohesive network. In contrast, Albini, Smith and Hess deny any such cohesion and thus fail to fully explain much evidence to the contrary.[35] In short, most evidence feeds the myths more than the facts about organized crime.

* * *

It is evident that the most commercially successful gangster films after the 1960s, such as the *Godfather* trilogy, *Goodfellas* and *The Sopranos*, fulfill the criteria identified as the primary elements of Mafia myths. They all prioritize the importance of Sicilian heritage (or in the case of *The Sopranos* Italian) and thus, at first glance, appear to consider Mafia as determined by race. For instance, the Corleone family hail from Sicily, and the narrative often makes allusions to Tom Hagen (Robert Duvall) as an outsider, due to his Irish German identity. He is the family's *consigliere* (legal adviser) and adopted brother to Sonny, Mike, Connie and Fredo. However, he is rejected by Michael, in Part I, when Michael wants to build the family's strength. In Part II, Michael reverses this and picks Tom to be his deputy rather than Fredo. This is a significant factor in signalling the breakdown of family loyalties. Fredo has betrayed Michael, but Michael also betrays the family unity by ignoring his brother and thus the Sicilian heritage: "I was passed over" explains Fredo later, in defense of his subsequent betrayal of Michael, "I shouldda had respect." *Part III* focuses on Michael's desperate attempts to rekindle connections with his Sicilian roots and his family, but to no avail.[36] Similarly, in *Goodfellas*, it is explained that only those with an unblemished heritage, "Whose Sicilian blood can be traced right back to the home country" (Henry Hill's narration), can become made men, or full Mafia members. Henry is half–Sicilian, half–Irish; Jimmy Conway is Irish, and Tommy DeVito is Sicilian. Thus, even though Tommy is the least competent in that his unpredictable temper is dangerous and he has little respect for fellow Mafiosi, he is the only candidate for full Mafia membership. In character, he is an exaggerated version of Sonny Corleone (James Caan), heir to the Corleone family by birth, but someone who Vito always maintained was a "bad Don."

* * *

Sicilian heritage in the Mafia is akin to royal lineages, wherein birthrights determine future rulers. *The Godfather* and *Goodfellas* identify two flaws in this system. Firstly, in a system based on Sicilian or Italian heritage, the inclusion of outsiders weakens the traditions on which unity is based. Outsiders Jimmy Conway and Henry Hill corrupt and eventually destroy the Mafia family in *Goodfellas*, first by their involvement in drug business, and second through Henry's testimony. Secondly, the insistence on birthrights means that, occasionally, bad men will rise to be leaders. In both films, the bad men are killed: Sonny by a rival family, and Tommy by his own family for the unauthorized killing of a "made man." Michael does not destroy the family in that its power survives, but he destroys the unity, and thus the foundations of his family, by denying his heritage.

The Sopranos avoids many of the problems associated with the first issue by not involving non–Italian forces. However, it does enjoy developing and destroying its own bad seeds, especially Ralph Cifaretto (Joe Pantoliano), who is such a parody of perverted authority that his violent death and dismemberment by Tony encourages audiences to cheer rather than admonish Tony's authoritarianism. A connection between Mafia heritage and mental illness is presented not only in *Analyze This* and *The Sopranos*, but also in *The Funeral*. In my opinion, the emotional angst portrayed in *The Funeral* is epic in nature. While it can appear hysterical at times in that the brothers are portrayed as victims of their Mafia heritage, the level of emotional turmoil does reflect the violent tragedy of their family's fate. Almost in homage to the great German Expressionist films of the 1920s, the brothers' inheritance and personal choices are displayed as a complex web of destiny and personal responsibility. For them, "this thing of ours" is a living nightmare full of monsters both real and imagined. In many of these films, Sicilian heritage is identified as a binding force for the Mafia family and perpetuates the myths of Sicilian origin. However, it also suggests ethnic determinism, which is the next topic this chapter will discuss.

Stories of the production of *The Godfather* are more concerned with the financial details of the film than with the aesthetic history.[37] However, it is noted that political groups such as the Italian American Friendship Association caused difficulties for the shoot (Biskind: 157). One of the areas of protest was the fact that so few genuine Italian American actors were used in the main cast. *Variety* (February 17, 1971) reports pickets outside the Paramount Studios. One placard read, "More Advantages for Italian Actors," thus drawing attention to the ethnic bias in casting, but also to another ethnic issue: Mafia. These are important issues. It is evident that although most films about the Mafia allude to ethnic traditions associated with Mafia activity, they do not always adhere to any particular racial boundaries in casting or in narratives. In other words, Mafia is not only racially defined. A film such as *Goodfellas* may declare that only those with pure Sicilian blood can be "made men" and thus defines the "true" Mafia racially, something I call the Mafia Ideal and will discuss later. However, this doesn't mean that those films without Italian, or Sicilian narratives cannot be gangster or Mafia films.

* * *

What films like *The Godfather* and *Goodfellas* do achieve is to construct a hierarchy of Mafia activity, placing the Italian or Sicilian ideal at the pinnacle. This direct connection with Italian and Sicilian heritage and Mafia activity is also a contradictory "ideal," because while it romanticizes the race, it also links it directly with criminal activity, thus suggesting that all Italians, or Sicilians are part of it. For this reason alone I think it is necessary to concentrate on Mafia activity as an ethnic discourse rather than a racial one. It is evident that Mafia activity is most commonly associated with Italian and Sicilian heritage, but this does not mean it is a biological trait. It is part of their culture and therefore can be connected to their ethnicity, but not with the whole race. Coppola is noted in *Screen International* (2/7/71) as saying that accusations of ethnic bias, or allusions to Mafia in his films were all "fuss over nothing." However, it is also suggested that negotiations between the studio and the Italian American Civil Rights League and the Italian American Unification Council resulted in the omission of any references to Mafia or *Cosa Nostra* from *The Godfather* (Cowie, Lebo). This did not end all of the complaints, and *The Daily Mail* (March 23, 1972) details how pickets delayed the opening of the film in a cinema in Kansas. It is not noted whether this was an isolated incident, but it does suggest that ethnic tensions surrounding the film remained in evidence.

Such debates have also occurred during the broadcast history of *The Sopranos*. Richard Vetere (*New York Times*, February 12, 2000), Camille Paglia (*The Times*, October 13, 2000) and Bill Tonelli (*New York Times*, March 4, 2001) offer just some of the diverse reactions to the series. Tonelli notes how an e-mail discussion group attached to an Italian American association of academics and historians is constant in their calls for action against the TV producers. It is also noted though, for every group that is outraged by Italian American stereotyping there are plenty who enjoy the presentations. Vetere refuses to be placated by those Italian Americans who are happy to focus on its positive side, while Paglia accuses the show to be full of "loathsome slurs and outdated stereotypes." Tonelli states, compared to the ethnic slurs against other groups, "Being thought of as a cunning, quite possibly murderous people with a robust scepticism where the rules are concerned isn't the biggest defamation imaginable." He suggests, "The Mafia stereotype sticks because Italians are good at turning all their impulses, good or evil, into highly organized, fiercely efficient enterprises," citing the Roman Empire, the Catholic Church and the Rudy Giuliani administration! In short, discourses remain irreconcilable while popular culture remains enamored with the stereotypes.

Tony Soprano and most of his crew are truly Italian Americans in that their characters are a fusion between asserting their Italian heritage but within specifically American cultural parameters. The notion of Italy as a romantic or nostalgic ideal is presented through Furio Giunta (Frederico Castellucio), one of Tony's crew summoned from Naples to help instill some order in the operations. Furio is not only a romantic ideal, De Stefano suggests he looks like he has stepped straight from the cover of an Italian romance novel (174), and Carmela is instantly attracted to him,. However, he also represents nostalgia for the Old Country, where traditions and ideals still exist untainted by the frustrations associated with American identity. This simplistic view of European character is not uncommon in American popular culture, but *The Sopranos* does manage to imbue it with a certain amount of irony. Furio is both Italian stereotype and a comment upon that stereotype, in that he is at the mercy of what Tony, Carmela and others want him to be. In this sense he is the epitome of the Italian American dilemma, which is the desire to assert one's European character, but only the attributes that one finds attractive. This of course is common to all ethnic identities, but is extremely telling in the case of Italian Americans who face the constant associations, especially in popular discourses, with the positives and negatives of Mafia mythology.

These competing desires in mainstream Italian American culture are explored mainly through the character of Dr. Melfi (Lorraine Bracco). Dr. Melfi has to endure not only her own but also her colleagues' and extended family's contradictory feelings about Italian identity and the Mafia. There are multiple scenes wherein Dr. Melfi finds herself at the receiving end of preconceptions of Italian American Mafia identity. In Season Six, part II, she is goaded by her own therapist, Elliot Kupferberg (Peter Bogdanovich), to face the possibility that Tony Soprano is a sociopath and is using her therapy sessions to justify his own actions. This is not only worrying to her on a professional level, but also through her ethnic identity. At a dinner party with other therapists, Elliot reveals the name of her Mafia client. Furious, she accuses him of receiving pleasure from it. The two reactions by people at the table echo the standard response to Italian ethnicity's association with the Mafia. The first combines lurid fascination and a suggestion of Mafia chic: "Tony Soprano is your patient! That's pretty cool." The second is less positive as it assumes Dr. Melfi's Italian identity to include an understanding of, and therefore her implied complicity in, Tony Soprano's Mafia identity. A diner implies ethnic determinism through the joke, "All Italians have big noses." Melfi responds with the accusation, "If I had made that joke about other groups represented at this table, I would have been called a bigot." *The Sopranos* constantly draws attention to the contradictions of ethnic heritage and its positive and negative associations. While it is "cool" for Dr. Melfi to be Tony Soprano's therapist and therefore have insights into his darker secrets, it also suggests that her ethnic identity makes her best suited for understanding those secrets.

In similar ways, Tony's ethnic identity delves deeper than the Italian/Mafia stereotype. His Mafia identity is a family inheritance, but his "proud

Italianità" (De Stefano: 178) is more than that. He truly wants to retain a connection with his Italian heritage and pass that identity onto his children. Carmela is the perfect partner to this because her connection to Mafia is defined more through the personal choice of marriage. She is best placed to attack the hypocrisy of Italian Americans who are fascinated with the Mafia, or accept the profits of a familial association with the organization, but who then also feel compelled to judge it as "different," or "lower" than their own morals. Her memorable outbursts to the priest (Season 1 Episode 6: "Pax Soprano") and to her mother (Season 5 Episode 8: "Marco Polo") in protest at their self-assured moralizing are powerful examples of the hypocritical nature of immigrant identities.

The expertise with which *The Sopranos* deals with immigrant contradictions is evident in Season 2 episode 4: "Commendatori." Tony, Paulie and Christopher visit Naples to secure a car import deal. The complex relationship between Italian and American identity is played out through each character's attitude to the trip. Paulie's romanticism is amusing to audiences as much as it is a source of irritation to Tony. Paulie is desperate to connect with every idealized fantasy of Italian culture. It is not long before the reality falls short, as the food is different and the bathrooms are not to his liking. Paulie then represents the American tourist stereotype: fascinated with the exotic, but unable to explore outside their "comfort zone." Christopher simply connects to the nearest junkie and thus stays firmly cocooned in his comfort zone. His experience best exemplifies the image of American cultural imperialism, or the blurring of cultural barriers. This is further evidenced in the rap music that booms out of the picturesque Italian villa. Naples is not the Old Country; it is a living, breathing part of the twenty-first century.

Tony's experience in essence reverses the viewpoint. He appears more "old country" than the Italians. His attitude towards Annalisa Zucca (Sofia Milos) is traditionalist to the extreme. A woman boss "would never happen in America," he sneers. His disrespect appears childish and ignorant. In this sense, his version of Italian American identity is stuck in the past, an antiquated posturing of ethnic and masculine identity. This caricature is echoed in other scenes, such as Janice's (Aida Turturro) suggestion that Mafia guys are "big babies," and Angie Bompensiero's (Toni Kalem) distress that husbands "come and go without a word." This episode is at pains to point out that these men's attitudes are just plain selfish rather than a product of a particular ethnic background, or that they are stuck in a fictionalized past. In this way, the episode underscores *The Sopranos* characters as preoccupied with mythical versions of Mafia identity, and that those versions are at odds with the realities of modern culture and society.

* * *

To summarize, the Mafia is simultaneously romanticized and condemned in film and other cultural discourses. The association between Italian ethnicity and organized crime is also contradictory. In one sense it has created "Mafia Chic," where Italian American identity is applauded as a signifier of family loyalty and respect for an exclusive ethnic heritage. Conversely, it is condemned for aligning Italian American identity with criminal activity, murder and outdated patriarchal values. Therefore, possessing the mantle of Mafia ideal is both a positive and a negative for the Italian American community as a whole.

Ruth maintained that early images of gangsters treated ethnicity from a voyeuristic standpoint that soothed the public's fears by isolating deviance within immigrant populations.[38] Munby asserts that *Little Caesar* reveals the ways in which assimilation is withheld from the immigrant classes. Any attempt to move up the social ladder is derided as simulation, or aping that which they can never "really be" (49). The films of the seventies and beyond can also be viewed as voyeuristic, in that they claim to offer a unique insight into the exclusive worlds of Mafia. However, they no longer work to simply soothe white audiences' fears; they also project an insight into ethnic communities that whole-heartedly reject WASP American ideals of assimilation. In fact, Michael is punished in *The Godfather Part II* for his attempts at assimilation. Quart and Auster note (*Cineaste*, v6n.4, 1975: pp. 38–39) that the early Lake Tahoe party scenes in *The Godfather Part II* lack the ethnic warmth of Connie's wedding in *The Godfather*. The essentially American façade of choirs and ballroom dancing sets the tone of a film that catalogues Michael's continuing disconnection from his cultural heritage and the safety that involves. He tries to escape his heritage, and thus destroys his identity and the unity of his family. In other words, ethnic solidarity and exclusion from WASP society can often be presented as preferable to assimilation, especially when, as described in *The Sopranos*, American culture persistently intertwines Italian heritage with Mafia myths.

Corporate Structures

The *Godfather* trilogy, *Goodfellas*, *Gotti* and *Donnie Brasco* focus on the extended family and business. In *The Godfather*, the family is mainly blood-related, but bolstered by various other Capo-regimes led by Sicilians. Business is about assimilating Mafia money away from gambling and prostitution into the fabric of America's economy, in order to become legitimate (or at least immune to prosecution). *Goodfellas* is led by Sicilian "made men," but focuses more on the "wise guys" (street men or foot soldiers) who work for the bosses. These wise guys are loyal, but are not always Sicilian, and therefore reasons for their loyalties are more likely to be explored within the narrative. In *Goodfellas,* business revolves around basic criminal activities, such as extortion, robbery and drug dealing. The narrative focuses on how bosses get rich on the work of wise guys, while wise guys profit from the protection and organization the bosses represent. Both films focus on the extended family as non-blood related and the binding force as corporate-style criminal activity. Many articles on *The Godfather* have focused on this aspect of the narrative (Yates, 1975; Latimer, 1975; Ferraro, 1989; Papke, 1996). Ferraro suggests that the Corleone family mirrors the increasingly corporate nature of American business. *Goodfellas* has also been viewed (Murphy, 1990) as a parody of Reaganite America's obsession with material wealth. The capitalist subtexts of each film are apparent, but for this discussion of Mafia myths, the corporate nature of criminal activity is most useful in linking both narratives to the political concerns of the 1950s and beyond which focused on organized crime as a national network.

While individual enterprise is applauded in American society (Webster) and often associated with the classic gangster films (Warshow, McArthur, Cawelti), it is less easily defined in postclassical films. It could be argued that individual enterprise is stifled in films such as *The Godfather, Goodfellas* and *Donnie Brasco.* The emphasis is on individual sacrifice in favor of first the criminal family and second the national network: Michael Corleone sacrifices his legitimate career, Henry Hill's individual enterprise brings about his downfall, and Lefty Ruggiero identifies himself as merely a cog in the criminal system rather than a key player. Allusions to a wider criminal network are also prevalent, especially through Hyman Roth (Lee Strasburg) in *The Godfather Part II,* and through trips to Florida to negotiate with other families in both *Goodfellas* and *Donnie Brasco.* It could be argued that these films lament the loss of individual freedom against the increasingly corporate nature of modern business practices. The notion of corporate identity alienates individuality, in that Henry's criminal ambition is stifled within the corporate style of Mafia business, which has the older generation dictating acceptable and unacceptable criminal activities to its lower orders. In this sense individual enterprise is applauded within the films, but is also shown to be under threat from the Mafia's emphasis on corporate styles of business.

*   *   *

I would assert that *The Sopranos* contradicts the earlier idea of Mafia as corporate because while it presents Tony as part of a corporate style business, his extended crew and business deals still have more individuality than the "everytown" labels that are shown as gradually undermining the character of his old neighborhood. In Seasons 5 and 6 especially the nostalgia for family businesses in the face of corporate consumerism is a recurrent theme. While Tony profits from these changes when he sells one of his own buildings (housing Caputo's poultry store) to Jamba Juice, the narrative suggests such short term profit for businessmen is also part of their eventual demise as large multinational conglomerate businesses move in and transform old neighborhoods. The uniform branding of all aspects of American culture is robbing communities of their individuality, and the Mafia and its attendant associations with ethnic American communities is presented as a possible victim of such transformation.

There are other ways of reading the Mafia as a corporate-style organization that don't necessarily undermine their familial or community identity. Cressey maintains that the Mafia operates as a business, with coherent national networks of associates. Most gangster films perpetuate that mythology. Furthermore, the corporate nature of criminal activity combines notions of extended family loyalties with business tactics. Albert Fried (1980), who chronicled the rise and fall of the Jewish gangster in American culture, notes, "Italian Americans have tended to keep their vocation going inside their families, often marrying into similar families, thus perpetuating the institution generation after generation, much as skilled craftsmen once did through guilds" (Fried: xiv). Fried suggests that Jewish gangsters during prohibition were as powerful as the Italians, but they had no notable successors to carry on the business. A logical conclusion from this is that an attention to Sicilian heritage and family ties bound within corporate-style operations accounts for the success and longevity of Italian Mafia culture. Furthermore, it is the emphasis on criminal groups or families that provides success for the Mafia, rather than individual enterprise. This also accounts for its seeming superiority during the late twentieth century as the oldest Mafia tribe in terms of ethnic identity. As such, the Mafia as corporation is still based on familial ties. Therefore, it is not surprising that audiences are encouraged to sympathize with its struggle against 21st-century capitalism in *The Sopranos*, because the corporate Mafia family is now fighting for existence against the multinational conglomerates that defy any sense of individuality or ethnic heritage. In all of these films the Italian Mafia ideal is presented through Sicilian ethnic identity and the acceptance of patriarchal Mafia rules and traditions as essential for the family business's continued existence. The fact that all of these narratives question, disrupt, or endanger those same traditions does not alter the fact that it is Mafia traditions that bind the family business together.

Sicilian heritage and family loyalties are positive forces. It may be suggested that such themes romanticize the Mafia on screen. In my opinion, internet forums have done much to perpetuate cultural discourses on Mafia myths. One thread on *The Godfather* page of imdb.com asks, "Is The

Godfather a real life story by any chance?" While some argue that the film's narrative is implausible, others point to many true life references. One reply notes that the book blurb suggests Mario Puzo had little knowledge of real-life Mafia activity (Archangelmetatron). Another reply argues that the intricate detail of Mafia hierarchy and real-life events must dispute that claim (sidley 86). Within the discussion of "truth" there is always a comparison between realism and romanticism. A discussion thread on the *Goodfellas* page asks, "Is the Mafia glorified?": "So much screen time is spent in movies like these showing how 'respect' through fear is given to the wiseguys" (posted by Randy 144). This is an interesting topic and receives some considered replies. However, most adhere to the general belief that while *The Godfather* is romantic other films, such as *Goodfellas*, are "gritty and realistic" (strider 01) and "by the end of the movie it is made clear just how terrible and murderous it really is" (ssj raditz2). One reply reminds us that the end image in *Goodfellas* of Tommy shooting at the screen is "intended as a parody, a repudiation of the romanticized image of la cosa nostra that was perpetuated by *The Godfather*" (posted by printsofdarkness). As stated in my discussion above, such beliefs ignore the romanticism at the heart of Scorsese's films. While criminality is definitely presented as selfish and dangerous, Mafia as a system formed through ethnic heritage and family loyalties is not undermined. Instead it is shown as in danger from the same sources and influences that threaten many aspects of American society; self-interest, drugs and consumerism.

It is not that I completely disagree with these discussion thread replies; it is just that I believe that romanticism still exists, even in the more "gritty" films. Furthermore, I would argue that the mix of family loyalties versus selfish behavior has developed post–*Godfather* to become a dominant aspect of Mafia myths. Part of the appeal of gangster films is that characters break the rules. Many internet discussion threads focus on the cause-and-effect logic of Mafia behavior and killings. Mafia codes and rules have become so prevalent in mainstream media that it is not surprising that modern gangsters covet as well as rebel against them. In the years since *The Godfather*, gangster films, perhaps unknowingly, have created a Mafia ideal. The generalized acceptance of structure, codes, rules and ethnic heritage pervades most American films even when Mafia is not the primary focus of the narrative.

Mafia Ideal

Films that do not focus on Sicilian families often make reference to the Italian Mafia ideal as powerful opponents, or the epitome of organized crime's strength. It is evident that the most enduring images of Mafia activity are associated with Italian or Sicilian culture. In *State of Grace* Frankie Flannery (Ed Harris) recognizes the need for an alliance with the Italian Mafia, in order to make his own family powerful. Although a ruthless boss of an Irish Mob, he is shown as genuinely frightened of the Italians and this is emphasised by his nervously deferential manner during all meetings.[39] In *New Jack City*, Nino Brown's biggest enemies are the Italian Mafia. One of the many reasons for his downfall is his obsessional desire to beat the Italians at their own game. This is the same for Frank White (*King of New York*), whose murder of an old Italian associate (Frank Gio) begins his own descent to destruction. In contrast, *Carlito's Way* has Carlito meeting with older Puerto Rican bosses, who show their respect for him.[40] Even though this is not the ideal, the notion of cultural heritage affirms his gangster hero status in a similar way to the Italian ideal. Plus Pacino's star persona also encourages such respect, through the memory of his previous gangster roles. The notions of tradition, or accepted rules of conduct, are the key elements missing from the gangsters of different ethnicities. Many films of the nineties use the stereotype of Italian Mafia to provide images of stable and untouchable corporate criminal activity. These "backroom men"[41] remain secondary characters, but often survive the narrative conclusion. Mafia boss Joey Morolto (Paul Sorvino), who is behind Mitch McDeere's (Tom Cruise) troubles in *The Firm*, does not manage to defeat Mitch's integrity. However, although Mitch effectively beats the Mafia at their own game, it is evident that this event does not severely damage the Mafia either. In *Leon/The Professional*, Leon's boss Tony (Danny Aiello) remains aloof from the violence he pays Leon (Jean Reno) to conduct, and he also agrees to look after young Matilda's (Natalie Portman) upbringing after Leon's death.[42] The young lovers of *True Romance* escape the clutches of the Mafia, but the Mafia is not destroyed. In short, the Italian Mafia is identified as a huge organization with many bosses, hit men, wiseguys and "wannabes." In consequence, its existence in a particular narrative is supported by an acceptance of a larger organization or tradition. If a Mafia boss is killed, this does not defeat the Mafia. Another example of this is the perception that Italian American identity and Mafia are intricately married. Scorsese's film *Mean Streets* epitomizes this perception.

As previously discussed, *Mean Streets* represents the Italian American community on the fringes of Mafia activities. Mafia membership is viewed as a career opportunity for Charlie, a way to make something of himself. In short, the Italian Mafia is presented as one of the pinnacles of Italian community. This connection works in two ways. It emphasizes the fusion between Italian American identity and the Mafia, but it also focuses on the extent to which the community element of Mafia myths is founded in Italian ethnic identity. The fusion between the two suggests that as long as an Italian American community exists, the Mafia will also exist in one form or another. This is evident in the later film, *A Brooklyn State of Mind*. Marketed as a gangster film, the narrative focuses on a young man's discovery of the true nature of his father's death twenty years earlier. Set in New York's Little Italy, the patronage of Danny Parente (Danny Aiello) as a Mafia man is accepted without question. He is also the leading voice in the assertion of traditional family and community ideals. As part of the Mafia myths, this character embodies the contradictory nature of such ideals. He is one of the few people who cares about family loyalty and his cultural heritage, but he is also unveiled as the murderer of the boy's father and a leading extortionist of local business men; this one character represents both the romance and the brutality of Mafia myths.

Conversely, *Miller's Crossing* parodies the Sicilian heritage through a comic but extremely distasteful Italian character. Johnny Caspar (Jon Polito) is a psychotic but comic Mafia boss who constantly claims his actions are based on "et'ics."[43] He is mainly agitated by what he perceives as other gangsters' lack of respect for him and encroachment upon his territory. All other gangsters in this narrative are Jewish or Irish and corrupt, but willing to share their gains and not sadistic in their violence. Consequently, in *Miller's Crossing*, the Italian Mafia is shown to be an unworthy ideal, obsessed with status, possessions, and a perception of ethics that functions primarily to maintain their superiority. This may be rooted in the directing team's own ethnic identity. The Coen Brothers are Jewish and thus may take a personal delight in undermining the Italian Mafia ideal, especially as the Jewish Mafia has been eclipsed by it in Hollywood narratives. *King of New York* also presents a grotesque portrait of the Italian Mafia as fat, egotistical back room bosses. Frank White's assassination of the boss is presented as a heroic act, in that he releases younger Italians from "getting screwed by guys like that" (White in *King of New York*). In consequence, it is an attack on the old regime, similar to that suggested in Scorsese's films. Frank White's desire for a multi-ethnic team (white boss with African American workers) is on one hand shown as more tolerant than the Mafia ideal, who call him a "nigger lover," but on the other as exploitative of the ethnic minorities it includes.

The tendency to prioritize Italian imagery is further evidenced in reactions to *Once Upon a Time in America*, directed by Italian-born Sergio Leone. Vincent Canby in the *New York Times* suggests, "Even though about Jews, this film looks and sounds more authentically Italian" (January 6, 1984). He does not explain why, but it would appear that the images and sounds of urban criminality in early twentieth-century America are so firmly associated with Italian ethnic identity for Hollywood's audiences that a Jewish or Irish counterpart merely dissolves against the number of Italian examples. In the case of *Once Upon a Time in America*, Leone's ethnicity and the inclusion of Robert De Niro as a lead character only enhance the Italian identification.

This is similar to the ways in which a star director or actor may influence the recognition of generic markers, as discussed in Chapter 2.

Bound provides another parody of Italian heritage as the backbone of Mafia identity. Caesar (Joe Pantoliano) fears and respects his boss, Gino Marzzone (Richard Sarafian), but has contempt for the heir apparent, Johnnie Marconi (Christopher Meloni). This influences events, in that Caesar does not trust Johnnie or Johnnie's intentions towards himself. Violet (Jennifer Tilly) uses this distrust for her own advantage by suggesting that Johnnie is the real thief of some missing money. This works partly because Caesar understands that birthright makes Johnnie's word stronger than his in the eyes of the boss. It is useless for him to plead innocence if Johnnie accuses him of theft. This stereotype of Sicilian heritage influences the ensuing murders and Caesar's own destruction. In consequence, as with Scorsese's films, the ethics of bosses can be viewed as misguided and narrow and thus loyalties become fuelled by fear and distrust, rather than respect. *Bound* shows the way in which the fixed hierarchy of the Mafia can be used to undermine it. For this reason this film will be discussed further in an examination of fears and loyalties in Chapter 4. For the purposes of the present discussion of Mafia myths, films such as *Miller's Crossing* and *Bound* offer antidotes to the Italian Mafia ideal, but they do not undermine Mafia myths, or the overwhelming association between Italian ethnicity and Mafia activity.

Crime films that feature Mafia characters in marginal roles draw upon Mafia myths as shorthand for their criminal identity and power. This has occurred thoughout the postclassical period, but has been even more prominent since the nineties. Julie "Baby Feet" Balboni (*In the Electric Mist*) is an "insta-gangster" in that his Italian name, large physique and gaudy displays of wealth are all the evidence the scriptwriters need to identify him through genre and Mafia myths. Like the parodies, such insta-gangsters are antidotes to the Italian Mafia ideal, but they are also instantly recognizable because of the myths and genre conventions. The Mafia ideal is undermined because Balboni is introduced as a parody; it is suggested he killed his own father and he asserts his business legitimacy through investment in the movie industry. He is also unwittingly harboring a serial killer. His business provides the legitimacy, opportunity and means for the film's real terror, a deranged ex-cop. In this sense, Balboni as Mafia suggests that the ideal is not scary for itself anymore, but for the environment it provides in which other criminals operate. This use of the Mafia ideal as stereotype has fuelled the impression that, as *The Sopranos* has developed, the cinema Mafia has declined. It is true, as stated in Chapter 1, that the Mafia has dispersed into the backroom shadows now that the Italian American directors have moved on to other subjects. However, the myths that have created the ideal are alive and well in the presumptions such short hand characters as "Baby Feet" Balboni draw on.

Gang films also draw upon the Italian Mafia ideal. *Mean Streets* is similar to the classic gangster films of the thirties and also foreshadows some of the later gang films, such as *Boyz n the Hood* and *Clockers*, rather than other postclassical films about the Mafia. This highlights the similarities between films about street gangs and other gangster films. While films about street gangs involve organized crime and thus can be identified as part of the Mafia trend in postclassical gangster films, they differ from films specifically about Mafia because of ethnicity and history. Scorsese's film focuses on Italian Americans and thus draws upon a mythology of Mafia operations, but the characters are not active Mafia members. Charlie wants to be part of the Mafia, but has yet to be given any responsibility. Thus, the film resembles gangster films through the association of ethnicity. In contrast, Nino Brown (*New Jack City*) is exempt from this mythology by virtue of his ethnicity. Nino craves material wealth and the respect that criminal power will give him, but he can never blend in to such a white-ruled world.[44] Nino shoulders the social exclusion experienced by classic gangsters such as Tony Camonte (*Scarface*, 1932) or Rico (*Little Caesar*, 1930), who reminds us that we need to point our fingers at him and identify the "bad guy." Ethnicity is part of this easy identification. In this sense *New Jack City* reflects Munby's claim that the only true gangster films of the postclassical era are the black gangsta films, because they correspond to the ghetto-dwelling immigrant identity of the 1930s films.[45] Films such as *New Jack City* reflect the "outsider" ethnicity of the classical 1930s films most directly, but they do so in a new way. The thirties gangsters were Other to white, law-abiding society, whereas the postclassical "outsiders" are Other to the Italian Mafia ideal, as well as white law-abiding society. *New Jack City*, along with other films such as *Goodfellas*, reflects the phenomenon of wannabe gangsters that inhabit postclassical crime films. These wannabes emulate the style and costume of gangsters, but do not operate within a specific organization or ethnic tradition. Examples also include the white[46] heroes of *Reservoir Dogs* and *King of New York*, the African American characters in *Pulp Fiction,* and the multi-ethnic gang in *Heat*. These gangsters operate alongside or within the Mafia ideal, but are identifiably different to the ideal, mainly through ethnic identity and the conscious non-observance of Mafia traditions. The Italian ideal is the mythical original against which all other gangsters are measured: "Wannabes" and black gangs resemble the films of the 1930s in terms of narrative and ethnic exclusion, but they do so in a way that accepts an Italian Mafia ideal.

The Italian Mafia ideal, then, dominates post–*Godfather* films. Sicilian heritage is both romanticized and condemned, but it is nevertheless promoted as the original and most powerful. The importance of family is maintained by focusing on the disastrous results of any lapses in unity. Ethnic identity is identified as the dominant signifier of heritage and unity. Italian ethnicity has become the Mafia ideal, against which all others are measured. This is partly due to the commercial success of *The Godfather* trilogy and Scorsese's films, but it is also due to the focus on Italian communities in Senate hearings and biographies since the 1950s. Thus Italian Mafia now represents the mainstream in gangster films, yet remains Other to law-abiding society. Here, then, is yet another persistent contradiction. The exclusivity of the Italian Mafia family keeps them as Other in relation to white society, but this aspect is also romanticized to the point of cliché. Exclusivity and romanticizing ethnic heritage form part of the allure of the Mafia. *Reservoir Dogs*, which focuses on the inability of an arbitrarily-picked group of criminals to trust each other, shows the ineptitude of non-unified ethnicity. This example romanticizes the ethnic unity of the Mafia and their emphasis on loyalty, by showing the absence of it in non–Mafia organized crime. Ethnic unity is a prominent aspect of Mafia myths. It is featured in many of the films of the postclassical period. For this reason, notions of ethnic unity and the romanticism associated with exclusive environments will be discussed in detail in Chapter 4.

Allusions to Factual Events

Mario Puzo's novel *The Godfather* draws some of its detail from Joe Valachi's testimony. The Capo-regime structure of the Corleone family is a replica of Valachi's description of Mafia hierarchies, which in turn is based on the Roman Empire's military structure. On a more anecdotal level, in *The Godfather Part I*, Clemenza explains to Michael that after he kills the Police Chief McClusky and Sollozo, the family will "hit the mattresses," as there will be a gang war. The phrase "going on the mattress" is explained in Valachi's testimony: "You see, during the Catellammarese trouble [a Mafia war] we had to take mattresses with us as we were moving from one apartment to another. Sometimes we only had a minute's notice, and so you needed a mattress to sleep on. This is our meaning of going on the mattress" (Maas, 1968: 110). Films after *The Godfather* that are based on biographies, testimonies, or autobiographies also concentrate on the intricacies of Mafia life. For example, we learn about the selection process and power of "made men" in *Goodfellas*, based on Henry Hill's testimony and Nicholas Pileggi's biography, *Wiseguy* (1984). Various modes of torture and execution appropriate to certain crimes are explained in *The Godfather Part II* and *Casino*. We discover the fatal meaning of being "sent for" in *Donnie Brasco*, based on the published experiences of FBI agent Joe Pistone, *Donnie Brasco: My Undercover Life in the Mafia* (1989), in that your own execution is most often dealt out by your closest associates. Films such as *Honor Thy Father*, based on Guy Talese's biography of Joe Bonanno, or *Gotti*, based on contemporary headlines, provided details on the bosses of high-profile Mafia families, the Bonannos and the Gambinos, their heritage, their rules and business operations. Thus, Mafia dialogue operates as a signifier of genre convention, but this also develops Mafia myths, in that it operates as a discourse across different films. In the same way that Tarantino suggests that the characters of *Reservoir Dogs* and *Pulp Fiction* inhabit a world that exists beyond the individual films, so postclassical gangster films refer to the existence of Mafia traditions and hierarchies beyond the films. It is not so much the allusion to fact that underscores the films, but rather allusions to mythologies that interact between notions of ethnic identity, historical events, biographies, fictional literature, television, and even advertising, as well as cinema. Popular concepts of Mafia are so prevalent in recent American cultural history that their validity defies scrutiny. It is impossible to ascertain the truth; what remains and is perpetuated is myth.

Allusions to factual events and the structure and workings of the Mafia are so common that films that do not advertise a specific recourse to factual events can also add to the ever-developing network of Mafia mythologies. The narrative of *The Funeral* is woven around popular Italian superstitions, for example that a dead man's wounds will bleed if his killer enters the room where the coffin sits. This, according to Ray Tempio, is why rival gangsters do not attend each other's funerals. This premise provides both the tension and the naïve motivation for revenge killings in the film. However, it also functions as a reminder of the interaction between Mafia identity and Italian historical culture. The parodies *Analyze This* and *Mickey Blue Eyes* rely on popular understandings of Mafia myths, and also make allusions to such popularity in two ways. Dr. Ben Sobel (Billy Crystal) has enough understanding of Mafia mythologies to know how to behave when forced to take Paul Vitti's (Robert De Niro) place at a "sit down" between Mafia bosses.[47] His use of stereotypical Italian phrases and gestures is clearly used for comic effect and to reflect his preconceptions of Mafia dialogue, but he knows the importance of the event and the need to negotiate peace with the fellow families. It is also assumed that audiences possess this knowledge since this set scene, reminiscent of the meeting of the five families in *The Godfather*, is not overtly explained. Similarly, in *Mickey Blue Eyes*, Davenport's attraction to and understanding of his fiancée's Mafia relatives are fueled by knowledge of previous Hollywood films. Davenport learns enough to be able to convincingly pass himself off as a wise guy, thus suggesting, albeit through parody, that real Mafiosi are just like their Hollywood counterparts.

Postclassical gangster films are fuelled by mythologies of the Mafia, but in turn the films influence the continuing development of those mythologies.

The distinction between fact and fiction is blurred to the extent that both romanticise the Mafia. One of the most important examples of how allusions to factual events are used to romanticize the Mafia and its power appears in *The Godfather Part II*. This example also foregrounds the importance of *omertà* as one of the ultimate displays of loyalty in Mafia mythologies. Michael Corleone is indicted to appear before a Senate Committee hearing on charges of organized criminal activity. His old associate Frankie Pentangeli (Michael V. Gazzo) has provided testimony against him that will almost certainly guarantee a conviction. The film version of the hearings resembles newsreel footage of the original Kefauver and McClellan hearings. The layout of the courtroom, the crowds, the inclusion of journalists, the constant noise and the charts of Mafia family hierarchies are based on actual events.[48] The inclusion of such scenes also echoes the previous year's *Lucky Luciano*, which employed realist filmmaking techniques and included the recreation of discussions from The International Conference on Drug Traffic (1952) at the United Nations Headquarters. However, the cinematography used in *The Godfather Part II* senate hearings is in line with the rest of the film. The lighting is colder than the rich sepia tones used in *Part I* and the flashback sequences in *Part II*, but still richly defined and employing deep focus to emphasize the crowded arena and the centrality of Michael's presence. The film makes use of realist techniques, but combines them with the choreographed mise-en-scène associated with *The Godfather* films, thus emphasizing the interaction of fact with mythology.

The scenes that cover the day of Pentangeli's testimony show Michael arriving in the courtroom with Pentangeli's brother (Salvatore Po), who has flown in from Sicily. This man is shown in traditional Sicilian rural costume and speaks no English. Thus we are encouraged to assume that he represents both Michael's and Pentangelo's heritage. Upon seeing his brother, Frankie Pentangeli retracts his statement and the case against Michael instantly collapses. Further information is provided in a subsequent conversation between Michael and his wife Kay (Diane Keaton). Kay finds it incredible that Pentangeli's brother simply being there could alter Frankie's testimony. She asks how it was that "all he had to do was show up." Michael explains that the brother was there to help Frankie: "It was between the brothers Kay, I had nothing to do with it." Kay's questions are there for the purpose of expressing possible audience concerns: was Pentangeli's brother a hostage, who would be killed if Frankie went ahead and testified? The more ethical reason, in line with Mafia mythologies, is suggested later by Frankie's conversation with Tom Hagen. Frankie's brother was a Don in Sicily and lived by the old traditions of Mafia. One of the oldest and most powerful forces in Mafia mythologies is *omertà*. Pentangeli's brother was there to remind Frankie of his oath of silence till death. To break the code meant dishonoring his family name, thus dishonouring his brother, their wives and all their children. These scenes express the strength of honor and loyalty that are thought to exist in Mafia traditions.

The function of these scenes in *The Godfather Part II*, as part of the development of Mafia mythologies in gangster films, is to suggest the Mafia as a powerful force that evades scrutiny and destruction through its code of *omertà*. Allusions to the Kefauver Committee Hearings, which were held during the same years in which the narrative is set, work on two levels. Firstly, they suggest that Puzo's scripted events are based on fact, which in turn gives credence to other featured events, such as the bribing of a senator for a gambling license and pre-revolutionary Cuban business deals. The outcome of such a narrative is mythology. Secondly, the inclusion of such scenes in the film also adds credence to the notion that the Mafia exists and that it beat the Kefauver Committee by upholding its code of *omertà*, as suggested in William H. Moore's account of the hearings detailed earlier. Frankie's instant retraction and subsequent suicide, in order to restore his family's honour, offers a romantic insight into the power of Mafia heritage and loyalties. It uses allusions to factual events to promote the romance of Mafia honor as real and workable codes. The Mafia is promoted as an organization that can really exist, and furthermore its moral standards are superior to American democracy, because politicians and law enforcement agencies cannot comprehend or undermine such loyalties. In turn, such mythologies underscore a romanticized and homogenous view of ethnicity, in that an identifiable ethnic identity and unity through the upholding of traditional values is an effective weapon against WASP imperialist values.

Obviously, such idealism is undermined or interrogated in the post–1970s films. Most films since *Goodfellas* deal with the break-up of such loyalties especially through informants. However, as much as Tony Soprano is at the mercy of the RICO statute and the constant fear, real or imagined, of FBI informants, this does not completely undermine the importance of *omertà*. In fact, it reinforces its value as a code of honor and loyalty. Informers have always been portrayed as weak characters in American popular culture. They serve to make the other criminals appear more honorable. The only whistle-blowers that pop culture admires are those that expose government corruption, not those that inform on their own kind. As I have stated before, Paul Cicero (*Goodfellas*) constantly warns his younger crew against going against traditional Mafia values. He appears all the more honorable at the end when he is convicted by Henry Hill's testimony. It is evident too that Tony Soprano would never cooperate with the FBI (although, to be honest, he is never really tested on that score in the series). Tony's adherence to Mafia traditions incorporates many of the contradictions I have outlined before, but his recognition of traditional values such as *omertà* are evident.

Mafia Myths as Fantasy Narratives

In one sense, Italian Mafia is the ideal against which all others (Jewish, Irish, African American, Mexican, Chinese, Japanese, Russian, etc.) are measured in America culture. If this is the case, compared to all other ethnic crime, it could be said that the Italian Mafia is so much a part of American culture that it represents normalcy, or it has been assimilated into the mainstream so much that it is indistinguishable from WASP male ideals. This is the argument Vera Dika appears to make, suggesting that *The Godfather* is essentially a white male fantasy. She argues that *The Godfather* promotes white male identity as tribal, or identifiable as a homogenous entity, at least on a fantasy level. This is achieved because, she argues, Italianicity in the film is submerged beneath the universal themes of male bonding and business. When added to the possibility of the Italian Mafia as assimilated into mainstream culture, it would appear that Dika has a valid argument. However, it is not true to say that ethnicity is submerged. This is not because *The Godfather* cannot be viewed as a white male fantasy, but such a reading misses the fact that it is the very foregrounding of Italian identity that makes it possible for the films to function as "safe" white male fantasies.

The fantasy of a secret society with masculine rituals, not dominant but under threat, can be traced back to Warshow's original assessment of the popularity of the gangster film. Audiences identify with the freedom, while simultaneously separating themselves from the actions. However, this separation relies on the identification of difference between the audience and the criminals. It is evident from the studies featured here so far that all gangster films are displayed as Other to mainstream American society. It is also evident that responses to *The Godfather* have changed over the past four decades. The iconography and con-

Michael Corleone (Al Pacino). *The Godfather Part II* © 1974, Paramount.

ventions of the films have been circulated in popular culture to the extent
that the Corleones are no longer unique or distinct from mainstream identity in the same way they were in the early seventies. Consequently, for Dika
to suggest that the film is a white male fantasy narrative from a 21st-century
perspective can be accepted as an optional reading, but to say as she does that
this has always occurred for all audiences is misleading. I have already noted
in Chapter 2 how responses to the film at the time centered on ethnicity as
a primary element of the film's appeal. Furthermore as with most gangster
films the narrative structure focuses on the exclusivity of this world in opposition to mainstream society. It has been noted that the use of gestures, dialogue and costume in isolating Mafia identity as distinct from mainstream
society works to the extent that dialogue or actions often require explanation
within the text. Just as Eurocentric narratives in Hollywood Westerns that
promote Native Americans as their central characters employ devices to explain
Native American culture and habits, the gangster film employs similar tactics to explain the uniqueness of the Mafia to a multi-ethnic audience.

Further examples of the mediation between Mafia exclusivity and mainstream audiences can be found in *Gotti* and *Donnie Brasco*. As already noted,
Kay functions as the voice of concern in *The Godfather* trilogy and her ignorance allows for tactics to be explained. Henry Hill's voice-over narration in
Goodfellas provides working knowledge of dialogue and the rules of his Mafia
family. *Gotti* and *Donnie Brasco* include the mediation of FBI surveillance on
the Mafia, featuring wall charts of family structures, explanations of historical
vendettas and allegiances, and taped Mafia conversations, with the added help
of FBI interpretation. One reviewer (*Sight and Sound*, v7, n.5, 1997) has noted
that Lefty Ruggiero's (Al Pacino, *Donnie Brasco*) fascination with wildlife doc-
umentaries reflects the point of view of the film. The Mafia is viewed like a dangerous but endangered species, through a telephoto lens, with expert
interpretation added in voice-over or by a mediating character such as Joe Pis-
tone/Donnie Brasco (Johnny Depp). There is always someone who operates
between the ethnic criminal group and audiences, even in *The Godfather*. This
is not unique to postclassical gangster films, as there is often a mediating character from the position of law enforcers in classical films, but the exclusivity of
the Mafia collective in postclassical films is unique. Mediation functions both
to emphasize the difference of these groups from mainstream society, and to ren-
der that difference knowable and thus less frightening and alien. The fact that
Italian Mafia has been the prime target of such narratives makes that group
appear less alien, and thus partly assimilated into American mainstream culture,
but the very fact that their culture is still explained makes them similar to the
Native American: a culture that is inherent to the consciousness of American
identity, but remains different from it. In a similar vein to narratives focused on

Native American tribes, Mafia is viewed in the past tense, as a dying tribe: at once powerful, romantic and dangerous, but rendered safe by their separateness from ordinary society and their confinement to the past.

One of the primary manifestations of nostalgia in the gangster film can be summarized through the main themes of loyalty and betrayal. These aspects of the gangster film often appear as the essence of the narrative for reviewers, and the poignancy of these themes is heightened by the fact that postclassical gangster films often focus on the past. Characters yearn for past loyalties or claim adherence to them, but these ideals are shown as no longer attainable, under threat, or as false. For example, a review of *Once Upon a Time in America* identifies the film as employing "a time-honored formula for gangster films with a melodrama of loyalty and betrayal" (*Times*, May 22, 1984). Mostly, the themes of loyalty and betrayal are modified. For instance, *The Godfather* is spoken of as a narrative of "family loyalties" (*Mail on Sunday*, October 28, 1990), while *State of Grace* is about "tribal loyalties" (*Evening Standard*, June 13, 1991). *New Jack City* is about "betrayal and revenge" (*Guardian*, August 29, 1991), *Donnie Brasco* is about "trust and friendship" (*Times*, May 1, 1997), while *Mean Streets* displays "loss, guilt and betrayal" (*Village Voice*, October 25, 1973). This is not to assert that the exact wording of these reviews is significant, nor is it to say that these themes are unique to the postclassical era, as loyalty and betrayal are also prominent themes in classical gangster films.

The significance of these inter-textual consistencies only becomes clear when added to another tendency of reviewers, which is to position the reviewed film in relation to the narrative of earlier ones. For example, the film identified as opening the second cycle of film production, *Scarface*, is often compared to *The Godfather* in press reviews. For example, "While not in the same class as *The Godfather*, *Scarface* is nonetheless a vigorous melodrama" (*Sunday Express*, February 2, 1984). On some occasions reviewers go a little further. For instance, "the most chilling scene in *The Godfather* was the boss meeting about going into drugs. *Scarface* seems to be the inevitable sequel to that meeting" (*Guardian*, February 2, 1984), or *Mean Streets* "echoes the grander Mafia higher up the social scale" (*The Listener*, April 11, 1974). It is inevitable that *The Sopranos* encourages similar connections. Paul Hoggart calls it a "peculiar hybrid of *Goodfellas* and *All in the Family*" (*The Times*, October 13, 2000). Caryn James noted in 1999 how Tony's mob all "model themselves on movie mobsters" (*New York Times*, March 25, 1999).

Mafia Myths as a Continuous Text

What these reviewers suggest is that the narratives follow on or refer to other films, as if they are part of a larger over-arching narrative. Arguably, this larger narrative is the progression of Mafia myths. For instance, the end

Tony Montana (Al Pacino). *Scarface* © 1983, Universal.

of the narrative in *The Godfather Part II* includes details of the revolution in Cuba. The opening of *Scarface* involves the immigration of thousands of political prisoners, including Tony Montana, from Cuba to the United States. Thus, the narratives have a tenuous connection. This suggests that although *Scarface* can be identified as opening a new cycle of gangster film production and is a very different film in terms of narrative style, ethnicity and sense of family, it can still be connected to the earlier film in terms of historical detail. Furthermore, as stated in Chapter 2, *Mean Streets* alludes to *The Godfather* through the character of Uncle Giovanni, "an old world gangster, full of cold resolve and ponderous advice" (*New York Times*, October 3, 1973). This description makes him sound like a cross between Michael and Vito Corleone. Add to these references the use of stars, and the films appear to cross-reference their aesthetic styles, narratives, characters and stars to a high degree.

This does not occur to the point where particular elements can be said to define the gangster narrative, but exists enough to trace the development of mythologies. For instance, the characters in *Casino* are carbon copies of those in *Goodfellas*. Some reviewers like this (i.e. *Sunday Express*, February

25, 1996) and some do not (*Village Voice*, November 28, 1995). However, even though this occurrence can be defined as authorial in that Martin Scorsese directed both, or due to star presence in that Robert De Niro and Joe Pesci star in both, it also reinforces character types, especially as both films are supposedly based on factual events. Allusions to facts combined with the use of stereotyping in characters, costumes, gestures, dialogue and settings result in a continually blurred interaction between fact and fiction. This contradictory state, just like the media publicity surrounding the Senate Hearings of the 1950s, simultaneously romanticizes and condemns the Mafia, but more importantly denies resolution. Therefore, the Mafia remains part of mythology and able to produce further heroes and villains that straddle reality, fiction and most importantly, myths. The "insta-gangsters" that dominate crime narratives since the nineties are identified as Mafia through the use of crude stereotyping, but their crudeness does not undermine the Mafia ideal because, while these marginal characters are two-dimensional, their very presence as shorthand for organized crime reiterates the strength of those myths. The wide variety of Mafia images that have developed over the past 40 years is proof that Mafia myths are dominant and complex. In summary, Mafia myths are developed through inter-textual allusions, some of which are made in the narratives (such as sequels) or character stereotyping, while some are assumed by reviewers and other audiences, such as allusions to factual events.

In conclusion, Mafia myths appear to be confused by the conflicting interaction of many contributors. The political and law enforcement agenda seems often to be at odds with images shown in popular entertainment. Even though the Kefauver Committee and other agencies failed to provide conclusive evidence one way or another about the Mafia, no one seems to have been "really" listening anyway. The media loved Valachi's testimony in 1962 and the public loved Puzo's story in 1969. The myths remain consistently flexible to provide meanings across different decades and cultural domains. They provide feasible evidence of a counter culture, an underworld that exists within society that defies and maybe even influences national politics and law enforcement. This in turn suggests that no matter how wealthy, powerful or respectable the face of America becomes, it still may provide an environment for outlaws to exist under the surface. Furthermore, these outlaws or networks are not threatening to the ordinary citizen. The films both acknowledge a social climate of inexplicable and random violence while also offering safe explanations. The violence is shown to be the work of others, and we cannot be victims of it, unless we become involved, probably through our own actions, within this world. No matter how tenuous or romantic these assumptions may appear, they provide the backbone for countless film and television productions, novels, biographies and true crime testimonies published in America.

Myths also give particular film narratives credibility as realistic portrayals. For instance, myths of Sicilian culture and heritage mean that films such as *The Godfather, Mean Streets, Goodfellas, Casino, The Funeral, Donnie Brasco* and *The Sopranos* appear as credible examples of how the Mafia has developed in American society through the Sicilian, or Italian American community. As stated, the fact that Mario Puzo credits Joe Valachi's testimony as a primary influence for the book, *The Godfather*, or the fact that *Goodfellas* was based on the testimony of Henry Hill, and *Donnie Brasco* on the memoirs of FBI agent, Joe Pistone, gives the resulting films a credibility as realistic portrayals of Mafia life, even though as this chapter has shown the line between fact and fiction is irrevocably blurred by the prominence of Mafia myths.

*   *   *

Mafia myths also operate to define boundaries between the criminal and ordinary society. Whether the Mafia is romanticized or condemned in its actions, it is always defined as different or separate from ordinary society through its exclusivity, secrecy and ethnic heritage. Therefore, the cultural imperative of Mafia myths is similar in postclassical films as it was in the classical era in that it defines boundaries between the criminal world and the rest of society. As stated at the beginning of this chapter, the function of myth is to make sense of an unstable concept within more stable narratives. This is an illusory practice, in that myths are constantly subject to changes as part of discourse. However, the cultural problems that Mafia myths address and temporarily resolve are firstly the boundaries between criminality and the law, but secondly notions of individual enterprise and the increasing corporate nature of American business, assimilation and anti-assimilationist ideals. It is not the case to say that one side is always prioritized over the other. In *The Godfather* law-abiding society is suggested to be as corrupt and based on similar ideals as the family's criminal activities. In contrast, *The Funeral* shows the criminal community to be a brutal, unpredictable arena, which encourages the feeling that in comparison the world outside this community must be safer and more stable. The loss of individual enterprise is lamented in *Goodfellas*, but Mafia unity as corporate strength is also romanticized. Sicilian culture and heritage is shown to be oppressive and brutal in *The Godfather, Mean Streets, Goodfellas, Casino, The Funeral* and *Donnie Brasco,* and thus encourages the notion that assimilation would rid communities of such archaic practices and superstitions. However, these same films also show Sicilian heritage and culture as nurturing and offering individuals a sense of identity and belonging in comparison to the alienating, false homogeneity of assimilationist society that offers no security for anyone.

Mafia myths provide an extra-textual history for postclassical gangster films, in that they are cultural discourses that operate alongside but are not solely reliant on cinema history. They constantly blur any distinctions between historical accuracy and fiction. Within each film, though, myths do present boundaries between law-abiding and criminal behavior, or ethnic and white identities, but they also provide some of the inconsistencies that encourage films to be read in different ways. The notion that Mafia myths offer points of identification for characters within the films, as well as identification for viewers, is one of the topics that informs the discussion of masculinity and ethnicity in the following chapter.

4

Masculinities and Ethnicities

The previous chapters have dealt with the development and analysis of the Hollywood gangster film as a genre and as an articulation of Mafia myths. This chapter is concerned with the ways in which these two elements interact to construct a sense of collective identity within postclassical gangster films. The discussion will focus on two key elements of identity positions: masculinity and ethnicity.

The main focus of this chapter is to show how articulations of masculinity in postclassical gangster films arise from the conflicts between key elements within conceptions of masculinity as a subject position (notions of competitiveness, aggression and individual supremacy) and the structures of Mafia communities as collective hierarchies. While articulations of the classical gangster as a lone individual dominated early film studies, it is more appropriate to articulate postclassical gangster identity as a collective. This aligns perfectly with post-structuralist sociological and cultural studies that view masculinity, not as having an absolute or definable character, but as a site of flux (Pfeil, 1995; Uebel, 1997; Petersen, 1998; Whitehead, 2002), or as Tim Edwards (2006) suggests, imbued with "a sense of artifice, flux and contingency" (3). In addition to this, cinematic representations of the gangster operate within recognizable hierarchies. These hierarchies include male groups within the films, but also include references to Mafia myths and cinema history (including notions of genre) operating around and influencing each film. As such, masculinity in postclassical gangster films is a site of conflict, operating in similar ways to those indicated in the previous discussions of genre and Mafia myths. They refer to previous cinema, including the classical era, but they also articulate notions of collectivity that reflect concerns in recent American history and American identity through issues such as community, heritage and hierarchy within male groups.

Alongside the discussion of masculinity, there will be an exploration of how ethnicity is articulated through another conflict: a move towards assimilation versus a constant denial of such assimilation through criminal and ethnic identification. Again, this refers back to issues discussed in respect to the classical era where a gangster's isolation was connected to his immigrant identity. However, as stated in Chapter 3, the rise of Italian ethnicity as the Mafia ideal in postclassical films coincided with charges that the narratives are examples of "white male fantasy," thus blurring the distinction between the Mafia and mainstream society. As such, ethnic identity is another site of conflict within gangster films. The ambiguities of white ethnicity, which itself is a site of conflict in that it blurs boundaries of white and black signification, coincide with but contradict the competing desire for ethnic purity, which relies on the identification of difference, in many postclassical gangster narratives. Articulations of ethnicities are ambiguous, in that they are both a primary source of identification for audiences (through male fantasy, cultural heritage and Mafia myths) and often also sites of distanciation. This occurs through the fact that most postclassical gangster narratives are set in the past, and either foreground particular ethnic identities or highlight character flaws within individuals in the narrative.

* * *

Of course, as with any cultural texts, postclassical gangster films can be read in many different ways. The interactions of masculinity and ethnicity articulate identity in the following ways. The Mafia group is a place where masculinity can be explored, expressed and asserted because it can be positioned as both "like us" and "not like us." The notion of "other" and "like us" characters in the Mafia group allow the group to be both distanced from the contemporary viewer (further distanced by the fact these are Italian Americans, Mafia, of a past era), while at the same time playing out the contemporary contradictions or difficulties of a society that is still male-dominated, but where masculinity has lost its sense of certainty in its own rightness and immutability. Exclusively male groups such as the military or the Mafia, operate as sanctuaries both for the assertion of key elements of masculinity and for the exploration of what have been traditionally seen as non-masculine traits (Jeffords, 1989). Furthermore, myths of Italian ethnicity allow for a greater range of masculine personalities in the criminal group. This final chapter will map these particular elements onto postclassical gangster films in order to show how these films can be read as white-male supremacy narratives as well as assertions of ethnicity. To begin, I shall give a brief summary of some of the relevant debates within studies of masculinity. Then I will discuss similar debates on ethnicity before moving on to combine the two elements as they are articulated in postclassical gangster films.

Crime and Masculinity

Romantic notions of the gangster as some way embodying "an impression of profound worldly wisdom" (Warshow, 1954: 453) possibly stemmed from many attributes personified in the archetypal Westerner: a loner, in tune with his environment, confident and assertive. The limitations of the urban environment and the gangster's excessive nature, which refused to accept limits, meant that his ambitions were doomed to failure. However, the self-confidence and courage that spurred him to try in the first place were, as with the Westerner, identified as positive traits. The gangster was labeled a tragic hero, because these initially positive character traits were flawed by an inability to "accept the limits of individual aggression in a society which tolerates and even encourages a high degree of personal enterprise and violence" (Cawelti: 508). The tragedy occurred "not because he [was] inherently evil, but because he fail[ed] to recognise these limits" (*ibid.*). In consequence, the gangster can be defined in some ways as a positive character. He displays a "manliness" that is reminiscent of the frontier men idolized in cultural mythologies and pulp fiction since the nineteenth century,[1] a "manliness" that almost, if it were not for his criminal and immigrant status, approximates the ideal form of masculinity, both physically and mentally.

Robin Wood's ever-popular essay on American capitalist ideology in classical Hollywood cinema[2] identifies the "ideal male" in cinema as "the virile adventurer, potent, an untrammelled man of action" (Wood, 1977: 289). His alter-ego is the "settled husband/father," "dependable but dull" (*ibid.*). He goes on to explain how neither of these positions is satisfactory, as the "ideal male" wants to but can never settle, while the "settled male" always yearns to wander. Furthermore, both positions are constructed in direct opposition to the female. The "ideal female" is a homemaker and temperate, while the "erotic woman" is exciting but dangerous. Hence, gender ideals combine to make an incompatible couple. Wood's view concentrates on representations of gender in classical Hollywood and insists on male and female characteristics as binary opposites. More recent examinations of cultural discourses about representations of masculinity suggest a more complex situation. Studies note that even when biological determinism positions man and woman within a binary scheme, gender personalities cannot ever be distinguished in this way; "Between masculine man and feminine woman lie a broad landscape of intermediate states" (Edley and Wetherell, 1995: 75). Having said this, Wood's identification of the "ideal male" corresponds, in essence, to many theoretical discussions of masculinity.[3]

Alan Petersen notes that Western philosophy in general has favored dualisms that always involves the privileging of one side over the other: "Western philosophy is seen to be built upon a foundation of first principles which involves the ordering of reality into 'dualisms': identity and difference, reason and unreason, being and negation, nature and culture, self and other, mind and body, and male and female" (Petersen, 1998: 21). Wood's binary framework is too simplistic to be useful for my discussions of masculinity, because this book is dealing with an era in which gender classifications have become more uncertain. However, the notion of an ideal male is something that still appears in popular culture. For instance, much has been written about *The Sopranos* and Tony's nostalgia for a masculine identity based on Gary Cooper as the ideal male (De Stefano, Kocela, Pattie, Walker Fields). It is as if popular culture reacts to the ever-increasing complexities of modern identity by promoting nostalgia for a lost simplicity. It is my intention to show how postclassical gangster films articulate the conflicts between this nostalgia for the concept of the ideal male and also the crises in masculine gender identities. Therefore, I shall return to this discussion and possible reasons and functions for these conflicts later.

Inquiries into a "masculine crisis of identity" (Petersen, 1998: 1) have been developing since the 1970s. Theorists such as Harvey Goldberg (1976), Harry Brod (1987) and Kenneth Clatterbaugh (1990) have sought to map a range of masculine identities along a social/political axis, a range which resembles that constructed by feminist theorists as a mapping of feminine/feminist identities. This theoretical interest emerges at the same time as the re-appearance of the gangster genre in Hollywood in the forms this book is discussing. As stated in the introduction, issues such as feminism, the Vietnam war and civil rights all contributed to a crisis in American identity during this period, which in turn influenced the emergence of an interest in crises in American masculine identity. These issues are then played out in popular entertainment such as the gangster film.

While any attempt to fix identity within typologies is limiting, work such as Clatterbaugh's encouraged a more complex theorizing in of masculine identities and ideals, from the simplicities of gendered dualisms to more complex constructions of gender identities through psychology (Rutherford and Chapman, 1988; Horrocks, 1995) and gender performance (Butler, 1993: Petersen, 1998). New writings on masculinity[4] offer a "general understanding of identities as constructed and negotiated within and against a complex historical matrix of alterities, against a web of differences" (Uebel, 1997: 12). It is accepted that masculinity as a collective concept exists in a process of constant dialectical exchange within itself as well as in relation to the surrounding world. Such analyses deny a stable or fixed set of coordinates against which an individual element can be defined. This is a positive move, in that it frees identity from the reductive impulse of the either/or of self and other. However, it can also suggest identity as a constant re-evaluation of shifting differences, resulting in possible anxieties, or confusions. Collective identity is one aspect of constructed identity, in that it exists through the interaction, or discursive practices of individuals. The postclassical gangster film reflects notions of collective identity in its focus on the male group and the development of generic conventions and Mafia myths, and therefore it is an excellent source for examining how concepts of masculine identity can be opened out. I will discuss how this works in practice in more detail later in this chapter, but first it is necessary to assess examinations of cultural discourses of ethnicity.

The influence of ethnicity on discussions of masculinity (Hoch, 1979; Wiegman, 1995; Stecopolous and Uebel, 1997) is very important to this book. Writings on the gangster had, until recently, minimized ethnic backgrounds. This is not to say it was not addressed at all, but in the main the cinematic gangster was characterized as a reflection of a generalized western male experience.[5] Warshow maintained that the gangster was "without culture" (Warshow, 1954: 453). In one sense, this suggests that he lacked the cultural graces of civilized society. However, it also suggests that he lacks *any* cultural identity, which in fact is not true. The earliest gangster films always implied the protagonists' ethnicity. Rico Bandello and Tony Camonte were undoubtedly Italians, while Tom Powers' Irish background was implied in the film, and further amplified by James Cagney's star persona. That this understanding is commonplace now[6] is due mainly to the writings on ethnicity that have appeared over the past few decades.

Discussions of ethnicity have developed alongside those of masculinity. Writers such as Steve Neale (1979) and Homi K. Bhabha (1983) initially questioned the notions of "Self" and "Other" in relation to racial and national boundaries. Western philosophies operating in dualisms such as "self" and "other" essentialize self as white and European and thus "Other" as anything outside of that. One of the most evident ways of re-promoting an established order is to identify and contain "Otherness," and within this, cultural difference (whose signifiers can include skin color, religion and often sexuality) remains a key marker of such "Otherness." The notion that white is the norm by which all others are measured has been discussed by cultural theorists since the 1960s.[7] Whiteness has enjoyed similar claims to natural superiority as masculinity. Richard Dyer's "White," in *Screen* (1988) and later his book of the same name (1997), makes the point that "the colourless multi-colouredness of whiteness secures white power by making it hard, especially for white people and their media, to 'see' whiteness" (Dyer, 1988: 46). Dyer argues that, because Western culture has developed from a white subjectivity, it becomes impossible for that culture to see its own position as anything but the "natural order." In a similar way, Peter Middleton's (1992) view of studies in masculinities argues that masculinity still uses male dominated Western philosophies to analyze itself. Stuart Hall (1981) describes Western narratives as products of "the absent, but imperialising 'white eye,' the apparently unmarked position from which all these "observations are made and from which, alone, they make sense" (Hall: 38–9). This is one of the main reasons Dika assumes *The Godfather* as a white supremacist text, as discussed in Chapter 3. She does not qualify her initial identification of white skin beyond the banner of "imperialising." This simplification of male experience will be addressed throughout the analyses in this chapter.

Paul Hoch (1979) notes, "Racism [also] begins as an assertion of masculinity — the claim that the superior warrior manhood of the conquerors justifies their economic exploitation of the conquered" (Hoch: 115). Cultural theory has summarized this historical form of racism as Eurocentrism: the process of prioritizing European cultural history to the exclusion of all others. Thus, racism is an integral part of traditional notions of masculinity and the "ideal male." An ideal place to focus a study of the cultural power of Eurocentrism is through the narratives and images of ethnicity in Western cinema. Hollywood cinema, along with its fascination with the "ideal male," is also the most widespread modern producer of Eurocentric narratives. Nowhere is this more evident than in the genre of the Western. The Eurocentric structure of Hollywood Westerns does not deal with Native Americans in any way but the past tense:

> The elimination of the Indian allows for elegiac nostalgia as a way to treat Indians only in the past tense and thus dismiss their claims in the present, whilst posthumously expressing thanatological tenderness for their memory [Shohat & Stam, 1994: 118].

The Western genre, as a stylistic allusion to the past, is Hollywood's most successful genre. It has established itself as a convention outside of "real" history, almost in a self-perpetuating category of its own, even though the basic premise of the genre is the *"very real"* colonization of America. It has been suggested by Ella Shohat that Hollywood narratives work to locate the "other" in a temporally distinct space. In the case of Native Americans, this space is permanently located in the past. Hollywood narratives constantly re-enact a moment in history that marks the colonization and destruction of Native American culture. Thus, as Shohat and Stam suggest, expressing tenderness for its memory is rendered safe through the fact that narratives cannot alter the historical outcome. In my view postclassical gangster films can operate in similar ways.[8] This is because many of the narratives are situated in the past, thus distancing events from audience temporalities. Combine this with the fact that these narratives are also often portrayed as "exclusive universes" at the point of destruction or extinction and, as argued in Chapter 3, the structure of postclassical gangster films is reminiscent of the Eurocentric nature of Hollywood Westerns.

The Mafia world is presented as separate from ordinary society, in that it is a distinct feature of postclassical narratives, in comparison to those of the classical era, to deal with moments in history prior to the film's production.[9] For instance, films of the 1990s and beyond may deal with the 1970s, as do *The Godfather Part III, Goodfellas, Carlito's Way, Casino, Donnie Brasco, Gotti* and *American Gangster,* or the 1920s–30s in *Miller's Crossing* and *The Funeral.* In consequence, on the one hand these films display nostalgia on the part of assimilated, feminized (Italian) American man for his non-assimilated, "natural," defeated Other, while on the other hand, for the (non–Italian) American male, distancing events through history and ethnicity. Therefore, the films display a conflict between identification and distance. Mafia activity is distanced from the audience through an historical narrative. However, the films also offer points of identification by displaying nostalgia for particular ethnic and masculine identities.

White Ethnicity

In my discussion of Mafia myths, Italian/Sicilian origins were identified as a key characteristic. As stated, before gangster films of the 1960s the notion of a specifically Italian American stereotype was not fundamental. Ethnicity was generalized under the mantle of "immigrant," in that gangsters have always displayed some kind of immigrant identity. This was mainly Italian, Jewish or Irish, but the cultural specification was less important than the overall premise of the gangster as an immigrant, or "other" to American.[10] This is where the particular racial connotation of film gangsters is different to that of Native Americans, or blacks.[11] As previously stated, the ideal male is white and European. Therefore, the Italian, or Irish gangster should not fear rejection on the pretext of race. However, by the early twentieth century, a particular American WASP[12] identity, which had developed from the European, had asserted itself through the colonization of the Western frontier. This meant firstly that immigrants from Europe arriving to help progress the industrialization of the northeast were not part of this essentially American vision and colonization of the west. Secondly, many were not of either Anglo-Saxon or Protestant heritage. Thus, they occupied an ambivalent position of "white ethnicity."[13]

*   *   *

White ethnicity is a useful term to distinguish the interim position of immigrants, who have entered the United States but have yet to assimilate themselves into American culture. White ethnicity is as much reliant on cultural differences as it is on physical ones. For instance, although Italian racial characteristics can sometimes be defined as dark skinned, this is not an insurmountable barrier to assimilation into white culture as in the case of say African American racial characteristics.[14] Therefore, assimilation for such as Italian Americans is determined as much by an individual choice of whether they "act" Italian, as much as whether they "look" Italian. Andrew Greeley attempts to summarize white ethnicity as "essentially an attempt to keep some of the values, some of the informality, some of the support and intimacy of the communal life in the midst of an impersonal, formalistic, rationalized, urban and industrial society" (Greeley, 1973: 11).

Therefore, it is mainly a desire to retain distinct cultural and linguistic traditions that marks such immigrants as different to mainstream society. The Italian immigrants who congregated in northeastern cities clung to the traditions and culture of their Italian history and traditions as a support mechanism for dealing with the new and initially alienating American culture. This may account for some of the sociological studies referred to in Chapter 3 that have suggested the Italian Mafia came into America in the hearts and minds of immigrants and blossomed in the self-contained colonies initially established there.[15] The influx of Italians into America between 1899 and 1910 involved nearly two million men. The Irish had arrived much earlier, with numbers peaking in the 1850s (during the Irish famine) and Jewish immigration nearer the end of the century.[16] A main distinctiveness in the style of Italian immigration was the high proportion of men to women. Along with the two million men there were fewer than half a million women.[17]

*   *   *

Ruth suggests that images of the gangster in popular culture evolved from an American distrust of the city. The new urban environments at the turn of the century were the antibook of the safe small town: "The city was a disorderly place of dangerous strangers, of rapacious capitalists, of 'unmanly men,' and unwomanly women, of seekers of pleasure and shirkers of responsibility" (Ruth: 8). He does not explain what is meant by the term "unmanly men," but it could include those that fail to live up to the populist ideal of law-abiding, white heterosexual and European masculinity (Wood, Hoch), in one form or another. From this, it is apparent that the gangster in America originates from an environment of "tainted" masculinity. This would account for the constant assertions that the gangster character is in some way flawed (Warshow, Cawelti) and therefore brings about his own demise.

The underworlds of America's new cities, like any apparently lawless environment, were "places of exciting possibilities" (*ibid.*). They provided opportunities for American culture to attempt to control or reform them, while simultaneously revelling in their illicitness. Comparisons to the Western frontier can be drawn from the proposal that these environments were areas of danger, but also of freedom. However, just like the lawless frontier, this danger and freedom is a fantasy constructed by outside observers rather than the actual inhabitants. This can be linked with postclassical gangster narratives that isolate their characters within fictional environments of the past. Popular culture encouraged fantasies of urban heroes with similarities to the Westerner. Warshow writes that the gangster was the modern urban equivalent of the Westerner. However, he doesn't believe the gangster is attractive, whereas the Westerner is the "last gentleman, and the movies which over and over again tell his stories are the last art form in which the concept of honour retains its strength" (Warshow, 1954: 457), the gangster is an urban, crude tycoon, without culture and whose ambitions, in a grotesque caricature of the American spirit of free enterprise, know no limits. In postclassical narratives this view is no longer appropriate, because the gangster, as part of the Mafia, has an identifiable culture of his own. In addition, the American spirit of free enterprise is readily accepted as a façade for all manner of illegal activity, of which organized crime is merely one example. One factor remains however, and that is the notion that boundaries between criminality and the law operate as a relationship of "fascination and fear." In history, the ghettos provided boundaries that "seemed at the same time blurry and crucially important" (*ibid.*). In postclassical films, pastness and Mafia myths provide those boundaries. The difference is constantly reaffirmed, but so is the fascination. Notions of masculine identity can also provide these boundaries, in that gangster narratives often encourage displays of aggressive masculinity deemed unacceptable in law-abiding society. Simultaneously, though, the exclusivity of Mafia environments also encourages displays of a gentler, more nurturing masculinity. Thus, the boundaries between the gangsters and law-abiding society may remain both blurry and important, but it is important to note that it is not only the boundaries that are blurry, but also the reasons *why* those boundaries occur that are indistinct or changeable. In other words, the reasons why gangsters are positioned as different from law-abiding society are not fixed or stable.

Assimilation Desires

Sociologists have long maintained that the ethnic immigrants' ultimate goal was cultural assimilation into the American "melting pot" ideal. However, as Steven Steinberg notes, by the 1960s attitudes were beginning to change:

> For decades the dominant tendency among the nation's ethnic and racial minorities had been toward integration into the economic, political and cultural mainstream. Now the pendulum seemed to be swinging back, as these groups repudiated their assimilationist tendencies [Steinberg: 3].

This ethnic identification took a more pluralist turn and individuals looked to their cultural heritage again for security in similar ways to the "support and intimacy" Andrew Greeley maintained was sought by the early immigrants. However, by the 1960s the notion of clearly defined ethnic boundaries in second and third generation immigrants was suffering from confusions and discrepancies of its own. Italian American neighborhoods still remained in places such as New York City, but they could no longer claim any isolation from America. At the same time, discussions of ethnicity evolved into two definable theories. It is either a pre-determined, immutable condition, or it is a "self-determined, changeable condition subject to situations and personal taste" (Friedman: 18). Max Weber (1961) believed that "ethnic group membership is a subjective belief rather than a blood connection" (Weber, cited in Friedman, 1991: 17). Friedman seconds this by stating, "If one claims to be part of an ethnic group and is willing to be treated by outsiders and judged by insiders as such, then one is part of that group" (*ibid.*: 15). This suggests, in a similar way to new writings on masculinity (Butler, Petersen), that ethnicity is a kind of performance or role. It is debatable as to whether it is as subjective as Weber; or Friedman assert. It is more likely, as with all identity, that it is a mixture of self-assertion, cultural and historical influence, and performance.

The extent to which postclassical narratives confine their subjects to the past, allude to real events and use stereotypes have already been noted. White ethnicity is an important factor in maintaining the ambivalence of these elements of the postclassical narrative. This is due to the contradictory impulses of assimilation desires. Assimilation is possible for Italian Americans more easily than some others, because of the absence of any overt physical signifiers of difference. Thus, assimilation depends on the extent to which individuals assert their ethnic identity. Excessive emotional display, family loyalties and even an over-love of food have been identified as indicative of cultural difference: "The Italian soul is simple and its heart possessed of unsuitable emotions which are always excessive [...] Excess is inappropriate in American society because it is inefficient, using too much energy for its needs" (Papaleo, 1978: 93). For instance, the controlled sureties of Vito or Michael Corleone appear less stereotypically Italian than the excessive emotion of Sonny. The same could be argued of Pauly Cicero in comparison to Tommy De Vito (*Goodfellas*), Neil Dellacroce compared to John Gotti (*Gotti*), or Silvio Dante to Paulie Gualtieri (*The Sopranos*).

*   *   *

Defining the Italian character in such a way does not mean that the more controlled characters do not articulate their cultural heritage; they simply do not display it in the same way, or to the same degree. Having a stereotypical Italian within the narrative serves to assimilate other characters. For instance, Michael Corleone is a less impulsive character than Sonny, and thus it is not surprising that he takes control of the family. Henry and Jimmy appear comparatively sane against the behavior of Tommy (*Goodfellas*). Lefty Ruggiero is a sympathetic character when measured against Sonny Black (*Donnie Brasco*). Such comparisons can be made even in groups or characters not specifically identified as Mafia. For example, Mr. Blue (Michael Madsen) is the uncontrollable torturer/murderer who makes the rest of the *Reservoir Dogs* cast appear more ethical. Carlito Brigante appears positively angelic in comparison to the corrupt dealings of his lawyer Kleinfeld (*Carlito's Way*) and Caesar encourages sympathy when faced with the callousness of his rival Johnny Marzzone (*Bound*). These comparisons can be summed up by Tony Montana (*Scarface*), when he proclaims, "You need me, so you can point your fuckin' finger and say 'there's the bad guy.'" It is as if certain characters take the ethnic spotlight away from others by exaggerating certain negative masculine and ethnic character stereotypes. Even Tony Montana is more ethical than Sosa and his henchmen, as shown in the attempt to assassinate a senator (discussed in Chapter 2). Montana has a set of morals even within his violent world, and this makes helps to make him at least partly sympathetic. However, as is clear with Tony Montana such arguments are not intended to imply that the sympathetic characters are then devoid of ethnic signifiers. They blur the distinction between cultural difference and assimilation, in that they do assert their ethnic identity, but in comparison to the exaggerated type, in a less pronounced way.

Tony Soprano is the central figure in *The Sopranos* and is sympathetic often through comparison to other less palatable presentations of Italian American masculinity. A primary example of this is found in his relationship to Ralph Cifaretto. Ralph is a "bad" gangster stereotype. His violence is arbitrary and his loyalties are ambivalent. The audience is encouraged to anticipate and desire Ralph's inevitable demise. Tony's violent and messy fight with Ralph in Season 4, Episode 9 is cathartic revenge for all the innocent people we have witnessed suffer at Ralph's hands. Ralph embodies many negative masculine and ethnic stereotypes, especially sexual deviance, which I would argue is one of the ultra-conservative undercurrents in the later seasons. Tony's violence towards him is not only justified within the narrative, but can also be viewed as an attempt to annihilate the possibility of that aspect in Tony's own identity. Tony may be associated with violence and intimidation, but he's not as bad as Ralph. Ralph is there for the audience to point their finger at and say, "here's the bad guy."

More subtle comparisons can be made across Tony's crew. Silvio is the most Italian character and arguably the most old-fashioned gangster associated with the Mafia ideal: a good *consigliore*. Paulie is childish but loyal to Tony V and, Christopher is gullible and weak. Bobby is probably the most sympathetic as the all-around good guy. They are all cultural aspects of modern American masculinities as much as they are Italian. It is interesting that Richard Vetere in *The New York Times* laments the Sopranos' lack of refinement. He describes Tony as a "cursing, belching, caveman" in comparison to Vito Corleone, who at least "knew about Caravaggio, Dante and Puccini" (February 12, 2000). First, it shows how *The Godfather*, which was once derided as a defamation of Italian heritage, is now viewed through the distortive lens of nostalgia; but second, as always we have to ask the question, is it really Italian ethnicity that is at the root of *The Sopranos* or the image of American masculinity? In my view, the central factor that makes *The Sopranos* an intelligent show is its value as an exercise in cultural displacement: Italian ethnicity is simply the scapegoat for white male prejudices. This is the reason it has gained so much attention as a comment upon suburban life, because Tony Soprano acts out the supposed desires of American males. It is not that I disagree with Vetere's point of view, it's just that I wonder why there aren't more American males asking why Tony Soprano is suggested as representing them? Is it the idea that, in the end, his Italian heritage retains him in the land of Otherness? I think the series blurs that boundary far too many times to keep that claim.

Assimilation is a major theme in *The Godfather* trilogy. As stated in Chapter 3, Michael is punished in *The Godfather Part II* for his attempts to assimilate and the consequent denial of his cultural heritage. The films move from the desire to assimilate, that even Vito articulates in Part I, through the futility of such desires in Part II, to the final desperate attempts to combine the two in Part III. Cultural heritage and American idealism are shown to be at odds from the very opening scene, when Bonasera proclaims, "I believe in America," but then goes on to explain the extent to which the country has failed him. Furthermore, Sonny embodies all the negative stereotypes of Italian behavior, as does Tommy De Vito in *Goodfellas*. However, it is interesting to note how Sonny is still viewed as one of the most popular characters, and as most like the classical gangster (*Sunday Mirror* February 3, 1991). It is perhaps the generic conventions carried forward from the classical era that allow characters such as Sonny, Tommy, John Gotti, Mr. Blue, and others to be easily identified as gangsters. Their deaths encourage nostalgia for the classical gangster, whose fate is secured through his excessive behavior. They are unproblematic signifiers of a certain unreclaimed masculine and ethnic character type and thus rendered safe by this identification.

Gangster identity is one of negotiation between cultural heritage and assimilationist ideals. On the one hand Italian American Mafia identity is positive and can be seen as assimilated within American society through its dominance within popular culture. It is a symbol of strength, unity and enterprise, which are all laudable attributes in American society. However, these same characteristics are connected with Mafia ideals of violence, oppression and criminality, which in turn keep their identity different from the American ideal. In addition, as discussed in Chapters 2 and 3, the blurring of ethnic boundaries is often dependent upon the reception of films: whether the characters are seen to be expressing their difference to, or association with, American ideals. For instance, an anti-assimilationist desire for ethnic authenticity is suggested in a response to *The Godfather Part III*; the reviewer notes, "It is a melancholy thought that no Italian American could be found for the part [of Vincent (Andy Garcia)] and Hispanics seem to be taking over the brotherhood" (*National Review*, January 28, 1991: 65). Another example, *Donnie Brasco*, is not unique in distancing the Mafia from ordinary society by placing its narrative in the past, but this film also emphasises distance through the use of voyeurism and allusion to wildlife documentary which gives the narrative an "anthropological quality" (Wrathall, *Sight and Sound* v7 n.5, 1997: 41) Both of these responses suggest the ethnic heritage of gangster films as some kind of distinct national treasure, uniquely Italian, which must be preserved, albeit in the past, from infiltration by other ethnicities.

Throughout this book it has been noted how generic conventions, Mafia myths of the Italian ideal and stereotyping have identified the Italian Mafia as the template against which all other criminal gangs are measured. This allows shortcuts to be made in narratives (*New Jack City, State of Grace, The Firm, Leon* and *Bound*) that don't require detailed explanation of character motivation. However, it also suggests, as Papaleo notes, that "Mafia killers kill because they are Italian, not because they are insane" (94), thus firmly entrenching violence within the Italian psyche. In contrast, *Goodfellas* has been viewed, without recourse to ethnicity, as "a buddy film, a male fantasy in which the guys have all the fun [but also] it's about the reality that drives street kids like Henry — in every poor neighborhood in America — to choose gangs over gainful employment" (*The Progressive*, March 1991: 38). Here we find the notion that the film is about male fantasies rather than ethnic identity, rather like Dika's assertion of *The Godfather* as a white male fantasy narrative.[18] In my view this is because white ethnicity is a problematic identity. On the one hand it can be identified as Other through articulations, such as gesture, dialogue and actions; on the other it can just as easily be assimilated into white male identity because it is not perceived as irrevocably different.

* * *

Assertions of male identity through ethnic identity became more important after the Civil Rights movements of the 1960s. Assimilation, for an ethnic identity, meant denying one's own cultural identity and heritage. However, if skin color still marks an individual out as physically different, then true assimilation is rendered impossible and an individual faces the prospect of being bereft of any coherent cultural identity.[19] Black Civil Rights groups[20] noted this discrepancy and worked to raise the importance of black identity as separate from the white, rather than to accept assimilation, which skin color will always contradict. Furthermore, white identity has been shown as socially and politically diverse, especially through opposing attitudes to the Vietnam War. Whites are not always treated collectively, but are often differentiated by class and education. Therefore, the stability of "white" as a dominant or secure identity is undermined and specific ethnic identities become a more appealing point of stability amid the conflicts of identifying a meaningful collective American consciousness. In this context, Italian American identity as it appears in *The Godfather* presents a coherent set of rules, traditions and a family unit that mainstream white America can no longer offer.

It is noted in Chapter 3 that there was unease at the time of *The Godfather*'s production from the Italian American Unification Council about the association between Italians and organized crime, plus demonstrations from the Italian Friendship Association about the under-representation of Italian actors in the main roles. Issues of ethnic stereotyping were raised again in response to the popularity of *The Sopranos*. These events and discussions further emphasize how sensitive issues of ethnic identity remain within American culture. In the forties and fifties, gangster films declined or were diluted to cop-thrillers, not only because censorship insisted on the promotion of the law-abiding hero, but because organized crime could not be associated with any specific ethnic minority. The relaxation of censorship allowed *The Godfather* to be made and the theme of ethnic unity becomes a key aspect of postclassical narratives. However, as discussed, the blurred distinctions between assimilation and anti-assimilation desires allow for a considerable amount of negotiation as to the extent to which gangster narratives relate to specific ethnicity, or whether they are more focused on masculine identity as a whole.

Male-Male Intimacy

One of the ways in which issues of ethnic and masculine identity are merged in postclassical gangster films is through the display of male-male intimacy. The Mafia's exclusively male environment offers a sanctuary for the male psyche, in that it justifies displays of intimacy and exclusivity by constantly reaffirming the goal-orientated nature of their unity, through activities such as criminal business and continuous protection of the organization. The exclusivity of Mafia groups also allows for displays of physical intimacy that would be generally derided in wider society. Physical contact between WASP men in American culture is often asserted as playfully aggressive. Physical contact, such as backslaps, bear hugs, even the handshake, is vigorous to the extent that such displays almost subvert the show of friendship that provides the reason behind the contact in the first place. In Hollywood film, such activity has been suggested as an assertion of opposite, but often linked drives: homoeroticism and homophobia.

* * *

Cynthia Fuchs' work on "The Buddy Politic" (1993)[21] suggests that the extraordinary virility displayed in the actions of film heroes in buddy films, such as the *Lethal Weapon* series (1987, 1989 and 1992), is sexually charged, but oscillates between homoerotic and homophobic, in that the heroes are "in love with their self-displays and at odds with their implications" (Fuchs: 195). However, she states that such anxieties are displaced by the fact that the heroes are of different ethnic backgrounds: "The transgressiveness of black-white difference displaces homosexual anxiety" (*ibid.*: 203). This is useful for a discussion on gangsters, as displays of male-male intimacy are frequent and yet anxieties about homoeroticism are diffused both by ethnicity and by the pervasiveness of Mafia myths. However, this is further confused by the fact that Italian American ethnicity is white, as discussed earlier, and thus blurs the boundaries of racial difference.

Male-male intimacy is a distinct feature of postclassical gangster films for three main reasons. Firstly, the relaxation of censorship has allowed for greater freedoms in expressing both intimacy and violence. However, this fact does not change the mainstream aversion to intimacy between men. As suggested earlier, advertising for *The Brotherhood* (1968) used an image of the "kiss of death" scene from the film showing the brothers kissing on the lips. A review for the film was adamant that such publicity suggested it as "a fag film" and "without denying the necessity to provoke audience interest, the pitch does a disservice to the film" (*Variety*, November 20, 1968). Thus, even after the end of the censorship, there remained a need to contextualize male intimacy in order to allay homophobic fears. This context is found in the pervasion of Mafia myths, as discussed in Chapter 3, which was boosted by *The Godfather* to the extent that the "kiss of death" scene from *The Brotherhood* would now be less likely to raise comment, especially after two similar scenes in *The Godfather Part II*. Michael Corleone kisses his brother Fredo initially to signal Fredo's betrayal and then to seal his death sentence. Thus, the second reason for believing that male-male intimacy is less threatening in postclassical gangster films is due to the prevalence of Mafia myths as an integral part of the films' cultural meaning. Kissing is used as a show of respect or brotherly unity, but it can also signal violence or death. In *The Godfather Part III*, Vincent (Andy Garcia) kisses Joey Zasa (Joe Montagna) on Michael's command, but the show of respect turns into a display of aggression when Vincent bites part of Joey's ear off. Therefore, scenes of physical intimacy are displaced by the constant threat of violence. This is similar to the displacement suggested by Fuchs, in that Mafia characters are in love with their displays of intimacy, but homosexual anxiety is dispelled by the ever-present threat of violence.

The Sopranos developed its own homosexual storyline in Season 6. Vito is a sympathetic character, a good earner and a respected captain in Tony's crew. However, the narrative focuses less on Vito's sexual identity and much more on the crew's homophobia. Vito's experiences are reduced to homosexual stereotyping: the leather night at the gay bar, the biker boyfriend and rural antique stores. There is no attempt to treat Vito's story as anything other than a cliché: it is almost as if the images we see of him are filtered through the imaginations of the mob crew. The narrative attempts to diffuse homophobia through various discussions between Tony and Dr. Melfi (Episode 5) and Tony and Silvio (Episode 6): Silvio suggests that at the core Vito's situation is "bad for business," but in truth what is "at the core" is the fact that Vito's storyline is nothing more than an excuse for a lot of bigoted jokes. As Renee Graham in *The Chicago Tribune* (May 13, 2004), points out in terms of the series' racism, "Bigoted thoughts or opinions are never far from the surface," and in my opinion Vito's storyline exemplifies that. In short, Vito's story is tucked in as an attempt to address an issue related to masculine groups, but only insofar as to reassert heterosexuality. Within the context of the series Vito's death is inevitable.

In my opinion, Tony and the gang, while essentially "Other" to mainstream America due to their ethnic and criminal behavior, can also be suggested as acting out the supposed desires of mainstream American males. Discussions on such forums as sopranoland.com, thesopranos.com, thechaselounge.net and sopranos.yuku.com include topics such as, "which Soprano are you most like?" or "Which Soprano's character are you?" (both from sopranos.yuku.com),[22] as well information on cause-effect logic in most characters' behavior. Homosexuality is discussed in relation to Tony Blundetto (Steve Buscemi) in a sopranoland thread titled, "Hugs Anyone? (Could Tony B be gay?)" (Season 5). Most replies defended Tony's behavior as a simple portrayal of Italian American identity through physical affection, but one post foreshadowed a later *Sopranos* plotline by citing a real-life news story about a Mafia Don executed by his own family for being gay: "Secret gay life leaves Capo capped" (*www.smh.com.au/articles/2...96372.html May 2003*, posted by flyonmelfiswall). As such, physical affection is accepted as a specifically Italian American cultural practice, but it is also suggested that homosexuality is something Mafia families fear.

Vito's story in Season 6 was bound to encourage some heated discussion on internet forums. It is important to note that not all discussion was negative. Some forums, especially thechaselounge.net, are very detailed in their responses, even dedicating a specific messageboard to symbolism and subtext. It should be noted that their episode forum discussed the season 6 episode "Live Free or Die" by comparing Vito's journey to New Hampshire to some of Tony's dream sequences. It was suggested that these sequences linked both characters and demonstrated projections of alternative lives outside the mob. The episode was also suggested as focusing on the revelation of secrets: "coming out of the closet." Debate was equally weighted as to whether Tony's defence of Vito was a weakness or strength. Duke of Mantua suggests Tony reveals himself as a "homosexual apologist," which will "undo his feeble attempt at gaining control of the crew." Jeff41954 argues that Tony is "showing his strength by trying to change the old ways." Other forums were more emotional. Sopranoland.com have threads titled "Disgraceful," "This is worse than Brokeback Mtn," "homophobe?" and "I'm still disappointed." Discussion of Vito's storyline is interspersed with other comments about Season 6, but the comments about homosexuality are mainly negative. "As a diehard fan of the sopranos this whole storyline of Vito and his new bum buddy is just too much" (posted by Pablo Picass0). I am "weary of the 'Queer as Folk detour myself" (posted by gnimat). Zillajay4life found it irritating to have the homosexual plot "shoved in your face over and over." Marta18 "could have done without the bedroom scenes." It's interesting that one poster (Unregistered(d)) laments, "Must it be force fed to us," "I wanted to throw a brick thru my T.V. in the Vito and Johnny Cakes scenes," and "The season is on a political crusade for gays," but then he also asks the forum about the inherent contradictions in such responses. "I'm confused how can you guys be 'ok' or at least tolerable of murder and all the other horrible things that are done on this show. But gayness is a no no?" I find this an interesting question, because it lies at the heart of the many discussions (his or her own included) featured on forums that express disgust at the explicit nature of such scenes. *The Sopranos* features many explicit sex scenes, some of which include violence against women. It is fair to say that most are voyeuristic and treat women simply as sexual toys for the men. It is hard to find any discussion that considers such scenes as "disgraceful." This attitude would possibly be defended by stating, that "This is what mob life is like," and so the series is simply adhering to realism. However, my point (and possibly the crux of the post from [U]nregistered[d]) is that if the scenes are simply adhering to realism then Vito's homosexuality is a part of that. Expressing one's personal distaste at such an inclusion only reveals one's own discomfort and therefore is a discussion mainly of yourself and your own personal identity rather than its place in *The Sopranos'* narrative.

What is interesting is that Vito's story line is unveiled just after Tony leaves hospital from the bullet wound and Johnny Sack attends his daughter's wedding. Homosexuality is woven into other presentations or anxieties about masculine weakness. Tony fears his authority may be undermined by his physical injury. Johnny Sack's authority is undermined by his emotional outburst at his daughter's wedding. Therefore, one of the many driving forces behind the violence against Vito is a continuation of Tony's personal anxieties about his own masculine identity. Aggressive heterosexuality is promoted at a hysterical level throughout the Sopranos. Tony's many conquests are presented in graphic detail. As much as those instances make *The Sopranos* almost a parody of masculine desires and anxieties, the continuation of that through racial and sexual bigotry is what damages the series' critical credibility. Furthermore, when discussion forums react with hostility towards a homosexual plotline it encourages the question of why the series included it in the first place. Rocky1993 asks on thesopranos.com if "Chase is jumping on the Hollywood political agenda hot button issues, such as terrorism and homosexuality?" It's not possible to answer that here of course; maybe he is, but in doing so in such a clichéd way surely Chase is dangerously close to poking fun not only at homosexuality and the mob's ultra conservative reaction, but also at the series' fan base. It promotes a perception that *The Sopranos* appeals to a predominantly male conservative audience and therefore such a plotline is bound to invite hostile audience reactions in much the same way as it did on screen. As stated, while most discussions were not in favor of the Vito plotline, it was for various reasons, such as it developed too fast, was badly written and was too sexually explicit. While I agree that the narrative did feel forced and clichéd, I found it interesting simply because it struck at the heart of some unspoken fears and anxieties about male-male intimacy and masculine groups.

The third point concerning male-male intimacy in postclassical gangster films simplifies Fuchs' notions of racial transgressiveness. Images of intimacy are diffused by the ethnic identity of Mafiosi in Hollywood cinema. As non–WASP Americans, gangsters can transgress the restrictions on white masculine display, because this simply reasserts their difference and distances all of their actions, including intimacy and criminality, from white heterosexual identity. This is different from Fuchs' explanation of "the buddy politic," in that the Mafia does not transgress racial boundaries in order to displace intimacy. Instead physical intimacy is asserted as an element within Italian American identity, linking Mafia myths with ethnic identity and thus justifying transgressive displays of intimacy within the boundaries of ethnic conventions and cultural heritage. Male relationships in gangster films operate under the same rubric as other mainstream examples, in that aggressive activity is used in order to displace intimacy. However, they also convey the uniqueness of the Mafia identity in that combining Italian American ethnic identity with ideals of a collective male identity allows for more intimate displays of male-male affection within a specific environment. This is because the Mafia is displayed as a collective identity, which has appeal across racial boundaries, but also signifies the difference between Mafia groups and mainstream society. Thus, it also reinforces a stereotyped image of Mafia ethnicity that renders it knowable and thus safe. In turn, these stereotypes serve to assert mythologies of the Mafia. These mythologies also allow for a certain amount of male intimacy on the part of the Mafia group. In short male-male intimacy is both encouraged and displaced within the postclassical gangster film, but the reasons for this are not reducible to a single impulse. As stated, the Mafia is displayed as a collective identity, which has appeal across racial boundaries because it does not fix identity within one typology. However, this does reflect a desire for an ideal identity within the collective, and so it is now necessary to move on to discuss notions of collective identity in postclassical gangster narratives.

*　*　*

The Collective Ideal

As previously stated, the imagined community of an exclusively male Mafia offers a sanctuary for the male psyche. It offers an all-male domain with a specific purpose, albeit criminal, that justifies the intimacy and exclusivity of the unit. Many writings on masculinities suggest that men need to be apart from women in order to reassert their masculinity.[23] It is a contradictory state, as Roger Horrocks explains: "Men need women to assert their masculine side, yet they must also keep their distance, in order to evade domestication" (Horrocks, 1988: 64). This corresponds to Robin Wood's definition of the ideal male, whose very nature is defined in relation to the ideal female, but is also under threat from her influence. The problems of an all-male environment, such as a fear of male-intimacy,[24] are avoided by foregrounding the purpose of the domain. Drury Sherrod (1987) finds sociological studies of male friendships have concluded that it is a demand for a specific purpose, goal, honor or code that justifies their unity. This means that "men's relationships are a constant contradiction, or disavowal of intimacy through the prioritisation of action, or goals" (Sherrod: 221).[25] Susan Jeffords (1989) continues this notion of contradictory unity in her discussion of interracial camaraderie during the Vietnam War. She explains how firsthand accounts of soldiers' experiences on the battlefield present an "imagery and rhetoric of collectivity" (Jeffords: 55). She goes on to say, "The collectivity of war, we are to understand, encompasses all men who engage in battle on any battlefield and overcomes all barriers between races" (*ibid.*: 57). There is an understandable hesitation in her acceptance of this harmonious collectivity, but it does show how comforting the notion of "brotherly love"[26] is in male groups, especially in times of conflict. Susan Faludi's article, "The Naked Citadel" (1994), also focuses on life in a military academy, and she suggests that an exclusively male environment allows men to explore beyond traditional masculine roles: "The military stage sets a false front and a welcome trap door — an escape hatch from the social burdens of traditional masculinity [..] where rules of gender could be bent or escaped" (Faludi: 81–2). She notes how the mastery of women's work (ironing, sewing, polishing) is part of military training and that squad camaraderie is bolstered by sitting around "like a bunch of hausfraus, talking and gossiping" (*ibid.*).

Postclassical gangster narratives reflect the notion of men exploring beyond traditional masculine roles. For instance, cooking is used as a display of masculine affection and unity. *The Godfather* has Clemenza teaching Michael to cook as part of his initiation into the trade: "You never know when you might have to feed a group of men." It is important to note that Mafia men only cook for other men, thus it is an articulation of masculinity. It is also evident that good Mafia men are good cooks. For instance, in *Goodfellas* the wise guys in prison take pride in their cooking and share tasks, indicating their unity as well as their ability to take care of each other.

In contrast, disasters in the kitchen can often signify a gangster's downfall. For instance, Henry Hill (*Goodfellas*) is supposed to be cooking for his family, especially his brother, on the day he is finally arrested for drug smuggling. The day spirals into a maelstrom of cocaine deals, taxiing and attempts to control his special tomato sauce. Henry's identity is shown as out of control, in that he is pulled between too many competing forces: individual gain from drug dealing, a selfish desire to run a family and a mistress at the same time, plus the Mafia life. The competing crises reach their climax through a montage centered on cooking and his attempts to stop the sauce from burning. His tomato sauce is a symbol of his Mafia training. If he had concentrated on this aspect of his life, rather than attending to drug deals and his mistress, he might have eluded capture. Similarly, Lefty (*Donnie Brasco*) attempts to cook Christmas dinner for Donnie and instead sets fire to the frying pan. Such culinary incompetence is representative of Lefty's ineffectual status within the Mafia as a whole. An ideal gangster is self-sufficient, both emotionally and physically, and thus resembles ideal masculinity in that he does not need women around him in order to function effectively. However, this does not mean that the gangster is emotionally reticent. An ideal gangster is a protector and a provider for his fellow men.

Italian American and mainstream American comfort food hold equal value in Tony Soprano's world. His love of ice cream sundaes while watching old Westerns or gangster movies is equaled only by his sharing of Italian sandwiches at the Bada Bing or Satriale's. Food is often the first offering from the crew in times of stress. It is an offering, alongside the money and the loyalty, to show respect to the boss. However, in a particularly graphic example of gastronomic revenge, one of Tony's captains Gigi Gestone (John Fiore) finds that stress, bad food and new responsibilities can put a stop to the toughest constitution. Gigi suffers a heart attack and dies while in the bathroom (Season 3, Episode 8), an ending some might say Tony Soprano should fear for himself. However, food remains one of the ties that bind Tony's crew. It is a measure of their ethnic identity both at home and abroad. While Carmela typifies the Italian American stereotype of hearth and home, Paulie's dismay at "real" Italian food (Season 2, Episode 4) is testimony to the cultural assimilation these twenty-first century gangsters have soaked in. Tony's crew are true "Italian Americans" and as such their association with food and each other is fluid blend of both influences.

The role of male as protector and provider is used to justify male intimacy in an all-male group. Faludi notes that male intimacy is still obscured by intense displays of virile showmanship: "Every display of affection must be counterbalanced by a display of sadism" (*ibid.*: 80). Furthermore, masculine unity that outweighs any individual prejudice over race is only cohesive when the group is defined in opposition to an enemy, for instance women. Movie Mafias seemingly contradict this premise, in that ethnicity is a primary focus of its particular collectivity, *especially* in times of conflict. For instance, in *The Godfather*, the family "go to the mattresses"[27] during the five-family-war, when family unity and isolation is at its most intense. Also, movie Mafias are obviously very different from the army, in that they are an aggressive community operating outside of the only domain where aggression is applauded, that of military combat.[28]

The notion of the Mafia as a homogeneous collective is expounded through myths of the Mafia. The suggestion that *the* Mafia originates from Sicily and now operates as a cohesive network across the United States and beyond, as suggested by the Kefauver Committee and criminologists such as Cressey detailed in Chapter 3, also suggests that the characters of Mafiosi are cohesive. If all members abide by the same strict rules of honor and loyalty, this is likely to promote a single masculine identity or at least an ideal. This is evident in some of the more romantic examples of postclassical gangster films, such as the *Godfather* trilogy, *Goodfellas, Casino, The Funeral, Gotti, Donnie Brasco* or on TV in *The Sopranos*. All of these include explicit discourses around acceptable behavior, demeanor and respect. A significant articulation of this is found in the extent to which a single character is asked to compromise an assertion of individual identity or ambition in favor of collective unity. Perhaps the clearest example is Michael Corleone's gradual absorption into the family firm (*The Godfather*). The narrative is that of the prodigal son returning to his family, but this process also displays an

Lefty Ruggiero (Al Pacino). *Donnie Brasco* © 1997, Mandalay/Baltimore.

assimilation of Michael's identity into the Mafia community. His identity is initially represented by difference, in that his assertion of self-identity is situated in opposition to the rest of the family. This is evidenced in the opening scenes at Connie's wedding. Michael is dressed in his army uniform rather than the black suits worn by the rest of his family. His costume signifies an allegiance to the military rather than the Mafia hierarchy, and thus his American rather than Italian cultural heritage. Michael's visual appearance confirms his position in his statement to Kay, "That's my family, Kay, not me."

However, his alliances are tested by the attack on his father, and the initial identity-through-opposition is gradually replaced by an assertion of unity and assimilation into the Mafia identity. Michael's nighttime visit to the hospital, in which he and Enzo pretend to be bodyguards outside the hospital doors, begins Michael's transformation from Ivy League student/war hero to Mafia Don. He instructs Enzo how to assume the Mafia persona. Turning up the collars of their overcoats and keeping their hands within visible reach of implied handguns, the young men take on the appearance of Mafia bodyguards. This scene provides evidence of Mafia identity as performance, in that Enzo and Michael protect his father through the suggestion of a Mafia presence at the hospital rather than having to prove any individual abilities. As noted in Chapter 2, costume and settings convey the threat of Mafia activity and violence to the extent that characters are able to use this threat as a personal shield. Michael uses the implication of Mafia presence at the hospital to protect his father, and this performance also operates as the first signal of Michael's immersion into a Mafia role. While Enzo trembles to the extent that he can hardly hold a cigarette, Michael calmly and steadily offers his lighter. The camera lingers upon this act and Michael's contemplation of his steady hands. This and other pivotal scenes, such as the plan to kill Sollozo and McClusky[29] in which the camera steadily focuses on Michael to the exclusion of all others, guide attention towards Michael as the central figure. He has assumed a Mafia identity, firstly through costume by discarding his army uniform and college clothes for overcoats and Fedora hats, and secondly through presence, by displaying a more solemn and guarded persona in his gestures and dialogue. As such, Michael gradually submerges his personality into the collective identity of the Mafia by assuming the conventions of costume and character.

In contrast, Sonny Corleone, who initially operates as the heir apparent in the family, is shown to be at odds with the collective identity. He is aggressive, disloyal to his wife and speaks without thinking. Vito Corleone explains the need for Sonny to control his own aggression for the benefit of the family identity as a whole, as in the meeting with Sollozo, where Sonny's temper nearly destroys the delicate negotiations.[30] The embarrassment of Sonny's outburst is registered within the scene by a long silence and individual close-ups of each participant. Vito explains to him afterwards, "Never tell anyone outside the family what you are thinking." The scene reflects a need for the Mafia family to censor individual concerns in order to project unity, and thus strength, to outsiders. After Sonny's death, Vito states that he always thought of Sonny as a "bad Don." Here Vito is lamenting Sonny's inability to submerge his own identity, ambition, or aggression for the benefit of the collective identity of the Mafia. In this sense, it was Sonny's unwillingness to submerge his individualism that made him a "bad Don."

The fragility of a large organization that requires all of its members to project a unified identity is reflected in later films, such as *Casino* and *Gotti*. John Gotti is a similar character to Sonny, in that his own ambitions encourage him to operate without recourse to the collective. Neil Dellacroce (Anthony Quinn) reminds Gotti of the fragile nature of Mafia unity, by stating that rules are there to protect everyone: "You break the rules and this whole damn thing of ours cracks and crumbles." In *Casino* Remo is anxious to know if Nicky is messing around with Sam's wife, Ginger. Frankie's (Frank Vincent) narration explains: "There's one thing about these old timers, they don't like any fucking around with other guy's wives. It's bad for business." The difference here is that the unity is shown as a means for profit. Dissension within the group is bad for business, because it means the group is no longer working together. These later films all concentrate on the destruction of Mafia unity, whereas *The Godfather* still had time to bask in its security. However, as with Sonny Corleone, it is often the failure in the main characters, such as Henry Hill (*Goodfellas*), Nicky Santoro (*Casino*), or John Gotti (*Gotti*), to compromise their own identity within the collective of the Mafia that brings about their own or the family's downfall. Thus the collective identity, despite its non-achievability in these films, is still admired as an ideal.

It is the desire for a homogeneous masculine collective operating within an otherwise fractured society — secure, strong and based on an identifiable set of codes — which underscores the appeal of the Mafia (Tillman). However, notions of collectivity require individuals to discard their individuality in order to safeguard the ideals of the collective. An example of individual identity operating on behalf of the collective appears in *The Untouchables*, in which Al Capone (Robert De Niro) steals the show because his criminal character is more compelling than Costner's righteous and understated law enforcer. Ruth maintains that classical gangsters reflected reactions against modernist impersonal societies formed through corporate bureaucracies, denying personal agency.[31] Conversely, postclassical gangsters display their strength precisely because they *do* operate within notions of corporation and bureaucracy. De Niro's Al Capone has the strength and cooperation of his criminal organization behind him, while Eliot Ness, as the representative of morality, has only a small band of righteous law enforcers. Ruth suggests that gangsters embody an individualism whereby they seemingly construct or live by rules of their own devising, as opposed to the establishment slave, who abides by the laws set down by a bureaucratic system. This may be true of the pre–1970s gangsters, but by the 1970s, gangsters in films have fully embraced the bureaucratic system and turned it around to make it their own. It now exists as a representation of their collective identity and national/international power. In contrast, the individual law enforcer, Eliot Ness, is now the isolated one, in that he struggles to find allies or a coherent set of values in his organization.

Postclassical gangster films display and develop notions of a collective Mafia identity within a more general structure of hierarchy and tradition. This collectivity is partially achieved by constantly replaying genre conventions of costume and dialogue, but through new characters. The repetition of conventions encourages audiences to recognize characters and situations, but each narrative adds further information regarding genre, Mafia myths, masculine and ethnic identity. Postclassical gangster films display collective identities, firstly because they reflect the multiplicity of masculine identities through groups of men, rather than through the less comfortable notion of a fracturing of individual masculine identity. This also happens as a result of a nostalgic desire for a lost masculine ideal or omnipotence that has always been represented in cinema (Wood), but is not acceptable in social reality. Secondly, postclassical gangster films display collective identities because each film text refers to and builds upon previous films, a feature which has been referred to before in Chapter 2 as continuous narratives across films, and in Chapter 3, as the continuation of Mafia myths. All these influences develop collective notions of gangsters and Mafia identities through cinema history.

Recent approaches to masculinity suggest that white heterosexual identity is no longer so distinctly the norm by which everything else is measured. White masculinity is now making its own claims upon marginal identity. This coincides with theoretical interests in identity as performance (Judith Butler, 1993; Alan Petersen, 1998). Edley and Wetherell suggest that "manliness" is something that is learned: "A set of lines and stage directions which all males have to learn in order to perform" (Edley & Wetherell: 71). Obviously, these lines and directions will be slightly different based on the social positions of individuals, and most importantly these roles are often not recognized as such; most men would consider themselves as "being" rather than "playing" masculinity (73). However, this distanciation between biological determinism (man/woman) and gender personality (masculine/feminine) allows for the complexities and inconsistencies of gender behavior. The fact that those who display inappropriate behavior, "effeminate" men, or "masculine" women are noted as deviant or inverted (75) does not alter the fact that these gender positionings exist. Therefore, gender identity is performance, in that while it is influenced by biology and the social expectancies associated with that, it is not confined to these factors. Different environments and situations can encourage a more diverse range of gender behavior such as the all-male environment in the armed forces, or the Mafia. Inappropriate gender behavior is a social judgment influenced by the context in which this behavior is displayed, or by whom. Cinematic representations of gangsters show them as existing in an environment where intimacy and aggression can operate simultaneously and can offer points of both identification and distanciation. On the one hand gangster narratives operate as fantasies of white male omnipotence, while on the other simultaneously foregrounding racial otherness and pastness. Identification and distanciation are in a state of constant flux, which allows for viewers to move in and out of specific identifications — in other words, to "pick and choose" the elements they wish to applaud while distancing themselves from those they find uncomfortable. One way in which identification is encouraged in cinema is through stereotyping.

Stereotyping

Notions of collective identity in postclassical gangster films on the one hand suggest a multiplicity of character identity that would seem to be at odds with the role of stereotyping. However, stereotyping is still a fundamental part of gangster identity in that it is possible to identify stereotypes in postclassical gangster films that relate to genre conventions, masculinity and ethnicity.

One of the ways stereotyping appears in gangster films is through particular assertions of stable or fixed identification within the otherwise blurred collective identities. These draw upon genre or cultural stereotypes that reaffirm the boundaries between the Mafia and ordinary society. These can be boundaries of time, placing the Mafia narrative in history, or boundaries of identity through articulations of masculinity and ethnicity. It is suggested that popular culture narratives employ an "essentialising and ahistorical discourse to mask the fact that no group exists in a vacuum" (Shohat, 1991: 216). Boundaries of identity in the "real world" are permeable and not fixed or stable. However, mainstream Hollywood has tended to utilize particular ethnic stereotypes in order to make the boundaries between ethnic and white easily identifiable. The exclusive universes represented in gangster films focus on their difference from "ordinary society." For instance, as stated in Chapters

2 and 3, voice-overs are often employed, especially in Scorsese's films, to explain events. Distancing devices of voyeurism are employed in *Donnie Brasco* through the recurring use of long shots and freeze frames to suggest the images as examples of FBI surveillance. Lefty's fascination with nature programs on TV is also an important allegory for the film's presentation of the Mafia as a dangerous but endangered species. Just like the lion prides Lefty loves to watch, his own involvement in the Mafia is an exercise in the survival of the fittest. These devices emphasize the boundaries between the ethnic criminal identity and ordinary society. Furthermore, the fact that gangster films' characters are easily identifiable, even in films that are not recognized as part of the genre,[32] suggests that stereotyping is a major source of character identification.

The term "stereotype" is meant to convey a "standardized image" that operates in order to simplify recognition and thus reduce the necessity for complex narrative explanations of character traits and backgrounds. However, it is a problematic term due to its role in helping to essentialize particular groups within Western culture. It is most often seen as "a stable and repetitive structure of character traits" (Neale, 1979: 33), but as Richard Dyer has noted, it suffers from negative connotations and is "today almost always a term of abuse" (Dyer, 1993: 11). With regard to Hollywood cinema it is important to note, as Neale states,

> Within any one text, or within any one corpus of texts, a character or character type always assumes its identity and its meaning insofar as it is distinguishable from other characters and other character types. It assumes its identity and meaning insofar as the differences are marked — textually — as pertinent ones [Neale: 36].

This corresponds to Shohat's assertion that Hollywood cinema essentializes existence, in that a character type, such as the Indian warrior, assumes an identity in relation to the white settlers that inevitably occupy the same narrative.[33] As all Hollywood Westerns employ Eurocentric discourse, the Indian warrior is forced into the position of enigmatic or aggressive "Other." This extends to the black "mammy," or Uncle Tom figures that often occupy the rhetorical position of passive conscience in the case of Hollywood films. Italians Richard Gambino (1978), Joseph Papaleo (1978) Laurence Friedman (1991) and George De Stefano (2006) have noted how the Italian stereotype involves mainly waiters, barbers and laborers as well as gangsters. Character traits are "composed of overreactions: after bowing, smiling and being funny, the Italian loses control" (Papaleo: 93). Stereotypes are useful narrative aids, but they reduce the complexity and heterogeneity of culture. Bhabha (1983) maintains that colonial discourse is dependent on "the concept of 'fixity' in the ideological construction of otherness" (Bhabha: 18). Characters such as

Tommy DeVito, Nicky Santoro (Joe Pesci, in *Goodfellas* and *Casino*) or Paulie (*The Sopranos*) are Italian stereotypes in that they perpetuate the myth of overreaction. They can also be positioned within a construction of "Otherness" in that their behavior is excessive to the point of psychotic caricature and thus can be identified as 'abnormal.' However, the stereotype is "a form of knowledge and identification that vacillates between what is always 'in place,' already known, and something that must be anxiously repeated" (*ibid.*). As such, stereotyping is a process of ambivalence, whereby the stereotype's characteristics are simultaneously known and yet still to be fixed, proof and yet unproved.[34] Tommy and Nicky are not the only stereotype of Italian American gangsters, and they are identified as abnormal within the context of Mafia life. Even though the Italian stereotype of "overreaction" can be located within gangster narratives, it can be disproved by other gangster characters and so the stereotype is both anxiously repeated and also revealed to not be the whole of the Italian American male identity. This helps to explain why ethnicity is such a contentious area in Hollywood cinema and why the gangster film can operate as both a white male fantasy and a distancing device. As Gina Marchetti states, Hollywood is a contradictory force in that "it is based on the melting pot ideal, but tries to cater for different cultures in order to retain a mass market" (Marchetti, 1991: 278). Hollywood wishes to minimize racial difference, yet continuously draws attention to it through its (Eurocentric) narratives.

Neale states that a stereotype "assumes its identity and meaning insofar as the differences are marked — textually — as pertinent ones" (Neale: 36). For instance, the character of Rocco (Edward G. Robinson) in *Little Caesar* is different because of his dialogue, accent, gestures and costume. These are marked textually through an exaggerated emphasis upon his manner. He is clumsy, rude, arrogant and gaudy, thus drawing attention to his inability to assume his desired role as a "swell." Both Tommy Powers (James Cagney in *Public Enemy*) and Tony Camonte (Paul Muni in *Scarface*) also retain their aggressive manners in "polite" society, which also sets them apart as different, no matter how financially successful they become. Consequently, the development of gangster stereotypes at this stage includes references to class or immigrant status. Criminal activities aside, all these characters are marked as different from ordinary society through their inability to assume the dress, accent and manners culturally associated with politeness. Warshow's description of the gangster as "without culture, without manners" (Warshow, 1954: 453) is a reference to this stereotype, but his assertion that society encourages "individual aggression — personal enterprise and violence" to a limited extent and that the gangster's flaw is founded in the fact that "he fails to recognize these limits" (*ibid.*: 508) only delivers part of the reasoning.

The limits that the gangster fails to realize are also bound by racism. The gangster fails to recognize his immigrant status and thus his inability to assume a position of status in American society of that time. The differences marked by texts of this era provide gangster stereotypes based on loud-mouthed, aggressive immigrants, who refuse to remain in the ghettoes but roam across invisible boundaries into polite society and thus become a threat. This is pertinent to my discussion, because gangster stereotypes from the classical era influence the postclassical era, but the ethnic identity of postclassical gangsters is more distinct. Before I proceed it is also necessary to remember that, as Dyer (1993) notes, stereotypes are not simple substitutes, but depend upon a receiver's cultural associations of the images or phrases. Therefore, the reference "gangster" may conjure images of tommy guns, fedora hats and spats if the receiver's main reference point is the classical era. However, it may conjure images of silk suits, darkened rooms, or clubs and groups of men discussing business if the receiver's reference point is *The Godfather* or *Goodfellas*. In short, it is not the intention here to assume the cultural associations of gangster stereotypes, but to assert some of the reference points suggested by particular film texts.

* * *

The importance of stereotypes for this analysis is the way in which stereotypes "invoke a consensus" about the images, structure and activities of the Italian Mafia. Furthermore, stereotypes encourage a spontaneous collective agreement that these people are "like this." The inclusive and yet invisible "we" operates to ensure that recognition of the type unconsciously encourages us to believe in the "truth" and "simplicity" of stereotyping (Dyer). As discussed in Chapter 2, popular films such as *The Godfather* and *Goodfellas* provide a consensus on images of Mafia, which are then invoked in such films as *The Firm*, *Leon*, *True Romance* and *Bound*. In order to re-emphasize how this occurs, it is necessary first to outline the stereotypes utilized in *The Godfather* and *Goodfellas*. As stated earlier, a stereotype is a confirmation of difference: it is not a fully formed representation of an individual, but a homogenised reference or projection of a group.

Chapter 2 detailed the ways in which gesture, costume and dialogue operate as generic iconography and convention in gangster films. Both can be seen as another form of stereotyping, in that the repetition of similar images across texts works to project these images as "known," or the "truth" about gangsters. However, with this in mind, *The Godfather* is more original than *Goodfellas* in its conception of character, as its characters do not draw upon any easily identifiable gangster stereotypes, as discussed above. This is not to say that the film does not draw upon notions of Italian stereotyping.

It prioritizes the closeness of an extended family unit, and the importance of food and religion to their everyday life, but their Italian ethnicity is not marked within the text as different. The film offers an insight into an exclusive society, but not one that is marked as explicitly different or dangerous to mainstream society. Having said this, Kay occasionally operates as a mediator in that her presence as an outsider, a doubter, or a threat[35] operates as a reminder of difference and can encourage actions and events to be explained, or marked as unusual or dangerous. In *Part II* especially, Kay symbolizes Michael's loss of control concerning family matters. Her presence becomes a threat as she constantly doubts his actions and intentions and thus her involvement encourages audiences to judge him.[36] However, in general, Italian ethnicity is the defining element of the narrative rather than an oppositional one. In the few street scenes in which we see, for instance, Tom Hagen shopping, Michael and Kay shopping, or Vito buying fruit, the characters are not marked as different by their costume or manner. Therefore, the characters do not fit into the general assertion of stereotype. The one character who does display elements of the gangster stereotype is Sonny Corleone (James Caan) who is shown as aggressive and misguided in his loyalties. His one street scene involves the brutal beating of his brother-in-law, Carlo Rizzi (Giani Russo). Such practices are marked textually as different from those of the rest of the family. Their disapproval is shown through reprimands from his father, arguments with Tom Hagen and the increasing prominence of Michael as the central character of the *mise-en-scène*.[37] In short, Sonny's actions emphasize his role as stereotype against which the rest of the criminal family are shown as collective identities.

Goodfellas relies more upon stereotypes, mainly because the narrator marks the Mafia out as different from mainstream society. The term "wise guys" is used to assert the difference between those involved in organized crime and the "schmucks" who have to wait in line for second-rate service. Thus the text marks such differences as pertinent through the fact that the story is mediated; the Mafia is a projection of a group, from Henry's point of view. It is an exclusive society, in similar ways to *The Godfather*, but the characters' exclusivity is differentiated through their gestures, dialogue and manners.[38] As stated before, Henry's mother identifies the gangster imagery immediately in his new suit. Furthermore, they assert their dominance over ordinary citizens by taking the best seats in a club and intimidating businessmen. On a date with Karen, Henry does not know how to behave at a health club and is rude to Karen's friends. These characterizations make this film similar to the classical examples noted earlier. None are given the fully formed character of an individual, as they are all introduced and mediated through Henry's eyes. In consequence, Pauly is an image of a Mafia boss, which relies on an audience's cultural references to decide whether he is a good or a bad character. His quiet authority and loyalty to tradition suggests him as similar to Vito Corleone, but his coldness towards Henry later suggests the older Michael Corleone, or the corporate impersonality suggested in syndicate movies. Tommy DeVito reflects the psychotic aggressiveness of the gangster stereotype, from Rocco, Tommy Powers and Tony Camonte through Cody Jarrett (James Cagney in *White Heat*), Vince Stone (Lee Marvin in *The Big Heat*), Sonny Corleone and many more. *Goodfellas* combines stereotypes from the classical and postclassical era, and it does not de-mythologize such forms.

Stereotypes are used in later films without the need for explicit explanation. Audiences are encouraged to identify their role and strength mainly through the identification of ethnicity. Papaleo notes that, in contrast to other psychotics whose motivation will be investigated, the Italian Mafia killer "kills because he is Italian [...] He is not insane [but] his lack of self control comes from him being Italian" (93–94). Such stereotyping confirms the view argued in Chapters 2 and 3 that the Italian Mafia ideal has gradually developed over the twentieth century to the extent that Italian and Mafia identity have become inextricably combined. Some wear silk suits and always appear with at least two bodyguards (*State of Grace, True Romance, Bound*). Some are businessmen (*The Firm*). Others operate from their Italian restaurants (*King of New York, Leon*). Some are playboys with more money than sense (*In the Electric Mist*). Most importantly, their criminal activities, or role within the narrative, do not include explanation, because they do not require it. They are not only connected with Mafia activity through ethnicity and cultural associations, but they are seen as the pinnacle of Mafia authority. Thus other ethnicities, such as the Irish in *State of Grace* or Puerto Ricans in *Carlito's Way*, must defer to them. The most effective de-mythologization of this dominance appears in *Miller's Crossing* and *Last Man Standing*, where the authority of the Italian Mafia is shown to be based purely on their own megalomania.

Both of these films revert back to an individual hero who defeats the warring gangs or families mainly because of their vanity. Tom Reagan (Gabriel Byrne) is Irish, but has no loyalty to any crime family. The loyalties of the Italian, Jewish and Irish gangsters are shown to be false and their aggressions are based on paranoia rather than justifiable conflicts. Tom gradually becomes ensnared in their operations and brutal revenge tactics. When he is initially told to execute Bernie Bernbaum (John Turturro) in the forest, he cannot bear to do it, especially as Bernie pleads for his life. Later, Bernie comes back to taunt him for his lack of guts: "I know you won't shoot me, all I have to do is blub a bit and you'll let me go." At this point, Tom shoots him. Tom shoots him because Bernie is questioning his masculine identity, as well as his allegiance to Mafia ideals. Tom is a lone operator, something that is antithetical to the Mafia ethic of collective identity and hierarchy that has been shown in this book to dominate postclassical gangster films. Michael Sullivan (Tom Hanks) in *Road to Perdition* operates from a similar position. These characters are more akin to Western or *noir* heroes rather than gangsters. In essence, the films suggest Tom and Michael as saved from the corresponding paranoia suffered by gangsters. Similarly, the lone gunman (Bruce Willis) in *Last Man Standing* is not troubled by a Mafia conscience and mows down every last gangster in a spectacularly violent and depthless narrative. However, as a genre production, like *Miller's Crossing*, which attempts to unsettle the Mafia myth, it shows the extent to which stereotypes can alleviate a need for time-consuming contextual narratives.

Stereotyping is both a shortcut to character identification and a reaffirmation of popular beliefs concerning particular groups. For Italian American identity in gangster films, stereotyping is both a negative and a positive component. The negative aspects are that it firmly associates Italian identity with criminality, violence and out-moded patriarchal values. However, as noted in Chapter 3, it also suggests a strong sense of community, loyalty and honor within a modern ethnic identity unashamed to embrace its heritage, rather than sacrificing it to the American ideal of assimilation. Thus, Mafia stereotyping has given Italian American identity prominence in popular culture and a sense of status, which, as previously noted, Richard Gambino has termed "Mafia chic."

Fears and Emotional Instability

The flip-side to notions of Mafia chic is that the constant link between Italians and organized crime simply perpetuates an image of aggressive, male-orientated ethnicity that is obsessed with honor and revenge. The notion that violence and criminality are linked directly to portrayals of Italian ethnic identity or cultural heritage has been continually debated throughout this book. The discussion will now move to consider the extent to which ethnic and masculine identity combine violence and criminality in the later films of the chosen period to express fears and emotional instability. It has already been noted how Sonny Corleone and Tommy DeVito are shown to represent the excessive nature of gangster behavior. Their lack of control brings about their own downfall and they are both described within the context of their actions as "bad gangsters." However, later films show an increasing interest in the ways violence and criminality, as articulations of masculinity and ethnicity, bring about particular displays of emotional distress in gangster characters.

Loyalty and family are important themes within postclassical gangster films. In fact, Tillman[39] lists these elements as seductions into the romance of the Mafia. However, the discussion will now proceed to consider some of the alternative aspects of this seduction. It will concentrate on how violence both maintains and corrupts masculine and ethnic identities within the Mafia.

* * *

It is noted that in an exclusively male environment physical and emotional strength are valuable traits (Jeffords, Faludi): "In cultures of masculinity, the demonstrated willingness to fight and the capacity for combat are measures of worth and self-worth" (Toch, 1998: 170). Violence within the Mafia is both a demonstration of masculine prowess and also a display of loyalty. For these reasons violence is highly regarded and prevalent in gangster films. However, such associations of loyalty with violence suggest that fear is as much part of notions of male collectivity as trust. As discussed earlier, hierarchies within the Mafia are built upon the contradictory impulses of fear and trust. In addition to this, violence is shown as a corruption of masculinity in many postclassical films. The primary example would be *The Funeral*, where Mafia tradition is portrayed as a heritage of violence and insanity; but *The Godfather Part III* also questions the Mafia traditions upheld by Vito Corleone, as Michael laments the loss of family and personal esteem. His heartbreaking confession to Cardinal Lamberto (Raf Vallone) of his sins, including fratricide, is the clearest example of how the rigid traditions of loyalty and revenge, which made Vito a hero, have gradually eroded Michael's emotional strength. Rather than this being an example of Michael's inability to rule, this display of excessive emotion suggests the extent to which a life devoted to the Mafia can damage even the strongest masculine identity. Michael's distress can be associated with the complex struggle within an individual between acceptable and excessive masculine traits, or between an outmoded and newer (post-feminist) masculinity.

* * *

The Funeral sees the Tempio brothers, Ray (Christopher Walken) and Chez (Chris Penn) mourning the murder of their brother, Johnny (Vincent Gallo). The *Sunday Times* suggested it as a standard plot with "the burden of Catholic guilt" (April 20, 1997). This links the narrative, which centers on the surviving brothers' neuroses, with Michael's guilt in *The Godfather Part III*. However, the narrative is much more about the sins of the father as displayed in the sons. It is made explicit that Chez's mental instability is inherited from his father who, it is hinted, committed suicide. Furthermore, Ray's propensity for violence is explained as a result of early training. A flashback reveals his father compelling a twelve-year-old Ray to murder an enemy of the family. "If he leaves here alive he will eventually return to kill, because he'll be driven by the fear that one day we'll change our minds," his father (Gian Di Donna) explains. "Either you do it, or we set him free and you can wait for him to return." Catholic guilt makes its appearance in the fact that the adult Ray believes the first murder condemned his soul to eternal damnation. Therefore, within Ray's particular belief system, any more killings can't make things worse. His notion of masculine identity is shown to be taught as much as inherited, and focuses on the necessity for violence as a mode of survival. This links with some sociological examinations of masculinity and violence that suggest that historically, in the context of war but also in the context of the male role as protector, those who "show themselves incapable of physical retaliation when the occasion calls for it [..] justify victimisation" (Toch: 170). Suzanne Hatty (2000) also notes, "The use of force and violence is viewed as one of the instruments of power and as one of the modes of [masculine] behavior by which hierarchy is perpetuated in society" (181). In this context, Ray is taught to either be a perpetrator or a victim; there is no other option for a man. However, this type of masculinity is firmly associated with Mafia identity. Revenge is a primary motivator for Mafia violence. A Mafioso has no choice but to direct proportional violence against any person who threatens his family. Therefore, Ray's emotional inheritance, like Michael Corleone's, can be seen as a specifically ethnic as well as a masculine identity.

Ray's father's teachings focused on fear as the antithesis of masculinity: "The faster he conquers fear, the faster he becomes a man." Both Ray and Chez caress their dead brother, suggesting not only their closeness, but also their lack of fear or even their affinity with death. No other characters venture so close to the body. In fact, Gaspare Spoglia (Benicio Del Toro), the suspected killer, displays his only moment of fear when made to enter the room where the body lies. This is partly due to the superstition, as stated in Chapter 3, that the dead man's wounds will bleed if the killer enters the room, but it also emphasizes the brothers' ease around death. They mourn the loss of their brother, but death is very much part of their lives: for Ray it is murder and for Chez it is suicide. At one point Ray calmly debates the need for revenge with Johnny's killer and Chez is shown contemplating an open razor while in the bath. The narrative shows that it is not the revenge for Johnny's death nor simply Mafia rivalry that causes the family's downfall. These elements are undermined by the revelation that the killer was in fact a young man, humiliated in front of his girlfriend by Johnny. In essence, the motivation for Johnny's murder reflects the film's primary theme, masculinity as the perpetrator or victim of violence. Johnny beat the young man in front of his girlfriend, thus undermining his masculinity. The young man's only option is to avenge that act, also in front of his girlfriend, in order to resurrect his self-esteem. Initially, the young man states that Johnny raped his girlfriend and Ray appears to accept Johnny's death as justifiable revenge. However, when the real motivation is revealed Ray is relieved, not only because it restores his brother's reputation, but because he now knows that the young man is operating within the same construction of masculinity as Ray and understands the motivations of revenge. At this instant Ray and the young man fully understand each other, even if this understanding also includes recognition of the stupidity or destructiveness of such masculine traits.

Carlito's Way displays a similar recognition of the role of violence in the construction of masculinity. Carlito Brigante has proved his masculinity and is the hero of the neighborhood. However, this has provided him with a reputation that he has to uphold if he is to survive long enough to earn the money to escape. His decision not to kill the young usurper, Benny Blanco (John Leguizamo) is not only a narrative convention that sets up his own demise, but also reflects a similar theme to that displayed in *The Funeral*. Carlito chooses to let the young man go free, and thus generic conventions encourage audiences to wait for him to return. It is inevitable that the young man must prove his masculinity through violence, as Carlito has humiliated him in front of his friends. This Darwinian world, which Mitchell describes as a generic convention of gangster films, is also a generic convention of popular concepts of masculine identity, in that it is masculine character at its basic Darwinian survival of the fittest level: kill or be killed. However, as already stated with regard to *Donnie Brasco*, sympathy for a character raises the narrative above simple Darwinian drives. Carlito is a sympathetic character, in that he shows a capability for violence when necessary, but also displays an awareness of the limitations and destructiveness of violence. He yearns to escape from the arena that demands such behavior, but is still able to accept the Darwinian codes of revenge, such as when he discovers Kleinfeld's (Sean Penn) disloyalty and consequently abandons him to a violent end. Carlito's story adheres to genre conventions in that his own demise is both inevitable and linked to a specific choice. However, he is an unusually sympathetic gangster hero because his downfall is isolated to a momentary weakness (which may be perceived as strength in another cultural context). He chooses not to act as the perpetrator of violence against Benny Blanco and so, within the context of Mafia myths and generic conventions, he inevitably becomes the victim.

As a comedy, *Analyze This* draws upon many gangster stereotypes in order to invert them. Paul Vitti (Robert De Niro) is suffering under the pressure of being the Mafia boss. It is revealed that he was accompanying the old boss when he was murdered. This factor has two possible implications within the narrative: either he was traumatized by witnessing the murder, or he fears the beliefs of his rivals, who suggest he may have been involved in the crime.

Both motivations justify his emotional insecurity, but they say very different things about his masculine and ethnic identity. The first is a weakness, in that it suggests him as expressing his role as a possible victim rather than perpetrator of violence, and as denying the revenge impulse of his cultural heritage. The second is simply part of Mafia business and justifies his insecurity as part of an ever-shifting hierarchy.

* * *

The comedy stems from the fact that Vitti attends therapy sessions as a result of the very activities and characteristics Mafia myths and generic conventions have suggested as inherent within Italian Mafia identity. Initially, it is suggested that Vitti is attempting to regain these stereotypical and masculine traits, but it is later revealed that the very behavior he has lost is the reason behind his problems in the first place. Thus, Vitti is questioning both his masculine and his ethnic identity. The pressure of always having to kill people, make decisions and act tough, in essence to perform gangster identity, has brought about his illness. In this sense, *Analyze This* is a clear of example of identity as performance. However, the film's attitude towards ethnic identity is contradictory, in that audiences are encouraged to laugh at Vitti, the Italian American gangster, and his excessive emotions, while simultaneously engaging with the Jewish Doctor's opportunities for performing a gangster identity in his place. This makes the structure of *Analyze This* similar to that of *Goodfellas*, where Henry Hill is allowed to perform a gangster identity at the expense of others. The final scenes of *Analyze This* show Dr. Ben Sobel (Billy Crystal) attending a sit-down in Vitti's place and acting out a medley of conventional phrases and gestures from gangster cinema history. In this sense, the film becomes a prime example of the interaction between genre conventions and Mafia myths. Sobel is shown to have more courage and self control than Vitti, who fails to control any emotion throughout. Thus, the film is perpetuating a specifically Italian gangster stereotype, while allowing an ordinary schmuck to perform a gangster identity, which necessarily includes the performance of aggressive masculinity. This film then operates as an antidote to such Mafia angst as is found in *The Funeral*, but also acts as a backlash against the Italian Mafia ideal. It does not show the Mafia ideal itself as oppressive, so much as the Italian character's inability to control his excessively emotional personality.

Depression and anxiety are central to the development of Tony's character in *The Sopranos*. While most therapy sessions attempt to explore the various aspects of these illnesses, it is best summarized in Tony and Carmela's argument in Season Six (Part II, Episode 7). Tony calls his depression a hereditary illness and thus echoes the Tempio brothers' (*The Funeral*) association of organized crime and mental instability as irrevocably entwined. Carmela, in contrast, responds that she is "intimately aware of the Soprano curse" and calls it "bullshit." What she may be arguing against here is the central argument of hereditary personality. Just like the wives in *The Funeral*, she refuses to accept organized crime or the associated character traits that inform Mafia identity as hereditary. She is challenging Tony to accept personal responsibility for the choices he has and continues to make. She is possibly representative, not only of mainstream America womanhood who are tired of masculine excuses for bad behavior, but also Italian American identity that is tired of the suggestion that somehow Mafia is an indelible part of their ethnic identity.

In summary, although later films attempt to address the fears and emotional instabilities associated with criminal activity and masculine and ethnic heritage, they also address the inadequacies of the masculine ideal and displace them onto a specific ethnicity and cultural heritage. *Analyze This* and *The Sopranos* do not successfully de-mythologize the Mafia, because the myths and conventions are too widely applauded in American society. However, emotional distress and/or insanity are often traced back through the oppressive idealization of masculine heroes, or an attempt to align criminal behavior specifically to Italian cultural heritage.

Male Melodrama

The discussion will now move away from the extremes of insanity or the scapegoating of ethnic character to the ways postclassical gangster films reflect issues of masculine identity as a whole. Masculine identities, as filtered through notions of collectivity, are bound by definition to be sites of conflict. Notions of individual masculine identity, as detailed earlier, identify aggression as a primary element. Therefore, masculine hierarchies, which insist on a certain amount of humility as well as assertion, are bound to cause conflict within and between individuals. Such conflicts make postclassical gangster films operate as male melodramas[40] in that they represent sanctuaries for the male psyche, away from feminine influence, and as such are narratives that deal with emotional relationships between men. In consequence, this space allows individuals to articulate a wider variety of gender characteristics.

Julian Stringer's (1997) work on Hong Kong action films[41] explores traits of anxiety in the modern gangster. His analysis focuses on the extent to which Hong Kong cultural experience just prior to the hand-over to China (1997) encourages anxieties in the main protagonist's character. The subject matter and settings of the films make this appropriate, but they also portray the gangster in the classic form: as a lone figure, not part of an organization.[42]

Stringer's analysis is useful for me in that he links the gangster more closely with the emotional complexities associated with melodrama by focusing on the character's emotional as well as physical disintegration. Drawing on Geoffrey Nowell Smith's analysis of American genres in terms of a distinction between male (active) genres and female (suffering) genres, Stringer's article suggests that the Hong Kong gangster film straddles both. Even though this is not a new approach to the crime film, especially since the noir films of the 1940s and beyond, it does rekindle the notion that the hero is a site of complex identification that is not always stable or sure. This approach is appropriate to the American postclassical gangster film, in that the emphasis on the crime family, rather than the powerful individual, gives rise to a more contradictory discourse of power and authority — to use Stringer's terms, one that is based both on active agency and masochism.

Contradictory discourses of active agency and masochism are articulated in various ways within postclassical gangster films, but a significant example of how this melodramatic form can articulate Mafia identity is found in *Donnie Brasco*. The hierarchical structure of the crime family in this film results in a complex construction of the individual masculine image that contains varying levels of power[43] and subjugation, courage and fear. This emphasis on family hierarchies relies on compromise and a sense of status that includes inferiority as well as superiority. Hierarchical structures are living entities in that they are constructed through the interrelationship of many individuals. An individual identity is thus subsumed by the identity of the collective, as stated earlier in the discussions of the collective ideal, but it is necessary to reassert that this submersion is not a passive process, but an active one. For instance, Michael Corleone's transformation occurs as an act of allegiance to his family and the collective Mafia identity therein.

As the process is an active one, a collective is not a stable structure, but a structure in constant flux. Therefore, a gangster operating within such a structure cannot be said to embody a fixed and stable notion of self-identity, as that identity is formed as a result of continual negotiation between the individual and the hierarchy.[44] Each operates in relation to the others, in a constant oscillation between the self and the collective. This is a useful explanation for why disruptions in the hierarchy are often at the heart of a film's narrative. For if identity is formed as a result of an ongoing process of negotiation, it is evident that identities are likely to shift in nature and cause changes to occur in the hierarchy. In *Donnie Brasco*, the murder of the boss leads to Sonny Black's promotion, which later leads to his murder of Sonny Red, which then makes Black an underboss. Shifts such as this are a result of particular individuals whose sense of identity leads them to believe that they are superior to the boss. In the terminology employed by the narrative, they no longer have *respect* for their boss. Again, this links these notions of hierarchy to the earlier discussion of collective identity. It was suggested that the submersion of individuality was at the heart of a collective ideal and forms the basis for a family's display of unity and strength. However, it is apparent that within that collective there will be the constant reassessment of individual identities against the collective, and this is achieved through notions of hierarchy. If individuals identify themselves within the hierarchy as it stands, then a shift will not occur, but if they change their perspective then disruption in some form is inevitable. The intricacies of hierarchy are a primary concern to many gangster films. An oft-repeated convention in gangster narratives is to signal the prospect of a family's destruction through examples of in-fighting, such as overzealous competition or the perceived loss of *respect* within the hierarchy. Even without these major disruptions the hierarchy in the Mafia collective is constantly reasserting itself by issuing orders, threats and the payment of tributes and respect.

For instance, an early portion of *Goodfellas* is devoted to explaining the hierarchy of the Mafia group. Henry, Tommy and Jimmy pay tributes (a percentage of their profits) to Pauly Cicero for the continued protection of the Mafia. This aspect of business is further explained in the opening scenes of *Casino*. The intricacies of casino business are shown to be primarily targeted towards paying the absent but controlling Mafia bosses a large percentage of the profits. Meetings between bosses in the *Godfather* trilogy, *Gotti* and *Casino* often focus on issuing orders for implementation by lower echelons of the hierarchy. The structure of buffers is most notably explained in the Senate Committee scenes in *The Godfather Part II*, wherein the investigators assert that Michael's orders are filtered through an intricate network of intermediaries before reaching the actual individual who implements them.

In *Donnie Brasco* the character of Lefty (Al Pacino) is employed as a narrative device to explain some of the rules of the crime family to audiences, through his explanations to Donnie (Johnny Depp). Lefty explains how Donnie is to be introduced, who the various family members are and where they fit in the hierarchy. However, these explanations do more than simply set the scene. They display Lefty's identity in relation to the hierarchy, as it oscillates between active agency and passive masochism. He has power and can be threatening. In fact, Lefty displays the contradictory forces of active agency and masochism, explained by Stringer, in the clearest sense. This is evident in the scene where he and Donnie first meet. Lefty gets angry at Donnie's apparent lack of *respect*. He explains that he is 'known' in the neighbourhood, meaning that he embodies an authority, one that Donnie would be wise to acknowledge. When Donnie tries to leave, Lefty tells him, "You don't leave, I tell you when you can leave." Lefty controls this scene and is thus identified as the active agent, a site of power and authority in relation to Donnie.[45]

The scene, which is primarily a verbal exchange, relies on the implication of violence rather than a specific threat. Audiences already know Donnie to be an undercover agent. Therefore, Lefty's character is based on Donnie's antibook, the object of the FBI's hunt. Lefty has not been introduced in any depth and has yet to display any violence. His threatening behavior in this initial scene carries depth only to the extent of audiences' cultural knowledge of the gangster. The threat is evident in his words "known" and "respect," plus the Italian American trademark shrug as a non-verbal but recognizable gesture of confidence.[46] However, the extent to which those words and gestures articulate the real danger to Donnie may also depend on the level to which audiences are aware of gangster narratives and/or Pacino's previous gangster roles. Pacino's star persona, as discussed in Chapter 2, is an extra-textual influence, in that it does not stem from the text itself. However, if audiences are aware of previous roles — e.g. Michael Corleone (*Godfather*), or Tony Camonte (*Scarface*) — then the line "I am known" has a deeper significance and the threat of violence is conjured from previous displays. It is almost impossible to extricate this influence from the text once it is known. Pacino's career has been built on gangster roles and therefore each character is bound to induce echoes of others. These influences become less important (although they always remain) as the narrative progresses and Lefty is developed as a specific character.

In a subsequent scene, almost directly after this initial meeting with Donnie, Lefty's power is undermined by his peers and bosses and begins to subdue the extratextual knowledge concerning Pacino's persona in favor of Lefty's particular experiences. Lefty takes Donnie along to meet Sonny Black. He explains that he is taking responsibility for Donnie's behavior by introducing him as a "friend of mine." While Lefty's peers virtually ignore Donnie's presence, their immediate boss, Sonny Red, verbally belittles Lefty with a threat concerning recent conduct. Lefty tries to deny the threat, after Sonny passes, but it is too late; his low status in the crime family has already been observed. Again, in comparison to the previous scenes and Pacino's previous roles, the pathos of Lefty's humiliation, albeit in a brief scene, undermines his authority. He is not a powerful individual, but simply a "spoke in a wheel" (an analogy he later uses himself). Lefty's persona has been literally contextualized against the truly powerful authority of the hierarchy.

When Edward Mitchell[47] suggested that gangster films were a display of social Darwinism, he observed an individual's rise and success that was then violently stolen by another. *Donnie Brasco*, along with many other postclassical gangster films, shows that the gangster's success is always relative in the first place. The criminal world is much larger than a single individual's reach and there is always someone who is more powerful. Furthermore, success and failure are concurrent themes throughout the narrative, rather than consequential (as suggested by a rise-and-fall narrative); success can be undermined by a look, or an order from the hierarchy. Lefty, along with Jimmy Conway (*Goodfellas*), Ace Rothstein (*Casino*), and even Michael Corleone (*Godfather*), operates in a specifically Italian American Mafia hierarchy that always appears as greater than any one individual, or any one film for that matter. As Tommy DeVito (*Goodfellas*) explains, "You know what the rules are, if you step outta line, you get whacked — no questions asked." A hierarchy based on continual aggression could not have survived as long as the Italian Mafia appears to have done (based on even cinema history alone). There has to be a consensus, whereby most of the time the threat of aggression serves only to emphasize the combined power and strength of the group to outsiders. Therefore, if the hierarchy is in a constant state of flux, the construction of an individual's identity is bound to reflect this as well.

The Sopranos draws on this notion of hierarchy to place Tony in his organization in a similar way to an average successful mainstream business man. His success is relative to a complex web of external factors most of which constantly avoid his control by evolving into new threats and new ventures. Some reviewers of the TV series suggest Tony's stress-related symptoms are a reflection of the modern American male experience. While not aligning himself with Tony's criminal activities, Allan Johnson and Bob Condor (*Chicago Tribune*, September 15, 2002) sympathize with Tony's irritability in the home. When Tony blows up at Carmela for interrupting his TV viewing, Johnson and Condor note this anger as a justifiable response in the context that Tony as a stressed, overworked male sitting down "on the sofa to watch a Wild West Musical, only to be promptly interrupted by his spare-no-makeup wife" is identifiable as the harassed husband; "Admit it or not, most of us feel the same way about our lives some nights (even most nights)." This view is echoed in part by Tom Shales, who characterizes Tony as "so much, the guy next door [whose] big goal in life is to be left alone" (*Washington Post* September 15, 2002). Through the convergence of Mafia activity and domestic melodrama, Tony Soprano as both gangster stereotype and guy next door reflects the Mafia experience as a white male fantasy: like us, yet not like us.

Internet forums consider the contradiction of "like us, yet not like us" in many discussion threads. Sopranos.com features two threads, "Do you like Tony?" and "Maybe Tony wasn't so bad after all." The discussion is varied. Many people find him despicable and greedy. However, a recurring view (featured on sopranoland.com too) suggests such views as, "Tony was someone I could vicariously live through. He said and did things that most of us, deep down, wanted to but couldn't" (Rollatomazi). A discussion on imdb.com asks "What makes gangster movies so good?" Chrisasiama suggests, "I wonder if it's because the characters in gangster films operate above the laws that most normal people in real life have to obey." There is no doubt that a great deal of enjoyment appears to come from watching men behave badly. A discussion thread on sopranos.com titled "Ralph" laments his demise: "He was a great character it's a shame he got killed" (posted by the riddler). This was qualified by the comment "He was one of those guys you love to hate" (posted by ScottC). It is evident that, while audiences do not condone the violence, racism, misogyny and homophobia on screen, they do enjoy watching it occur. An angry interaction on sopranos.com began on a thread titled "Which of these 3 broads would you give a beating?" The choices were "Tony's sister, Tony's daughter, or the Chef's wife (the one with the tits).' Most posters stated they were uninterested in the topic, to which the original poster replied, "Why are you watching the show if you disagree with women getting a beating once in a while?" (posted by Frankie Carbone). Again, as with the discussions on homosexuality, this altercation highlights the contradictions of watching a show that features exploitative sexual practice and graphic violence, while also actively distancing oneself from condoning such practices. It is important to many fans that they draw the line between liking such narratives on screen while distancing them selves from it in real life. In response to "What makes gangster movies so good?" a person responds, "The people portrayed are meant to be low and despicable, yet they're not too dissimilar to us law abiders. Also, for me they're objects of interest not role models" (posted by eight days). This is similar to an article posted on mafiaflix.com that states that secretly, "We'd like to punch out those in authority [..] if we knew we wouldn't get caught would we act out our darkest emotions?" As such, characters like Tony Soprano are the everyman insofar as they are the repository of society's deepest and darkest desires. However, at the same time they can be presented as quite ordinary through their revelations of personal fears and weaknesses.

* * *

Films that show the fragility of masculine power through the intricacies of hierarchy encourage sympathies from audiences. Lefty is a sympathetic character because he is simultaneously aggressive yet pathetic. Michael Corleone is also a sympathetic character throughout the *Godfather* trilogy. This is because his transformation into a Mafia Don not only endows him with power and status, but also makes him vulnerable, as it places him within a hierarchy that is constantly in flux. The Mafia, as an organized network of criminals, is ever-changing, dangerous and impossible for one individual to control. Audiences can sympathize with Michael's realization in *Part II* that his father's omnipotence was an illusion, a display of power to ward off enemies or usurpers, but also combined with a respect for his peers. Michael discovers through his negotiations with Hyman Roth (Lee Strasbourg) that a Don cannot operate alone and that he is always vulnerable. As stated earlier, that motivation for Mafia members is based on a collective rather than individual ambition. The security of the Mafia as an organized criminal network is as important as an individual's success within it; the individual and the collective need to interact in order to survive.

Sympathy for Michael in *The Godfather Parts II* and *III* is directed through Connie, who returns to the ideals of the family because it is suggested that she realizes Michael's actions are guided by a desire to protect the family. She states, "I know now you are just being strong for the family, like Papa." The protection of the collective is encouraged as more important than individual actions or desires. Thus, Mafia membership represents as much a sacrifice as an assertion of ambition. This in turn reflects notions of masculinity anxiety in that it suggests masculine as a site of flux, no longer able to define itself within a fixed, stable set of ideals. The only way for masculinity to be asserted as a positive strength is through a coherent collective. The male community of the Mafia can project its power through asserting its unity and shared goals. This allows for the more aggressive masculine traits to be dispersed throughout the collective, rather than pinpointed within an individual identity, but also allows aggression to be displayed as a necessary function of survival. Lefty is a primary example of this notion, in that his identity is constructed within a hierarchy and is thus ever-shifting. He is capable of brutality, but this aspect of his gender personality is diffused by the equal presence of a more passive and suffering character. Connie's actions in *The Godfather Part III* foreground the need for unity, which at times requires an individual not only to deny his or her own ambitions, but also to ignore the actions of others. Her continual assertion that Fredo drowned, rather than died at the hands of his brother, Michael, is a denial of the brutal reality behind the collective ideal of family unity. Similarly, in *Goodfellas* and *Casino* bosses maintain that disrespect is bad for business, in that it lets your enemies know that your family is not unified. In interviews, Scorsese[48] suggests that this unmasks the callous, self-serving nature of the Mafia, but in my view it also offers another example of how unity, as the culmination of a coherent collective identity, is the only chance for a family's survival. Furthermore, unity is shown to be extremely tenuous as it relies on individual sacrifice, a trait that is in opposition to the American ideals of individual enterprise. This contradiction is the flaw behind many of the gangster narratives discussed in this book. Unity may demand the submersion of individual identity for the good of the collective, but in the Darwinian world of postclassical Mafia identity—united they stand, divided they fall.

Fathers

It is important to remember once again that this book is not attempting to isolate a single unifying theme within postclassical gangster films. So far, discussions have concentrated on the Italian American Mafia in postclassical cinema and its articulations of a particular type of collective masculine identity. However, it is also necessary to address the significance of those postclassical films that focus on the lone gangster. Munby has quite rightly suggested that such films emulate the classical narratives, but they also correspond to notions of collectivity and are influenced by the Mafia myths and genre conventions identified throughout this book.

Having asserted the belief that postclassical gangster films tend to prioritize the community, rather than individual gangsters, it is necessary to explain how some of the films that have isolated characters fit into this rubric. For this, the discussion will concentrate mainly on *Scarface* and *New Jack City*. These two films employ central protagonists who assert their masculine identity in aggressive and exaggerated ways. Tony Montana (*Scarface*) witnesses and employs violence without remorse, and his language is peppered with constant expletives. Nino Brown (*New Jack City*) exaggerates his body shape through the clothing he wears, and his movements and gestures are sexualized. Thus the films offer two different displays of powerful masculinity. They are primarily influenced by race, but also by inter-textual references to classical and postclassical gangster films. Firstly, Tony Montana is a Cuban gangster, but the character is played by Al Pacino, who at this point was best known for his roles in *The Godfather* and *The Godfather Part II*. Reviewers make links between the films, as shown in previous chapters. Tony is viewed as "a physically bloated Pacino supplanting his spiritually blank self" (*Monthly Film Bulletin*, 1984), while the film is "a coarsened proletarian remake" of *The Godfather* (*ibid.*). Another reviewer suggests that it is "a fascinating operation of drip feeding movie history intravenously into social history" (*Standard*, February 2, 1984).[49] These inter-textual references are created by reviewers, as much as encouraged within the text itself, but these references position Tony Montana's identity within a hierarchy of Hollywood gangsters, especially *The Godfather*, because of Al Pacino's star persona. Inter-textual references are further encouraged by suggestions that Tony Montana is an exaggerated caricature whose actions, as one reviewer notes, are "so numbing and brash that it turns to pastiche" (*Scotsman*, February 4, 1984).[50] Reviewers appear to have difficulties explaining Montana's actions as an individual. It is easier to compare him to previous examples of gangster identity.

Asserting postclassical Mafia narratives as collective identities articulated across many texts suggests that Tony Montana is an offspring of previous narratives. It has already been noted in the discussions of continuous narrative in earlier chapters that the Cuban storyline in *The Godfather Part II* ends at the moment of the Cuban revolution. This coincides with the year of Montana's birth. As such, it could be suggested that he is the offspring of the Corleone activities in Cuba. More importantly, he operates as a man without a sense of cultural identity, but with a perverted sense of family. This is mainly due to the re-working of Ben Hecht's original screenplay, but it also draws attention to itself as an exaggerated parody of the lone gangster. Montana does not belong to an ethnic community, such as the Italian, that can teach him the effective ways of organized crime. He has no father figure to guide him, but he also has no uncles or brothers. This is brought to the foreground when he kills his brother-substitute, Manny. The narrative suggests that Montana kills him because of an over-protective attachment to his sister, with whom Manny has had an affair. However, the murder also shows a severe miscarriage of loyalties by Montana, in that the Mafia group is one where relationships between men take precedence over heterosexual alliances. Montana's greatest weakness is the fact that he operates alone, without the security of a wider organized network. His willingness to kill all other males (most notably his boss, which enables him to possess Elvira) reveals his Darwinian nature and aligns his character with those of the classical era. In terms of identity, Montana lacks the cultural heritage or father figure to guide him towards the benefits of collectivity.

Nino Brown is African American. As such, his tendency for sexual display and a heightened awareness of his own physical beauty is reminiscent of African American male stereotyping. Nino is the leader of a small criminal group, so is not positioned within the wider hierarchy of organized crime. However, there is reference to an inter-textual, and also a cultural hierarchy. The inter-textual hierarchy is displayed on the huge television screen in Nino's office. Brian De Palma's *Scarface* is displayed directly behind Nino's semi-clad posturing, as Nino declares, "The world is mine." This inter-textual reference to De Palma's film not only declares Nino's ambition and hero worship, but also positions him within the history of Hollywood gangster films. The cultural hierarchy is displayed through the interconnection of gangster film history and ethnicity. *New Jack City* is an African American film, directed by an African American, but it displays its influences not as the blaxploitation gangster films, such as *Black Caesar* (1973), but the classic gangster figure. I am not concerned here with the politics of choosing white-ethnic gangsters rather than black gangsters as the film's reference points; what is important is that Nino's assertion of masculine identity is based on denying his black-identity and it is this factor that brings about his downfall.[51] The reference to *Scarface* has significance within the narrative, as it displays his misdirected idolatry. However, it also positions Nino's assertion of his own identity against a cultural history of gangsters. This not only signals Nino's doom through genre convention, but also signals his doom through racial inadequacy; his attempt at emulating the Mafia ideal is doomed to failure because of his skin color and because such a desire is disrespectful to his own cultural identity. The film emphasizes this in the final scenes. After being acquitted at trial Nino is gunned down by an elderly black man (Bill Cobb) who explains himself by claiming Nino as an enemy to the principles of black culture.

American Gangster replays the stereotypes, but in this case, it is Frank Lucas' display of blaxploitation-style behavior that brings about his downfall. When he wears his wife's fur coat to the boxing match he becomes the loudest person in the room visually. This display undermines all his previous control and business acumen by revealing him as the stereotypical black gangster unable to suppress the desire to flaunt his wealth in a gaudy and overt manner. The ease with which Richie Roberts (Russell Crowe) abuses Frank's vulnerability is testimony to the long history of using such stereotypes as representations of weakness and criminal stupidity. As such, Lucas' downfall is signalled through similar tropes of racial inadequacy as displayed in Nino Brown.

Racial inadequacy is not unique to these films, it has already been noted that Tony Montana suffers from an absence of father figures in his pursuit of the gangster dream, which could also be suggested as an absence of cultural heritage in that particular example of organized crime. Other examples include Frank White (*King of New York*) and Frankie Flannery (*State of Grace*). All of these gangsters operate outside of the Italian Mafia. As already noted in Chapter 3, the Italian Mafia is recognized in film as the ideal to which all others aspire, or wish to emulate. It would seem that an absence of cultural heritage, or an associated denial of one's own cultural identity, hastens the demise of these lone or "wannabe" gangsters. Nino Brown is shot dead by an older black man. The reasoning is that Nino represents a misguided direction for African American identity and thus is an inappropriate role model for black youths. Frank White runs a mixed-race organization, which angers his Italian rivals. So, when the law closes in on him, he lacks a secure network in which to hide. Similarly, Frankie Flannery desires acceptance from the Italian Mafia. Unfortunately, his desire for assimilation into the Italian heritage takes precedence over loyalty to his own family. The Mafia manipulate his anxieties so that he murders his own brother, thus signalling Frankie's and his family's downfall.

Carlito Brigante is less insecure in his ethnicity. However, he operates as a bad father, in that he refuses his responsibilities as an elder statesman. Firstly, he fails to protect his nephew during a drug deal. This is suggested to be a result of Carlito's reluctance to accept his role as gangster hero, his explanation being that he has retired now. The younger gangsters are therefore not sufficiently intimidated by his presence and slit his nephew's throat. It is only then that Carlito reverts to type, issuing threats to the terrified group while he pretends to reload an empty gun. This exaggerated display, which concentrates around a silhouetted Carlito (used as the main publicity image for the film) shouting, "Prepare to die!" allows Carlito to escape. The group are sufficiently convinced of his superiority to allow him to leave, even though he has no bullets. Secondly, he rejects his role as an elder statesman, or father figure, when the young Benny Blanco (John Leguizamo) insults him in the nightclub: "I know I should have him killed, as now he will have to return to kill me." Not only is this an allusion to generic convention, but it also underscores the Darwinian brutality beneath Mafia hierarchies and the conflict

Carlito Brigante (Al Pacino). *Carlito's Way* © 1993, Universal.

between individualism and collectivity. As Tommy states in *Goodfellas*, "You step outta line, you get whacked, no questions asked." Carlito ignores that rule, and thus declines his role as the father figure. Therefore it is inevitable that the same youth will bring about Carlito's downfall at the end of the narrative. The moral of this narrative convention is that no matter how much you may lament your role in the hierarch, your survival is based on the maintenance of such; this refers directly to my previous discussions about collective identities and male melodrama. Similarly, in *The Funeral* Ray Tempio recounts his boyhood lesson in revenge killing. His father explains that Ray, aged twelve, must kill a man, because this man has stolen from the family: "If you let him go, he will return and kill you one day." As such, survival is once again reduced to Darwinian aggression. However, such practices focus on the extent to which these attributes are taught by fathers to their sons, thus emphasizing the extent to which gender personality can be constructed in this way. Furthermore, such actions reiterate the ethnic stereotype linking Italians to organized crime and confirm Lawrence Fried's comment that the Italian Mafia are the most successful and still prevalent, because the business is passed down through the family.[52]

* * *

Jonathan Rutherford (1992) notes that inherited languages of masculinity are bound up with longings for a "good father," in the hope that he will operate as a "figure who will ensure a sense of destiny and becoming" (143). Tillman echoes this sentiment by suggesting an appeal of *The Godfather* as "a wish for some ultimate authority to relieve me of the burden of conscience" (33). Narratives that include hierarchy or cultural tradition allow for masculine fantasy narratives of retributive violence, without recourse to guilt. Aggression can be blamed on the Mafia tradition of revenge: kill, or be killed. Furthermore, the urge to take part in Mafia activities can also be blamed on cultural heritage. For instance, in *The Godfather Part II*, Connie remembers her father not as an oppressive patriarch, but as someone who did his best to protect his family. She remembers his role as leader of a community, which requires a man to be protective and promote unity, a unity which is constantly threatened by the very competition that structures the hierarchy in the first place. Mafia myths cling to or maintain the old beliefs that a masculine hierarchy can be maintained through loyalty. This is a desirable fantasy for masculine identity because it is based on a collectivity of fathers and sons, rules of behavior and honor that are identifiable and unchanging. It is a fact that many of the narratives that focus on the Mafia as a collective are based in the past, and this shows how difficult it is to maintain that fantasy in the present. Narratives can deny culpability in the downfall of such collectives by reveling in a lost time when men were "allowed" to be men and did not have to feel guilty for their actions: the Gary Cooper era, as Tony Soprano would call it. As discussed earlier, some of the late-nineties comedies that focus on gangsters in therapy are a natural progression of views that men are unduly punished for their innate male characteristics, while simultaneously emphasizing the fact that men are taught these violent codes of behavior. Therefore, it is evident that these films simultaneously refer to a "natural" masculinity while also recognizing its cultural construction.

Recent work on representations of masculinity in American film have identified ways in which white heterosexual masculinity can be viewed as displaced within modern American society. These can be categorized into three different types and associated star personae: the displaced man of action (Jeffords, 1989; Rutherford, 1992; Tasker, 1993) or the "angry white male" (Gabbard, in Lehman 2001) typified by Rambo/Sylvester Stallone (*First Blood*, 1982; *Rambo: First Blood Part II*, 1985; *Rambo III*, 1988), Bruce Willis (*Die Hard*, 1988; *Die Hard 2*, 1990; *Die Hard with a Vengeance* (1995); *Live Free or Die Hard*, 2007) and Mel Gibson (*Ransom*, 1996); the displaced heterosexual hero (Davis & Smith, 1997; Knee, 1993)[53] typified by Michael Douglas (*Fatal Attraction*, 1987; *Basic Instinct*, 1991; *Falling Down*, 1993); and the displaced ideal father (Rutherford & Chapman, 1988; Horrocks, 1995) typified by Robin Williams (*Dead Poets Society*, 1989; *Mrs. Doubtfire*, 1993; *Good Will Hunting*, 1997).[54] It is suggested by Rutherford that Rambo issues retributive violence, and that this is "a common fantasy of masculinities" (Rutherford: 193). He states that the spectacle of violence is a "negation of desire" (*ibid.*: 191), both homosexual and heterosexual, because Rambo represents the misfit son of America. He is "trained to kill in her [America's] defence and [is] now abandoned and alone" (*ibid.*). Therefore, his violence is a consequence of both the desire for and denial of emotional contact with another. As Jeffords notes, violent masculinity is applauded in war time. In consequence, the very skills that made Rambo a hero in Vietnam make him a threat back in his home country. His desire to be loved by his country (stated at the end of *Part II*) is at odds with his identity as a military hero: lone, silent and deadly. In relation to Mafia identity, Rambo represents a comparable violent masculinity that is both applauded and derided. Both embody aggressive masculinity that is desirable, but not appropriate in modern society. However, Rambo is a lone hero, whose violence is said by Rutherford to be a denial of emotional contact, whereas gangster narratives focus on the emotional contact between men as much as the violence. Thus, a comparison between the displaced man of action with the gangster is relevant, but the focus on the collective differentiates the gangster narrative and allows a place (for instance, the past, or the Mafia) where such a masculinity can be expressed.

Michael Douglas, especially in *Falling Down*, represents the white heterosexual call for "access to discourses of victimhood" (Davies and Smith: 34). While the films are over fifteen years old now, the discourses remain part of American culture and I would say inform the narratives of such as *The Sopranos*. In *Disclosure* Douglas is the victim of "anti-discrimination legislation" (*ibid.*: 46). In *Fatal Attraction* and *Basic Instinct* he is the victim of sexuality

Paulie Gualtieri (Tony Sirico, standing, left), Silvio Dante (Steve Van Zandt, seated, left), Tony Soprano (James Gandolfini, standing, right), and Christopher Moltisanti (Michael Imperioli, seated, right). *The Sopranos* © 1999-2007, HBO.

as power: he has the sex, women have the power. In short, these films offer discourses of masculine anxieties in the family, in the workplace, in heterosexual relationships and in modern society in general. They are all narratives of sociopolitical victimization, in which the white heterosexual male is represented as the harassed, victimized, or marginalized identity. Such narratives are easily identifiable as an understandable desire to deny responsibility on an individual and a collective level. In response to the accusation that sexual harassment is about power rather than sex, Sanders (Douglas) in *Disclosure* asks, "When did I have the power?" Sanders does not align his own identity with that of the privileged white male. As such, his argument is that it is not fair to punish him for a privilege he has never had access to. Later Mafia narratives, such as *The Funeral, Donnie Brasco, Analyze This* and *The Sopranos* can be viewed in the same way. Mafia men are represented as damaged egos, struggling to live up to their reputation in popular culture. In each case, the individual is shown as incapable of enacting the callous behavior Mafia tradition dictates without significant damage to his own psyche. For the Tempio brothers (*Funeral*), this brings about insanity and death. In the case of Lefty (*Donnie Brasco*), it allows him to fall prey to an FBI trap. Paul Ricci (*Analyze This*) resorts to psychotherapy and retirement from the Mob. Tony Soprano hovers closely to all of these, although he finally avoids succumbing to any particular flaw.

Finally, the ideal father is offered in *Dead Poets Society* as a welcome alternative to the emotionally detached father (Rutherford). He is the "good, helpful object [...] used as a screen for the son's projections of perceptions of his capacity to be, to live, to create" (Rutherford: 158). The fact that Williams is forcibly ejected from the boys' lives and education, plus the fact that one boy still ends his life due to the actions of the more isolated oppressive father, highlights the marginality of good or ideal fathers. In *Mrs. Doubtfire* and *Good Will Hunting*, Williams' character is also identified as different from the norm. He is punished and separated from his children in the first and offers comfort to the already psychologically damaged in the second. Good fathers in the Mafia are those that teach you how to survive; Vito Corleone (*The Godfather*), Pauly Cicero (*Goodfellas*), Neil Dellacroce (*Gotti*) are wise men. They can read the actions of others, and thus little appears to shock them. Even Sonny's death (*The Godfather*), although tragic, is not a surprise to Vito, as he recognized his son's "hot-headedness." However, Mafia good fathering encompasses the isolated oppressive father figure too, in that the role the father teaches is one of violence and compliance. Again it is quite easy to see how postclassical gangster narratives coincide with popular conceptions of masculine experience. Gangster narratives are articulations of masculinity in crisis, ones that are relevant to all male experience and not restricted to particular ethnicities or criminal deviances.

Tony Soprano's father remains a ghost in his head, in that he haunts Tony's conscience. A good contrast to Tony's experience appears in HBO's companion series *Six Feet Under* (2001–2005), in which a funeral director's dead father often appears and speaks to him. However, whereas Nathaniel Fisher (Richard Jenkins) offers his son Nate (Peter Krause) friendly advice from beyond the grave, Tony's father is a memory that offers little comfort. Tony's filial duty is bound up in discourses of bravery and loyalty. The stories that surface about Tony's father include his leadership, his sexual prowess and his violence. In some ways, Tony's idealization of the Gary Cooper persona is a way of justifying his father's antiquated masculinity. Like the displaced man of action, Gary Cooper's attributes as a man of strength and action are appropriate to his fictional time and place. Perhaps Tony believes that in the same time and place his father's and his own attributes would be valued as much and less of an emotional burden. In this sense, Tony is no more than Rutherford's displaced male, both blaming and yearning for the powerful father figure and the idealized masculinity of cultural mythologies.

Instead of being the privileged homogeneous mass, white masculinity is broken up into a myriad of experiences and performances that deny interaction or homogeneity. In essence the "privileged white male" is represented as a misnomer, constantly displaced onto some abstract identity: corporate business, absent fathers, military service, etc. In other words, such representations can be seen in the light of contemporary conceptualizations of masculinity, especially those which acknowledge masculinity as powerful and aggressive against women but deny culpability by placing this type of masculinity in the past. Furthermore, these approaches to masculinity suggest white male individuals to be victims of this kind of aggressive masculinity too.

In my opinion, the "performance" of hyper-masculinity in many gangster movies is nostalgic for a masculinity that is acknowledged as no longer appropriate. It is as if the earlier ideals of masculinity have now been criminalized. Individual gangsters refer to cultural history or cinema history for their inspiration and ambitions based upon a projected hierarchy or set of ideals. Masculinity as performance is another way of spectacularizing ideal masculinity and separating it from ordinary experience. Confined to the screen, it operates as a fantasy, which male audiences can enjoy without feeling culpable. Similar distancing devices (criminality, ethnicity, etc.) are used as in the classical era. However, the pleasures are distinct in that the post-classical gangster film offers notions of collectivity, a shared cultural heritage to be proud of, which is something contemporary white males may see themselves as being denied.

Masculinity and Ethnicity as Nostalgia

To conclude, the discussion will now focus on the ways in which post-classical gangster films offer nostalgia for particular types of masculinity and ethnicity. Some of these resemble the ideal male as put forward by Robin Wood, or the aggressive, Darwinian masculine nature defined by many writers on the gangster genre. It is what Kenneth Clatterbaugh (1990), discussing different types of masculinity, terms the conservative legacy[55] that most resembles the initial glorification of gangster images: a single minded pursuit of ambition, plus the Darwinian nature of underworld violence that is seen to strip male nature down to its barest aggressive function. Early critical work suggested that the gangster provided a modern industrial glimpse of the Westerner's principles: The gangster is the "man of the city" (Warshow: 86). Thus, the gangster is viewed as an example of male nature, whose brutality is a necessary attribute for success in the urban environment: "Brutality itself becomes the means to success and the content of success" (Warshow: 87). Warshow notes that this is an "agreed conception of human life" between the audience and the film, a principle that "belongs to the city; one must emerge from the crowd or else one is nothing" (*ibid.*). Warshow associates individuality with success and maintains that its achievement requires single-minded ambition, but most importantly aggression. Thus, the successful male is one who rises above the masses by whatever means necessary. The gangster has been viewed as a cultural representation of this successful male: "The gangster speaks for us, expressing that part of the American psyche which rejects the qualities and the demands of modern life" (*ibid.*: 86). Neither the criminal element of the gangster's persona, nor his ethnicity is at issue here. Warshow is applauding the gangster as a representation of masculine freedom, a freedom that modern civilization tries to tame, yet cannot eradicate. In this sense it is an unreclaimed masculinity, an example of gender behavior that resembles the masculine traits of frontier heroes. Views of masculinity such as "the conservative legacy" would agree with Warshow that the gangster is a representation of a male gender behavior that is at odds with the modern society it created.

Critics who appear to identify gangsters as examples of "unreclaimed masculinity" (Jameson, Dika) view the gangster as an archaic representation of repression, sexism and violence. Frederic Jameson's analysis of *The Godfather*[56] suggests such an archaic representation to be an important part of the appeal of the Mafia. It simultaneously revels in envying the mythical ethnic unity of the Mafia while unmasking the barbarity of it. The aggressive male nature can be enjoyed, but then distanced by placing it firmly in a specific ethnic past.

Culpability is another issue to be determined in relation to the gangster character: is a character's aggression a biological gender trait, or a symptom of the society he inhabits? Warshow maintains that the tragedy of the gangster narrative is rooted in the fact that society punishes him for attempting to rise above the crowd:

> At bottom, the gangster is doomed because he is under the obligation to succeed, not because the means he employs are unlawful. In the deeper layers of the modern consciousness, *all* means are unlawful, every attempt to succeed is an act of aggression, leaving one alone and guilty and defenseless among enemies: one is *punished* for success [Warshow: 88].

Warshow blames American society, in that it encourages ambition yet punishes those who display it. In this sense, the individual cannot be blamed for his actions. Society is to blame, for producing, encouraging and ultimately destroying him. Mitchell, who utilizes the Horatio Alger myth, Puritanism and Social Darwinism to explain the principles of the gangster genre, suggests, "While he somehow cannot succeed, the film gangster hero insidiously demands our admiration. His is a hostile environment. [...He] survives as long as he does against heavy odds because of his energy, cunning and bravura" (Mitchell, 1976: 207). None of these definitions suggest the gangster's gender behavior to be the primary fault. Society, or the gangster's immediate environment, forces his aggressive masculine behavior to the surface. We are called to sympathize with the gangster's plight in having to play out this masculine role.

Whether or not the gangster's gender behavior is at the root of his actions, aggressive masculinity can be viewed nostalgically, as it operates within seemingly stable binary oppositions of good and evil, male and female, where gender behavior and roles are unproblematic. Postclassical gangster films can encourage such nostalgic views of masculinity, especially in the fact that many narratives are confined to the past. As already noted, Frederic Jameson's view of *The Godfather* suggests it as an archaic representation of ethnic masculinity. Similar themes could be argued in relation to *Goodfellas* and *Gotti*. Audiences are encouraged to envy the mythical ethnic unity, while simultaneously denouncing the barbarity of it. These contradictory impulses encourage nostalgia, yet deny culpability through the distancing devices of both history and ethnicity. This is similar to Warshow's original claim that the gangster character encourages our sympathy for his individualism while simultaneously attracting disgust at his lack of moral discipline. But Warshow is discussing gangsters who exist in a narrative of the present. Most postclassical gangster films feature narratives of the past and, as such, offer narratives of nostalgia whereby criminal activities are displaced into history. In other words, history can take the place of ethnicity as the focus of distanciation.

Films that offer narratives of nostalgia include *Once Upon a Time in America*. This film has been labeled "a fable for adults"[57] in that Sergio Leone believes American cultural genres tap into a "universal collective consciousness" (Leone interviewed by Lomenzo, 1984: 22) and the gangster is a development of the Westerner, in that, if the Western is infancy, the gangster represents America in its urban childhood.[58] The antics of the gangster are confined and defended by their role in history. It is suggested by Roger Corliss (1984) that the main characters in *Once Upon a Time in America* are contemptible: "Wildcats and condors may patrol the West, [but] the urban Underground shelters nothing but rats" (Corliss: 20). In contrast, Chris Peachment (1984) suggests that Leone's characters are "ordinary" (Peachment, 1984: 301), as opposed to conventional "energetic" gangsters. Most importantly though, the film is suggested as nostalgic (Kael, *New Yorker*, May 27, 1985, McNab, *Time Out*, February 14–21, 1996). This can be seen in both Noodles' yearning for the past and Leone's evocation of the main prohibition-era setting. In terms of masculinity, the film offers a collective vision of adolescence, with all its contradictions. The gang members are both contemptible and ordinary, in that their crimes are petty and self-serving; they abuse women and betray each other. However, it is also suggested that the youthful antics of the gang represent an innocence that the older Noodles yearns for (McNab, Peachment). The narrative trajectory of the European version of the film,[59] which is the version discussed here, is about memory, or more importantly Noodles' guilt about his past actions.[60] A narrative of appeasement can be traced in *Once Upon a Time in America* that sidesteps culpability for actions of the past.

The young Noodles is a petty thief, a sexual abuser and an extortionist; however his overriding sense of guilt, when we first see him in 1933 and 1968, is focused upon a belief that he caused the death of his friends during a bank raid. A mixture of flashbacks (1922, 1933) and present day (1968) action slowly reveals that Noodles' friend Max had engineered the deaths so he could escape with the money. Noodles refuses to enact revenge on Max, possibly because his own relief is enough recompense, but it is suggested that Max commits suicide anyway. The important element of this conclusion, as Tony Rayns (1984) notes, is that the film then returns to the opening scene of Noodles in the opium den in 1933. Initially this scene had encouraged the audience to believe that Noodles had betrayed his friends. By the end, the same scene suggests a clear conscience, in that audiences now know that he was not the perpetrator. It also ends the narrative at a moment of youth and freedom. Rayns notes, "For Noodles, and the viewer, time has stopped at the moment he most fully enjoyed his life. The fantasy is intact and perfect" (Rayns, 1984: 296). Thus, the narrative has absolved the guilt of Noodles' earlier actions: firstly by confining them to the past and secondly by facing up to those memories in order to dissolve the feelings of guilt. The narrative structure effectively distances viewers from the actions of the young Noodles, while also suggesting nostalgia for them. Attention is diverted onto the issues of friendship, betrayal and memory, so that when Noodles is proven blameless in this respect the narrative returns to his youth without the guilt. Noodles' aggressive and unacceptable actions are confined to history, but they are not identified as abnormal or the cause of any downfall. It is his own feelings of guilt that have caused him pain, and these feelings are proven to be unfounded. Thus, both Noodles and his adolescent activities are absolved. This conclusion encourages nostalgia for the aggressive or unreclaimed masculinity displayed in the narrative flashbacks, in that it confines it to the past but also suggests that the guilt felt by the reformed Noodles concerning such activities is not only unnecessary, but misguided.

The same could be said for *The Godfather Part III*, where audiences are encouraged to sympathize with Michael's display of guilt. The flashback sequences that show his wedding to Appollonia are nostalgic for a seemingly innocent time, or at least a simpler, more knowable time for Michael. This obviously sidesteps the fact that such times included the gunning down of Michael's father and the murder of Appollonia, but they refer to a time where Michael's strength was increasing, which contrasts with and heightens the tragedy of Michael's decline in *Part III*. The narrative structure of *Goodfellas* and *Casino* isolate the narratives in the past. This means that the narrators always display the twin characteristics of hindsight: a glorification of past pursuits, coupled with a desire to distance themselves from some of the less laudable activities.

* * *

Another example of how audiences are encouraged to be nostalgic for the past is found in *Donnie Brasco*. Lefty is an aging, emotionally defeated mobster who constantly laments the loss of the power he once had (or was capable of), lost opportunities and the lack of respect within the modern Mafia. The narrative does not include any flashbacks, so that audiences cannot experience or judge his memories, but intertextual knowledge and star persona provide for that. As discussed before, Lefty is played by Al Pacino and thus references memories of previous gangster roles. Therefore, even though Lefty is a unique character within a specific Mafia narrative, the absence of visualized memories in the text encourages audiences to provide their own, which may include memories of previous Pacino roles in *The Godfather* trilogy, *Scarface* and *Carlito's Way*.[61] Thus, the power and respect Lefty mourns can be provided through the memory of these previous texts. Yacowar

(1997) notes, "Lefty teaches Donnie the ropes, on which most filmgoers are already well versed" (64). This then heightens the tragedy of Lefty's present situation near the bottom of the Mafia hierarchy, as Lefty conjures up memories of previous status and knowledge of the structure. Thus, *Donnie Brasco* encourages its audiences to be nostalgic for a lost masculine strength and power in similar ways to those suggested in Pam Cook's discussion of *Raging Bull*,[62] but in a more abstract way. Cook notes how the structure of *Raging Bull*, which begins and ends with images of the aging and physically bloated Jake La Motta (Robert De Niro), encourages audiences to be nostalgic for the physical beauty he once was, thus competing withs, if not overriding disgust at the egocentric activities he engaged in.

* * *

Postclassical gangster films, which are obsessed with the past, encourage the same kind of nostalgia, but not always necessarily within one text. Lefty is a pathetic character, but still a sympathetic one. As Yacowar notes again, "Pacino's casting evokes Hollywood's most illuminating film [*The Godfather*]" (65). In a similar way, Susannah Radstone's (1995) work on *Sea of Love* argues, "The film's nostalgic gestures towards a lost way of life (and towards older cop movies?) suggest that something of the past has been lost" (151). Thus, nostalgia is something that has already been associated with Pacino's aging star persona. In *Donnie Brasco* he still embodies myths of Mafia loyalty, explaining rules and conduct to Donnie. He also faces his death with the stoicism and heroism associated with Mafia loyalties. On the one hand, this fatalistic behavior emphasizes his powerlessness within the Mafia hierarchy, but on the other, in the context of Mafia myths, his unquestioning acceptance of his culpability in allowing the FBI agent, Donnie, into the Mafia is a display of integrity and is thus heroic. When contextualized within Mafia myths, discussed in Chapter 3, Lefty's actions reassert his honor. They encourage nostalgia for a time when Mafiosi lived and died by their honor and fix Lefty within that time. This is the point at which the film ends; thus, as with *Once Upon a Time in America*, it leaves the main character as a hero, even though in *Donnie Brasco* the ending also implies tragedy.

Conclusions

As stated earlier, recent approaches to masculinity suggest that white heterosexual identity is no longer secure as the norm by which everything else is measured. In addition, white masculinity is now making its own claims upon marginal and oppressed identity. A key aspect of this lies in the apportioning of blame which often revolves around a single but diverse premise of the "sins of the fathers," which includes absence, brutality and power, characterizing masculinity as damaged and a complex state of being or performing. Therefore, the postclassical gangster narrative, with its focus on the collective rather than the individual, provides a suitable environment in which the dominant concerns of modern American society can be played out, including displays of violence, homosexual and heterosexual desire, and ideal or absent fathers. The flaw in the gangster's character is no longer an individual problem, but can be displaced onto other aspects of the collective identity: for instance, onto cultural heritage, or sins of the fathers. Furthermore, the Mafia is identified as a marginal group by its ethnicity and/or criminality and this provides a masculine fantasy of unproblematic collective identity, in that it appears distanced from the complexities inherent within "real" or ordinary law-abiding society and from a dominant white society. Therefore, Mafia narratives operate as a contradictory discourse of both collective masculine ideals and ethnic unity. They feature all-male environments, allowing for the parallel existence of aggressive and vulnerable behavior (masculine ideals and fears), but also deny assimilation through the foregrounding of ethnic separateness.

As discussed in the introduction to this chapter, the figure of the ideal male is an unachievable goal, but this does not mean that all masculine identities exist in opposition to this ideal. Many gangster stereotypes reflect the gender characteristics of the omnipotent male. It is the reliance on binary oppositions as identifying axes that does not work. In reality, as Robyn Wiegman states, "The social subject cannot be aligned, without contradiction, on one side or another of the minority-majority divide" (Wiegman, 1995: 7). It is necessary to look beyond singular identifying practices, for instance identifying a complete cultural identity from a connection with a particular racial group. It is necessary to show how identities are constructed: to map out part of the web of differences in historical and cultural terms. This book has sought to do that, using postclassical gangster films as displays of such identities. As Foucault states, no text sits alone: "It is caught up in a system of references to other books, other texts, other sentences; it is a node within a network" (Foucault, 1976: 423). Gangster films articulate notions of masculinity and ethnicity as part of popular culture popular culture is part of cultural discourses and cultural discourses are part of how societies make sense of themselves. Therefore, individual identity is also caught up in cultural discourses, in a continual process; it is "re-invented again and again" (Campbell and Kean, 1989: 23). Contradictions within identity are central to American society, not least because American identity has always been constructed from connections with home countries, yet at the same time, the legitimacy of this connection is negated by space and time (Campbell and Kean). In particular, masculine identity, especially in America, is constructed from a web of historical and cultural discourses that include notions of race and class.[63]

Citing gangster masculine types in the past is a narrative device that is open to all the inflections noted here. Such a positioning can be viewed nostalgically, as a "natural" but now lost identity, or it can be viewed as archaic and either viewed or critically with nostalgia. In summary, postclassical gangster films offer white male fantasy narratives, but they also offer romantic notions of ethnic unity. They foreground assimilationist ideals, but are also nostalgic for ethnic identity. Therefore, ethnicity is shown to be both the flaw in the gangster identity, but also the source of its strength. Gangster films applaud displays of aggressive masculinity, but they also provide arenas wherein the more feminine gender personalities can be brought to the fore. They encourage nostalgia for an ideal masculinity that does not adhere to the constraints of law-abiding society, but also chart the crises of masculine identity in such a society. In short, postclassical gangster films are narratives that encourage very different and contradictory readings, which is perhaps why the films attract such diverse reviews and opinions and why they are so popular across a wide variety of audiences.

5

Conclusions

One of the initial intentions of this book was to show how postclassical gangster films are distinct from the earlier classical gangster films. I have shown that postclassical films refer back to the films of the classical era and are heavily influenced by these earlier films, but that they also offer different perspectives. I have identified various distinctive elements such as a tendency to place narratives in the past, to on focus groups rather than lone gangsters, to allow gangsters to survive at the end of narratives, and to on focus Mafia myths as developed since the 1950s. However, identifying these differences is only the beginning; this book has also focused on the ways in which gangster films have been previously analyzed, and to what extent these approaches are useful for understanding postclassical films. Four key aspects of gangster films were chosen: genre, myths, masculinity and ethnicity. I examined the ways in which they were articulated in gangster films, what were the functions of such articulations, what readings these films have generated and finally what points of tension can be discerned within these readings.

It was apparent that, until recently, interest in the gangster film has been mainly focused alongside the development of genre theory. In response, I have examined how useful such an approach is for postclassical gangster films, and made the following conclusions. While a structural analysis of genre is restrictive and cannot account for the multiplicity of film texts displaying gangster images, genre is still a process by which producers, publicists and reviewers identify films. Therefore, rather than attempting to reduce genre to a list of conventions, this book has identified some of the commonalities the films express and to which reviewers and internet discussion forums tend to refer. From this the conclusion is that postclassical gangster films still appear to operate as a unique genre mainly because of the subject matter of organized

219

crime, primarily identified as gangsters or Mafia. However, other factors, such as costume, dialogue, gestures, violence, star personae and historical settings also encourage allusions to the genre even in films that do not primarily focus on gangsters or the Mafia. Star directors, especially those of Italian descent, tend to influence the allocation of genre labels. For instance, Coppola's *Cotton Club* has been included in Gangster film histories mainly because of its director; its narrative did not primarily focus on gangsters or Mafia activity. It was also noted that reviews tended to allude to previous films to assess the authenticity or merits of the reviewed film. For instance, many reviews of *Scarface* compared it unfavorably to *The Godfather*: "Perhaps DePalma had aspirations of *The Godfather*, but *Scarface* lacks the generational sweep and moral ambiguity" (*Time Magazine*, December 5, 1983). It "strives too extravagantly for grand operatic style and ends up with gruesome grand guignol" (*Mail on Sunday*, February 5, 1984). A rare positive review suggests, "While not in the same class as *The Godfather*, *Scarface* is nonetheless a vigorous melodrama stylishly directed" (*Sunday Express*, February 5, 1984). The messageboard on imdb.com asks, "*King of New York* better than *Scarface*?" To which most agree. However, another board suggests the film "captures the streetlife mentality better than any other gangster movie" (posted by BruceSmith78)" also, "It is a masterpiece [..] untouchable in its genre with *The Godfather* movies" (posted by aleo999). In summary, genre is an oft-used label in discussions of film but that does not make it a stable form.

*   *   *

Allusions to previous films are not surprising, as reviewers and internet discussion forums are always likely to make comparisons in order to convey an evaluative judgement of a film. However, an important discovery in examining the reviews and discussions was that allusions to previous films often compare issues of authenticity. References to Mafia myths corresponded to claims of authenticity and tended to result in positive reviews in terms of genre. This also coincided with less discomfort about displays of violence. In comparison, films that did not allude to Mafia myths tended to be viewed as non-authentic and tended to attract concern over what was seen as unsubstantiated glorification of gangster violence. The combination of all of these findings raised more questions about how the connections between film narratives operated.

The functions of genre are influenced by the fact that audiences, critics and all forms of publicity can embrace very different interpretations in any film. Therefore, it is appropriate to note, as Maltby does

> The boundaries of a genre dissolve not only to admit new movies, but also to incorporate the surrounding discourses of advertising, marketing, publicity,

press and other media reviewing, reporting and gossip, and the "word of mouth" opinions of other viewers [Maltby: 113].

By the release of *The Godfather* (1972), surrounding discourses not only included the history of the gangster film, but also the history of gangsters in other media: for example, in news reporting, fiction and political propaganda. Film characters were compared to historical figures or events, and narratives were based on biographies or at least film producers who publicized their research amongst the real-life Mafia were always noted. Furthermore, genre criticism itself was a powerful factor in assessing a new film's credibility. I concluded that the function of genre is mainly to provide an easily understood label or category for a film, which is socially constructed but unfixed. Identifying a unique genre form from a purely textual, text and reviewer point of view is unpractical, because genre is used in different ways, by different people, at different times. Therefore, it can only ever operate as a guide to films, never as an enclosed category. However, genre remains a meaningful term in discourses in and around film, in that I have identified the ways in which films display similarities in their structure and aesthetic styles. This analysis showed that it is still possible to identify consistencies in textual elements (narrative, conventions, iconography) within gangster films, but that this approach alone was insufficient in defining a genre. A more discursive approach to the texts and reviews succeeded in uncovering a wide range of structural and thematic conventions that reference each other, but are never static. Therefore, the gangster genre exists on a discursive level and can incorporate films that employ very different narratives, characters and themes. The analysis of some of the focal points of narratives and reviews of postclassical films did show that the films and responses to them often made connections across films, or referenced historical events in such a way as to suggest the gangster genre as a continuous narrative. I identified Mafia myths as a significant source behind many such connections.

I began my discussion of Mafia myths in Chapter 3 by providing an overview of the development of the term Mafia, from its origins in nineteenth-century Sicily to the Kefauver Committee hearings in 1950s America. This showed how the belief in the Mafia as an organized criminal network across America, while prevalent since the mid–nineteenth century, really took hold in the 1950s and beyond. The extent to which novels and biographies since Joe Valachi's testimony at the McClellan Committee Hearings (1963) also tended to focus on the Mafia as a real and prevalent form in America was also noted. It was concluded that such reports, testimonies, biographies and novels, rather than facts, are responsible for the development of Mafia myths, because none of the material observed can completely verify its findings. As such, the structure, traditions, or even the existence of the Mafia cannot be proved or denied. Basing the analysis on Roland Barthes' description of myths in popular culture, this chapter also examined how postclassical gangster films provided illusions of stable and identifiable facts in the display of Mafia myths, by foregrounding and explaining concepts of structure and tradition within their narratives. Mafia myths, as cultural discourses, are some of the most important influences upon postclassical gangster films. Such myths exist in the era of the classic films, but not in the form that has developed since the 1950s. The belief in a nationwide network of organized crime that cannot be proved or denied is reminiscent of many conspiracy theories that have entered popular discourses during the Cold War and beyond. In this environment Mafia myths serve two purposes: on the one hand they are anti-establishment and thus offer a powerful alternative to the American government that gives the impression it no longer cares for the ordinary individual. On the other hand Mafia myths provide a scapegoat for those looking for something to blame for the increasing instability or fracturing of American society. In this sense, Mafia myths operate in the same dualistic ways that gangster films have always done: They are simultaneously romanticized and condemned. However, since the fifties, these myths are on a much grander scale in that they no longer concern just individual gangsters, but nationwide networks. *The Godfather* trilogy is by far the most influential set of films in the chosen era, because it offers the widest, most intricate picture of Mafia activity in the United States and beyond.

The critical and box office success of *The Godfather* films has meant that their focus on corporate business and extreme wealth that, most importantly, is not destroyed by the end of the narrative, has encouraged a perception of the Mafia as a world-wide network. Individuals may die or be imprisoned, but the network remains. The Mafia myths encouraged by *The Godfather* films are important, because the initial film was such a critical and box office success and because no later film has completely undermined the images produced in these films. For instance, *Goodfellas* is suggested as a more realistic portrayal of the lower echelons of the Mafia (*Guardian*, October 25, 1990). However, this film does not undermine the romanticism of *The Godfather*, firstly because, as stated in Chapter 2, *Goodfellas* does romanticize the traditions of the Mafia, but secondly because it offers a view of just one Mafia group. Therefore, it does not undermine a belief in the upper echelons in other parts of the Mafia that might operate alongside senators or business executives. The film merely offers a view of some of the workers or "wise guys" operating at street level, as in *Mean Streets*, *Once Upon a Time in America*, *State of Grace*, *Donnie Brasco*, or *The Sopranos*. Mafia myths are greater than any one film, book, or senate hearing, in that they are ever-evolving discourses concerned with notions of the Mafia. These discourses influence particular films and also the responses to these films, including references to genre. However, the films and the responses also influence later myths, and thus discourses on Mafia myths and films constantly evolve.

Postclassical gangster films influence each other and in certain aspects operate as a continual narrative in respect of Mafia myths. This occurs in various ways: firstly, the star personae of actors and certain directors make reference to Mafia myths and hint at real-life experiences of the Mafia. For instance, Coppola includes a scene in *The Godfather Part II*[1] of his own father, Carmine Coppola, as a young boy, playing a flute while Vito Corleone buys guns from his father, Francis Ford Coppola's grandfather. Scorsese, DePalma, Ferrara and Leone are all Italian, and thus are generally accepted in reviews as legitimate, or appropriate directors of gangster films. However, as stated in Chapter 3, Mike Newell's Britishness was noted (*Guardian*, May 2, 1997, *Sight and Sound*, May 1997) in the production of *Donnie Brasco* and used to explain the documentary "outsider looking in" feel of the film. By comparison, this attention to nationality suggests that Italian or Italian American directors have insider knowledge of the Mafia purely because they share its ethnic heritage. Such assumptions strengthen notions of authenticity in their films, not because they have any foundation in fact, but because they have foundation in the myths. The myth in this case is that Italian ethnicity and an understanding of Mafia activity are somehow inextricably linked.

On a textual, or more appropriately intertextual level, postclassical gangster films often refer to factual events or previous fictional narratives. For instance, as noted in Chapter 3, *The Godfather Part II* includes scenes of a Senate hearing, which may be referring to the Kefauver Committee Hearings of the same decade. The character of Willie Cici (Joe Spinell), who appears to enjoy the notoriety of testifying against the Mafia, can be said to allude to Joe Valachi (although, in real life, that occurred a decade later). The fact that the Senate is defeated by the Mafia rule of *Omertà* in the film, can also be associated with the real hearings, which failed to prove or deny the existence of a Mafia network in America. In terms of suggesting connections between film narratives, it has been noted throughout the book how narratives interconnect across different films. Stories of street level gangsters complement *The Godfather*'s focus on the bosses, by simply showing another aspect of the same criminal network. Furthermore, *Scarface* features a young man fleeing Cuba twenty years after Michael and Fredo Corleone fled the country in *The Godfather Part II*, thus suggesting Tony Montana to be an offspring of that era, if not an offspring of one of the brothers themselves. Many non–Italian narratives make reference to the Italian Mafia (*King of New York*,

State of Grace, New Jack City), which further acknowledges the Italian Mafia as a constant presence in narratives on organized crime.

My analyses have shown that Mafia myths are the closest thing to authenticity that reviewers can refer to. This is because any reference to actual reality is not possible when the subject matter is constructed from so much hearsay and contradictory evidence. The development of Mafia myths is one of the reasons why postclassical gangster films enjoy the critical credibility that classical examples were often denied. The articulation of Mafia myths in postclassical gangster films, whether in positive or negative ways, further encourages their perpetuation in wider cultural discourses. If reviewer responses to a film wish to condemn the Mafia, then Mafia myths suggest that organized crime has infiltrated corporate businesses and government departments, and that it is mainly responsible for the growth in drug trafficking in America. If reviewer responses wish to romanticize the Mafia, then Mafia myths suggest that strict codes of family loyalty and respect are attractive opposites to the cold impersonality of corporate America. They suggest that an "eye for an eye" revenge code, free of the bureaucracy-led legal system, offers almost immediate satisfaction for an individual who seeks justice. Furthermore, narratives often focus on the extent to which Mafia bosses deplore any involvement in drug trafficking, stating the extent to which it ruins families and communities thus implying a sense of morality and desire for family values. In short, Mafia myths provide an extra-textual backdrop to the development and uses of genre, but they are also the primary source material for narratives, either to condemn or romanticize Mafia activity.

The Sopranos operates in both of these arenas. On the one hand, Tony Soprano is representative of how organized crime has infiltrated the mainstream America. On the other he remains separate from that mainstream through ethnicity and criminality. He and his crew can be charged as acting out some of the most racist, misogynistic, homophobic, ultra-conservative practices mainstream society professes to abhor, while also garnering sympathy as embodying the fears and anxieties of modern American masculinity. As such, *The Sopranos* is not scary because these men are the Mafia, it is scary because in many books, reviews and discussion forums these underlying social and political aspects are not sufficiently questioned. The tribal structure contained in Mafia myths may be romantic to some, especially when contained in narratives based in the past, but the attendant ideologies are not romantic. Reviewers and viewers are not blind to the nastiness of their behavior, but they do defend it as appropriate in terms of genre and Mafia myths. It is evident to me that the vicarious pleasure involved in watching such men behave badly is the most important, yet least explored aspect of modern American masculinity. In response to "Why do people like [Scarface]?" ChrisSmith

78 suggests, "People watch a gangster movie to let loose and root for the bad guy." Mafia myths are part of the fabric of American history, like Western outlaws. As myths they reflect aspects of American identity, maybe even vents for unacceptable behaviors. As such, we need to ask more challenging questions about "why" the myths have become mouthpieces for such extremist views.

The structure of family provided a backdrop for the discussions of masculine identity. The final chapter showed how representations of masculinity in postclassical gangster films were articulated as collective identities, ever-shifting in relation to each other within the criminal group and within notions of Mafia myths or genre. Different environments and situations, such as the all-male environment in the Mafia, can encourage a more diverse range of gender behavior. Inappropriate gender behavior is a social judgment influenced by the context in which this behavior is displayed and by whom. The gangster exists in an extremely interesting environment where intimacy and aggression can be viewed almost simultaneously as points of identification and distanciation. On the one hand films operate as omnipotent white male fantasy narratives, while at the same time they foreground racial difference and pastness. Identification and distanciation are once again in a state of constant flux, which allows for viewers to "pick and choose" the elements they wish to applaud while distancing themselves from those they deplore.

Masculinity and ethnicity interconnect as articulations of identity in postclassical gangster films. It has been noted that identity remains a site of immense confusion and nowhere is this more evident than in cultural representations of the male. Fred Pfeil states that although masculinities are seen as a product of a dialectical process between men and women and thus socially constructed, there remains a contradiction in the fact that cultural representations of men still assume that *all* white straight males are "promised recognition and a secure place in the world" (Pfeil, 1995: ix). While it is accepted that masculine identity is a fluid concept, "Cultural productions are viewed as reflections of the flux they seek simultaneously to exploit and arrest" (*ibid.*: xv). Consequently, conflicting representations of masculinity in gangster films — such as expressions of dominance or frailty, the desire for comradeship or isolation — are all possible identification points, but they are also suggested as solved by the outcome of the narrative. Dika's assertion of *The Godfather* as a white male fantasy narrative can be accepted as a reading that attempts to arrest the fluidity of masculine identity within one particular expression of white supremacy.

In terms of the representation of ethnicity in film, postclassical cinema has offered a more open environment than the classical period. Postclassical Hollywood mainstream directors such as Martin Scorsese have made their own particular ethnic experience an important part of their films. Houston A. Baker Jr. (1993) explores how the transnational commercial success of another director, Spike Lee, has developed to make certain aspects of ethnicity hip. He maintains that this hipness is still based on assumptions of difference at times, but that the assimilation of such directors as Spike Lee into the Hollywood mainstream has made Black American culture palatable to a multicultural audience. The commercial success and, perhaps more importantly, the critical acclaim of the *Godfather* trilogy (1972, 1974 and 1991), *Goodfellas* (1990) and *Donnie Brasco* (1997), are some of the reasons the mainly Italian American Mafia myths have been raised to a global level.

Italian ethnicity is often used as evidence to back up opinion on internet discussion forums, especially *The Sopranos* forums. If behavior, dialogue, or narrative authenticity is challenged it is not uncommon for posters to detail their Italian roots in order to authenticate their opinions. This is understandable as the show is at pains to be authentic in its presentation of many aspects of Italian American identity.

Italian Mafia and Italian American identity in film and TV relies on blurry distinctions between not only between criminals and non-criminals but also fact and fiction, which, as Clancy Sigal has noted, is the nature of modern ethnic identity. He draws attention to the ever-shifting discursive nature of ethnic identity, especially as it is articulated through film, by examining the attitude of people on Mulberry Street, New York, the area of Little Italy where *Mean Streets* (1972) was filmed: "It was hard to know who was copying whom — probably a little of both" (Sigal, 1979, cited in Wilkinson, 1984: 123). Gangsters and policemen imitate their fictional screen counterparts, and moviemakers then use these imitations. It is impossible to trace where the original influence came from: reality, or fiction? As noted in the discussion of genre, gangster films have always had an ambiguous relationship with real history. Stuart Kaminsky (1985) maintains that the use of *real* gangsters as subjects of the films necessarily blurs the distinction between fact and fiction. *The Sopranos* is as much about modern Italian American identity as it is about organized crime. This, of course, is bound to have the knock-on effect of perpetuating the belief that they are synonymous with each other.

Postclassical gangster films provide environments where multiple masculine gender characteristics can be displayed. Confined to the past, gangster films can glory in the excesses of aggressive masculinity without having to defend such activities against contemporary social values. While *The Sopranos* is set in the present, it is a narrative that is obsessed with the past. Tony's obsession with old-world values, traditions and Gary Cooper's masculinity is testimony to this fact. Furthermore, the show's love affair with the *Godfather* mythology is also heavily nostalgic. The guys want to live their own

Corleone fantasy. In this sense, they are not only like Henry Hill (*Goodfellas*), but also like the modern TV and film viewer, who fantasizes about the Mafia life and wishes to "live vicariously through Tony Soprano" (rollatomazi on sopranos.com).

The exclusive male environment allows for more feminine gender personalities to be displayed through acts of nurturing or protection between father and son figures, or concepts of masculine self-reliance through displays of house-keeping, especially cooking. The structure of all-male Mafia environments display masculinity as a collective construct, in that the stereotyping of particular identities complement each other depending on the narrative to build a picture of a Mafia identity that is at once known and yet constantly changing. For instance, the overly emotional, aggressive gangster is not the only stereotype associated with postclassical gangster narratives. It is often used as an indicator of "bad behaviour," or a trouble-maker within Mafia groups (Sonny Corleone, Tommy De Vito, Nicky Santoro, Chaz Tempio, Ralph Cifaretto), whereas the colder, more business-like stereotype is the stronger, more successful character (Michael Corleone, Pauly Cicero, Ray Tempio, Tony Soprano).

The function and construction of stereotypes is different in each narrative, but the continual development of stereotypes has meant that a collective ideal of Mafia identity in postclassical films has evolved. The result is that films such as *State of Grace*, *King of New York*, *Leon* and *The Firm* display Italian gangster characters that are instantly recognizable as the ideal and thus do not require explanation as to their strength or power in relation to other criminals. Furthermore, the hierarchical nature of Mafia environments also allows for different masculine gender personalities through the display of strength and passivity. It was noted, especially in relation to *Donnie Brasco*, the extent to which Lefty's identity is constructed through his interaction with the surrounding hierarchy. Furthermore, the Mafia as a criminal group relies on the acceptance of hierarchy in order to survive. The function of such multifarious articulations of masculine identities is once again linked to responses to films. Gangster characters can be both condemned and romanticized in respect of their display of masculine gender personalities. Thus, it is as valid for Gow to suggest that the garden scene in *The Godfather* is like "watching Hitler play with his grandson" (*Scotsman*, August 23, 1972), as it is for Tillman or Wood to proclaim it "a romance." It is as justifiable for reviewers to suggest these films as tragedies or melodramas as it is to suggest that they are brutal or amoral. In short, postclassical gangster films offer simultaneous points of identification and distanciation in their articulation of masculine identities so that individual characters, like Tony Soprano, can be viewed as both heroes and villains.

As stated in Chapter 3, Richard Gambino (1973) has suggested that since the 1960s the power of the media has raised the Mafia myth to the status of Mafia chic. This is an ambiguous position for the Italian American individual, because "at least the *Mafioso* is taken seriously as an individual of some importance, an improvement over being considered a buffoon, or being ignored" (Gambino, in Ryan: 1973: 48). This newfound credibility has led to some seeking "to get some public-relations mileage out of [it]" (*ibid.*). Thus, the connection with the Mafia that was once thought to haunt the ordinary law-abiding Italian American has evolved to also offer a kind of credibility for them. This is not to suggest that the criminality of the Mafia is an identity most Italian Americans want to be associated with, but that the courage, loyalty and secrecy of the Mafia myth has its attractions. The notion that there still exists an essence of ethnic security and stability within a complicated and alienating modern urban society is a desirable myth.

Francis Ianni maintains that the immigrant colonies of early twentieth century America were self-contained. He further claims that the police were indifferent to the crimes within particular colonies, as long as none ventured outside of its borders. This would account for the exclusivity of these areas. The Mafia is said to have blossomed in the American city because of the need for these immigrant colonies to police themselves. Ianni states: "In Italy, the custom had been to go to a 'man of respect'—a leader in the Mafia or Camorra—for redress of ills and protection from the vagaries of peasant life; in the American ghetto it was the same" (Ianni, 1972: 53). American Mafia families are said to have grown from this practice. The nostalgic notion of community and ethnic stability that accounts such as these conjure up not only influences my analyses of postclassical gangster narratives, but suggest new ways of viewing classical gangster films.

The stereotype of the Italian immigrant emerged as masculine, urban and associated with the ghetto underworld, with all its connotations of vice. The gangster in fiction and early film mainly took the form of an individual attempting to break out of the ghetto and into mainstream American culture. It is not surprising then that gangsters should be a focus of fascination and fear. The "melting pot" ideal of American culture meant that cultural assimilation should be the ambition of all immigrants. As Stephen Steinberg has stated, the dominant cultural message was, "You will become like us whether you want to or not" (Steinberg: 42). The problem with the gangster narrative was that his attempt at assimilation simply reaffirmed his difference. Both Ruth and Munby have argued that the gangster was a tragic hero because he represented the beleaguered individual who could not fit into the American ideal. Munby argues, "As films that found their audiences in the Depression metropolis they testified to the polyglot American reality that was increasingly at odds with the rarefied discourse of official society" (Munby: 50).

The reality of American urban society was a multicultural one, not the homogenous ideal encouraged by any social and political elite. In consequence, both Ruth and Munby should take issue with earlier analyses of gangster films over ethnicity, but their overall approach is not dissimilar to the viewpoint of scholars such as Robert Warshow or Jack Shadoian. They both highlight the gangster's entrepreneurial ambition as a reflection of the ideal American male principle of individual success. His eventual demise is justified in the text by some immoral act, but he remains the hero because his basic characteristic is seemingly "American." The general view of the gangster's ambiguous ethnicity in these early films seems to be a multifarious one of recognition and difference. In other words, it is open to multiple interpretations. Ethnicity highlights the gangster's difference from an ideal American male and thus helps to justify his demise, but it also works to promote a social message of exclusion that many Americans can identify with.

Ethnicity in postclassical gangster films develops the dual forces of recognition and difference through the ambiguities of white ethnicity. As stated in Chapter 4, post–Civil Rights America embraced anti-assimilationist ethnic identities as positive contributors to a multi-racial American society. Thus, postclassical gangster films, with their attention to Italian ethnic heritage and traditions, can be viewed as positive displays of non–WASP American identities. Family loyalties, desires to keep business within the family, and the continuation of traditional Italian culture encourage positive portrayals of Italian ethnicity in modern America. However, as the narratives are mainly confined to the past, such ethnic purity could be viewed as out-dated: a nostalgic memory of a lost sense of community. For instance, an ambition stated by Vito Corleone in *The Godfather* was to make his son, Michael, a senator. Michael echoes this in that film and *The Godfather Part II*, by asserting his belief that in five years he can make the Corleone family business legitimate. Thus, the Corleone ambition is to assimilate itself into the mainstream fabric of American society. They no longer wish to stand out as criminals, or indeed as members of a distinctive ethnic group. The narratives show the extent to which such an assimilation ideal is flawed, either through the loss of ethnic heritage, or the bland, isolating coldness of an assimilated society that, without diversity, lacks any sense of identity at all. Having said this, it is also evident that as "white ethnics," Italian, Irish, or Jewish gangsters can be viewed as indistinguishable white males, and thus viewed as "white supremacy narratives." Ethnicity is both condemned and romanticized in different ways. Attachments to ethnic heritage can be viewed as archaic and brutal, but also as articulations of security or stability. Ethnicity is most often condemned as the character flaw behind aggressive behavior, or the destruction of a family. However, ethnicity also provides the impetus for the family to exist in the first place and the reasons for it to be protected.

While the connection between Mafia and madness is suggested in *The Funeral* and to a certain extent in *The Sopranos*, it is mainly suggested as an excuse for egotistical and greedy behaviour. Clara Tempio (Isabella Rossellini, *The Funeral*) describes it as the family curse, while Carmela Soprano (*The Sopranos*) perhaps more accurately suggests to Tony that it is "bullshit." The boundaries between ethnic identity and mainstream white masculinity are both blurred and defined in gangster narratives. Bad behavior is both inherent in gangster narratives, and applauded and derided in reviewers and fan discussion. While *Goodfellas* maintains many of the myths of Mafia structures and rules, it does highlight the inherent nastiness of the regular street guys. Therefore, as David Pattie has asserted, it is not surprising that the characters in *The Sopranos* ignore *Goodfellas* in favor of *The Godfather*, because they want to view themselves through Coppola's golden glow rather than Scorsese's neon glare. Audiences, like Clara Tempio and Carmela Soprano, may view gangsters as tragic heroes or idiots depending on their own beliefs or perspectives.

Rather than attempting to provide singular conclusions or an ultimate definition of postclassical gangster films, this book has opened out discussions on them to embrace new analyses of genre, extra-textual discourses, and articulations of masculinity and ethnicity. That is why I chose to discuss such a wide range of topics: all of these topics draw out the complex nature of gangster films and show how these films encourage a diverse set of responses from reviewers. Other topics, such as the changing roles of women in gangster narratives, the articulation of religious beliefs, wider social or political motivations for criminal activities, and the international influences of gangster films upon each other are important and rich areas for further study. It is evident that TV has not killed the gangster film, although like many influences before it has contributed to its development. Mafia mythology remains intact and there is sure to be some new critically acclaimed text before too long. This book has provided the evidence to show that postclassical gangster films, while distinct from the classical era, are developments of traditional myths and conventions. Therefore, it is most likely that developments will continue to occur. This book has also shown that, far from being easily categorized, gangster films articulate a wide range of issues associated with American identities and concerns, and as such remain popular and socially relevant.

In conclusion, it is evident that films about gangsters, the Mafia, or criminal gangs are simultaneously known and unknown, loved and deplored by many different audiences. They are narratives that appear to applaud displays of unreclaimed masculinity. However, they also provide arenas for more feminine gender attributes to reside. They offer scapegoats for the concerns of law-abiding citizens, while applauding the spirit of free enterprise. They are about white male supremacy, while also offering post–Civil Rights ethnic pride. They are narratives that typify all that is American in late twentieth-century popular culture and yet are also non–American. For this reason, they are films that can be enjoyed by diverse audiences, in that, as previously stated, an audience can pick and choose the elements they wish to identify with, or distance themselves from. In this sense, the conclusions of this book are a clear example of how meaning in film texts is in constant flux and can appear to be encouraged by certain aspects of production or consumption, but never fixed. To return to Gledhill for a moment, she states that critical activity, rather than providing complete evaluations of a text, "generates new cycles of meaning production and negotiation" (175). Meaning is constantly evolving, and this book has been an assessment of some of these negotiations. Post-classical gangster films, like the myths that influence them, cannot be satisfactorily isolated within one definition (nor denied by one condemnation). This book has shown how films reflect and encourage discourses on genre, Mafia myths, masculinity and ethnicity to the extent that gangsters and the Mafia remain some of the most popular antiheroes and romantic myths in American culture.

Selected Filmography

Post–1967

Chronological Order

Bonnie and Clyde	(1967)	Dir. Arthur Penn, Warner Bros./Seven Arts.
Point Blank	(1967)	Dir. John Boorman, MGM.
Le Samurai	(1967)	Dir. Jean-Pierre Melville, Filmell/Cicc/Fida Cinematografica.
The Saint Valentine's Day Massacre	(1967)	Dir. Roger Corman, 20th Century–Fox.
The Brotherhood	(1968)	Dir. Martin Ritt, Paramount Pictures.
Bloody Mama	(1970)	Dir. Roger Corman, American International.
Get Carter	(1971)	Dir. Dir. Mike Hodges, MGM.
Every Little Crook and Nanny	(1972)	Dir. Cy Howard, MGM.
The Godfather Part I	(1972)	Dir. Francis Ford Coppola, Paramount Pictures.
Prime Cut	(1972)	Dir. Michael Ritchie, Cinema Center.
The Valachi Papers	(1972)	Dir. Terence Young, Columbia Pictures.
Black Caesar	(1973)	Dir. Larry Cohen, Larco.
Crazy Joe	(1973)	Dir. Carlo Lizzani, Bright-Persky/Produzioni De Laurentiis.
Dillinger	(1973)	Dir. John Milius, American International.
The Don Is Dead	(1973)	Dir. Richard Fleischer, Universal Pictures.
Honor Thy Father	(1973)	Dir. Paul Wendkos, Metromedia Producers Co.
Lucky Luciano	(1973)	Dir. Francesco Rosi, Vides Films La Boetie.
Mean Streets	(1973)	Dir. Martin Scorsese, Taplin-Perry-Scorsese.
The Outfit	(1973)	Dir. John Flynn, MGM.
Big Bad Mama	(1974)	Dir. Steve Carver, Santa Cruz.
Chinatown	(1974)	Dir. Roman Polanski, Long Road Productions.
The Godfather Part II	(1974)	Dir. Francis Ford Coppola, Paramount Pictures.
The Yakuza	(1974)	Dir. Sydney Pollack, Warner Bros.
Capone	(1975)	Dir. Steve Carver, Santa Fe Productions.
Crazy Mama	(1975)	Dir. Jonathan Demme, New World Pictures.
Lepke	(1975)	Dir. Menahem Golan, Amerieuro Pictures Corp.

Bugsy Malone	(1976)	Dir. Alan Parker, Bugsy Malone Productions.
Atlantic City	(1980)	Dir. Louis Malle, Cine-Neighbor Montreal/ Selta Films-Elie Kfouri Paris.
Gloria	(1980)	Dir. John Cassavettes, Columbia Pictures.
The Long Good Friday	(1980)	Dir. John MacKenzie, Calendar/Black Lion.
True Confessions	(1981)	Dir. Ulu Grosbard, United Artists.
Scarface	(1983)	Dir. Brian De Palma, Universal Pictures.
The Cotton Club	(1984)	Dir. Francis Ford Coppola, Zoetrope/Orion.
Johnny Dangerously	(1984)	Dir. Amy Heckerling, Fox.
Once Upon a Time in America	(1984)	Dir. Sergio Leone, Ladd/Embassy International.
Prizzi's Honor	(1985)	Dir. John Huston, ABC Pictures.
Year of the Dragon	(1985)	Dir. Michael Cimino, Dino De Laurentiis/ MGM/United Artists.
Tough Guys	(1986)	Dir. Jeff Kanew, Touchstone/Silverscreen Ptnrs.
Wise Guys	(1986)	Dir. Brian De Palma, MGM/United Artists.
A Better Tomorrow	(1987)	Dir. John Woo, Atlas/Cinema City.
City on Fire	(1987)	Dir. Ringo Lam, Cinema City/Golden Princess.
Matewan	(1987)	Dir. John Sayles, Cinecon/Film Gallery.
The Sicilian	(1987)	Dir. Michael Cimino, Gladden Entertainment Corporation.
The Untouchables	(1987)	Dir. Brian De Palma, Paramount Pictures.
Colors	(1988)	Dir. Dennis Hopper, Orion.
Married to the Mob	(1988)	Dir. Jonathan Demme, Mysterious Arts/Demme/ Orion.
The Killer	(1989)	Dir. John Woo, Cinema City/Film Workshop.
LA Takedown	(1989)	Dir. Michael Mann, Ajar/WIN.
Dick Tracey	(1990)	Dir. Warren Beatty, Touchstone/Silver Screen.
The Freshman	(1990)	Dir. Andrew Bergman, Tristar Pictures.
The Godfather Part III	(1990)	Dir. Francis Ford Coppola, Zoetrope/Paramount Pictures.
Goodfellas	(1990)	Dir. Martin Scorsese, Warner Bros.
The Grifters	(1990)	Dir. Stephen Frears, Cineplex/Odeon.
King of New York	(1990)	Dir. Abel Ferrara, Augusto Caminto/Reteitalia/ Scena.
The Krays	(1990)	Dir. Peter Medak, Fugitive Features.
Miller's Crossing	(1990)	Dir. Joel Coen, Circle Films.
State of Grace	(1990)	Dir. Phil Joanou, Orion/Cinehaus.
Billy Bathgate	(1991)	Dir. Robert Benton, Warner Bros./Touchstone.
Boyz 'n the Hood	(1991)	Dir. John Singleton, Columbia Pictures.
Bugsy	(1991)	Dir. Barry Levinson, Columbia Pictures.
City of Hope	(1991)	Dir. John Sayles, Esperanza.
Mobsters (The Evil Empire)	(1991)	Dir. Michael Karbelnikoff, Universal Pictures.
New Jack City	(1991)	Dir. Mario Van Peebles, Warner Bros.
American Me	(1992)	Dir. Edward James Olmos, Universal Pictures.
Hoffa	(1992)	Dir. Danny DeVito, Fox/Jersey.
Sister Act	(1992)	Dir. Emile Ardolino, Touchstone/Touchwood Pacific Partners.
Reservoir Dogs	(1992)	Dir. Quentin Tarantino, Live Entertainment.
American Yakuza	(1993)	Dir. Frank Cappello, Overseas/First Look/Ozla Neo Motion.

A Bronx Tale	(1993)	Dir. Robert De Niro, Price Entertainment/ Tribeca.
Carlito's Way	(1993)	Dir. Brian De Palma, Universal Pictures.
The Firm	(1993)	Dir. Sydney Pollack, Paramount Pictures.
Mad Dog and Glory	(1993)	Dir. John McNaughton, Martin Scorsese/ Barbara Defina.
Sonatine	(1993)	Dir. Kitano Takeshi, Office Kitano/Yamada Right Vision/Bandai/Schochiku-Fuji.
True Romance	(1993)	Dir. Tony Scott, Morgan Creek.
Bullets Over Broadway	(1994)	Dir. Woody Allen, Buena Vista.
Leon	(1994)	Dir. Luc Besson, Gaumont/Les Films Du Dauphin.
Pulp Fiction	(1994)	Dir. Quentin Taratino, A Band Apart/Jersey/ Miramax.
Bound	(1995)	Dir. Andy & Larry Warchowski, De Laurentiis/ Summit/Newmarket.
Casino	(1995)	Dir. Martin Scorsese, Universal Pictures.
Clockers	(1995)	Dir. Spike Lee, 40 Acres and a Mule/Filmworks.
Heat	(1995)	Dir. Michael Mann, Warner Bros.
The Usual Suspects	(1995)	Dir. Bryan Singer, Polygram/Spelling.
A Brooklyn State of Mind	(1996)	Dir. Frank Rainone, Norstar/Storm
The Funeral	(1996)	Dir. Abel Ferrara, October.
Get Shorty	(1996)	Dir. Barry Sonnenfield, Jersey.
Gotti	(1996)	Dir. Robert Harman, HBO Pictures.
Last Man Standing	(1996)	Dir. Walter Hill, New Line Pictures.
Original Gangstas	(1996)	Dir. Larry Cohen, Po' Boy.
Sugartime	(1996)	Dir. John N. Smith, HBO Pictures
Cosa Nostra	(1997)	Dir. Tony Spiridakis, NuImage/Chase the Moon Inc.
Donnie Brasco	(1997)	Dir. Mike Newell, Mandalay/Baltimore.
Hoodlum	(1997)	Dir. Bill Duke, United Artists.
L.A. Confidential	(1997)	Dir. Curtis Hanson, Warner Bros.
Trigger Happy	(1997)	Dir. Larry Bishop, Ring-a-Ding.
Underworld	(1997)	Dir. Roger Christian, Underworld Pictures.
The Winner	(1997)	Dir. Alex Cox, Feature/Village Road-show/Clipsal.
Jerry and Tom	(1998)	Dir. Saul Rubine, Lions Gate Films.
The General	(1998)	Dir. John Boorman. Sony Pictures.
Analyze This	(1999)	Dir. Harold Ramis, Warner Bros.
Mafia!	(1999)	Dir. Jim Abrahams, Touchstone Pictures.
Mickey Blue Eyes	(1999)	Dir. Kelly Makin, Simian Films.
Gun Shy	(2000)	Dir. Eric Blakeney, Firtis Films.
Gangster No. 1	(2000)	Dir. Paul McGuigan, British Screen Productions/BSkyB/Film Four.
Love, Honor and Obey	(2000)	Dir. Dominic Anciano, Keystone Pictures.
Sexy Beast	(2001)	Dir. Jonathan Glazer, Recorded Picture Co./ Filmfour/kanzaman
Boss of Bosses	(2001)	Dir. Dwight H. Little, Bleeker St. Films.
Friends and Family	(2001)	Dir. Kristen Coury, Belladonna Productions.
Mulholland Drive	(2001)	Dir. David Lynch, Les Films Alain Sarde.
Gangs of New York	(2002)	Dir. Martin Scorsese, Miramax.
Road to Perdition	(2002)	Dir. Sam Mendes, Dreamworks SKG.
Charlie	(2004)	Dir. Malcolm Needs, 21st Century Pictures.

The Business	(2005)	Dir. Nick Love, Vertigo Films.
The Departed	(2006)	Dir. Martin Scorsese, Warner Bros.
American Gangster	(2007)	Dir. Ridley Scott, Universal Pictures.

TV Series

| *The Untouchables* | (1993–1994) | Dir. Paramount TV. |
| *The Sopranos* | (1999–2007) | Dir. David Chase, HBO. |

Pre–1967

Chronological Order

The Musketeers of Pig Alley	(1912)	Dir. D.W. Griffiths, Biograph Co.
Outside the Law	(1921)	Dir. Todd Browning, Kino International.
The Doorway to Hell	(1930)	Dir. Archie Mayo, Warner Bros.
Little Caesar	(1930)	Dir. Mervyn LeRoy, First National.
The Public Enemy	(1931)	Dir. William A. Wellman, Warner Bros.
Scarface, Shame of a Nation	(1932)	Dir. Howard Hawks, Caddo Co.
The Mayor of Hell	(1933)	Dir. Archie Mayo, Warner Bros.
Jimmie the Gent	(1934)	Dir. Michael Curtiz, Warner Bros.
Manhattan Melodrama	(1934)	Dir. W.S. Van Dyke, MGM.
The Glass Key	(1935)	Dir. Frank Tuttle, Paramount Pictures.
G Men	(1935)	Dir. William Keighley, Warner Bros.
Bullets or Ballets	(1936)	Dir. William Keighley, First National.
The Petrified Forest	(1936)	Dir. Archie Mayo, Warner Bros.
The Last Gangster	(1937)	Dir. Edward Ludwig, MGM.
Pepe Le Moko	(1937)	Dir. Julien Duvivier, Paris Films.
You Only Live Once	(1937)	Dir. Fritz Lang, Walter Wanger/United Artists.
Angels with Dirty Faces	(1938)	Dir. Michael Curtiz, Warner Bros.
The Roaring Twenties	(1939)	Dir. Raoul Walsh, Warner Bros.
The Corsican Brothers	(1941)	Dir. Gregory Ratoff, Edward Small/United Artists.
The Glass Key	(1942)	Dir. Stuart Heisler, Paramount Pictures.
Dillinger	(1945)	Dir. Max Nosseck, Monogram.
The Killers	(1946)	Dir. Robert Siodmak, Universal Pictures.
Brighton Rock	(1947)	Dir. John Boulting, Associated British.
Kiss of Death	(1947)	Dir. Henry Hathaway, Fox.
I Walk Alone	(1948)	Dir. Byron Haskin, Paramount/Hal B. Wallis Productions.
Key Largo	(1948)	Dir. John Huston, Warner Bros.
They Live by Night	(1948)	Dir. Nicholas Ray, RKO.
Gun Crazy	(1949)	Dir. Joseph H. Lewis, King Brothers.
White Heat	(1949)	Dir. Rauol Walsh, Warner Bros.
The Asphalt Jungle	(1950)	Dir. John Huston, MGM.
The Big Heat	(1953)	Dir. Fritz Lang, Columbia Pictures.
On the Waterfront	(1954)	Dir. Elia Kazan, Columbia Pictures.
The Big Combo	(1955)	Dir. Joseph H. Lewis, Security-Theodora.
Baby Face Nelson	(1958)	Dir. Don Siegel, Fryman-ZS/United Artists.
I, Mobster	(1958)	Dir. Roger Corman, E.L. Alperson Productions.
Machine Gun Kelly	(1958)	Dir. Roger Corman, American International.

A Bout de Souffle	(1959)	Dir. Jean-Luc Godard, Imperia Films.
Al Capone	(1959)	Dir. Richard Wilson, Allied Artists.
Inside the Mafia	(1959)	Dir. Edward L Cahn, United Artists.
Murder Inc.	(1960)	Dir. Burt Balaban, Fox.
The Rise and Fall of		
Legs Diamond	(1960)	Dir. Budd Boetticher, Warner Bros.
Shoot the Pianist	(1960)	Dir. Francois Truffaut, Films de la Pleiade.
Underworld USA	(1960)	Dir. Samuel Fuller, Globe Enterprises.
The George Raft Story	(1961)	Dir. Joseph M. Newman, Allied Artists.
Portrait of a Mobster	(1961)	Dir. Joseph Pevney, Warner Bros.
Le Doulos	(1962)	Dir. Jean-Pierre Melville, Rome-Paris Films.
Salvatore Guiliano	(1962)	Dir. Francesco Rosi, Lux Film/Vides/Galatea.
The Killers	(1964)	Dir. Don Siegel, Revue.
Robin and the 7 Hoods	(1964)	Dir. Gordon Douglas, P-C Productions.

TV Series

The Untouchables	(1959–1963)	Dir. Phil Karlson, Desilu Productions.

Chapter Notes

Introduction

1. This is the date of the Paramount decree (Paramount case decision) that ruled against the major studios' control over distribution and first-run exhibition. This U.S. Supreme court decision effectively marked the end of the studio system. See R. Maltby, *Hollywood Cinema: An Introduction* (1995) and D. Gomery, "Hollywood Corporate Business Practice and Periodizing Contemporary Film Industry," in S. Neale and M. Smith, eds., *Contemporary Hollywood Cinema* (1998).

2. Changes in the Hollywood film industry and product have been explored in one form or another since the early 1970s, especially by T. Elsaesser, "The American Cinema 2: Why Hollywood," in *Monogram* n.1 (1971), S. Neale, "New Hollywood Cinema," in *Screen* v17 n.2 (1976), T. Schatz, *Old Hollywood/New Hollywood* (1983), and more recently by T. Corrigan, *A Cinema Without Walls: Movies and Culture After Vietnam* (1991), J. Lewis, *The New American Cinema* (1998), Y. Tasker, "Approaches to the New Hollywood" (1996) and P. Krämer, "Postclassical Hollywood" (1998). However, the existence of such changes has also been called into question by Bordwell and Thompson (1985) and Cowie (1998).

3. The term "postclassical" coexists with the term "New Hollywood." Both have grown from debates about the changing structures, both textual and extra-textual, in the cinema industry since the late sixties.

However, some recent debates concerning "New Hollywood" (T. Schatz, "The New Hollywood," 1993), J. Wyatt, *High Concept: Movies and Marketing in Hollywood*, 1994) have suggested it is more appropriate to use this term to distinguish cinema production and consumption after 1975.

4. See D.E. Ruth, *Inventing the Public Enemy: The Gangster in American Culture 1918–1934* (1996) and J. Munby, *Public Enemies, Public Heroes: Screening the Gangster from Little Caesar to Touch of Evil* (1999).

5. See for example Ianni's account of immigration and the ghettoes in *A Family Business* (1972) or S. Ostendorf and S. Palmié, "Immigration and Ethnicity," in M. Gidley, ed., *Modern American Culture: An Introduction* (1993).

6. F. Ianni, *A Family Business: Kinship and Social Control in Organized Crime* (1972), W. Balsamo and G. Carpozi Jr., *Crime Incorporated: The Inside Story of the Mafia's First 100 Years* (1991), and J. Morton, *Gangland International: The Mafia and Other Mobs* (1998) all provide details on how these lotteries operated.

7. See especially his discussion of the plays of David Mamet in "American Crime: Debts No Honest Man Could Pay," in D. Webster, *Looka Yonder! The Imaginary America of Populist Culture* (1988).

8. I will discuss the work of these authors in more depth in Chapter Three.

9. See for example D.C. Smith, *Mafia Mystique* (1975) Chapter 4, or G. Grella, "The

Gangster Novel: The Urban Pastoral," in D. Madden, ed., *Tough Guy Writers of the Thirties* (1968).

10. See Ruth, *Inventing the Public Enemy*.

11. This era has been extensively explored in Munby's work.

12. For the most recent studies of genre in Hollywood see R. Altman, *Film/Genre* (1999) and S. Neale, *Genre and Hollywood* (2000).

13. For detailed analyses of American culture and politics in the sixties see M.J. Heale, *The Sixties in America: History, Politics and Protest* (2001), W.H. Chafe, *The Unfinished Journey: American since World War II*, 4th edition (1999), W.E. Leuchtenburg, ed., *A Troubled Feast: American Society Since 1945* (1983) and D. Farber, *The Age of Great Dreams: America in the 1960s* (1994), who summarizes the decade thus:

> [In the 1960s] Americans questioned the rule makers and rule enforcers who formally and informally governed their lives. Specific events in the 1960s — like those associated with the civil rights and liberation movements, the failed war in Vietnam, and the chaotic violence that engulfed America's cities — sprang from America's changing cultural values, national economic and political system and international role. Such events also intensified many Americans' "doubts about the legitimacy and responsibility of their leaders and the authority and wisdom of their cultural arbiters" [5].

14. See for example the Kefauver Committee Hearings of 1950–2, the McClellan Hearings 1963, or the President's Crime Commission 1967.

15. Gangster films of the classical era did include criminal groups, but they were less pronounced than in the postclassical era and not discussed in detail by critics. Films such as *Little Caesar*, *Public Enemy* and *Scarface* focused on the individual hero against a backdrop of the criminal organization. Postclassical films foreground the criminal organization as much as the individual hero, making the personality of the group as a whole as important to the narrative as the individual personalities within it.

Chapter 1

1. A. Bazin, "On the *politique des auteurs*" (1957), translated by P. Graham, in J. Hillier,

ed., *Cahiers du Cinema I: The 1950s Neo-Realism, Hollywood, New Wave* (1985).

2. See P. Biskind, *Easy Riders, Raging Bulls: How the Sex, Drugs and Rock 'n Roll Generation Saved Hollywood* (1999). While much of this book is based on gossip, it still provides an interesting viewpoint on the shifts in production styles of films in the late sixties and seventies.

3. *Time* magazine, cited in Biskind, 46.

4. See J. Munby, *Public Enemies, Public Heroes* (1999), and also the discussion on Dillinger and Bonnie and Clyde in Chapter Two of this book. W. R. Burnett (author of *Little Caesar*) is cited in Munby as stating of Dillinger, "Such men are not gangsters, organized crime, Mafioso. They were a reversion to the Western bandit. [...] an entirely different breed" (Burnett, cited in Munby, 46). For a historical account of the real-life criminals that influenced these films, see P. Kooistra, "The Heroic Criminals of the 1930s," in *Criminals as Heroes: Structure, Power and Identity* (1989).

5. Hardy (1998) notes that the real Bonnie and Clyde were part of a rural crime wave in the early thirties that was said to be influenced by cinema representations of urban gangsters, but also the rural crime and cinema representations of John Dillinger. Thus, *Bonnie and Clyde* is a portrayal of real criminals who constructed their own personae from the cinema.

6. A more detailed discussion of costume in gangster films will occur in Chapters Two and Three. However, it is interesting at this point to note how the costume from *Bonnie and Clyde* became popular on the high street, which further emphasizes the cultural influence of the film. (See P. French in *Sight and Sound* v37:1 1968, 3–8.)

7. This film is said to have influenced Truffaut and Godard in their depictions of gangsters. See P. French in *Sight and Sound* (1968).

8. See Hardy (1998).

9. This approach is not restricted to the postclassical era. Warshow (1954) was one of the first to suggest the isolation of the lawman or Western hero. Later analyses of the classical era, such as F. Krutnik's *In a Lonely Street: Film Noir, Genre, Masculinity* (1991), have discussed masculine anxieties expressed in film noir. Lastly, S. Neale, "Masculinity as Spectacle" and C. Fuchs, "The Buddy Politic," both in S. Cohan and I.R. Hark (1993), include dis-

cussions of the anxieties about male friendship and violence within law enforcement in post-classical film.

10. *Death Wish* (1974), *Death Wish II* (1981), *Death Wish III* (1985), *Death Wish IV* (1987) and *Death Wish V* (1993). *Dirty Harry* (1971), *Magnum Force* (1973), *The Enforcer* (1976), *Sudden Impact* (1983) and *The Dead Pool* (1988).

11. These types of criminals and crimes tend to be politically as well as personally motivated. They are characterized mainly as single-issue terrorist groups.

12. *Die Hard* (1988), *Die Hard II* (1990) and *Die Hard with a Vengeance* (1995). *Lethal Weapon* (1987), *II* (1989), *III* (1992) and *IV* (1998).

13. In the last of these, Joe Pistone (Johnny Depp), like Eliot Ness (Kevin Costner) in *The Untouchables*, is no match for the persona of Lefty Ruggiero (Al Pacino). *Donnie Brasco* and *The Untouchables* will be discussed later in this chapter.

14. See Cowie, 1997, 70–74. He details *The Godfather*'s box office success during its first year of release as surpassing previous record holders *Gone with the Wind* (1939) and *The Sound of Music* (1965).

15. Like the outlaw films, later examples of revenge narratives against gangster activities can be found in films such as *The Outfit* (1973) and *No Way Out* (1987).

16. The unquestioning henchmen may be less evidently psychopathic in *The Godfather* trilogy, but Luca Brasi (Lenny Montana), Al Neri (Richard Bright) and Michael's unnamed bodyguard in *Part II* (Amerigo Tot), who shadows both Michael and his enemies like an angel of death, all embody a necessary single-minded brutality, without which the upper regimes would not retain their authority.

17. It could be argued that Kay Adams (Diane Keaton) always remains an outsider emotionally, but she is part of the Mafia family as Michael's wife.

18. In Hollywood representations of the Mafia (see especially the Senate hearings in *The Godfather Part II*), buffers are intermediaries between bosses and the lower ranks. Orders are passed down via various "buffers," so that crimes cannot be traced back to those in charge.

19. Admittedly, he carries rather than wears the trench coat in the scenes of Carlo and Tessio's murders near the end of the film.

20. See P. Maas, *The Valachi Papers* (1968).

21. See discussions on the Senate hearings in Chapter Two and Three.

22. Both Munby and Ruth discuss the influence of factual events on Hollywood narratives, but also the effect of real-life events, such as the hunt for John Dillinger and Bonnie and Clyde from 1932 to 1934, that are said to have influenced the genre's popularity.

23. E. Shorter (*Daily Telegraph* 16/5/75) wished he had a family tree to refer to when viewing the film, as he found the constant flashbacks confusing. K. Robinson (*The Spectator* May 24, 1975) stated, "There is no justification for the intrusive flashbacks," and noted the general frustration from viewers concerning the film's structure.

24. In interviews, Scorsese alludes to *The Godfather* as a "whitewash," eliciting sympathy for the characters in a "phony way." He sees *Mean Streets* as "anthropology—that idea of how people live, what they ate, how they dressed" (Smith, 1990, 68).

25. *Gloria* (1980) is an interesting film in that it features a female protagonist who takes on the mob and beats them at their own game. I have chosen not to identify this as the most dominant opening of the next cycle, because like *The Outfit* (1973), it is a film that concentrates on the effect of the Mafia on an outsider, rather than a film about the Mafia itself.

26. A photograph of President Jimmy Carter is shown clearly in the background of the immigration office scene, perhaps placing the blame for an influx of Cuban criminals into America on the unpopular president's policies, thus reflecting the Reagan era to which this film belongs.

27. Forster Hirsch's afterword in C. Clarens, *Crime Movies: An Illustrated History of the Gangster Genre from D.W. Griffith to Pulp Fiction* (1997), barely mentions the film at all.

28. Voted the best gangster film ever by *Neon*, November 1998. However, the editors recognize this as a "bone of contention." The film is applauded as a "searingly honest vision of all-American anarchy."

29. Interestingly, this is another film ignored Clarens in his history of the Gangster genre, adding weight to Neale's argument (in *Genre and Hollywood* 1999) that many attempts to map the development of a specific genre suffer from selectivity. This will be discussed in Chapter Two.

30. David "Noodles" Aaronson discovers that Max and Deborah have built a business empire since the Max's faked death in 1935.

31. De Niro's face was used to promote the film as much as Costner's (*Newsweek* June 22, 1987, *Observer* September 20, 1987) which is significant, considering the fact that De Niro's character has so little screen-time.

32. See E. Hobsbawm, "Robin Hoodo: Mario Puzo's *The Sicilian*," in *The New York Review of Books* (1985), 12–17.

33. See Brode (1995), 151–156 for a detailed discussion of *The Freshman* and its references to *The Godfather*.

34. Having said this, when the prospect of a *Part IV* began hitting the headlines in 1999, the general view can be summarized by Andrew Collins' headline in *The Observer* (June 27, 1999): "Don't Do It, Francis."

35. I use the term "white" here because, even though Christopher Walken's star persona is associated with Italian-American ethnicity, this is not dominant within this particular narrative.

36. This provides another instance of intertextual Mafia mythology, in that Michael Corleone has one of Bugsy's contemporaries, Moe Greene (Tony Giorgio), assassinated during the bloody finale of *The Godfather Part I*.

37. *The Glass Key* was originally filmed in 1935 (Dir. Frank Tuttle) and starred George Raft. It was later remade in 1942 (Dir. Stuart Heisler), starring Alan Ladd and Veronica Lake.

38. For a discussion on the alleged dumbing down of movie narratives in favor of style, see R. Schickel, "The Crisis in Movie Narrative," in *Gannett Center Journal* (1989), 1–15.

39. See G. Peary, *Quentin Tarantino: Interviews* (1998), plus Tarantino interviews in *Film Comment*, v30: 4 (1994), *Empire* no.65 (1994), no.75 (1995), no.100 (1997) and no.106 (1998), *Sight and Sound* v2: 8 (1992), and *Positif* n405 (1994). In every interview Tarantino talks about influential directors, genres and cultural events.

40. See *Observer* 8/1/93 and *Time Out* 30/12/92; plus Tarantino mentions *Reservoir Dogs* and *Pulp Fiction* as allusions to the gangster genre in *Film Comment* v30: 4 (1994).

41. Discussion of ethnic and historical authenticity will occur throughout this book.

42. *American Me* (1992) offers a similar realistic portrayal of the Mexican Mafia in America.

43. Hardy notes how the urban jungle is "governed not by street level gangsterdom but by pure pragmatism and market forces and with all the horrors of 'decent' society — such as rigid class divisions, moral bigotry and racial prejudice — still intact" (388). The cold business style emulates *The Godfather Part II*, but the film's realism denies Coppola's epic romanticism.

44. RICO stands for the Racketeer Influenced and Corrupt Organizations Act of 1970 that helped the government successfully prosecute members of organized crime (Stefano: 161).

45. See Ruth's discussion of the cultural reference points for the 1930s gangster films.

46. For example, *Crime Inc.* (1945), *I Walk Alone* (1948) and *Force of Evil* (1949).

47. In the same ways that black gangstas are suggested now (Munby).

Chapter 2

1. Kitses' work was later taken up by J. Cawelti, *The Six Gun Mystique* (1971), and W. Wright, *Six Guns and Society* (1975).

2. This is not to say that films such as *Little Caesar* et al. do not recognize organized crime as a business. Yet in these films the business of crime is a less defined structure of rival gangs, which features mainly as background motivation for the protagonist's ambitions.

3. See R. Cohen, "History and Genre," *New Literary History* (1986), quoted in Neale (1991).

4. See the work of George De Stefano, especially *An Offer We Can't Refuse: The Mafia in the Mind of America* (2006), for a comprehensive discussion on the contradictory impulses of Italian-American identity and Mafia myths in American culture.

5. See for example *White Heat* (1949), *The Lavender Hill Mob* (1951), *The Killing* (1956) *The Italian Job* (1969).

6. See for instance *Dirty Harry* (1971) and *Badlands* (1973).

7. Also, see most reviews of *Miller's Crossing*, as they refer to these nightmares as a main theme of the film.

8. In the classic gangster films, the gangster is presented as a dandy in his attention to his dress. This is continued throughout the '40s and '50s noir films, where the gangster is differentiated from the hero by subtle differ-

ences in costume. The cut or general sharpness of the suited gangster is often shown in contrast to the more disheveled appearance of the hero. See for example *Kiss of Death* (1947) or *The Big Heat* (1953).

9. As already stated, previous films had alluded to Mafia mythologies (for example *The Brotherhood*), but the commercial success of *The Godfather* is a significant factor in suggesting it as a more prominent influence.

10. A "made man" is a senior member of the Mafia. First used in Scorsese's *Goodfellas*, it is an honor reserved for those of pure Sicilian blood only. A made man can only be killed (also referred to as "clipped" or "whacked") with the consent of other made men within the family or consortium.

11. For example, see interviews with Martin Scorsese about the dialogue in *Goodfellas* (Smith, 1990; Christie and Thompson, 1996), or interviews with Mike Newell about *Donnie Brasco* (*Total Film*, No.4, 1997) and a review (*Guardian*, 2/5/97).

12. See R. Maltby, "Grief in the Limelight..." (1993), Ruth (1996) and Munby (1999).

13. See J. Capeci and G. Mustain, *Gotti: Rise and Fall* (1996), or P. Maas, *Underboss* (1998).

14. Hearsay suggests that George Raft established the coin-flipping gesture and that Bugsy Seigel copied it. See for example the TV series *Gangsters: The Bootleg Years*, Aimimage Productions Ltd. (1997).

15. Disclaimers include the kind of on-screen claims that "Crime doesn't pay," or "Tom Powers in *Public Enemy* and Rico in *Little Caesar* are not two men, nor are they merely characters — they are problem that sooner or later we, the public, must solve" (Opening Titles of *Little Caesar*).

16. Such as speeches from District Attorneys about the inevitability of the criminal's eventual downfall in *Little Caesar* and *Scarface*, or the potential young criminal shown the "real consequences of crime" in *Angels with Dirty Faces* or *The Rise and Fall of Legs Diamond*.

17. See also G. Newman, "Popular Culture and Violence: Decoding the Violence in Popular Movies," in F. Bailey and D. Hale, eds., *Popular Culture, Crime and Justice* (1998).

18. There is a significant amount of innocent or periphery victims in *The Sopranos*, but they operate as pawns within the main cause-effect narrative. For instance, the brutal killing of the prostitute by Ralphie is not inserted so that audiences would dwell on the horror of such a murder for the victim or her young child. It is merely there as an action that develops the justification for Ralphie's own violent demise later.

19. For example, see "The savagery of *Scarface*" (*The Sun*, December 22, 1983), "Comic strip nasty" (*Daily Mail*, February 2, 1984), "Gruesome" (*Mail on Sunday*, February 5, 1984), "Numbing and brash" (*Scotsman*, February 4, 1984), "Macho ritual and mayhem" (*New York*, December 19, 1983), plus "Swearing three times a minute is the most prominent part of the narrative" (*Spectator*, February 2, 1984).

20. For example, "Scorsese has arguably hijacked the genre and simply told the truth" (*Western Mail*, on *Goodfellas*, October 27, 1990), or the use of Scorsese's childhood in New York's Little Italy to authenticate his narratives as "realist" [in this case, more than Coppola's narrative] (*Times Saturday Review*, October 3, 1990).

21. A review of *The Untouchables* refers to him as "the ketchup king" (*Today*, September 11, 1987).

22. See M. Bliss, *Brian De Palma* (1983) — pre-*Scarface*, but also Yaquinto (1997) and McCarty (1993).

23. See also G. Murdock, "Reservoirs of Dogma: An Archeology of Popular Anxieties," in M. Barker and J. Petley, eds., *Ill Effects: The Media/Violence Debate* (1997).

24. The release of *Reservoir Dogs* on video in 1995 attracted a rash of publicity against violent films, especially in the *Daily Mail* with headlines such as, "It is time to stop glorifying brutality" (*Daily Mail*, October 26, 1994), "Sick films turned my son into a gangster" (*Daily Mail*, August 3, 1995), plus "Beware of the Dogs" and "Reservoir Dogs boys turned to robbery" (*Daily Telegraph*, June 9, 1995 and June 10, 1995). Links between this film and violent crime are still made. For instance, a man convicted of killing his girlfriend was described as acting out a scene from the film: "*Reservoir Dogs* torturer set girlfriend alight" (*Times*, May 11, 2000). Similarly, it is suggested that four young boys accused of murder in Liverpool "copied *Reservoir Dogs* scene to kill rival" (*Independent*, July 5, 2000), while another headline reads, "Teenagers killed

boy in *Reservoir Dogs* frenzy" (*Times*, July 5, 2000).

25. As stated earlier, Neale (1999) also later declares the limitations of such critical practices.

26. See A. Bazin, "The Evolution of the Language of Cinema," trans. H. Gray, in *What is Cinema?* In two volumes (1951/1967): in G. Mast, M. Cohen, and L. Braudy, eds., *Film Theory and Criticism* (1992).

27. As discussed in the Introduction.

28. Rather than acting as competent technicians (*Metteurs-en-scene*) of an imposed, formal storytelling structure, some film directors were seen to imprint their own unique identity within their work (as *auteurs*).

29. J. Kitses, *Horizon's West* (1969), R. Wood, "Ideology, Genre, Auteur," in *Film Comment* v13 n.1 (1977).

30. Rather than list all the writings on Coppola here, it is sufficient to reference two of the best: J. Chown, *Hollywood Auteur: Francis Coppola* (1988), and J. Lewis, *Whom God Wishes to Destroy: Francis Coppola and the New Hollywood* (1995). It is also not necessary to all writings on Scorsese. Interviews with the director have influenced much of the critical work. See for example: D. Thompson and I. Christie, eds., *Scorsese on Scorsese* (1989); M. P. Kelly, *Martin Scorsese: A Journey* (1992); L. Friedman, *The Cinema of Martin Scorsese* (1997); P. Brunette, ed., *Martin Scorsese Interviews* (1999); and R. Casillo, *Gangster Priest: The Italian American Cinema of Martin Scorsese* (2007).

31. Obviously, stars are not an absolute guarantee of box office success. However, they can be useful advertising images.

32. Especially since the success of Coppola's *The Godfather* and Scorsese's *Mean Streets*.

33. In addition to the interviews noted earlier, see M. Scorsese and M. H. Wilson, *A Personal Journey with Martin Scorsese Through American Movies* (1997), or M. Bliss, *Martin Scorsese and Michael Cimino* (1985).

34. The inclusion or exclusion of films in this category is arbitrary. As with the attribution of star status to actors, it is practically impossible to define at what point the crossover takes place.

35. See the bibliography of reviews of Tarantino's films, *Reservoir Dogs* and *Pulp Fiction*; also G. Peary, ed., *Quentin Tarantino: In-*

terviews (1998), and G. Smith, "When you know you're in good hands: Quentin Tarantino interviewed," in *Film Comment* (1994).

36. This is also complicated by the fact that studio heads often oversee the final editing process — a practice that can result in very different films being released. Furthermore, this has resulted in an extra merchandising area of "director's cut" films, often released a few years after the original.

37. Many reviews of *Reservoir Dogs* and *Pulp Fiction* use interviews as their primary sources, as detailed in the Introduction.

38. Scorsese often appears in his films as an observer or cameraman (e.g. watching Betsy [Cybil Shepherd] walking down the street in *Taxi Driver* [1974], or as the TV director in *The King of Comedy* [1980]). Tarantino appears in both *Reservoir Dogs* and *Pulp Fiction* in small roles. These directorial influences can be extended even further by noting how Scorsese and Coppola also often include close family members in their films. This will be addressed in more detail in Chapter Two.

39. The extent to which Coppola and Scorsese are presented as the authors of their films has already been noted. For examples of Sergio Leone's status as a star director see C. Frayling, *Sergio Leone: Something to Do with Death* (2000). Pressbooks for *Once Upon a Time in America* concentrate on interviews with the director, plus reviews of the film, such as "A Fable for Adults: Sergio Leone interviewed by Elaine Lomenzo," in *Film Comment* v20: 4 (1984).

40. Oliver Stone's persona (as writer) dominated both the press pack and reviews for *Scarface*. De Palma was rarely quoted in reviews. However, this does not alter the fact that most reviews introduce *Scarface* and *The Untouchables* as De Palma films. His name appears in the first paragraph of all reviews, before references stars Al Pacino, Kevin Costner, or Sean Connery. The only significant example of an actor eclipsing De Palma's role is *Newsweek* (22/6/87) which has Robert De Niro on its cover as its headliner for *The Untouchables*.

41. For example, many reviews of Tarantino's films are based on interviews with the director, as stated in the Introduction.

42. Dyer uses the work of Levi Strauss in similar ways to Alloway (1971) and V. Sobchack (1977) in genre theory.

43. For work that does address issues of audiences at particular points in time and place, see R. Dyer, *Heavenly Bodies: Film Stars and Society* (1986), M. LaPlace, "Stars and the Star System: The Case of Bette Davis," in C. Gledhill, *Home Is Where the Heart Is* (1987), J. Stacey, "Feminine Fascinations: Forms of Identification in Star-Audience Relations," in C. Gledhill, ed., *Stardom* (1991), or J. Staiger, *Interpreting Films: Studies in the Historical Reception of American Cinema* (1992).

44. For an interesting appropriation of Dyer's theoretical model, see S. Cohan, *Masked Men: Masculinity and Movies in the Fifties* (1997), including analyses of how the star images of Cary Grant, Humphrey Bogart and Glenn Ford "contributed to but also resisted and problematized the postwar articulation of masculinity as a universal condition" (Cohan: xv).

45. Based on a true story, this film documents an attempted bank robbery engineered by Sonny (Al Pacino) in order to raise the money for a sex change operation for his lover (John Cazale).

46. *The Insider* has Pacino playing the idealistic TV producer Lowell, who eventually resigns his post in order to maintain a belief in his own journalistic integrity in the face of increasing commercial intervention.

47. He has been nominated four times for Academy Awards. He has won only one, in 1993 for his role in *Scent of a Woman* (1992). He has also recently begun to be honored with Lifetime Achievement Awards, as at the Golden Globe Awards 2001.

48. A publicized piece of Hollywood gossip includes the story that a scene in *Frankie and Johnny* (1991), which involved Johnny (Pacino) being mugged by some young thugs, was edited out after test screenings because audiences refused to accept that a Pacino character would not fight back — and win. (*Empire*, Production News, May 1991.)

49. An aging, blind war hero (Pacino) seeks to end his life during a weekend trip to New York. However, his relationship with his young caregiver (Chris O'Donnell) leads him to see how much his life is still useful.

50. An aging football coach (Pacino) questions his own ability to inspire a team in the face of increasing commercial intervention and young/female management. A young player leads him to see how much he still has to offer

as a coach, albeit through a move to a less prominent (and thus less money-orientated) team.

51. The notion of nostalgia is crucial to an understanding of Pacino's star persona and specifically important to the discussion in Chapter Four.

52. This discussion will be focused on in more detail in Chapter Two.

53. *Righteous Kill* (2008) was marketed on the strength of Pacino and De Niro's previous roles in *Heat*. As they played two cops, allusions to gangster roles were minimal. The film was not critically successful. However, the narrative employs an interesting twist that is primarily achieved through their star personae.

54. As noted in the Introduction, this also applies to more minor actors, who appear across many films.

55. Neale also acknowledges and cites the work of H.R. Jauss, *Towards an Aesthetic of Reception* (1982), and R. Cohen, "History and Genre," in *New Literary History,* 17:2 (1986), 203–18.

56. T.J. Roberts, *An Aesthetics of Junk Fiction* (1990), cited in Neale (2000).

57. He uses the historical period 1930 to the mid–1950s as the parameters for the studio era.

58. See J. Staiger, *Interpreting Films: Studies in the Historical Reception of American Cinema* (1991), J. Mayne, *Cinema and Spectatorship* (1993), and M. Stokes and R. Maltby, eds., *Identifying Hollywood's Audiences: Cultural Identity and the Movies* (1999).

59. See G. Turner, *Film and Social Practice,* 2nd Edition (1993), I. Ang, *Living Room Wars: Rethinking Media Audiences for a Postmodern World* (1996), and A. Ruddock, *Understanding Audiences: Theory and Method* (2001).

60. See for example R. Maltby, *Hollywood Cinema: An Introduction* (1995), and his work on censorship, *Harmless Entertainment: Hollywood and the Ideology of Consensus* (1983).

61. William S. Pechter called *Jaws* "a mind-numbing repast for the sense-sated gluttons" (cited in Halliwell, 1997). Pre-release merchandising and perceptive holiday timing made *Star Wars* one of the top-grossing films of all time. *Batman Returns* (1992) proved more successful than the previous *Batman* (1989), taking over $333 million worldwide.

62. This subject also preoccupies the re-

view in *Films and Filming* v15: 5, February 1969).

63. It is regarded that "the Mafiosi in *The Godfather* have dwelt in America long enough to imitate the behavior of the civilized; the competing bands in *Scarface* are too primitive to have acquired even this" (*Sunday Times*, 5/2/84).

64. J. D. Pistone, with R. Woodley, *Donnie Brasco: My Undercover Life in the Mafia* (1987).

Chapter 3

1. *Compareggio* is the Italian word for non-blood family relationships, especially relevant to the godfather-godson relationship.

2. Roughly translated, it denotes the code of silence by which all *Mafiosi* abide. It also translates as a suspicion of all government and law. Both of these can be traced back to the distrust that exists, according to popular conception, within the Sicilian psyche towards the government and official law enforcement agencies over many centuries.

3. RICO: Racketeer Influenced and Corrupt Organizations Act of 1970.

4. *The Oxford English Dictionary* definition is as follows: "In Sicily, the spirit of hostility to the law and its ministers prevailing among a large portion of the population and manifesting itself frequently in vindictive crimes; the body of those who share in this illegal spirit. In the U.S. and elsewhere, an organized secret society existing for criminal purposes" (*Oxford English Dictionary*, 2nd Ed., 1989: 180–1). Derivatives include Mafioso: a member of such an organization (plural: Mafiosi).

5. First revealed publicly by Joe Valachi in his 1963 testimony to the McLellan Committee Hearings. See Nancy E. Marion (2008), Robert J. Kelly (2000).

6. See D.C. Smith Jr., *Mafia Mystique* (1975) and J.L. Albini, *The American Mafia: Genesis of a Legend* (1971).

7. See J.R. Davis, "Things I Couldn't Tell Till Now," *Collier's*, August 19, 1939, 35–36, cited in D.R. Cressey, "The National and Local Structures of Organized Crime," in D.R. Cressey and D.A. Ward, eds., *Delinquency, Crime, and Social Process* (1969). However, *The Oxford English Dictionary* also notes an *Encyclopedia Britannica* entry (referencing an article in *New Orleans*: XXXI 163/1) of 1902,

relating most probably to the murder of the Superintendent of Police David C. Hennessey in 1890, that states, "It was popularly believed that his death was the work of a maffia, or sworn secret society." (*O.E.D.*: 181). Allusions to "stiletto societies" (*New York Times*, Oct 19, 1890, 1) and "Black Hand Organisations" (*ibid.*) in turn of the century America are also detailed in Smith Jr. (1975), but the use of the term Mafia is not widespread.

8. See Marion (2008), Kelly (2000), Kenney and Finckenauer (1995).

9. The five families were as follows: Luciano/Genovese, Minco/Gambino, Reina/Lucchese, Bannano, Profaci/Colombo (Marion: 59).

10. For a detailed discussion of the political pressure for senate investigations into crime see D. C. Smith Jr., *Mafia Mystique* (1975).

11. W. H. Moore, *The Kefauver Committee and the Politics of Crime 1950–52* (1974), 119.

12. Special Committee to Investigate Organized Crime in Interstate Commerce (Kefauver Committee), *Third Interim Report*, U.S. Senate Report No. 307, 82nd Congress, 1951, p.150, quoted in D.R. Cressey, "The National and Local Structures of Organized Crime" in D.R. Cressey and D.A. Ward, eds., *Delinquency, Crime, and Social Process* (1969).

13. Joseph Bonnano is said to have later taken over control of part of the notorious Gambino family, one of New York's wealthiest crime families, after the death of Joseph Profaci.

14. See also Marion (2008)m *Government Versus Organized Crime.*

15. It's important to note that Smith's work, published in 1975, was probably influenced by the popularity of *The Godfather* book and film. Smith fiercely disagreed with the idea of the Mafia as a significant force in American society and therefore the popularity of such fictions and the widespread belief that they reflected real criminal organizations must have been an irritation to him.

16. See specifically J. Albanese, *Organized Crime in America* (1989), and J. Bonnano, *A Man of Honor* (1983), both quoted in J. Morton, *Gangland International: The Mafia and Other Mobs* (1998).

17. See P. Maas, *The Valachi Papers* (1968). The blurb includes references to it as a "story making headlines across America" and "The first inside account of life in the Cosa Nostra."

18. See *The Valachi Papers* (1972), Columbia Pictures. Neither the book nor the film was an international bestseller, but their basis in supposed fact makes them interesting fuel for myths.

19. For a detailed description of *Capo Regime*, see Maas (1968), and also Ianni (1972) and Cressey (1969). In brief, it structures the Mafia hierarchy along similar lines to ancient Roman legions.

20. By 1971 the book had sold over 1 million copies in hardback. It was yet to be released in paperback. See P. Cowie, *The Godfather Book*, New York: Faber and Faber, 1997.

21. See *The Godfather* (1972), Paramount Pictures. This film, according to Cowie in *The Godfather Book*, earned more than a billion dollars in world-wide sales and also, "in critics' and audience polls would consistently rank in the top half-dozen motion pictures ever made" (Cowie, 1997: xxii).

22. On the popularity and function of conspiracy theories, Palmer and Riley (1981) state the following: "Those who look at their own world, seeking explanations for the confusion, or mischief that apparently surrounds them, often seem to find more comfort in notions of conspiracy than of chance, for chance is amorphous and impersonal, unnerving in its apparent meaninglessness. Conspiracy, on the other hand, is villainy and villainy is reassuringly concrete, subject to exposure and confrontation. Such a conviction tells U.S. that if we have battles to wage and enemies to oppose, at least we know where we stand and what safety requires" (21).

23. See for example Balsamo and Carpozi (1991), R. Siebert, *Secrets of Life and Death: Women and the Mafia* (1996), and Morton (1998).

24. These claims, which were fairly common in films for the period, appeared in the trailer for *Outside the Law*.

25. See Maas (1968).

26. See in particular J. L. Albini (1971), Chapter 4, "The Mafia and the Camorra."

27. *Vendetta*; a process of revenge in equal parts to the crime. For example, "If you kill my brother, I will kill yours."

28. Reviewers have helped to promote Mafia myths by constantly alluding to films such as *Goodfellas* as a true depiction of gangster life — "how it really was." Of course this is not true, but it does strengthen the mythology.

29. This is not an attempt to split the films into specific categories here, as this will not work. For instance, *Miller's Crossing* is in no way a realist film, but it is brutal. It is merely to suggest a connection between films that are viewed as realistic and the lack of family loyalty.

30. T. Hutchinson, (*Mail on Sunday*, October 28, 1990) calls *Goodfellas* "un-romantic" in a review entitled, "Ruthless reality of life inside the mob" (21).

31. One who lives by the rules and traditions of the old world Mafia.

32. The Catholic tradition of issuing godparents at baptism is recounted as one of the binding forces of extended families in Italy and those of Italian descent. See especially Ianni (1972), G. Talese, *Honor Thy Father* (1971), Balsamo and Carpozi (1991).

33. Albini (1971), Smith (1975) and Hess (1998) do not state that a form of Mafia has never existed, but they do assert that the myths are much larger and impressive than the reality. Hess states, "*Mafia* has to be understood as a plethora of small, independent criminal organisations rather than as the secret society of common belief" (Hess: xi).

34. Hess' work, written in Italy and not America, was originally published in 1970.

35. For example, the Apalachin incident, discussed earlier in this chapter.

36. An example of Michael's disconnection from his cultural heritage is evidenced when he struggles to pronounce the title of the most famous of Sicilian Operas, Mascagni's *Cavelleria Rusticana*. He apologizes for this by explaining, "I've lived in New York too long."

37. For the best and most detailed accounts of behind-the-scenes arguments and financial wrangles, see P. Cowie, *The Godfather Book* (1997), P. Biskind, *The Godfather Companion* (1990), H. Lebo, *The Godfather Legacy* (1997) or P. Biskind, *Easy Riders, Raging Bulls: How the Sex Drugs and Rock 'n' Roll Generation Saved Hollywood* (1998).

38. Ruth notes, "Categories of defect and criminality blurred into categories of economic class, race and ethnicity. [...] Respectable Americans need neither deny nor take responsibility for the disorder around them: it emanated from others" (15).

39. The crucial meeting between Flannery and the Italians requires Flannery to call his men to halt an assassination attempt on the

Italian boss. Flannery's inferiority in the face of the Mafia results in them denying him permission to make the call. The ensuing mix-up reveals the assassination plot and results in Flannery's assassination of his own brother to appease the Mafia.

40. It is suggested that Carlito's prison sentence was a result of not testifying against an older Puerto Rican Mafia member. This gives a sense of honor to Carlito's character, as well as linking his persona to the generational aspect of Mafia myths.

41. This phrase is often used in gangster films to explain the bosses who do not get involved in the frontline activities of extortion or murder, but spend their days sitting in the backrooms of restaurants or clubs, making deals and giving out orders.

42. This fact possibly suggests the continuation of Matilda's training as an assassin, which would leave the narrative open for a possible sequel, as yet un-made.

43. He pronounces ethics with a silent "h."

44. It is significant that Nino is finally gunned down by an African-American grandfather and not the law. The narrative suggests Nino dies for betraying his own ethnic traditions as much as anything else, thus suggesting Nino's emulation of white gangsters denigrates black identity. This is not surprising considering the fact that Italian-American gangster films are often brutally racist in their perception of blacks as animals (*The Godfather*) or as incompetent criminals. See for example the portrayal of the getaway driver (Samuel L. Jackson) in *Goodfellas*.

45. See J. Munby, "Epilogue: From Gangster to Gangsta," in *Public Enemies, Public Heroes*....

46. The term is used here to indicate that the ethnicity of these characters is not emphasized in the narrative, in that they are simply "white" Americans.

47. A "sit down" is a meeting between rival bosses used to try to avoid bloodshed. The most famous example of this is the meeting of the five families in *The Godfather*, but the term is also reminiscent of syndicate films of the 1950s. An interesting example occurs in *The Rise and Fall of Legs Diamond* (1960), wherein Legs realizes his reign is over as he stumbles across a syndicate meeting between bosses who are conspiring against his activities. Examples such as these mark the transition from individual gangster successes to corporate Mafia narratives.

48. The Senate Caucus Room set was "a perfect reproduction of the real thing at ⅞ original scale" (Lebo, 1997: 229).

Chapter 4

1. See especially J. Tompkins, *West of Everything: The Inner Life of Westerns* (1992), which details the representation of male heroes in novels and films of the Western since the nineteenth century. Also, see R. Wilkinson, *American Tough: The Tough Guy Tradition and American Character* (1984), which focuses on American male character types in popular culture since the nineteenth century.

2. Wood's essay, "Ideology, Genre, Auteur" (1977) examines "the values and assumptions embodied in and reinforced by the classical Hollywood cinema." He isolates twelve ideological viewpoints, which include the Ideal Male, the Ideal Female, and their alter-egos; the Settled Husband and the Erotic female.

3. For a historical analysis of masculine/feminine dualisms in Western culture, see G. Lerner, *The Creation of Patriarchy* (1986).

4. See R. Weigman, *American Anatomies* (1995), S. Cohan, *Masked Men: Masculinity and the Movies in the Fifties* (1997) and H. Stecopoulos and M. Uebel, eds., *Race and the Subject of Masculinities* (1997).

5. This is not an oversight by the genre theorists. At the time Warshow (1948, 1954), McArthur (1971), or even Cawelti (1976) made their analyses, the plurality of male experience was not a primary concern in the area of film studies.

6. See for example J. McCarty, *Hollywood Gangland*, J. Munby, *Public Enemies, Public Heroes*, D.E. Ruth, *Inventing the Public Enemy*, and M. Yaquinto, *Pump 'Em Full of Lead*.

7. See for example F. Fanon, *Black Skin White Masks* (1968), S. Hall, *The Whites of their Eyes* (1981), H. K. Bhabha, *The Other Question... The Stereotype and Colonial Discourse* (1983), R. Stam and L. Spence, *Colonialism, Racism and Representation: An Introduction* (1983), and E. Shohat and R. Stam, *Unthinking Eurocentrism: Multiculturalism and the Media* (1994).

8. However, it should be noted that Hollywood Westerns are directed by white males, while postclassical gangster films have tended

to be directed by Italian-American males. Thus, there is a closer affiliation with their subject matter.

9. This is in contrast to popular conceptions of the gangster genre. As recently as 2000, Steve Neale asserted that a key characteristic of the gangster genre is that it is set in the present (Neale, 2000:227).

10. For discussions of American identity at the beginning of the twentieth century, see T. Roosevelt, *The Winning of the West* (1889), or E.A. Ross, *The Old World in the New* (1914). These essentially racist views can still be found in more recent works, such as A. Brimelow, *Alien Nation* (1995).

11. The racial connotations of Oriental gangster narratives, such as Chinese Bandits and Japanese Triads, are also different in this context because the "ideal male" against which the gangster is being measured is European.

12. This identity can be summarized in the often used acronym WASP (White Anglo-Saxon Protestant).

13. See J. Guglielmo and Salerno, eds., *Are Italians White? How Race Is Made in America*, New York: Routledge, 2003, and P. Boscia-Mulè, *Authentic Ethnicities: The Interaction of Ideology, Gender, Power, and Class in the Italian American Experience*, Westport: Greenwood Press, 1999.

14. Frantz Fanon (1968) writes that no matter how much an African American attempts to assimilate into white culture, his or her skin color and physical features will always mark him or her out as different.

15. See specifically F. Ianni, *A Family Business*.

16. *Report of the United States Immigration Commission* (1911), cited in S. Steinberg, *The Ethnic Myth: Race, Ethnicity and Class in America* (1981).

17. Sociologists believe this may have been due to Italian poverty. The cost of bringing the whole family to America was too high, so the men came first and sent for the women later. In the Jewish community the gender split was more evenly balanced, as most came in family groups, while the Irish had a slightly higher female-to-male ratio in immigration by 1900. The implication of this is that there would be more single Italian immigrant males in the early years of this century populating the urban ghettos and looking to establish themselves in business and communities generally.

18. See earlier discussions in Chapter Two and Chapter Three.

19. This is the basis for Fanon's seminal work *Black Skins, White Masks*, wherein he details the belief that the physical identity of blackness denies an individual's access to complete assimilation in white American culture.

20. See especially the work of Malcolm X, in A. Haley, *The Autobiography of Malcolm X* (1965) and S. Carmichael, "Black Power" (1967) reprinted in R. Griffith, ed., *Major Problems in American History since 1945: Documents and Essays* (1992), in which he states, "Integration is a subterfuge for the maintenance of white supremacy" (366).

21. See S. Cohan and I. Rae Hark, eds., *Screening the Male: Exploring Masculinities in Hollywood Cinema*, London: Routledge (1993).

22. "Which Sopranos character are you?" features a link to an on-line quiz at another site.

23. Male bonding has attracted a great deal of interest in relation to wider notions of cultural theory. See for example R. Horrocks, *Male Myths and Icons* (1988), D. Sherrod, "The Bonds of Men: Problems and Possibilities in Close Male Relationships," in H. Brod, ed., *The Making of Masculinities* (1987), S. Jeffords, *The Remasculinization of America: Gender and the Vietnam War* (1989) and R. Bly, *Iron John: A Book About Men* (1990).

24. Emotional reticence, according to Wood, is a prerequisite of the ideal male.

25. See also, P. Nardi, ed., *Men's Friendships*, Newbury Park: Sage (1992).

26. See W. Broyles Jr., "Brothers in Arms" (1986), cited in Jeffords.

27. See Chapter Three. This phrase, meaning to hide out in secure houses during gang wars, is used in Mario Puzo's original book, but is taken in turn from Joe Valachi's account of Mafia activity. See P. Maas, *The Valachi Papers*, 1968, 110.

28. J. Rutherford and R. Chapman discuss the role of machismo — whereby "the borderline between legitimate violence employed by the state and male violence that threatens social stability is quickly crossed" (31), in *Male Order: Unwrapping Masculinity* (1988). The very aggression that is applauded in army conflict is reviled in ordinary society.

29. This scene takes place in the study, where Michael, explaining his plan to kill both

Sollozo and McClusky, gains center stage from Sonny as the camera tracks forward to isolate him in the frame.

30. This scene also provides Sollozo's motivation for attempting to kill Vito. Sonny's outburst gives Sollozo the impression that with Vito gone, Sonny would be open to negotiation concerning the drugs business.

31. Ruth (1996) notes that in the early twentieth-century American economy, "Success seemed to depend less on character and hard work than on the ability to situate oneself within a promising professional or corporate bureaucracy. For many workers technology made obsolete the skills on which personal identity had been founded" (19).

32. See the discussion of character types in the Introduction and Chapter One.

33. Even if Native Americans occupy the major narrative position, the Eurocentric nature of Hollywood cinema asserts its "white" subjectivity. For detailed discussions see R.H. Pearce, *Savagism and Civilisation: A Study of the Indian and the American Mind* (1965), R. Stam and L. Spence, *Colonialism, Racism and Representation: An Introduction* (1983), E. Shohat and R. Stam, *Unthinking Eurocentrism: Multiculturalism and the Media* (1994) and S. M. Larke, *Geronimo Versus the American Legend: The Eurocentric Structure of Hollywood Westerns* (1995).

34. This work follows on from Edward Said's discussions (for example *Orientalism* (1978)) and F. Fanon *Black Skins White Masks* (1968).

35. In *Part I* she visits the house to find Michael, thus compromising the security of the family, and in *Part II* after the abortion she visits the house to see the children, before being rejected by Michael — who shuts the door in her face.

36. However, this same involvement also encourages audiences to sympathize with his increasing isolation and lack of family support.

37. After being assaulted by the police chief, Michael devises a plan to kill him and Sollozo. Sonny belittles his involvement, but the camera slowly centralizes and focuses in on Michael, ignoring Sonny's presence. From this moment on Michael takes center stage in the narrative, and Sonny is murdered not long after.

38. See Chapter Two and the discussion of costume, dialogue and gestures as iconography and conventions.

39. See Tillman (1992) in *Sight and Sound*, v2.2, 33.

40. As noted earlier in Chapter One, I am using melodrama to denote those films which foreground the emotional aspects of a character.

41. See J. Stringer, "Your Tender Smile Gives Me Strength: Paradigms of Masculinity in John Woo's *A Better Tomorrow* and *The Killer*," in *Screen* v38:1 (Spring 1997) 25–41.

42. John Woo's films focus on an emotional respect or affection between the criminal and the cop, as two similar characters isolated in their individual pursuits. The theme is common in many American films too. The most recent example, *Heat* (1995), includes Al Pacino as the cop, with Robert De Niro as the villain.

43. Julian Stringer uses the term omnipotence, which makes the binary opposition too extreme. However, he is suggesting that characters perform omnipotence rather than embody it. Even so, this book shall use the term power, which allows for a greater variation in the level of masculine performance of omnipotence.

44. This is referring to the construction of identity as negotiation through social discourse, as defined by Michel Foucault in such works as "The Subject and Power" in H. Dreyfus and P. Rabinow, *Michel Foucault: Beyond Structuralism and Hermeneutics* (1982). An individual constructs his or her own identity through interaction with others.

45. Of course this is slightly undermined by audiences' privileged knowledge of Donnie's real identity as an FBI agent, but while undercover Donnie is at the mercy of the Mafia hierarchy.

46. Gestures and multi-faceted phrases — such as "Forget about it" — are wonderful clichés, but also valuable in assessing a character's status in Mafia culture.

47. See E. Mitchell, "Apes and Essences: Some Sources of Significance in the American Gangster Film," in B. K. Grant, ed., *Film Genre Reader II* (1995).

48. See D. Thompson and I. Christie (1990), and G. Smith in *Film Comment* (1990 and 1996).

49. Many more reviews express the relationship between *Godfather* and *Scarface*, such as *New York* (December 19, 1983), *Guardian* (February 2, 1984), *Sunday Express* (February

5, 1984), *Sunday Times* (February 5, 1984), and *Time* (December 5, 1983).

50. He also displays the "bold, garish vitality of a comic strip nasty" (*Daily Mail*, February 3, 1984).

51. He is killed, not by the law, or rival gangs, but by an elderly African-American man, who despises the drug business and the harm it does to African-American communities.

52. See L. Fried, *The Rise and Fall of the Jewish Gangster*, discussed in Chapter Two.

53. See A. Knee, "The Dialectic of Female Power and Male Hysteria in *Play Misty For Me*," in S. Cohan and I. Rae Hark, eds., *Screening the Male*.... It is also important to note that the concept of the displaced heterosexual hero discussed here is similar to that discussed in relation to film noir; see for instance F. Krutnik, *In a Lonely Street: Film Noir, Genre, Masculinity* (1991).

54. There are other examples, but this book has chosen these three stars as representative of these categories.

55. Clatterbaugh outlines a conservative view of masculinity that maintains the male character is aggressive, single-minded and brutal. These are all attributes that could be applauded in an environment where men are required to battle hostile forces in order to protect themselves and their belongings, but these traits have become outmoded as society has become more civilized. However, the conservative view is that gender personalities are biologically determined, and thus men cannot be blamed for behaving or desiring to behave in these ways.

56. See F. Jameson, "Reification and Utopia in Mass Culture," in *Social Text 1* (Fall 1979) reprinted in *Signatures of the Visible*, London: Routledge, 1992.

57. See *Film Comment* v20 n.4 (1984), 21.

58. This development is evident in Leone's declaration in publicity materials and interviews that *Once Upon a Time in America* follows on from *Once Upon a Time in the West* (1969) and the unrealized *Once Upon a Time, the Revolution*.

59. The film was released in two versions.

The shorter American version ran chronologically. The European version moved between the three settings — the 1920s, 1930s and 1960s — in a non-linear narrative of flashbacks and flashforwards.

60. The main reason for not discussing the shorter, chronological version of the film is because it is not the film Leone intended. However, this is not advocating directorial authority, but merely aligning a similar preference for the narrative flashback structure of the full-length version for this discussion, as it foregrounds memory and guilt and is therefore a more emotion-led narrative structure. Furthermore, the European version provides narrative closure by ending the narrative at the point it began, which is central to the ways in which the film encourages nostalgia.

61. Reviews of *Donnie Brasco* allude to Lefty in relation to Pacino's previous gangster roles; see for example "An end to Mob rule," in *Independent* 24/497: 6; "Portrait of a Hit Man," in *Village Voice*, March 4, 1997: 69; "Review," in *Cineaste* v23 n.1, 1997: 43. Maurice Yacowar (1997) notes, "Pacino's casting evokes Hollywood's most illuminating Mafia film [*The Godfather*]. Where earlier Pacino grew from soft to hard, here his character moves from hard to soft. This role is a reversal to his earlier success" (*Queen's Quarterly*, 104/1: 65).

62. See P. Cook, "Masculinity in Crisis: Tragedy and Identification in *Raging Bull*," in *Screen* v23:3/4 (1982), pp. 39–46.

63. Even though race could be said to be America's signifier for class in that those further from the white ideal often suffer the greatest poverty, terms such as white trash, trailer trash, and redneck are beginning to emerge that distinguish on economic rather than racial lines.

Conclusion

1. This scene was cut from the original release of *The Godfather Part II*, but was reinserted in *The Godfather 1901–1959: The Epic*, released in a video box set (1991).

Bibliography

General

Alba, R.D. (1985) *Italian Americans: Into the Twilight of Ethnicity.* Englewood Cliffs, NJ: Prentice-Hall.

_____. (1990) *Ethnic Identity: The Transformation of White America.* London: Yale University Press.

Albanese, J. (1989) *Organized Crime in America.* Cincinnati: Anderson.

Albini, J.L. (1971) *The American Mafia: Genesis of a Legend.* New York: Meredith.

Allen, R.C., and D. Gomery. (1985) *Film History: Theory and Practice.* London: McGraw-Hill.

Alloway, L. (1963) "Iconography and the Movies." *Movie* no. VII: 4–6.

_____. (1971) *Violent America: The Movies 1946–1964.* New York: Museum of Art.

Altman, R. (1999) *Film/Genre.* London: BFI.

Ambrogio, A. (1978) "*The Godfather I* and *II*: Patterns of Corruption." *Film Criticism* vol. 3:1: 35–44.

Ang, I. (1996) *Living Room Wars: Rethinking Media Audiences for a Postmodern World.* London: Routledge.

Angus, I., and S. Jhally, eds. (1989) *Cultural Politics in Contemporary America.* London: Routledge.

Balio, T, ed. (1985) *The American Film Industry.* Madison: University of Wisconsin Press.

_____. (1990) *Hollywood in the Age of Television.* Cambridge, MA: Unwin Hyman.

Barker, M., and J. Petley. (1997) *Ill Effects: The Media/Violence Debate.* London: Routledge.

Barreca, R, ed. (2002) *A Sitdown with The Sopranos: Watching Italian American Culture on TV's Most Talked-About Series.* New York: Palgrave Macmillan.

Bartell, S.M. (1981) "The Chinese Bandit Novel and the American Gangster Film." *New Orleans Review,* 8. no. 1: 102–105.

Barthes, R. (1973) *Mythologies.* London: Paladin/Grafton.

Bell, D. (1953) "Crime as an American Way of Life: a Queer Ladder of Social Mobility." *The Antioch Review,* 13. Reprinted in D. Bell. (1988) *The End of Ideology: On the Exhaustion of Political Ideas in the Fifties.* Cambridge, MA: Harvard University Press. 127–150.

Bennett, T. (1983) "Texts. Readers. Reading Formations." *Literature and History,* 9 no2: 214–227.

Bennett, T., and J. Woollacott. (1987) *Bond and Beyond: the Political Career of a Popular Hero.* London: Macmillan Education.

Bergan, R. (1999) *Coppola: The Making of His Movies.* New York: Orion.

Berger, A.A. (1978) *Film in Society.* New York: Transaction.

Bernstein, M. (2000) "Perfecting the New Gangster: Writing *Bonnie and Clyde.*" *Film Quarterly,* 53, no. 4: 16–31.

Bhabha, H. K. (1983) "The Other Question ... The Stereotype and Colonial Discourse." *Screen,* 24, no. 6: 8–36.

Biskind, P. (1990) *The Godfather Companion.* New York: Simon and Schuster.

_____. (1999) *Easy Riders, Raging Bulls: How*

the *Sex-Drugs-and-Rock 'n' Roll Generation Saved Hollywood*. New York: Simon and Schuster.

Black, G.D. (1994) *Hollywood Censored: Morality Codes, Catholics and the Movies*. Cambridge: Cambridge University Press.

Bliss, M. (1983) *Brian De Palma*. Metuchen, NJ: Scarecrow.

_____. (1985) *Martin Scorsese and Michael Cimino*. Metuchen, NJ: Scarecrow.

Bordwell, D., J. Staiger, and K. Thompson. (1985) *The Classical Hollywood Cinema: Film Style and Mode of Production to 1960*. New York: Routledge.

Boscia-Mulè, P. (1999) *Authentic Ethnicities: The Interaction of Ideology, Gender Power, and Class in the Italian American Experience*. Westport, CT: Greenwood.

Bowker, L.H, ed. (1998) *Masculinities and Violence*. London: Sage Publications.

Brimelow, A. (1995) *Alien Nation*. New York: Random House.

Brittan, A. (1989) *Masculinity and Power*. Oxford: Blackwell.

Brod, H., ed. (1987) *The Making of Masculinities: The New Men's Studies*. London: Allen and Unwin.

Brode, D. (1995) *Money, Women and Guns: Crime Movies from* Bonnie and Clyde *to the Present*. New York: Carol Publishing Group.

Browne, N., ed. (1998) *Refiguring American Film Genres*. Berkeley: University of California Press.

_____. (2000) *Francis Ford Coppola's* The Godfather *Trilogy*. Cambridge: Cambridge University Press.

Bruce, B. (1986) "Martin Scorsese: Five Films." *Movie*. 31/32: 88–94.

Brunette, P., ed. (1999) *Martin Scorsese Interviews*. Jackson: University of Mississippi Press.

Bruzzi, S. (1995) "Style and the Hood: On Gangsters, American and French Style." *Sight and Sound*, 5:11: 26–27.

_____. (1997) *Undressing Cinema: Clothing and Identity in the Movies*. London: Routledge.

Butler, J. (1990) *Gender Trouble: Feminism and the Subversion of Identity*. New York: Routledge.

Campbell, N., and Kean. A., eds. (1997) *American Cultural Studies: An Introduction to American Culture*. London: Routledge.

Carroll, N. (1982) "The Future of Allusion: Hollywood in the Seventies (and Beyond)." *October*, 20: 51–81.

_____. (1998) *Interpreting the Moving Image*. Cambridge: Cambridge University Press.

Casillo, R. (1991) "Moments in Italian-American Cinema: from *Little Caesar* to Coppola and Scorsese." *From the Margins: Writings in Italian-Americana*. Edited by Anthony J. Tamburri, P. Giordano, and F. Gardaphe. West Lafayette, IN: Purdue University Press. 374–96.

Cawelti, J.C. (1971) *The Six Gun Mystique*. Ohio: Bowling Green University Press.

_____. (1975) "Myths of Violence in American Popular Culture." *Critical Inquiry*, 1:3: 521–541.

_____. (1976) "The Mythology of Crime and Its Formulaic Embodiments." *Adventure. Mystery and Romance*. Chicago: University of Chicago Press. 51–79.

_____. (1978) "*Chinatown* and Generic Transformation." *Film Theory and Criticism*. Edited by G. Mast, M. Cohen, and L. Braudy. Oxford: Oxford University Press, 1992.

Chafe, W.H. (1999) *The Unfinished Journey: America Since World War II*. 4th Edition. New York: Oxford University Press.

Chapman, R., and J. Rutherford. (1988) *Male Order: Unwrapping Masculinity*. London: Lawrence and Wishart.

Chown, J. (1988) *Hollywood Auteur: Francis Coppola*. London: Praeger.

Chubb, J. (1982) *Patronage, Power and Poverty in Southern Italy: A Tale of Two Cities*. Cambridge: Cambridge University Press.

_____. (1996) "The Mafia. the Market and the State in Italy and Russia." *Journal of Modern Italian Studies*, 1, no. 2: 273–91.

Chute, D. (1984) "Scarface." *Film Comment*, 20:1: 66–70.

Ciongoli. A.K., and J. Parini, eds. (1997) *Beyond* The Godfather: *Italian American Writers on the Real Italian American Experience*. Hanover, NH: University Press of New England.

Clarens, C. (1977) "Hooverville West: The Hollywood Man 1934–1945." *Film Comment*, May/June: 10–16.

_____. (1978) "The *Godfather* Saga." *Film Comment*, 14: 21–23.

Clarens, C., and F. Hirsch. (1997) *Crime Movies: An Illustrated History of the Gangster Genre from D.W. Griffith to* Pulp Fiction. New York: Da Capo.

Clatterbaugh, K. (1990) *Contemporary Perspectives on Masculinity: Men, Women and Politics in Modern Society*. Boulder, CO: Westview.

Cohan, S. (1997) *Masked Men: Masculinity and Movies in the Fifties*. Bloomington: Indiana University Press.

Cohan, S., and I.R. Hark, eds. (1993) *Screening the Male: Exploring Masculinities in Hollywood Cinema*. London: Routledge.

Cohen, D. (1990) *Being a Man*. London: Routledge.

Collins, J. (1993) "Genericity in the Nineties: Eclectic Irony and the New." *Film Theory Goes to the Movies*. Edited by J. Collins, H. Radner, and A. Preacher Collins. London: Routledge. 242–264.

Connell, R.W. (2005) *Masculinities*. 2nd Edition. Berkeley: University of California Press.

Combs, J., ed. (1993) *Movies and Politics: The Dynamic Relationship*. New York: Garland.

Cook, D.A. (1991) *A History of Narrative Film*. 3rd Edition. London: W.W. Norton.

Cook, J. (1969) "Bonnie and Clyde." *Screen*, 10, 4/5: 101–114.

Cook, R. (1998) *Sweet Land of Liberty?: The Afro-American Struggle for Civil Rights in Twentieth Century America*. London: Longman.

Corliss, M. (1984) "Once Upon a Time in America." *Film Comment*, 20:4: 18–21.

Corrigan, T. (1991) *A Cinema Without Walls: Movies and Culture After Vietnam*. Piscataway, NJ: Rutgers University Press.

Cowie, E. (1998) "Storytelling: Classical Hollywood Cinema and Classical Narrative." *Contemporary Hollywood Cinema*. Edited by S. Neale and M. Smith. M. London: Routledge. 178–190.

Cowie, P. (1997) *The Godfather Book*. New York: Faber and Faber.

Creed, B. (1993) *The Monstrous Feminine*. London: Routledge.

Creekmur, C.K. (1997) "On the Road and On the Run." in Cohan. S., and Hark. I.R., eds. *The Road Movie Book*. London: Routledge. 90–112.

Cressey, D. R. (1969) "The National and Local Structures of Organized Crime." *Delinquency. Crime and Social Process*. Edited by D.R. Cressey and D.A. Ward. New York: Harper and Row. 867–883.

_____. (1969) *Theft of a Nation: The Structure and Operations of Organized Crime in America*. New York: Harper and Row.

Davies, J., and C.R. Smith. (1997) *Gender, Ethnicity and Sexuality in Contemporary American Film*. Edinburgh: Keele University Press.

De Stefano, G. (2006) *An Offer We Can't Refuse: The Mafia in the Mind of America*. New York: Faber and Faber.

Denby, D. (1973) "The Sweetness of Hell." *Sight and Sound*, 43:1: 48–50.

Diawara, M. (1993) "The New Realism" in *Black American Cinema*. New York: Routledge. 3–25.

Dick, B.F. (1990) *Anatomy of Film*. 2nd Edition. New York: St. Martin's.

Dixon, W.W. (2000) *Film Genre 2000: New Critical Essays*. New York: State University of New York Press.

Durgnat, R. (1991) "Of Gangs, Gangsters and Genres." *Monthly Film Bulletin*, 58: 687. 93–96.

Dyer, R. (1986) *Heavenly Bodies: Film Stars and Society*. Basingstoke, UK: Macmillan.

_____. (1988) "White" *Screen*, 29(4): 44–65.

_____. (1993) *The Matter of Images: Essays in Representation*. London: Routledge.

_____. (1998) *Stars*. New Edition. London: BFI.

Easthope, A. (1992) *What a Man's Gotta Do: The Masculine Myth in Popular Culture*. London: Routledge.

Edley, N., and M. Wetherell. (1995) *Men in Perspective: Practice, Power and Identity*. London: Prentice Hall/Harvester Wheatsheaf.

Edwards, T. (2006) *Cultures of Masculinity*. New York: Routledge.

Elsaesser, T. (1971) "The American Cinema 2: Why Hollywood?" *Monogram*, no. 1: 4–10.

Faludi, S. (1991) *Backlash: The Undeclared War on Women*. London: Vintage.

_____. (1994) "Naked Citadel." *New Yorker*, September 5, 1994, 62–81.

Fanon, F. (1968) *Black Skin, White Masks*. London: MacGibbon and Kee.

Farber, D. (1994) *The Age of Great Dreams: America in the 1960s*. New York: Hill and Wang.

Farber, S. (1972) "Coppola and The Godfather." *Sight and Sound*, 41:4: 217–223.

Fender, S. (1993) "The American Difference." *Modern American Culture: An Introduction*. Edited by M. Gidley. London: Longman. 1–22.

Ferraro, T. (1989) "Blood in the Marketplace: The Business of Family in the *Godfather* Narratives." *The Invention of Ethnicity.* Edited by W. Sollors. New York: The Open University Press. 176–207.

Foucault, M. (1970) *The Order of Things: An Archaeology of the Human Sciences* London: Routledge.

Frayling, C. (2000) *Sergio Leone: Something to Do with Death.* New York: Faber and Faber.

French, P. (1968) "Incitement Against Violence." *Sight and Sound*, 37:1: 3–8.

Fried, A. (1993) *The Rise and Fall of the Jewish Gangster in American.* Revised Edition. New York: Columbia University Press.

Friedman, L., ed. (1991) *Unspeakable Images: Ethnicity and the American Cinema.* Urbana: University of Illinois Press.

_____. (1997) *The Cinema of Martin Scorsese.* Oxford: Roundhouse.

_____, ed. (2000) *Arthur Penn's Bonnie and Clyde.* Cambridge: Cambridge University Press.

Fuchs, C.J. (1993) "The Buddy Politic." *Screening the Male: Exploring Masculinities in Hollywood Cinema.* Edited by S. Cohan and I.R. Hark. London: Routledge. 194–212.

Gabbard, G. (2002) *The Psychology of* The Sopranos*: Love, Death, Desire and Betrayal in America's Favorite Gangster Family.* New York: Basic Books.

Gaines, J. (1994) "White Privilege and Looking Relations: Race and Gender in Feminist Film Theory." *Multiple Voices in Feminist Film Criticism.* Edited by Carson, Dittmar and Welsch. Minneapolis: University of Minnesota Press. 176–190.

Gambino, R. (1974) *Blood of My Blood: The Dilemma of the Italian Americans.* New York: Doubleday.

Geraghty, L., and M. Jancovich, eds. (2008) *The Shifting Definitions of Genre: Essays on Labeling Films, Television Shows and Media.* Jefferson, NC: McFarland.

Gidley, M., ed. (1993) *Modern American Culture.* London: Longman.

Glazer, N., and D.P. Moynihan. (1970) *Beyond the Melting Pot: The Negroes, Puerto Ricans, Jews, Italians, and Irish of New York City.* 2nd edition. Cambridge, MA: The M.I.T. Press.

Gledhill, C. (1988) "Pleasurable Negotiations." *Feminist Film Theory: A Reader.* Edited by S. Thornham. Edinburgh: Edinburgh University Press, 1999. 166–179.

Goldberg, H. (1976) *The Hazards of Being Male: Surviving the Myth of Masculine Privilege.* New York: Signet Books.

Goldstein, L., ed. (1994) *The Male Body: Features, Destinies, Exposures.* Ann Arbor: University of Michigan Press.

Gomery, D. (1988) *The Hollywood Studio System.* London: St. Martin's Press.

_____. (1998) "Hollywood Corporate Business Practice and Periodizing Contemporary Film History." *Contemporary Hollywood Cinema.* Edited by S. Neale and M. Smith. London: Routledge. 47–57.

Grant, B.K., ed. (1995) *Film Genre Reader II.* Austin: University of Texas Press.

Griffith, R., ed. *Major Problems in American History since 1945: Documents and Essays.* Lexington, MA: D.C. Heath.

Guglielmo, J., and S. Salerno, eds. (2003) *Are Italians White? How Race Is Made in America.* New York: Routledge.

Hall, S. (1981) "The Whites of Their Eyes: Racist Ideologies and the Media." *Silver Linings.* Edited by G. Bridges and R. Brunt. London: Lawrence and Wishart. 18–22.

_____. (1985) "The Rediscovery of Ideology: Return of the Repressed in Media Studies." *Subjectivity and Social Relations.* Edited by V. Beechey and J. Donald. Milton Keynes: Open University Press. 23–55.

Hardy, P., ed. (1998) *The Overlook Film Encyclopedia: The Gangster Film.* New York: Overlook Press.

Hatty, S. (2000) *Masculinities, Violence, and Culture.* Thousand Oaks: Sage.

Heale, M.J. (2001) *The Sixties in America: History, Politics and Protest.* Edinburgh: Edinburgh University Press.

Hess, H. (1998) *Mafia and Mafioso: Origin, Power, Myth.* 2nd Edition. London: C. Hurst.

Hess, J. (1976) "*Godfather II*: A Deal Coppola Couldn't Refuse." *Movies and Methods Vol. I.* Edited by B. Nicholls. Berkeley: University of California Press. 81–90.

Hill, A. (1999) "Risky Business: Film Violence as an interactive Phenomenon." *Identifying Hollywood's Audiences: Cultural identity and the Movies.* Edited by M. Stokes and R. Maltby. London: BFI. 176–186.

Hillier, J., ed. (1985) *Cahiers du Cinema I: The*

1950s. Neo-realism, Hollywood, New Wave. London: Routledge and Kegan Paul.

Hoberman, J. (1991) "Believe It or Not." *Art-Forum*, v. 29:5: 19–22.

Hobsbawm, E.J. (1969) *Bandits*. Harmondsworth: Penguin.

_____. (1985) "Robin Hoodo: Mario Puzo's *The Sicilian*." *The New York Review of Books*, February 14, 1985, 12–17.

Hoch, P. (1979) *White Hero Black Beast: Racism, Sexism and the Mask of Masculinity.* London: Pluto Press.

Hollows, J., and M. Jancovich, eds. (1995) *Approaches to Popular Film*. Manchester: Manchester University Press.

Horrocks, R. (1995) *Male Myths and Icons: Masculinity in Popular Culture*. London: Macmillan Press.

Ianni, F.A.J. (1972) *A Family Business: Kinship and Social Control in Organized Crime*. New York: Russell Sage Foundation.

_____. (1974) *Black Mafia: Ethnic Succession in Organized Crime*. New York: Simon and Schuster.

Isaacs, N. (1996) "Bathgate in the Time of Coppola: A Reverie." *Literature and Film Quarterly*, v.24:1: 109–110.

Jameson, F. (1992) *Signatures of the Visible*. London: Routledge.

_____. (1992) *The Geopolitical Aesthetic: Cinema and Space in the World System*. Bloomington: Indiana University Press.

Jeffords, S. (1989) *The Remasculinization of America: Gender and the Vietnam War*. Bloomington: Indiana University Press.

_____. (1994) *Hard Bodies: Hollywood Masculinity in the Reagan Years*. Piscataway , NJ: Rutgers University Press.

Johnson, R.K. (1977) *Francis Ford Coppola*. Boston: Twayne.

Jowett, G. (1991) "Bullets, Beer and the Hays Office: *Public Enemy* (1931)." *American History/American Film*. Edited by J. E. O'Connor and M.A. Jackson. New York: Continuum.

Kaminsky, S.M. (1983) "Narrative Time in Sergio Leone's *Once Upon a Time in America*." *Studies in Literary Imagination*, v. 16 no. 1: 59–74.

_____. (1985) *American Film Genres: Approaches to a Critical Theory of Popular Film* 2nd Edition. Chicago: Nelson-Hall.

Karpf, S.L. (1973) *The Gangster Film: Emergence, Variation and Decay of a Genre 1930–1940*. New York: Arno.

Kelly, M.P. (1992) *Martin Scorsese: A Journey*. London: Secker and Warburg.

Kenney, D.J., and J. Finckenauer. (1995) *Organized Crime in America*. Belmont, CA: Wadsworth.

Kerr, P., ed. (1986) *The Hollywood Film Industry*. London: Routledge.

Kitses, J. (1969) *Horizon's West*. Bloomington: Indiana University Press.

Klein, N. (1998) "Staging Murders: The Social Imaginary, Film and the City." *Wide Angle*, v. 20:3: 85–96.

Klinger, B. (1984) "Cinema/Ideology/Criticism Revisited: the Progressive Genre." *Film Genre Reader II*. Edited by B.K. Grant. Austin: University of Texas Press, 1995.

Kolker, P. (1980) *A Cinema of Loneliness: Penn, Kubrick, Coppola, Scorsese, Altman*. Oxford: Oxford University Press.

Konieczny, V. (1985) "On Film: Francis Ford Coppola." *West Coast Review*, v. 19 no. 4:. 4–8

Kooistra, P. (1989) *Criminals as Heroes: Structure, Power and Identity*. Bowling Green, Ohio: Bowling Green State University Popular Press.

Körte, P., and G. Seesslen, eds. (1999) *Joel and Ethan Coen*. Translated by R. Mulholland. London: Titan Books.

Krämer, P. (1998) "Postclasical Hollywood." *The Oxford Guide to Film Studies*. Edited by J. Hill and P. Church Gibson. Oxford: Oxford University Press. 289–309.

Kritzman, L.D., ed. (1988) *Michel Foucault: Politics, Philosophy, Culture, Interviews and Other Writings 1977–1984*. London: Routledge.

Krutnik, F. (1991) *In a Lonely Street: Film Noir, Genre, Masculinity*. London: Routledge.

LaPlace, M. (1987) "Stars and the Star System: the Case of Bette Davis." *Home Is Where the Heart Is*. Edited by C. Gledhill. London: British Film Institute.

Latimer, J. (1975) "*The Godfather*: Metaphor and Microcosm." *Journal of Popular Film and TV*, v. 4:2: 204–208.

Lavery, D., ed. (2002) *This Thing of Ours: Investigating the Sopranos*. New York: Columbia University Press.

_____. (2006) *Reading the Sopranos: Hit TV from HBO*. New York: Palgrave Macmillan.

Lebo, H. (1997) *The Godfather Legacy*. New York: Simon and Schuster.

Lehman, P., ed. (2001) *Masculinity: Bodies, Movies, Culture*. New York: Routledge.

Leong, I., M. Sell and K. Thomas. (1997) "Mad Love. Mobile Homes and Dysfunctional Dicks." *The Road Movie Book*. Edited by S. Cohan and I.R. Hark. London: Routledge. 70–89.

Lerner, G. (1986) *The Creation of Patriarchy*. Oxford: Oxford University Press.

Leuchtenburg, W., ed. (1983) *A Troubled Feast: American Society Since 1945*. New York: Harper Collins.

Levi-Strauss, C. (1966) *The Savage Mind*. London: Weidenfeld and Nicolson.

_____. (1968) *Structural Anthropology*. Translated by C. Jacobson and B.G. Schoepf. London: Allen Lane.

_____. (1978) *Myth and Meaning*. London: Routledge and Kegan Paul.

Lewis, J. (1995) *Whom God Wishes to Destroy: Francis Coppola and the New Hollywood*. Durham: Duke University Press.

_____, ed. (1998) *The New American Cinema*. Durham: Duke University Press.

Lindstrom, J.A. (2000) "*Heat*: Work and Genre." *Jump Cut*, no. 43: 21–30.

Lippe, R. (1996) "Style as Attitude: Two Films by Martin Scorsese." *CineAction!*, no. 41: 14–21.

Lomenzo, E. (1984) "A Fable for Adults: Sergio Leone Interviewed." *Film Comment*, v. 20:4: 21–23.

Lourdeaux, L. (1990) *Italian and Irish Film Makers in America*. Philadelphia: Temple University Press.

Lukow, G., and S. Ricci. (1984) "The Audience Goes 'Public': Inter-textuality, Genre and the Responsibilities of Film Literacy." *On Film*, no. 12: 28–36.

McArthur, C. (1972) *Underworld USA*. London: British Film Institute.

McCarty, J. (1993) *Hollywood Gangland: The Movies' Love Affair with the Mob*. New York: St. Martin's Press.

McClellan, J.L. (1963) *Crime Without Punishment*. New York: Duell, Sloan and Pearce.

McDonough, D. (1989) "Chicago Press Treatment of the Gangster 1924–1931." *Illinois Historical Journal*, 82:1: 17–32.

McNay, L. (1992) *Foucault and Feminism: Power Gender and the Self*. Cambridge: Polity.

Mac An Ghaill, M., ed.(1996) *Understanding Masculinities*. Buckingham: Open University Press.

MacInnes, J. (1998) *The End of Masculinity: The Confusion of Sexual Genesis and Sexual Difference in Modern Society*. Buckingham: Open University Press.

Madden, D., ed. (1968) *Tough Guy Writers of the Thirties*. London: Feffer and Simons.

Maltby, R. (1983) *Harmless Entertainment: Hollywood and the Ideology of Consensus*. Metuchen, NJ: Scarecrow.

_____. (1995) *Hollywood Cinema: An Introduction*. Oxford: Blackwells.

_____. (1998) "'Nobody Knows Everything': Postclassical Historiographies and Consolidated Entertainment." *Contemporary Hollywood Cinema*. Edited by S. Neale and M. Smith. London: Routledge. 21–44.

_____. (2001) "The Spectacle of Criminality." *Violence and American Cinema*. Edited by J.D. Slocum. New York: Routledge. 117–152.

Marchetti, G. (1991) "Ethnicity, the Cinema, and Cultural Studies." *Unspeakable Images: Ethnicity and the American Cinema*. Edited by L. Friedman. Urbana: University of Illinois Press. 277–307.

Marion, Nancy E. (2008) *Government versus Organized Crime*. Englewood Cliffs, NJ: Pearson/Prentice Hall.

Martin, M., and C.T. Mohanty. (1988) "Feminist Politics: What's Home Got to Do with It?" *Feminist Studies/Critical Studies*. Edited by D. De Laurentiis. Basingstoke: Macmillan. 191–212.

Mason, P. (1990) *Deconstructing America: Representations of the Other*. London: Routledge.

Mayne, J. (1993) *Cinema and Spectatorship*. London: Routledge.

Middleton, P. (1992) *The Inward Gaze: Masculinity and Subjectivity in Modern Culture*. London: Macmillan.

Miles, R. (1991) *The Rites of Man: Love, Sex and Death in the Making of the Male*. London: Grafton.

Minganti, F. (1981) "The Hero with a Thousand and Three Faces: Michele, Mike, Michael Corleone." *Rivista on studi angloamericani*, v. 3:4/5: 257–268.

Mitchell, E. (1976) "Apes and Essences: Some Sources of Significance in the American Gangster Film." *Film Genre Reader II*. Edited by B.K. Grant. Austin: University of Texas Press, 1995. 203–212.

Modleski, T. (1991) *Feminism Without Women: Culture and Criticism in a "Postfeminist" Age*. New York: Routledge.

Monaco, J. (1979) *American Film Now: The People, the Power, the Money, the Movies.* London: New American Library.

Moore, W.H. (1974) *The Kefauver Committee and the Politics of Crime 1950–1952.* Columbia: University of Missouri Press.

Morgan, D. (1992) *Discovering Men: Cultural Studies on Men and Masculinities.* London: Routledge.

Morley, D., and H.K. Chen, eds. (1996) *Critical Dialogues in Cultural Studies.* London: Routledge.

Morris, M. (1988) "Tooth and Claw: Tales of Survival and *Crocodile Dundee.*" *Universal Abandon?: The Politics of Postmodernism.* Edited by A. Ross. Minneapolis: University of Minnesota Press.

Mosse, G.L. (1996) *The Image of Man: The Creation of Modern Masculinity.* Oxford: Oxford University Press.

Munby, J. (1996) "*Manhattan Melodrama's* 'Art of the Weak': Telling History from the Other Side in the 1930s Talking Gangster Film." *Journal of American Studies.* v.30, no. 1: 101–118.

_____. (1999) *Public Enemies Public Heroes: Screening the Gangster from Little Caesar to Touch of Evil.* Chicago: University of Chicago Press.

Murdock, G. (1997) "Reservoirs of Dogma: an Archeology of Popular Anxieties." *Ill Effects: The Media/Violence Debate.* Edited by M. Barker and J. Petley. London: Routledge.

Murphy, K. (2000) "Al Pacino." *Film Comment,* v. 36, no. 2: 26–32.

Murphy, K., and G. Smith. (1990) "Made Men." *Film Comment,* v. 26 no. 5: 25–30 and 69.

Neale, S. (1976) "New Hollywood Cinema." *Screen,* v.17, no. 2: 117–122.

_____. (1980) *Genre.* London: British Film Institute.

_____. (2000) *Genre and Hollywood.* London: Routledge.

_____. (1990) "Questions of Genre." in *Screen,* v. 31 no. 1: 45–66.

_____. (1979) "The Same Old Story. Stereotypes and Difference." *Screen Education,* v. 32/33: 33–8.

Neale, S., and M. Smith, eds. (1998) *Contemporary Hollywood Cinema.* London: Routledge.

Neibaur, J.L. (1989) *Tough Guy: The American Movie Macho.* Jefferson, NC: McFarland.

Newman, G. (1998) "Popular Culture and Violence: Decoding the Violence of Popular Movies." *Popular Culture. Crime and Justice.* Edited by F. Bailey and D. Hale. London: West/Wadsworth. 40–56.

Nicholls, M. (2004) *Scorsese's Men: Melancholia and the Mob.* Melbourne, Victoria: Pluto.

O'Connor, J.E., and M.A. Jackson, eds. (1991) *American History/American Film.* New York: Continuum Books.

Ostendorf, B., and S. Palmié. (1993) "Immigration and Ethnicity." *Modern American Culture: An Introduction.* Edited by M. Gidley. London: Longman. 142–165.

Palmer, J., and M.M. Riley. (1981) "America's Conspiracy Syndrome: From Capra to Pakula." *Studies in Humanities,* v. 8 no. 2: 21–27.

Papaleo, J. (1978) "Ethnic Pictures and Ethnic Fate: The Media Image of Italian Americans." *Ethnic Images in American Film and TV.* Edited by R.M. Miller. New York: The Back Institute. 93–97.

Papke, D.R. (1996) "Myth and Meaning: Francis Ford Coppola and Popular Response to *The Godfather* Trilogy." *Legal Reelism: Movies as Legal Texts.* Edited by J. Denvir. Urbana. Illinois University Press. 1–22.

Parrish, R., and M.R. Pitts. (1987) *The Great Gangster Pictures II.* Metuchen, NJ: Scarecrow.

Pauly, T.H. (1997) "The Criminal as Culture." *American Literary History,* v. 9:4: 776–785.

Peary, G., ed. (1998) *Quentin Tarantino: Interviews.* Jackson: University of Mississippi Press.

Pease, B. (2000) *Recreating Men: Postmodern Masculinity Politics.* London: Sage.

Petersen, A. (1998) *Unmasking the Masculine: "Men" and "Identity" in a Skeptical Age.* London: Sage.

Pfeil, F. (1995) *White Guys: Studies in Postmodern Domination and Difference.* London: Verso.

_____. (1995) "Sympathy for the Devils: Notes on Some White Guys in the Ridiculous Class War." *New Left Review,* no. 213: 115–124.

Powers, J. (1996) "The Big Casino." *Sight and Sound,* v. 6:11: 18–22.

Prince, S. (1998) "A Disputed Legacy." *Savage Cinema: Sam Peckinpah and the Rise of Ultra Violent Movies*. Austin: University of Texas Press. 213–254.

Pye, M., and L. Myles. (1979) *The Movie Brats: How the Film Generation Took Over Hollywood*. London: Faber and Faber.

Quart, L., and A. Auster. (1991) *American Film and Society Since 1945*. London: Praeger.

Radstone, S. (1995) "Too Straight a Drive to the Toll-Booth: Masculinity, Mortality and Al Pacino." *Me Jane: Masculinity, Movies and Women*. Edited by P. Kirkham and J. Thumin. London: Lawrence and Wishart. 148–165.

Rafter, N. (2000) *Shots in the Mirror: Crime Films and Society*. Oxford: Oxford University Press.

Rapping, E. (1991) "Gangster Snow White, Gangster Sid Vicious." *The Progressive*, 55/3: 37–38.

Ray, R.B. (1985) *A Certain Tendency of the Hollywood Cinema. 1930–1980*. Princeton, NJ: Princeton University Press.

Reid, M.A. (1993) "The Black Gangster Film." *Film Genre Reader II*. Edited by B.K. Grant. Austin: University of Texas Press, 1995.

Restaino, K.M. (1998) "*Miller's Crossing:* the Politics of Dashiell Hammett." *The Detective in American Fiction, Film and TV*. Edited by J.H. Delamater and R. Prigozy. London: Greenwood Press. 103–110.

Rich, B. Ruby. (1992) "Art House Killers." *Sight and Sound*, v. 2:8: 5–6.

Richardson, J. (1990) "The Joel and Ethan Story." *Premiere*, v. 4:2: 94–101.

Rogers, R. (1993) "Pleasure, Power and Consent: The Interplay of Race and Gender in *New Jack City.*" *Women's Studies in Communication*, v. 16, no. 2: 62–85.

Roosevelt, T. (1889) *The Winning of the West*. New York: G.P. Putnam and Sons.

Rosow, E. (1978) *Born to Lose: The Gangster Film in America*. New York: Oxford University Press.

Ross, E.A. (1914) *The Old World in the New*. New York: The Century Company.

Ruddock, A. (2001) *Understanding Audiences: Theory and Method*. London: Sage.

Ruth, D.E. (1996) *Inventing the Public Enemy: The Gangster in American Culture, 1918–1934*. Chicago: University of Chicago Press.

Rutherford, J. (1992) *Men's Silences: Predicaments in Masculinity*. London: Routledge.

Ryan, J., ed. (1973) *White Ethnics: Life in Working Class America*. Englewood Cliffs, NJ: Prentice-Hall.

Ryan, M., and D. Kellner. (1990) *Camera Politica: The Politics and Ideology of Contemporary Hollywood Film*. Bloomington: Indiana University Press.

Said, E. (1978) *Orientalism*. Reprinted in J. Rivkin and M. Ryan, eds. *Literary Theory: An Anthology*. London: Blackwell, 1998.

Sarris, A. (1977) "Big Funerals: The Hollywood Gangster. 1927–1933." *Film Comment*, May–June: 6–9.

Schatz, T. (1993) "The New Hollywood." *Film Theory Goes to the Movies*. Edited by J. Collins, H. Radner, and A. Preacher Collins. London: Routledge. 8–36.

_____. (1983) *Old Hollywood/New Hollywood*. New York: UMI Research Press.

_____. (1977) "The Structural Influence: New Directions in Film Genre Study." *Film Genre Reader II*. Edited by B.K. Grant. Austin: University of Texas Press, 1995. 91–101.

Schickel, R. (1989) "The Crisis in Movie Narrative." *Gannett Center Journal*, Summer: 1–15.

Schneider, W. (1990) "Editorial: Blood Ties. Blood Shed: Finding the Meaning in Crime Movies." *American Film*, v.15:4: 4.

Scorsese, M., and M.H. Wilson. (1997) *A Personal Journey with Martin Scorsese through American Movies*. New York: Faber and Faber.

Seidler, V.J. (1997) *Man Enough: Embodying Masculinities*. London: Sage.

Shadoian, J. (1977) *Dreams and Ends: The American Gangster/Crime Film*. Cambridge, MA: The M.I.T. Press.

Shohat, E. (1991) "Ethnicities-in-Relation: Toward a Multicultural Reading of American Cinema." *Unspeakable Images: Ethnicity and the American Cinema*. Edited by L. Friedman. Urbana, IL: University of Illinois Press. 215–50.

Shohat, E., and R. Stam. (1994) *Unthinking Eurocentrism: Multiculturalism and the Media*. London: Routledge.

Simon, J. (1991) "The Mob and the Family." *National Review*, v. 43 no. 1: 63–65.

Simon, W. (1983) "An Analysis of the Structure of *The Godfather, Part One.*" *Studies in the Literary Imagination*, v. 16:1: 75–89.

Sklar, R. (1992) *City Boys: Cagney, Bogart,*

Garfield. Princeton, NJ: Princeton University Press.

Slocum, J.D., ed. (2001) *Violence and American Cinema*. New York: Routledge.

Smith, D.C. Jr. (1975) *Mafia Mystique*. New York: Basic Books.

Smith, G. (1990) "Moon in the Gutter: Abel Ferrara interviewed." *Film Comment*, v.26:4: 40–44.

_____. (1990) "Street Smart: Martin Scorsese interviewed." *Film Comment*. v. 26:5: 68–74.

_____. (1996) "Two Thousand Light Years from Home: Scorsese's Big *Casino*." *Film Comment*, v. 32:1: 59–63.

_____. (1994) "When You Know You're in Good Hands: Quentin Tarantino interviewed." *Film Comment*, v. 30:4: 32–43.

Sobchack, T. (1975) "Genre Films: A Classical Experience." *Film Genre Reader II*. Edited by B.K. Grant. Austin: Texas University Press, 1995. 102–113.

Sobchack, V. (1977) "Film Genre, Myth, Ritual and Sociodrama." *Film/Culture: Explorations of Cinema in Its Social Context*. Edited by T. Sari. Metuchen, NJ: Scarecrow, 1982. 147–165.

Stacey, J. (1991) "Feminine Fascinations: Forms of Identification in Star-Audience Relations." *Stardom: Industry of Desire*. Edited by C. Gledhill. London: Routledge.

_____. (1994) *Star Gazing: Hollywood Cinema and Female Spectatorship*. London: Routledge.

Staiger, J. (1991) *Interpreting Films: Studies in the Historical Reception of American Cinema*. London: Routledge.

Stam, R. and L. Spence. (1983) "Colonialism. Racism and Representation: an Introduction." *Screen*, v. 24(2): 2–20.

Stecopoulos, H. and M. Uebel, eds. (1997) *Race and the Subject of Masculinities*. Durham: Duke University Press.

Stein, M. (1995) "Violence in Recent American Movies." *Films in Review*, v. 46:3/4: 14–21.

Steinberg, S. (1989) *The Ethnic Myth: Race, Ethnicity and Class in America*. Boston: Beacon.

Stern, L. (1995) *The Scorsese Connection*. Bloomington: Indiana University Press.

Stokes, M., and R. Maltby, eds. (1999) *Identifying Hollywood's Audiences: Cultural Identity and the Movies*. London: British Film Institute.

Storey, J., ed. (1994) *Cultural Theory and Popular Culture: A Reader*. Hemel Hempstead: Harvester Wheatsheaf.

Stringer, J. (1997) "Your Tender Smile Gives Me Strength: Paradigms of Masculinity in John Woo's *A Better Tomorrow* and *The Killer*." *Screen*, v. 38, no. 1: 25–41.

Sutherland, J. (1981) "The *Godfather*." *Bestsellers*. London: Routledge.

Tasker, Y. (1996) "Approaches to the New Hollywood." *Cultural Studies and Communications*. Edited by J. Curran, D. Morley and V. Walkerdine. London: Arnold. 213–228.

_____. (1993) *Spectacular Bodies: Gender, Genre and the Action Cinema*. London: Routledge.

Thompson, D. (1993) "Death and Its Details." *Film Comment*, v. 29:5: 12–16.

_____. (1977) "Man and the Mean Street." *America in the Dark: Hollywood and the Gift of Unreality*. New York: William Morrow. 56–72.

Thompson, D., and I. Christie, eds. (1989) *Scorsese on Scorsese*. London: Faber and Faber.

Tillman, L. (1992) "Obsession: Kiss of Death." *Sight and Sound*, v. 2:2: 33.

Todorov, T. (1990) *Genres in Discourse*. London: University of Cambridge Press.

Tompkins, J. (1992) *West of Everything: The Inner Life of Westerns*. Oxford: Oxford University Press.

Tsalamandris, C. (1993) "Warehouse of Games." *Metro*, n. 96: 3–9.

Tudor, A. (1973) "Genre." *Film Genre Reader II*. Edited by B.K. Grant. Austin: University of Texas Press, 1995. 3–10.

Turner, G. (1988) *Film as Social Practice*. London: Routledge.

Vincent, C.J. (2008) *Paying Respect to* The Sopranos: *A Psychosocial Analysis*. Jefferson, NC: McFarland.

Vogelsang, J. (1973) "Motifs of Image and Sound in *The Godfather*." *Journal of Popular Film and TV*, v. 2:2: 115–135.

Von Gunden, K. (1991) *Postmodern Auteurs: Coppola, Lucas, De Palma, Spielberg and Scorsese*. Jefferson, NC: McFarland.

Walker, J., ed. (1997) *Halliwell's Film and Video Guide*. London: Harper Collins.

Warshow, R. (1946) "The Gangster as Tragic Hero." *The Immediate Experience: Movies, Comics, Theatre and Other Aspects of Popular Culture*. New York: Anchor Books. 83–88.

_____. (1954) "Movie Chronicle: The West-
erner." (1992) *Film Theory and Criticism.*
Edited by G. Mast, R. Cohen, and L.
Braudy. Oxford: Oxford University Press.
453–466.

Wasko, J. (1994) *Hollywood in the Information
Age: Beyond the Silver Screen.* London: Polity.

Webster, D. (1988) *Looka Yonder! The Imaginary America of Populist Culture.* New York:
Routledge.

Welsch, T. (1997) "At Work in the Genre Lab-
oratory: Brian De Palma's *Scarface.*" *Journal
of Film and Video,* v. 49:1/2: 39–51.

Wiegman. R. (1995) *American Anatomies:
Theorizing Race and Gender.* Durham: Duke
University Press.

Wilkinson, R. (1984) *American Tough: The
Tough Guy Tradition and American Character.* London: Greenwood.

Williams, A. (1984) "Is a Radical Genre Criticism Possible?." *Quarterly Review of Film
Studies,* v. 9, n. 2: 123–4.

Willis, S. (1997) "Borrowed Style: Quentin
Tarantino's Figures of Masculinity." *High
Contrast: Race and Gender in Contemporary
Hollywood Film.* Durham: Duke University
Press. 158–188.

_____. (2000) "Style. Posture and Idiom:
Tarantino's Figures of Masculinity." *Rein-
venting Film Studies.* Edited by C. Gledhill
and L. Williams. London: Arnold. 279–295.

Wood, R. (1977) "Ideology, Genre, Auteur."
Film Comment, v. 13, n. 1: 46–51.

_____. (1986) *Hollywood from Vietnam to
Reagan.* New York: Columbia University
Press.

Wright, W. (1975) *Six Guns and Society.* Berkeley: University of California Press.

Wyatt, J. (1994) *High Concept: Movies and
Marketing in Hollywood.* Austin: University
of Texas Press.

Yacowar, M. (1997) "Love vs Honor: *Donnie
Brasco* & *Sling Blade.*" *Queen's Quarterly,*
Spr. 104:1: 56–69.

Yaquinto, M. (1998) *Pump 'Em Full of Lead:
A Look at Gangsters on Film.* New York:
Twayne.

Yates, J. (1975) "The *Godfather* Saga: The
Death of the Family." *Journal of Popular
Film,* v. 4:2: 157–161.

Zavarzadeh, M. (1988) "The New Woman as
Mafia Hit Man: John Huston's *Prizzi's
Honor.*" *North Dakota Quarterly,* v. 56, n. 1.
154–164.

Mafia Biographies and Associated Literature[*]

Anastasia, G. (1998) *The Goodfella Tapes.* New
York: Avon Books.

Asbury, H. (1928) *Gangs of New York: An
Informal History of the Underworld.* New
York: Blue Ribbon Books. (Study of the rise
of organized crime in immigrant, mainly
Irish neighborhoods of New York City in
the 19th century.)

Balsamo, W., and G. Carpozi Jr. (1991) *Crime
Incorporated: The Inside Story of the Mafia's
First 100 Years.* Far Hills, NJ: New Horizon.
(Study by two journalists of gangster activ-
ity in Northern American cities.)

Block, A. (1983) *East Side. West Side: Organiz-
ing Crime in New York 1930–1950.* New
Brunswick: Transaction. (A historical
account of gang wars in New York focusing
on the fights for dominance by ethnic
groups in particular neighborhoods and
businesses.)

Bonnano, B. (1999) *Bound by Honor: My Life
in the Mafia.* New York: St. Martin's. (An
autobiography of the now-retired Bill Bonnano, one-time head of New York's Bonnano family.)

Bonnano, J. (1983) *Man of Honor.* New York:
Simon and Schuster. (An autobiography by
Bill Bonnano's father Joseph.)

Bonnano, R. (1998) *Mafia Marriage.* New York:
Avon. (A female point of view of life inside
the Bonnano family, by Bill Bonnano's wife.)

Cantalupo, J., and T.C. Renner. (2000) *Body
Mike: An Unsparing Expose by the Mafia
Insider Who Turned on the Mob.* http://
www.iuniverse.com.

Capeci, J., and G. Mustain. (1996) *Gotti: Rise
and Fall.* New York: Onyx. (Biography of
the "Dapper Don," head of New York's
Gambino family.)

Davis, J.H. (1994) *Mafia Dynasty.* New York:
Harper Perennial. (A history of the Gam-

* *This is only a selected bibliography. For a more extensive list of associated literature on organized crime
in America see the reference library at http://www.americanmafia.com.*

bino family from Carlo Gambino to John Gotti and beyond.)

Dickie, J. (2004) *Cosa Nostra: A History of the Sicilian Mafia.* New York: Macmillan.

Farrell, J., ed. (1997) *Understanding the Mafia.* Manchester: Manchester University Press. (Sociological study of the history of the Mafia.)

Feder, S., and J. Joesten. (1994) *The Luciano Story.* New York: Da Capo.

Hinkle, W., and W.W. Turner. (1993) *Deadly Secrets: The CIA Mafia War Against Castro and The Assassination of J.F.K.* New York: Thunder's Mouth.

Hoffman, W. (1993) *Contract Killer.* New York: Thunder's Mouth. (Based on real-life Mafia hitman "The Greek" operating in New York.)

Longrigg, C. (1998) *Mafia Women.* London: Vintage Books. (Real-life accounts of women connected with the Italian and American Mafia: "Instead of leading the tide of righteous citizens against crime, women turned out to be even more entrenched in Mafia values," p. 6.)

Maas, P. (1968) *The Valachi Papers.* New York: G.P. Putnam's and Son. (The book based on Joe Valachi's testimony to the McLellan Hearings.)

_____. (1997) *Underboss.* London: Harper Collins. (The story of Sammy "The Bull" Gravano. The man who worked under and later testified against John Gotti.)

Maloney, E., and W. Hoffman. (1995) *Tough Guy: The True Story of Crazy Eddie Maloney.* New York: Pinnacle. (Includes stories concerning Jimmie Burke — Jimmy Conway in *Goodfellas* — and Neil Dellacroce, mentor to John Gotti.)

Morton, J. (1998) *Gangland International: The Mafia and Other Mobs.* London: Little, Brown. (Includes brief histories of Mob families based all over the world, from the nineteenth century to the present day.)

Mustain, G., and J. Capeci. (1993) *Murder Machine: A True Story of Murder, Madness and the Mafia.* New York: Onyx.

Nellij, H.S. (1981) *The Business of Crime: Italians and Syndicate Crime in the U.S.* Chicago: University of Chicago Press. (An analytical survey of Mafia business throughout the 20th century.)

Pileggi, N. (1984) *The Wise Guy.* New York: Simon and Schuster. (Based on the testimony of Henry Hill and adapted as the screenplay for *Goodfellas* [1990].)

Pistone, J.D., and R. Woodley. (1987) *Donnie Brasco: My Undercover Life in the Mafia.* New York: Signet.

Repetto, T. (2004) *American Mafia: A History of Its Rise to Power.* New York: Henry Holt.

Scheim, D.E. (1989) *Contract on America: The Mafia Murder of President John F. Kennedy.* New York: Zebra. (Mainly investigates Jack Ruby's Mafia connections.)

Siebert, R. (1996) *Secrets of Life and Death: Women and the Mafia.* London: Verso. (Real-life accounts of women's roles within the Italian-based Mafia.)

Smith, J.L. (1998) *The Animal in Hollywood: Anthony Fiato's Life in the Mafia.* New York: Barricade. (Reviews question the credibility of this book, as it focuses on the point of view of wannabe gangsters rather than key players.)

Sterling, C. (1990) *The Mafia: The Long Reach of the International Sicilian Mafia.* London: Hamish Hamilton. (An observation of the political and economic power of the post-war Sicilian Mafia.)

Talese, G. (1971) *Honor Thy Father.* New York: Ivy Books. (Biography of Bill Bonnano. Later adapted as a screenplay for the TV film *Honor Thy Father* [1973].)

Turkus, B., and S. Feder. (1951) *Murder, Inc.: The Story of the Syndicate.* New York: De Capo. (Murder, Inc. is the moniker of the syndicate's firing squad. This book is promoted as relating true accounts of Mafia murders.)

Volkman, E. (1999) *Gangbusters: The Destruction of America's Last Great Mafia Dynasty.* New York: Avon. (Tracks the downfall of the Gaetano Lucchese family in New York and makes heroes out of the F.B.I. chiefs who led the investigation.)

Journal and Newspaper Reviews (by Film Title)

American Gangster (2007, Universal)

Dargis, M. "Sweet Bloody Smell of Success." *New York Times,* November 2, 2007, E1.

Roberts, K. "Denzel Washington is Riveting...." *Philadelphia Tribune,* November 2, 2007, 6.

Morgenstern, J. Review. *Wall Street Journal,* November 2, 2007, W1.

Gilbey, R. Review. *Sight and Sound*, v. 18:1 (Jan 2008): 56–57.
Review. *New York Times*, December 7, 2007, 32.
Review. *Evening Standard*, March 13, 2008.

Analyze This (1999, Warner Bros.)
Review. *Variety*, February 22, 1999, 49.
Review. *New York Times*, March 9, 1999.
Whittell, G. "De Niro's Genius Is as Clear as Crystal." *Times*, March 9, 1999, 19.
Hoberman, J. Review. *Village Voice*, March 9, 1999, 113.
Ojumu, A. "De-Mob Happy." *Observer: Screen*, May 6, 1999, 7.
Cliff, N. "Gangster, Killer, Hood? No, Just a Crazy Mixed-Up Guy." *Times*, August 16, 1999, 41.
Walker, A. "De Niro Gets that Shrinking Feeling." *Evening Standard*, September 23, 1999, 30.
Hoyle, M. Review. *Financial Times*, September 23, 1999, 28.
Mars-Jones, A. "You Talkin' to Me? Or My Inner Child?" *Times*, September 23, 1999, 39.
O'Hagan, A. Review. *Daily Telegraph*, September 24, 1999, 25.
Bradshaw, Review. *Guardian*, September 24, 1999, 5.
Quinn, A. "The Incredible Shrinking Mob." *Independent*, September 24, 1999, 12.
Caplan, N. "Crisis in the Family." *Metro: London*, September 24, 1999, 17.
Fisher, N. "Crazy Gang." *Sun*, September 25, 1999, 52.
Billson, A. Review. *Sunday Telegraph*, September 26, 1999, 9.
Taylor, C. Review. *Sight and Sound*, v. 9, n. 9 (September 1999): 40.
Review. *Empire*, Issue 124 (October 1999): 16.

Billy Bathgate (1991, Warner Bros/Touchstone)
Howe, D. "Billy Won't Be a Hero." *Washington Post*, November 1, 1991.
Mathews, J. "Dutch Schultz and Gang." *Newsday*, November 1, 1991.
Ebert, R. "Even Gangsters Lack Zip in Drab *Billy Bathgate*." *Chicago Sun-Times*, November 1, 1991.
Garneau, K. "Billy Bathgate: A Pretty Goodfella." *Chicago Tribune*, November 8, 1991.
Strauss, B. "Review." *Chicago Sun-Times*, November 10, 1991.

Review. *The Cincinnati Post*, November 10, 1991.
Walker, A. "A Gofer Goes to Gangland." *Evening Standard*, January 9, 1992, 26.
Malcolm, D. "Messing with the Mob." *Guardian*, January 9, 1992, 23.
Brown, G. Review. *Times*, January 9, 1992, 11.
Usher, S. Review. *Daily Mail*, January 10, 1992.
Johnston, S. "Tediumsgate." *Independent*, January 10, 1992, 16.
Lane, A. Review. *Independent on Sunday*, January 12, 1992, 19.
Hutchinson, T. "Crime Boss Hoffman's Killer Yawn." *Mail on Sunday*, January 12, 1992, 39.
French, Review. *Observer*, January 12, 1992, 44.
Tookey, C. Review. *Sunday Telegraph*, January 12, 1992, 41.
Johnstone, I. Review. *Sunday Times*, January 12, 1992, 5.
Wolfe-Murray, A. Review. *Scotsman Weekend*, January 18, 1992, 30.
Brett, A. Review. *What's On in London*, January 29, 1992, 11.

Bonnie and Clyde (1967, Warner Bros.)
Alpert, H. "Crime Wave." *Saturday Review*, August 5, 1967.
Sarris, A. Review. *Village Voice*, August 24, 1967.
Review. *Time*, August 25, 1967.
Pacey, A. Review. *The Sun*, September 5, 1967.
Benjamin, J., J. O'Mealy, *et al.* "Bonnie and Clyde — Facts? Meaning? Art?" *New York Times*, September 7, 1967.
Day-Lewis, S. Review. *Daily Telegraph*, September 8, 1967.
Wilson, D. Review. *Guardian*, September 8, 1967.
Hibbin, N. Review. *Morning Star*, September 9, 1967.
Review. *The Observer*, September 10, 1967.
Betts, E. Review. *The People*, September 10, 1967.
Hirschorn, C. Review. *Sunday Express*, September 10, 1967.
Robinson, D. Review. *Financial Times*, September 15, 1967.
Scott-James, A. "Why Bonnie and Clyde are more dangerous dead than alive." *Daily Mail*, October 5, 1967.
Lewis, J. Review. *New Statesman*, October 6, 1967.
Review. *The Observer*, October 8, 1967.

Harcourt, "You Bes' Keep Runnin." *The Queen's Journal*, November 24, 1967.
Review. *Variety*, December 13, 1967.
Johnson, A. Review. *Film Quarterly*, v. 21, n. 2 (1967): 41–48.
Review. *Monthly Film Bulletin*, v. 34, n. 405 (1967): 150.
French, "Incitement to Violence." *Sight and Sound*, v. 37, n. 1 (1967/8): 3–8.

The Brotherhood (1968, Paramount Pictures)
Review. *Variety*, November 20, 1968, 6.
Review. *Monthly Film Bulletin*, v. 35, n. 419 (December 1968): 198.
Austen, D. Review. *Films and Filming*, v. 15, n .4 (January 1969): 42–44.
"Banned Kiss." *Films and Filming*, v. 15, n. 5 (February 1969): 28.

Bugsy (1991, Columbia Pictures)
Hoberman, J. "Learning from Las Vegas." *Village Voice*, December 17, 1991, 65.
Mathews, J. Review. *Newsday*, December 13, 1991.
Clark, M. "*Bugsy* a Vegas Style Sure Bet." *USA Today*, December 13, 1991.
Blair, I. "*Bugsy's* Real Appeal." *Chicago Tribune*, December 15, 1991.
Howe, D. "*Bugsy*, Gangs Comic Spree." *Washington Post*, December 20, 1991.
Lyman, D. "Stylish *Bugsy* Much More Than a Gangster Movie." *Cincinnati Post*, December 20, 1991.
Walker, A. Review. *Evening Standard*, December 19, 1991, 24.
Rafferty, T. Review. *New Yorker*, December 30, 1991, 82–83.
Biskind, "Interview with Warren Beatty." *The Sunday Times*, February 16, 1992, 18–25.
"A Thriller You Can't Refuse." *The Sun*, January 17, 1992, 17.
Combs, R. "Gangster in Dreamland." *Observer*, March 1, 1992, 60.
Toback, J. "Interview with Warren Beatty." *Time Out*, March 18, 1992, 18–19.
Andrew, N. "Sweet and Sour Gangster Epic." *Financial Times*, March 19, 1992, 21.
Brown, G. "Bangs, Gangs and Warren Beatty." *The Times*, March 19, 1992, 1.
Francke, L. Review. *City Limits*, March 19, 1992, 23.
Usher, S. "Beatty Hosts a Deadly Funhouse." *Daily Mail*, March 20, 1992, 47.
Malcolm, D. "Mobster and His Moll." *Guardian*, March 20, 1992, 30.

Johnston, S. "Fear and Love in Las Vegas." *Independent*, March 20, 1992, 24.
Billson, A. "Las Vegas Nights." *New Statesman and Society*, March 20, 1992, 40–41.
Lane, A. "Starring an Immaculate Suit." *Independent on Sunday*, March 22, 1992, 22.
Wolfe Murray, A. "Tough Guise." *Scotsman Weekend*, March 28, 1992, 21–22.
Strick, Review. *Sight and Sound*, v. 1, n. 12 (April 1992): 45–46.
Vineberg, S. Review. *Film Quarterly*, v. 45 n. 4 (Summer 1992): 22–23.

Carlito's Way (1993, Universal Pictures)
Clark, M. "Acting and Action Energize *Carlito's Way*." *USA Today*, November 10, 1993.
Hinson, H. "*Carlito*: Blood and Gutless." *Washington Post*, November 12, 1993.
Howe, D. "De Palma Half-Way." *Washington Post*, November 12, 1993.
Siskel, G. "Gangster Clichés." *Chicago Tribune*, November 12, 1993.
Susman, G. "A Gangster of Love." *Chicago Sun-Times*, 14th November 1993.
Review. *Variety*, November 15, 1993, 30.
Hoberman, J. "Street Life." *Village Voice*, November 16, 1993, 59.
Curtis, Q. "Watching Us, Watching Him: Brian De Palma." *Independent on Sunday*, January 2, 1994, 16–17.
Brett, A. "Back on Track." *What's On in London*, January 5, 1994, 11.
Charity, T. Review. *Time Out*, January 5–12, 1994, 57.
Malcolm, D. Review. *Guardian*, January 6, 1994, 5.
Brown, G. Review. *Times*, January 6, 1994.
Tookey, C. Review. *Daily Mail*, January 7, 1994, 40.
Davenport, H. "Slick Suspense in Spanish Harlem." *Daily Telegraph*, January 7, 1994, 16.
Jackson, K. Review. *Independent*, January 7, 1994, 24.
Errigo, A. Review. *Today*, January 7, 1994, 30.
Curtis, Q. Review. *Independent on Sunday*, January 9, 1994, 23.
Leith, W. Review. *Mail on Sunday*, January 9, 1994, 23.
Morley, S. Review. *Sunday Express*, January 9, 1994, 54.
Review. *Sunday Times*, January 9, 1994, 54.
Falk, Q. "Pacino Unable to Resist the Lure of

a Life of Crime." *Daily Telegraph*, February 1, 1997, 3.

Casino (1995, Universal Pictures)
Review. *Variety*, September 5, 1994, 18.
Feinstein, H. "The Rules of the Game." Interview with Scorsese, *Guardian*, November 15, 1995, 4.
Jeffreys, D. "The Trouble with Wise Guys." *Independent*, November 16, 1995, 8–9.
Mathews, J. Review. *Newsday*, November 22, 1995.
Ebert, R. "Fascinating." *Chicago Sun-Times*, November 22, 1995.
Kopp, C. "Long, Bloody and Brilliant." *Cincinnati Post*, November 23, 1995.
Howe, D. "*Casino*: Scorsese's Losing Bet." *Washington Post*, November 24, 1995.
Vadeboncoeur, J.E. "*Casino* Puts Its Money on a Formula." *Syracuse Herald-Journal*, November 27, 1995.
Hoberman, J. "Cities on Fire." *Village Voice*, November 28, 1995, 59.
Wilmington, M. "Hell-Raiser in *Casino*." *Chicago Tribune*, December 10, 1995.
Christie, I. "Scorsese's Testament." *Sight and Sound*, v6 n.1, January 1996, 6.
Joseph, J. "You talkin' to him?" *Times*, February 3, 1996, 37.
Schiff, S. "The *Casino* Cut." *Independent on Sunday*, February 4, 1996, 17–18.
Gritten, D. "Too Many Crooks." *Daily Telegraph*, February 9, 1996, 25.
Cabrol, C. "The Original Sinner." *Times Magazine*, February 17, 1996, 8.
Malcolm, D. "An Odds-On Winner." *Guardian*, February 22, 1996, 8–9.
Mars-Jones, A. "Dice with Death." *Independent*, February 22, 1996, 10.
"Yearning for the Good Old Days of the Mafia." *Daily Mail*, February 23, 1996, 45.
Delingpole, J. Review. *Daily Telegraph*, February 23, 1996, 16.
Wright, S. Review. *Sun*, February 23, 1996, 16.
Curtis, Q. Review. *Independent on Sunday*, February 25, 1996, 11.
Grant, B. Review. *Sunday Express*, February 25, 1996.
Billson, A. Review. *Sunday Telegraph*, February 25, 1996, 11.
Shone, T. Review. *Sunday Times*, February 25, 1996, 7.
Romney, J. Review. *Sight and Sound*, v. 6. n. 3 (March 1996): 39.

Powers, J. "The Big Casino." *Sight and Sound*, v. 6 n. 11 (October 18–22, 1996).

The Departed (2006, Warner Bros.)
Caplan, N. "Scorsese Is Back on Form in Gangland." *Evening Standard*, October 5, 2006.
Dargis, M. "Scorsese's Hall of Mirrors, Littered with Bloody Deceit." *New York Times*, October 6, 2007, E1.
Morgenstern, J. Review. *Wall Street Journal*, October 6, 2006, W1.
Kass, J. "Mob Film Gets It Right, We Oughta Know." *Chicago Tribune* October 8, 2006, 2.

Donnie Brasco (1997, Mandalay)
Doherty, T. Review. *Cineaste*, v.23, n.1 (January 1997): 42–43.
Review. *Variety*, February 24, 1997, 75.
Italie, H. Review. *Asian Eye*, March 4, 1997, 10.
Hoberman, J. "Portrait of a Hit Man." *Village Voice*, March 4, 1997, 65.
Charity, T. "A Matter of Life and Depp." *Time Out*, April 2–9, 1997, 12–15.
Crisp, Q. "The Boy Don Well." *Guardian*, April 4, 1997, 9.
Katz, M. Article on Joe Pistone, *Evening Standard*, April 16, 1997, 24–25.
Curtis, Q. Review. *Daily Telegraph: Arts*, April 19, 1997, 1.
O'Toole, L. "Looking for Al Pacino." Interview, *Independent*, April 24, 1997, 4–5.
Hasted, N. "An End to Mob Rule." *Independent: Tabloid*, April 24, 1997, 6.
Queenan, J. "A Mob Hit." *Guardian: The Guide*, April 26-May 2, 1997, 14–15.
Andrews, N. "Mixing with the Mob." *Financial Times*, May 1, 1997, 23.
Mars-Jones, A. "Wise Guise." *Independent*, May 1, 1997.
Brown, G. "Pacino Makes an Offer You Can't Refuse." *Times*, May 1, 1997, 37.
Curtis, Q. "Getting to the Heart of the Mob." *Daily Telegraph*, May 2, 1997, 28.
English, C. "Englishman in New York." *Guardian: Section Two*, May 2, 1997, 2–3.
Malcolm, D. "Mob's Your Uncle." *Guardian*, May 2, 1997, 8.
Smith, J. "Here's Donnie." *Total Film*, No. 4 (May 1997): 24–28.
Review. *Total Film*, No. 4 (May 1997) 84–85.
McNab, G. "The Infiltrator." *Sight and Sound*, v. 7, n. 5 (May 1997): 6.
Wrathall, J. Review. *Sight and Sound*, v. 7, n. 5 (May 1997): 40.

Review. *Empire*, Issue 96 (June 1997): 36.

Goldman, S. "Donnie Brasco." *Empire*, Issue 96 (June 1997): 106–111.

Review. *Uncut* (June 1997): 130.

The Funeral (1996, October Films)

Review. *Variety*, September 9, 1996, 117.

Anderson, J. "Mobsters Not Just Bad but Berserk." *Newsday*, November 1, 1996.

Hoberman, J. Review. *Village Voice*, November 5, 1996, 71.

Howe, D. "Brother's Keepers." *Washington Post*, November 8, 1996.

Petrakis, J. Review. *Chicago Tribune*, November 8, 1996.

Ebert, R. "*Funeral* Goes Boldly into Gloom." *Chicago Sun-Times*, November 8, 1996.

Arnold, G. "*Funeral* Deserves a Burial." *Washington Times*, November 10, 1996.

Vadeboncoeur, J.E. "A Thoughtful Look at Mob." *Syracuse Herald-Journal*, December 6, 1996.

Hasted, N. "Sick Stories of Sin and Slaughter." *Independent*, April 3, 1997, 8.

Charity, T. Review. *Time Out*, April 16–23, 1997, 68.

Andrews, N. Review. *Financial Times*, April 17, 1997, 27.

Norman, N. Review. *Evening Standard*, April 17, 1997, 26.

Brown, G. Review. *Times*, April 17, 1997, 37.

Gilbey, R. Review. *Independent*, April 19–25, 1997, 8.

French, Review. *Observer Review*. April 20, 1997, 12.

Billson, A. "Greek Tragedy Among Sharp-Suited Mobsters." *Sunday Telegraph*, April 20, 1997, 12.

Perry, G. Review. *Sunday Times*, April 29, 1997, 5.

Smith, G. "Dealing with the now." *Sight and Sound*, v. 7, n. 4 (April 1997): 6–9.

Newman, K. Review. *Sight and Sound*, v. 7, n. 4 (April 1997): 42.

Review. *Total Film*, No. 4 (May 1997): 94.

Gangs of New York (2002, Miramax)

McCarthy, T. "Scorsese 'Gangs' Up for a Gotham Epic." *Variety*, December 9–15, 2002, 38.

Review *Morning Edition*, Washington, D.C., December 20, 2002, 1.

Scott, A.O. "To Feel a City Seethe." *New York Times*, December 20, 2002, E1.

Hunter, S. "A Bloodied Past." *Washington Post*, December 20, 2002, C1.

Wilmington, M. Review. *Chicago Tribune*, December 20, 2002, 1.

Chagollan, S. "Sign of the Times." *Variety*, December 15–21, 2002, 5.

Thompson, D. Review. *Sight and Sound*, v. 13:2 (February 2003): 44.

Gallman, J.M. Review. *Journal of American History*, v. 90:3 (December 2003): 1124–1126.

Get Shorty (1996, Jersey)

Review. *Variety*, October 9, 1995, 61.

Hoberman, J. "Double Dutch." *Village Voice*, November 24, 1995, 71.

"The Real Chilli Palmer." *Mail on Sunday*, January 28, 1996.

Walker, A. "The Funny Stuff." *Evening Standard*, March 14, 1996, 27.

Malcolm, D. Review. *Guardian*, March 14, 1996, 9.

Tookey, C. "Travolta Plays a Part to Rank with the Greats." *Daily Mail*, March 15, 1996, 42.

Wright, S. Review. *Sun*, March 15, 1996, 16–17.

Cohu, W. Review. *Sunday Express*, March 17, 1996, 64.

Shone, T. "A Touch of the Old Fever." *Sunday Times*, March 17, 1996, 6–7.

Wrathall, J. Review. *Sight and Sound*, v. 6, n. 3 (March 1996): 42.

Billson, A. Review. *Sunday Telegraph*, August 17, 1996, 8.

The Godfather (1972, Paramount Pictures)

Setlowe, R. "Production News." *Variety*, February 17, 1971.

Parker, J. "Opposition." *Screen International*, July 2, 1971.

Ebert, R. Review. *Chicago Sun-Times*, January 1, 1972.

Davis, I. "Brando's Shocker." *Daily Telegraph*, February 25, 1972.

"The Making of *The Godfather*." *Time Magazine*, March 13, 1972.

Canby, V. "Moving and Brutal." *New York Times*, March 16, 1972.

Sarris, A. Review. *Village Voice*, March 16, 1972.

Gagi, N. "A Few Family Murders, but That's Showbiz." *New York Times*, March 19, 1972.

Arnold, G. "*The Godfather*: Bene!" *Washington Post*, March 22, 1972.

McEwan, A. "Spaghetti Men Black Out Mafia Blockbuster." *Daily Mail*, March 23, 1972.

Cocks, J. "The Godsons." *Time Magazine*, April 3, 1972.

Roud, R. Review. *Guardian*, April 6, 1972.

Wiseman, T. Review. *Guardian*, May 31, 1972.

Zec, D. Review. *Daily Mirror*, August 22, 1972.

Malcolm, D. Review. *Guardian*, August 22, 1972.

Cashin, F. Review. *The Sun*, August 22, 1972.

Gow, D. Review. *Scotsman*, August 23, 1972.

Pileggi, N. Review. *Sunday Times Magazine*, August 23, 1972.

Hudson, C. "Into the Family Business." *The Spectator*, August 26, 1972.

Houston, "America's First Family." *New Statesman*, September 1, 1972.

Wood, M. "Myths of the Mafia." *New Society*, September 21, 1972, 17.

French, Review. *Sight and Sound*, v. 41, n. 4, (Autumn 1972): 217–223.

Gow, G. Review. *Films and Filming*, v. 19, n. 1 (October 1972): 56.

Chappetta, R. Review. *Film Quarterly*, v. 25, n. 4 (1972).

Strick, Review. *Monthly Film Bulletin*, v. 39, n. 464 (1972): 190–191.

Review. *Variety*, May 9, 1973.

Thomson, D. "Blood is thicker than water." (Review on re-release.) *Independent on Sunday*, June 16, 1996, 22.

Malcolm, D. "The Best Mob Story Ever." (Review on re-release.) *Guardian*, June 26, 1996, 7.

Malcolm, D. Review on re-release. *Guardian*, July 4, 1996, 9.

Curtis, Q. "Coppola's Ignoble Savages." (Review on re-release.) *Daily Telegraph*, July 5, 1996, 24.

Jackson, K. Review on re-release. *Independent on Sunday*, July 7, 1996.

Shone, T. "Keeping it in the family." (Review on re-release.) *Sunday Times*, July 7, 1996, 6–7.

Tonkin, B. "Cinematic offering you cannot refuse." (Review on re-release.) *New Statesman*, August 2, 1996, 39.

Pizzello, S. "Best Shot Films 1950–1997." *American Cinematographer*, v. 80, n.3 (March 1999): 132. (Listed as No. 2.)

The Godfather Part II (1974, Paramount Pictures)

Review. *Variety*, December 11, 1974, 16.

Schickel, R. "The Final Act of a Family Epic." *Time Magazine*, December 16, 1974, 48–49

Arnold, G. "And now comes the son of *The Godfather*." *Washington Post*, December 18, 1974.

Canby, V. "*Godfather Part II*: One Godfather Too Many." *New York Times*, December 22, 1974.

Ebert, R. Review. *Chicago Sun-Times*, January 1, 1975.

Hall, W. "Why you won't miss Brando." *Evening News*, May 15, 1975.

Walker, A. Review. *Evening Standard*, May 15, 1975.

Malcolm, D. Review. *Guardian*, May 15, 1975.

Shorter, E. "In Godfather's Footsteps." *Daily Telegraph*, May 16, 1975.

Combs, R. Review. *Financial Times*, May 16, 1975.

Coleman, J. Review. *New Statesman*, May 16, 1975.

French, "All in the Family." *Times*, May 16, 1975.

Davis, R. *Review. Observer*, May 18, 1975.

Hutchinson, T. Review. *Sunday Telegraph*, May 18, 1975.

Powell, D. Review. *Sunday Times*, May 18, 1975.

Robinson, K. Review. *Spectator*, May 24, 1975.

McArthur, C. "From Mafia Gangster to Tragic Hero." *Chicago Tribune*, June 6, 1975.

Milne, T. Review. *Monthly Film Bulletin*, v. 42, n. 497 (June 1975): 135.

Gow, G. Review. *Films and Filming*, v. 21, n. 10 (July 1975) 42–43.

Rosenbaum, J. Review. *Sight and Sound*, v. 44, n. 3 (Summer 1975) 187–188.

Quart, L. and A. Auster. Review. *Cineaste*, v. 6, n. 4 (1975): 38–39.

Malcolm, D. "The Best Mob Story Ever." (Review on re-release.) *Guardian*, June 20, 1996, 7.

Review. *Time Out*, July 24–31, 1996, 69.

Malcolm, D. "Get Married to the Mob." *Guardian*, July 25, 1996, 9.

Brown, G. (Review on re-release.) *Times*, July 25, 1996, 31.

The Godfather Part III (1990, Zoetrope/ Paramount Pictures)

Cowie, "Coppola: Remarried to the Mob." *Variety*, January 3, 1990, 10–11.

Cowie, "An Offer Coppola Couldn't Refuse." *Sunday Times*, January 14, 1990, 1–4.

Weatherby, W. "Making a Killing." *Guardian*, May 24, 1990, 30.

Camoro, M. "Phantoms of Omerta." *Mail on Sunday*, May 27, 1990, 44–46.

Goodman, J. "The Making of *Godfather III*." *Sunday Correspondent*, October 7, 1990, 18–28.

Boyer, "*Godfather 3*: When the Shooting Started." *Observer Magazine*, October 28, 1990, 24–31.

Kelly, J., and Ogle-Davis, S. "An Offer Coppola Couldn't Refuse." *Daily Mail*, November 9, 1990, 27–29.

Ogle-Davis, S. "My Godfather — An Offer We Can Refuse." Review. *Daily Mail*, December 17, 1990, 25.

Review. *Variety*, December 17, 1990, 41–42.

Walker, A. "God against the Mob." *Evening Standard*, December 20, 1990, 20–21.

Voedisch, L. "Unequalled Elegance." *Chicago Sun-Times*, December 21, 1990.

Clark, M. "Falls Short of Greatness." USA Today, December 24, 1990.

Review. "The Inexorable Corleone Whirlpool." *Newsday*, December 24, 1990.

Siskel, G. Review. *Chicago Tribune*, December 28, 1990.

Howe, D. "Godfather Puts on Heirs." *Washington Post*, December 28, 1990.

Ebert, R. "A Familiar Godfather: Part III Resumes Sins and Seduction." *Chicago Sun-Times*, December 25, 1990.

Kehr, D. "An Offer We Can Refuse." *Chicago Tribune*, December 25, 1990.

Maychick, D. "A Worthy Addition." *New Jersey Record*, December 25, 1990.

Hinson, H. "The Anticlimax." *Washington Post*, December 25, 1990.

Kael, "Vanity, Vanities." *New Yorker*, January 14, 1991, 76–79.

Simon, "The Mob and the Family." *National Review*, January 28, 1991, 65.

Stivers, C. "All in the Family." *Sunday Times*, March 3, 1991, 28–32.

Walker, A. "Blood Will Out." *Evening Standard*, March 7, 1991, 26–27.

Malcolm, D. "Desperate Don." *Guardian*, March 7, 1991, 29.

Brown, G. Review. *Times*, March 7, 1991, 21.

Usher, S. "Catholic Family Planning." *Daily Mail*, March 8, 1991, 32.

Orr, D. "Mob Rules." *New Statesman and Society*, March 8, 1991, 31–32.

Dunn, M. "The Naffia." *The Sun*, March 8, 1991, 13.

Heal, S. "The Plodfather." *Today*, March 8, 1991, 26–27.

Wolfe-Murray, A. "Family Fortunes." *Scotsman Weekend*, March 9, 1991, VI.

Hamer-Jones, B. "Perhaps Better to Let Sleeping Hoods Lie?" *Western Mail*, March 9, 1991, 2.

French, "Corleone Cortege." *Observer*, March 10, 1991, 56.

Tookey, C. "Striving Hard for Grandeur." March 10, 1991, 40.

Annan, G. "The Sins of the Fathers." *Spectator*, March 16, 1991, 46.

Combs, R. Review. *Monthly Film Bulletin*, v. 58, n. 687 (April 1991): 91–92.

Jaehne, K. Review. *Cineaste*, v. 18, n. 2 (1991): 41–43.

Coolidge, M. "Director's Cut: Angles and Godfathers." *Independent*, June 24, 1994, 26.

Collins, A. "Don't Do It, Francis." (Part 4.) *The Observer*, June 27, 1999, 8–9.

Goodfellas (1990)

Review. *Variety*, September 10, 1990, 56.

Keogh, "Scorsese Takes on the Mob Again." *Chicago Sun-Times*, September 16, 1990.

Siskel, G. "Dispelling the Mob Myth." *Chicago Tribune*, September 16, 1990.

McGrady, M. "Gangster Business from the Gutter Up." *Newsday*, September 19, 1990.

Simon, J. "A Mafia You Can Believe." *Buffalo News*, September 20, 1990.

Kehr, D. "Goodmovie: a Giddy, Amoral Comedy." *Chicago Tribune*, September 21, 1990.

Ebert, R. "Masterfully Examines Mafia Lifestyle." *Chicago Sun-Times*, September 21, 1990.

Barnigboye, B. "The Glamour Gangsters." *Daily Mail*, October 3, 1990, 36- 37.

Kael, "Tumescence as Style." *New Yorker*, September 24, 1990, 98.

Vadenboncoeur, J.E. "Goodfellas Is Too Much of Too Little." *Syracuse Herald-Journal*, September 24, 1990.

Robinson, D. "Apotheosis of the Ethnic Hood." *Times Saturday Review*, October 3, 1990, 16–17.

Review. *Independent*, October 4, 1990, 17.

Delingpole, J. "The Everyday Story of Mafia Folk." *Daily Telegraph*, October 15, 1990, 17.

Bremner, C. "Myths Resurrected as the Mafia Basks in Nostalgia's Golden Glow." *Times*, October 23, 1990, 18.

O'Brien, J. "Mob Saga on Target." *Chicago Tribune*, October 24, 1990.

Davenport, H. "Scorsese's Explosive Mafia Cocktail." *Daily Telegraph*, October 25, 1990, 3.

Walker, A. "Reared by the Mob." *Evening Standard*, October 25, 1990, 26.

Andrews, N. "Mobsters on a Carousel of Crime." *Financial Times*, October 25, 1990, 19.

Malcolm, D. "The American Nightmare." *Guardian*, October 25, 1990, 28.

Mars-Jones, A. "Keeping it in the Family." *Independent*, October 25, 1990, 15.

Usher, S. "The Poser Nostra." *Daily Mail*, October 26, 1990, 26.

Haver-Jones, B. "Scorsese Stunner." *Western Mail*, October 27, 1990, 8.

Lane, A. "The Mob Gets to Scorsese." *Independent on Sunday*, October 28, 1990, 21.

Hutchinson, T. "Ruthless Reality of Life Inside the Mob." *Mail on Sunday*, October 28, 1990, 39.

French, "Wise Guys in a Gang Show." *Observer*, October 28, 1990, 59.

Billson, A. "One Man's Mob Rule." *Sunday Correspondent*, October 28, 1990, 39.

Hirschhorn, C. Review. *Sunday Express*, October 28, 1990, 46.

Tookey, C. "Skull Behind the Smile." *Sunday Telegraph*, October 28, 1990, 4.

Stanbrook, A . "The Art That Coats a Poison Pill." *Daily Telegraph*, January 24, 1991, 14.

Simon, J. "The Mob and the Family." *National Review*, January 28, 1991, 63–64.

Anker, R. "Badfellas." *Christianity Today*, March 11, 1991, 45–47.

McKim, R. Review. *Cineaste*, v. 18, n. 2 (1991): 43–47.

Viano, M. Review. *Film Quarterly*, v. 44, n. 3 (1991): 43–49.

Hill, H. "Expert Witness." *Premiere* (U.S. Edition), December 1990, 148–149.

Honor Thy Father (1973, Metromedia Producers Co.)

Wilson, D. Review. *Monthly Film Bulletin*, v. 40, n. 479 (December 1973): 251.

Finch, S. Review. *Films and Filming*, v. 20, n. 6 (March 1974): 45.

King of New York (1990, Augusto Caminto/ Reteitalia/Scena)

Review. *Variety*, February 21, 1990, 306.

Clark, M. "King Has Lineage, but Lacks Legitimacy." *USA Today*, October 1, 1990.

Hinson, H. "Faith, Dope and Charity." *Washington Post*, November 20, 1990.

Klinghoffer, D. "Review." *Washington Times*, November 20, 1990.

Ebert, R. "Review." *Chicago Sun-Times*, December 7, 1990.

Caro, M. "Review." *Chicago Tribune*, December 11, 1990.

Grant, S. Review. *Time Out*, June 19, 1991, 24.

Anthony, A. Review. *City Limits*, June 20, 1991, 20.

Davenport, H. Review. *Daily Telegraph*, June 20, 1991, 16.

Walker, A. Review. *Evening Standard*, June 20, 1991, 35.

Malcolm, D. Review. *Guardian*, June 20, 1991, 26.

Grown, G. Review. *Times*, June 20, 1991, 17.

Usher, S. Review. *Daily Mail*, June 21, 1991, 30.

Johnston, S. Review. *Independent*, June 21, 1991, 18.

Heal, S. Review. *Today*, June 21, 1991, 29.

Wolfe-Murray, A. Review. *Scotsman Weekend*, June 22, 1991, 23.

French, Review. *Observer*, June 23, 1991, 48.

Tookey, C. Review. *Sunday Telegraph*, June 23, 1991, 41.

Mcnab, G. "Kingdom Come." *Time Out*, April 30–May 7, 1997, 7.

Francke, L. Review. *Sight and Sound*, v1 n.3, 1991, 46.

Last Man Standing (1996, New Line Pictures)

Review. *Variety*, September 16, 1996, 65.

Taubin, A. Review. *Village Voice*, September 24, 1996, 68.

Charity, T. Review. *Time Out*, September 25–October 2, 1996, 77.

Walker, A. "Bruce in the Shooting Booth." *Evening Standard*, September 26, 1996, 27.

Andrews, N. Review. *Financial Times*, September 26, 1996, 13.

Mars-Jones, A. "A Facial Hair Problem." *Independent*, September 26, 1996, 8.

Brown, G. Review. *Times*, September 26, 1996, 33.

Johnston, S. "Wanted: a Real Baddie." *Daily Telegraph*, September 27, 1996, 22.

Poole, S. Review. *Independent on Sunday*, September 29, 1996, 13.

Shone, T. "Man with No Aim." *Sunday Times*, September 29, 1996.

Newman, K. Review. *Sight and Sound*, v. 6, n. 11 (October 1996): 52.

Married to the Mob (1988, Orion Pictures)
Review. *Variety*, August 3, 1988, 10
Denby, D. "Hood Ornament." *New York Times*, August 15, 1988, 59.
Rafferty, T. "Family Business." *New Yorker*, August 22, 1988, 61–62.
Edelstein, D. "Gang Bang." *Village Voice*, August 23, 1988, 53.
Andrews, N. Review. *Financial Times*, June 22, 1989, 25.
Malcolm, D. Review. *Guardian*, June 22, 1989, 25.
Mars-Jones, A. "Something Tame." *Independent*, June 22, 1989, 16.
Robinson, D. Review. *Times*, June 22, 1989, 18.
Usher, S. "Shakespeare with Shooters." *Daily Mail*, June 23, 1989, 28.
"An Offer You Can Refuse." *Morning Star*, June 23, 1989, 8.
Heal, S. "Carry on Up the Corleones." *Today*, June 23, 1989, 32.
Wolfe-Murray, A. "Style in Bandit Territory." *Scotsman Weekend*, June 24, 1989, II.
Jenkins, S. Review. *Monthly Film Bulletin*, v. 56, n. 666 (July 1989): 209–210.
Wu, D. "Kiss and Shoot." *Sight and Sound*, v. 58, n. 3 (Summer 1989): 210–211.
Jacobsen, K. "Divorced from the Mob." *Guardian*, June 28, 1990, 25.

Mean Streets (1973, Taplin-Perry-Scorsese)
Ebert, R. Review. *Chicago Sun-Times*, October 2, 1973.
Canby, V. Review. *New York Times*, October 3, 1973.
Review. *Variety*, October 3, 1973, 15.
Kael, "The Current Cinema: Everyday Inferno." *New Yorker*, October 8, 1973.
Sarris, A. Review. *Village Voice*, October 25, 1973.
Schickel, R. Review. *Time Magazine*, November 5, 1973.
Review. *Daily Express*, April 5, 1974.
Thirkell, A. Review. *Daily Mirror*, April 5, 1974.
Shorter, E. Review. *Daily Telegraph*, April 5, 1974.
Andrews, N. Review. *Financial Times*, April 5, 1974.
Millar, G. Review. *The Listener*, April 11, 1974.
Coleman, J. Review. *New Statesman*, April 12, 1974.

Gow, G. Review. *Films and Filming*, v. 20, n.8 (May 1974): 45–46.
Review. *Monthly Film Bulletin*, v. 41, n. 484 (May 1974) 102–103.
Denby, D. Review. *Sight and Sound*, v. 43, n.1 (Winter 1974): 48–50.
Peachment, C. "Still crazy after all these years." (Review on re-release.) *Sunday Times*, November 22, 1992, 4–5.
Review on re-release. *What's On in London*, February 17, 1993.
Romney, J. Review on re-release. *New Statesman & Society*, February 19, 1993, 34–35.
Sawtell, J. Review on re-release. *Morning Star*, February 20, 1993, 19.
Shelley, J. "Down these mean streets many men have gone." (Review on re-release.) *Times: Saturday Review*. February 20, 1993, 12.
Review on re-release. *City Limits*, February 25, 1993.
Taubin, A. "The Old Hood." (Review on re-release.) *Village Voice*, March 17, 1998, 64.

Mickey Blue Eyes (1999, Simion Films)
Boshoff, A. "Hurley and Grant Meet Mafia Chiefs for Research." *Daily Telegraph*, May 18, 1998, 7.
Ojumu, A. "De-Mob Happy." *Observer*, May 6, 1999, 7.
Higgins, M. "Trailer Trash." *Independent*, July 7, 1999, 12.
Timms, J. Article on the premiere in London. *Daily Mail*, August 11, 1999, 3.
Review. *Variety*, August 16, 1999, 28–9.
Bradshaw, N. Review. *Time Out*, August 18–25, 1999, 80.
Walker, A. "Hugh Joins the Family." *Evening Standard*, August 19, 1999, 27.
Andrews, N. Review. *Financial Times*, August 19, 1999, 12.
Christopher, J. Review. *Times*, August 19, 1999, 38.
"Wise Guys, Stupid Guy." *Guardian* August 20, 1999, 5.
Quirke, A. Review. *Independent on Sunday*, August 22, 1999, 3.
Billson, A. Review. *Sunday Telegraph*, August 22, 1999, 10.
Hoberman, J. Review. *Village Voice*, August 31, 1999.
Kemp, Review. *Sight and Sound*, v. 9, n. 9 (September 1999): 50.

Miller's Crossing (1990, Circle Films)

Levy, S. "Shot by Shot." *Premiere* (U.S. Edition), v. 3 (March 1990): 64–68.

Review. *Variety*, September 3, 1990, 75.

Jameson, R. "Chasing the Hat." *Film Comment*, v. 26, n.5 (September/October 1990): 32–33.

Clark, M. "Crossing Soars Above the Mob." *USA Today*, September 21, 1990.

Richardson, J.H. "The Joel and Ethan Story." *Premiere* (U.S. Edition), v. 4, n. 2 (October 1990): 96–101.

Kempley, R. "Brutal Beauty." *Washington Post*, October 5, 1990.

Harrington, R. "Review." *Washington Post*, October 7, 1990.

Davidson, L. "A Crossing Worth Watching." *Chicago Tribune*, October 12, 1990.

Goodman, J. "Cinema's Blood Brothers." *Guardian*, October 18, 1990, 24.

Hunter, S. "An Essay in Irony" *The Baltimore Sun*, October 19, 1990.

Review. *Village Voice*, October 25, 1990, 18.

Vadeboncoeur, J.E. "Distinctive Movie" *Syracuse Herald-Journal*, October 25, 1990.

Review. *Screen International*, n. 780.27 (October 1990): 11.

Charity, T. Review. *Sight and Sound*, v. 60, n. 1 (1990/1): 64–65.

James, N. Review. *City Limits*, February 14, 1991, 28.

Norman, N. "A Hatful of Hoods." *Evening Standard*, February 14, 1991, 24.

Brown, G. Review. *Times*, February 14, 1991, 25.

Clarke, J. Review. *What's On in London*, February 13, 1991, 68.

Andrews, N. "Hammett Without the Prince." *Financial Times*, February 14, 1991, 19.

Malcolm, D. Review. *Guardian*, February 14, 1991, 56.

Mars-Jones, A. "Honour Among Thugs." *Independent*, February 15, 1991, 16.

Sawtell, J. Review. *Morning Star*, February 15, 1991, 5.

Heal, S. Review. *Today*, February 15, 1991, 24.

Annan, G. "Big, Black and Classy Joke." *Spectator*, February 16, 1991, 36.

Buss, R. Review. *Independent on Sunday*, February 17, 1991, 21.

Hutchinson, T. "A Thinking Person's Blood-letting." *Mail on Sunday*, February 17, 1991, 38.

French, "Mayhem for Full Orchestra." *Observer*, February 17, 1991, 56.

Johnstone, I. Review. *Sunday Times*, February 17, 1991, 16.

"Style Calls the Shots." *Scotsman Weekend*, February 23, 1991, 30.

Mobsters: The Evil Empire (1991, Universal Pictures)

Kaplan, E. "Young Tommy Guns." *Village Voice*, August 6, 1991, 65.

Brett, A. "One of the Mob." *What's On in London* April 29, 1992, 43.

Davenport, H. Review. *Daily Telegraph*, April 30, 1992.

Walker, A. "Brats of the Rat-Tat-Tat Pack." *Evening Standard*, April 30, 1992, 30–39.

Andrews, N. Review. *Financial Times* April 30, 1992, 19.

Usher, S. "Mob Handed Reality." *Daily Mail*, May 1, 1992, 34.

Jackson, K. Review. *Independent*, May 1, 1992, 18.

French, Review. *Observer*, May 3, 1992, 52.

Floyd, N. Review. *Sight and Sound*, v. 1, n. 11 (1992): 51 – 52.

New Jack City (1991, Warner Bros.)

Maslin, J. "Cops vs. Crack Formula." *New York Times*, March 8, 1991.

Kehr, D. "Son of 'Sweetback' Lacks Spirit of Revolt." *Chicago Tribune*, March 8, 1991.

Schleitwiler, V. "Real People Live in *New Jack City*." *Chicago Tribune*, March 15, 1991.

Bremner, C. Review. *Times*, March 18, 1991, 8.

"Flack over *New Jack*." *Variety*, March 18, 1991, 108.

Benjamin, "The Reel Deal: *New Jack City*, a Gangsta Chronicle." *Village Voice*, March 19, 1991, 49.

Ebert, R. Review. *Chicago Sun-Times*, May 1, 1991.

Campbell, A. "Rap Pack." *Scotsman*, May 25, 1991, 25.

Guilliat, R. "Why Is Ice-T Taking the Rap?" *The Sunday Times*, July 28, 1991, 18–21.

Hinson, H. Review. *Washington Post*, August 8, 1991.

McGregor, A. "It's a Rap." *Time Out*, August 28, 1991, 22–23.

Davenport, H. "A Crack Morality Tale." *Daily Telegraph*, August 29, 1991, 14.

Walker, A. "Painting Them Black." *Evening Standard*, August 29, 1991, 27.

Pulleine, T. "Gunning for the Drug End." *Guardian*, August 29, 1991, 23.

Brown, G. Review. *Times*, August 29, 1991, 15.

Johnston, S. "Crack Down In the Heart of the City." *Independent*, August 30, 1991, 14.

Newman, K. Review. *Sight and Sound*, v. 1, n. 5 (September 1991): 41–42.

Once Upon a Time in America (1984, Ladd/Embassy International)

Robbins, J. *Variety*, October 27, 1982, 3. (Arguments over European crew.)

Ebert, R. Review. *Chicago Sun-Times*, January 1, 1984.

Falk, Q. "And the Shooting Starts All Over Again." *Daily Mail*, February 2, 1984, 18–19.

"Sergio Leone Reacts to Threats to Trim *Once Upon....*" *Variety*, March 21, 1984, 3.

Variety, April 11, 1984, 14. (Arguments over running time.)

"So long Leone." *Daily Mail*, May 22, 1984, 22

Robinson, D. "Absorbing Creation." *Times*, May 22, 1984, 12.

Malcolm, D. Review. *Guardian*, May 24, 1984, 13.

Walker, A. "The Kosher Nostra." *Standard*, May 24, 1984, 2–4.

Andrews, N. Review. *Financial Times*, May 29, 1984, 13.

Canby, V. Review. *New York Times*, June 1, 1984, 8.

Siskel, G. Review. *Chicago Tribune*, June 1, 1984.

French, Review. *Observer*, June 3, 1984, 21.

Sarris, A. "Leone and Huston at Cannes." *Voice*, June 5, 1984, 59.

Davies, V. "Leone's Battle to Save His Savage Epic." *Daily Express*, August 1, 1984, 9.

Bell, I. "Unforgettable Leone." *Scotsman*, August 20, 1984, 5.

Van Gelder, L. "Picking the pieces off the cutting room floor." *New York Times*, August 24, 1984, 6.

Malcolm, D. "Chutzpah Nostra." *Guardian*, October 4, 1984, 11.

French, "The Ultimate Gangster Movie." *Observer*, October 7, 1984, 21.

Maslin, J. Review. *New York Times*, October 12, 1984, 8.

Ackroyd, "The Grand Scale." *Spectator*, October 13, 1984, 36–37.

Hoberman, J. Review. *Voice*, October 23, 1984, 57.

Combs, R. "A Movie Mausoleum." *Times Literary Supplement*, November 2, 1984, 125.

Rees, "Four Hour Gang Show." *Western Mail*, November 3, 1984, 8.

Rayns, T. Review. *Monthly Film Bulletin*, v. 51, n. 609 (October 1984): 295–297.

Peachment, C. Review. *Sight and Sound*, v. 53, n. 4 (Autumn 1984): 301.

Kael, Review. *New Yorker*, May 27, 1985, 82–85.

Billen, S. "Fairy Tale with No Happy Ever After." (Review on re-release.) *Daily Telegraph*, February 17, 1996, 3.

McNab, G. (Review on re-release.) *Time Out*, February 14–21, 1996, 155.

Pulp Fiction (1994, A Band Apart/Miramax)

Review. *Variety*, May 23, 1994, 52.

Malcolm, D. "Ideas gunned down." *Guardian*, May 23, 1994, 7.

Walker, A. "Stylish Edge from Man of Violence." *Evening Standard*, May 24, 1994, 18.

McClellan, J. "Interview with Tarantino." *Observer*, July 3, 1994, 26–30.

Pulver, A. "The Movie Junkie." *Guardian*, September 19, 1994, 8–9.

"Censorship Misses the Point." *Daily Telegraph*, September 24, 1994, 5.

Rankin, T. "Killing joke." *Time Out*, 21st – September 28, 1994, 24–26.

Norman, N. "Interview with Tarantino." *Evening Standard*, October 6, 1994, 29.

Hoberman, J. "Pulp and Gory." *Village Voice*, October 11, 1994, 61–75.

Kopp, C. "Tarantino Argues 'Violent Rap Unfair.'" *Cincinnati Post*, October 13, 1994.

Kempley, R. "*Pulp Fiction*: A Slay Ride." *Washington Post*, October 14, 1994.

Howe, D. "Truth Is: *Pulp Fiction* Rules." *Washington Post*, October 14, 1994.

Anderson, J. Review. *Newsday*, October 14, 1994.

Wilmington, M. "Bad to the Funny Bone." *Chicago Tribune*, October 14, 1994.

Ebert, R. "One-Stop Mayhem Shop." *Chicago Sun-Times*, October 14, 1994.

O'Hagan, S. "X Offender." *Times Magazine*, October 15, 1994, 13–14.

Green, T. "No Neutral Ground on Bloody *Pulp Fiction*." *USA Today*, October 17, 1994.

Andrew, G. "Fresco Kid." *Time Out*, October 19–26, 1994, 63.

Julius, M. Review. *What's On in London*, October 19, 1994.

Andrews, N. "Talent in Search of a Signpost." *Financial Times*, October 20, 1994, 23.

Malcolm, D. "A Cheap Thrill in a Minute." *Guardian*, October 20, 1994, 6.

Mars-Jones, A. "Reservoir Dregs." *Independent*, October 20, 1994, 25.

Brown, G. Review. *Times*, October 20, 1994, 37.

Kenny, M. Review. *Daily Mail*, October 22, 1994, 8–9.

Curtis, Q. "Blood and Guts in the Diner." *Independent on Sunday*, October 23, 1994, 26.

Leith, W. "The Scum Also Rises." *Mail on Sunday*, October 23, 1994, 27.

French, "Hell in the LA Twilight Zone." *Observer*, October 23, 1994, 15.

Billson, A. "Anorak Man and His Shaggy Dog." *Sunday Telegraph*, October 23, 1994, 6.

"It Is Time to Stop Glorifying Brutality." "Letters Page." *Daily Mail*, October 26, 1994.

Romney, J. "A Real Hamburger of a Movie." *New Statesman*, October 28, 1994, 29.

Asherson, N. "*Home Alone* Is More Disturbing Than Tarantino's Grisly Fiction." *Independent on Sunday*, October 30, 1994, 22.

Jones, K. "Time And Again." *Village Voice*, November 22, 1994, 22–24.

Bartley, L. "Dogged by a New Image." *Evening Standard*, November 15, 1994, 28.

Review. *Daily Telegraph*, November 19, 1994, 15.

Wood, J. "Dangerous Emptiness in the Films of Quentin Tarantino." *Guardian*, November 19, 1994, 31.

"Press Book." *Cannes Film Festival*. Buena Vista International Press Office, 1994.

Adair, G. "Nasty, Brutish and ... Stupid." *Sunday Times*, November 27, 1994, 10.

Dargis, M. "Interview with Tarantino." *Sight and Sound*, v4 n.11, November 1994, 16.

Lipman, A. Review. *Sight and Sound*, v4 n.11, November 1994, 50.

Brooks, R. "Violence Debate." *Observer*, October 26, 1997, 6.

"Greatest Cult Movie Ever Made." *Empire*, Issue 100 (October 1997): 108–114.

"*Pulp Fiction* 'May Have Increased Heroin Abuse.'" *Daily Telegraph*, November 11, 1998, 7.

Carroll, R. "Film Censor Says He Should Have Cut 'Irresponsible' *Pulp Fiction*." *Guardian*, November 11, 1998, 1.

Burton, J. "Censor: Film Was Drugs Ad." *Independent*, November 11, 1998, 11.

Gibson, J. "Screen Violence Seen as Fair Play in Right Context." *Guardian*, May 11, 1999, 6.

Reservoir Dogs (1992 Live Entertainment)
Review. *Variety*, January 27, 1992, 52.

Rafferty, T. "Men Overboard." *New Yorker*, October 19, 1992, 105–106.

Mathews, J. "The Last Laugh on Crime." *Newsday*, October 23, 1992.

Hinson, H. "*Reservoir Dogs*: Biting Wit." *Washington Post*, October 24, 1992.

Dougherty, R. "Honor Among Blue-Collar Thieves." *Chicago Sun-Times*, October 25, 1992.

Fine, M. "*Dogs* Is Funny and Horrifying." *USA Today*, October 26, 1992.

Ebert, R. "Looks Tougher Than It Really Is." *Chicago Sun-Times*, October 26, 1992.

Ryan, D. "Reinvents Gangster Flicks." *Albany Times-Union*, December 3, 1992.

Brown, G. "Odd Men Out." *Village Voice*, October 27, 1992, 62.

Usher, S. "Deadly Dogs." *Daily Mail*, December 22, 1992, 26.

Floyd, N. "Dark Star." *Time Out*, December 30, 1992–January 6, 1993, 16–18.

Usher, S. Review. *Daily Mail*, January 3, 1993, 28.

Andrews, N. "When Bloodletting Leads to a Moral Experience." *Financial Times*, January 6, 1993.

Davenport, H. Review. *Daily Telegraph*, January 7, 1993, 13.

Walker, A. "Dogs Off the Leash." *Evening Standard*, January 7, 1993, 30.

Malcolm, D. "Dogs of Gore." *Guardian*, January 7, 1993, 6.

Shelley, J. "The boys are back in town." *Guardian*, January 7, 1993, 7.

Brown, G. Review. *Times*, January 7, 1993, 35.

Review. *Independent*, January 8, 1993.

Romney, J. "Partners in Crime." *New Statesman*, January 8, 1993, 34–36.

Church, M. "Colours of the Charnal House." *Observer*, January 8, 1993, 33.

Heal, S. "Talk of the Wild Dogs Is Stylish, Violent and Empty." *Today*, January 8, 1993, 27–28.

Sawtell, J. Review. *Morning Star*, January 9, 1993, 7.

Billson, A. Review. *Daily Telegraph*, January 10, 1993.

French, Review. *Observer*, January 10, 1993.

Quinn, A. "It's Bleedin' Marvellous." *Independent on Sunday*, January 10, 1993, 18.

Hutchinson, T. "Drenched in Livid Shades of

Violence." *Mail on Sunday*, January 10, 1993, 39.

Billson, A. Review. *The Sunday Telegraph*, January 10, 1993, XII.

Iley, C. "New Man Turns to Life of Violence." *The Sunday Times*, January 10, 1993, 22–23.

Johnstone, I. "Bloody Good Start." *The Sunday Times*, January 10, 1993, 22- 23.

Newman, K. Review. *Sight and Sound*, v. 3 n. 1 (January 1993): 51–52.

Hilferty, R. Review. *Cineaste*, v. 19, n. 4 (March 1993): 79–81.

Collis, C. "Mad Dogs and Englishmen." *Empire*, n. 58 (1994): 20.

Walker, A. "Dogged by a New Image." *Evening Standard*, November 15, 1994, 28.

Davies, T. "Beware of the Dogs." *Daily Telegraph*, June 9, 1995, 23.

"*Reservoir Dogs* Boys Turned to Robbery." *Daily Telegraph*, June 10, 1995, 3.

De Lisle, T. "Debates on Violence." *Independent on Sunday*, June 11, 1995, 27.

"Channel 4 Faces New Storm over *Reservoir Dogs* Scoop." *Evening Standard*, June 22, 1995, 7.

"*Reservoir Dogs* for Channel 4." *Guardian*, June 23, 1995, 8.

Davies, J. "Sick Films Turned My Son into a Gangster." *Daily Mail*, August 3, 1995, 8.

McNab, G. "Debates on Violence." *Time Out*, June 4, 1997.

De Bruxelles, S. "*Reservoir Dogs* Torturer Sets Girlfriend Alight." *Times*, May 11, 2000, 9.

Herbert, I. "Teenagers Copied *Reservoir Dogs* Scene to Murder Rival." *Independent*, July 5, 2000, 6.

Jenkins, R. "Teenagers Killed Boy in *Reservoir Dogs* Frenzy." *Times* July 5, 2000, 3.

Moult, J. "The *Reservoir Dogs* Murderers." *The Sun* July 27, 2000, 31.

Burkeman, O. "Teenage Gang Guilty of *Reservoir Dogs* Murder." *Guardian* July 27, 2000, 5.

Road to Perdition (2002, Dreamworks SKG)

Larsen, J. "Sins of the Father — Gangster Drama Travels a Dark Road." *The Herald News* (Joliet, IL), July 11, 2002, D4.

Stuart, J. "A Gangster Epic's Road to Perfection." *Newsday*, July 12, 2002, B3.

Review. *Times-Courier* (Charleston, IL), July 27, 2002.

Guttenplan, D.D. "Dirty Rats and Dapper Dons." *The Times*, September 27, 2002.

G.M. Review. *Sight and Sound*, v. 13:5 (May 2003): 69.

Scott, A.O. "Vengeance Is Ours, Says Hollywood." *New York Times*. May 2, 2004, 24.

Jacobson, H. Review. *Film Comment*, v. 41:1 (Jan/Feb 2005): 20–21.

Scarface (1983, Universal Pictures)

Jaynes, G. "Miami Officials Object to Cuban Refugee Film." *New York Times*, August 24, 1982.

"*Scarface* Does Some Quiet Re-shooting in Miami." *Variety*, April 27, 1983, 40.

Scobie, W. "Film Angers Cuban Exiles." *Observer*, September 18, 1983, 12.

Harmetz, A. "Movie *Scarface* Receives X rating." *New York Times*, October 30, 1983, 66.

Harmetz, A. "De Palma Disputes Rating for *Scarface*." *New York Times*, October 26, 1983, 21.

Time Magazine, November 7, 1983. (X rating dispute.)

"*Scarface* Gets R Rating on Appeal." *New York Times*, November 9, 1983, 28.

Review. *Variety*, November 30, 1983.

Corliss, R. "Say Goodnight to the Bad Guy." *Time Magazine*, December 5, 1983.

Ebert, R. Review. *Chicago Sun-Times*, December 9, 1983.

Canby, V. Review. *New York Times*, December 9, 1983, 18.

Siskel, G. "Pacino's *Scarface* Does Have One Redeeming Factor: It Ends." *Chicago Tribune*, December 9, 1983.

Denby, D. "Snowed Under." *New York Times*, December 19, 1983, 70.

Dunn, M. "The Savagery of *Scarface*." *The Sun*, December 22, 1983, 14–15.

Kael, Review. *New Yorker*, December 26, 1983, 50–53.

Beam, R. Review. *Daily Mirror*, February 1, 1984, 2.

Malcolm, D. Review. *Guardian*, February 2, 1984, 11.

Walker, A. "Mainline Mobster." *Standard*, February 2, 1984, 22–23.

Christie, I. "Al Is Slob of the Mob." *Daily Express*, February 3, 1984, 24.

Hinxman, M. "The Good in the Bad and the Ugly." *Daily Mail*, February 3, 1984, 22.

Thirkell, A. "Cuban Heel." *Daily Mirror*, February 3, 1984, 19.

Andrews, N. "In Search of the American Dream." *Financial Times*, February 3, 1984.

Wigan, M. "Carnage Cuban Style." *Scotsman*, February 4, 1984, 3.

Hutchinson, T. Review. *Mail on Sunday*, February 5, 1984.

French, "Son of *Scarface*." *Observer*, February 5, 1984, 54

Hirschorn, C. "When a Bad Guy Makes One Mistake Too Many." *Sunday Express*, February 5, 1984, 22.

Castell, D. "Crime without a Point." *Sunday Telegraph*, February 5, 1984, 14.

Johnstone, I. Review. *Sunday Times*, February 5, 1984, 51.

"Failure with a Capital F." *Standard*, February 6, 1984, 7.

Ackroyd, Review. *Spectator*, February 11, 1984, 30–31.

Combs, R. Review. *Monthly Film Bulletin*, v. 51, n. 601 (February 1984): 51–52.

Jaehne, K. Review. *Cineaste*, v. 13, n.3 (1984): 48–50.

Review. *Movie*, n. 33 (Winter 1989): 56–62.

The Sopranos (1999–2007, HBO)
Season One
James, C. "No Horse Heads, but Plenty of Prozac." *New York Times*, January 8, 1999.

Vetere, R. "No, I'm Not with the Mob." *New York Times*, February 12, 2000.

Horwitz, S. Review. *Washington Post*, March 14, 1999, Y6.

Carter, B. "A Cable Show Networks Truly Watch." *New York Times*, March 25, 1999.

James, C. "Addicted to a Mob Family Potion." *New York Times*, March 25, 1999.

Johnson, A. Review *Chicago Tribune* June 6, 1999, 2.

Shales, T. Review. *Washington Post*, June 9, 1999, C1.

Dal Cerro, B. "*Sopranos* Just More 'Safe' Racism." *Chicago Tribune*, June 20, 1999, 2.

Goodwin, C. "They're Ganging Up on the Mafia Now." *Sunday Times*, July 4, 1999.

Canby, V. Review. *New York Times*, October 31, 1999.

James, M. "Critics Choice." *Sunday Times*, September 3, 2000.

"Famiglia Faces." *Sunday times*, October 1, 2000.

Thompson, D. "Wise Guys and Even Wiser Gals." *Independent on Sunday*, October 8, 2000.

"Mob Rules Make for Art of the Very Highest Order." *Independent on Sunday*, October 8, 2000.

"Psychopaths Among Us." *Daily Mail*, December 8, 2000.

Season Two
James, C. Review. *New York Times*, January 14, 2000.

Sharkey, J. Review. *New York Times*, January 15, 2000.

Carter, B. Review. *New York Times*, April 10, 2000.

James, C. Review. *New York Times*, April 12, 2000.

Paglia, C. "Columbus and the March for Italian Pride." *The Times*, October 13, 2000.

Hoggart, P. Review. *The Times*, October 13, 2000.

Rhodes, T. "Little Italy Goes Gunning for *The Sopranos*." *Sunday Times*, March 4, 2001.

Season Three
Tonelli, B. "A *Sopranos* Secret: Given the Choice, We'd All Be Mobsters." *New York Times*, March 4, 2001.

Tan, C.L. Review. *Chicago Tribune*, May 17, 2001, 8.

James, C. Review. *New York Times*, May 22, 2001.

James, C. Review. *New York Times*, May 27, 2001.

Pile, S. "How Can *The Sopranos* Cause Such Grief?" *Daily Telegraph*, February 23, 2002.

Buncombe, A. "It's Only TV Stoopid. How *The Sopranos* Took on a New Lease of Life." *Independent*, September 14, 2002.

Baxter, S. "*Sopranos* Blast Way into America's Heart." *Sunday Times*, September 22, 2002.

Dugdale, T. "Critics Choice." *Sunday Times*, October 20, 2002.

Season Four
Johnson A, and Condor, B. Review. *Chicago Tribune* September 15, 2002, Q2.

Shales, T. "The Crooks Who Steal Your Heart" *Washington Post*, September 15, 2002, G1.

Vincent, D. "The Curse of *The Sopranos*." *Mail on Sunday*, February 9, 2003.

Segal, V. "Critics Choice" *Sunday Times*, March 9, 2003.

Price, S. "TV Choice." *Independent on Sunday*, March 9, 2003.

Soave, D. "Pick of the Day." *Daily Mail*, March 11, 2003.

Joseph, J. Review. *The Times*, March 12, 2003.

Zurawik, D. Review. *Chicago Tribune*, August 29, 2003, 5.

Cox, T. "Incongruous and Out of Time, but

Never Reduced to Parody." *Daily Telegraph,* October 25, 2003.

Connolly, P. Review. *The Times,* November 1, 2003.

Season Five

Stanley, A. Review. *New York Times,* March 5, 2004.

Graham, R. Review. *Chicago Tribune,* May 13, 2004, 3.

Copeland, L. Review. *Washington Post,* June 5, 2004, C1.

Stanley, A. Review. *New York Times,* June 7, 2004.

Dugdale, J. "Pick of the Day." *Sunday Times,* August 15, 2004.

Longrigg, C. "It's Not Easy Being Married to the Mob." *Daily Telegraph,* August 31, 2004.

Orr, D. "With Tony Soprano as a 'Hero,' No Wonder George Bush Got Re-Elected." *Independent,* November 6, 2004.

Gill, A.A. Review. *The Times,* August 22, 2004.

Season Six, Part I

Segal, D. Review. *Washington Post,* March 9, 2006, C1.

Stanley, A. "Brutality and Betrayal, Back with a Vengeance." *New York Times,* March 10, 2006.

Johns, I. "Sex Therapists in Need of a Shrink." *The Times,* November 17, 2006.

Viner, B. "A Mafia Drama No-one Can Refuse." *Independent,* March 6, 2007.

Season Six, Part II

Schwarzbaum, L. Review. *Entertainment Weekly,* April 6, 2007.

Shales, T. Review. *Washington Post,* April 8, 2007, N1.

Stanley, A. "This Thing of Ours, It's Over." *New York Times,* April 8, 2007.

Bianculli, D. Review. *Chicago Tribune,* May 3, 2007, 9.

Reid, T. "Bookies Make a Killing on the Last Soprano." *The Times,* June 9, 2007.

Sherwell, "America Waits...." *Sunday Telegraph,* June 10, 2007.

Carter, B. "One Final Whack at That HBO Mob." *New York Times,* June 10, 2007.

Shales, T. Review. *Washington Post,* June 11, 2007, C1.

Usborne, D. "It's Finally the End ... Or Is It?" *Independent,* June 12, 2007.

"Fans Fume at Finale of *The Sopranos.*" *Daily Mail,* June 12, 2007.

Sutcliffe, T. "The Best Endings Have No End." *Independent,* June 15, 2007.

Macintyre, B. "Every Inch a Shakespearean Drama." *The Times,* June 15, 2007.

Segal, V. "Critics Choice." *Sunday Times,* September 2, 2007.

Pettie, A. "Poisonous Pleasure." *Sunday Telegraph,* September 9, 2007.

Sutcliffe, T. "Out with a Bada Bing! Not a Whimper." *Independent,* October 29, 2007.

Potton, E. Review. *The Times,* November 17, 2007.

Carter, B. "Tony Wasn't Whacked, but What about HBO?" *New York Times,* December 23, 2007.

State of Grace (1990, Orion/Cinchaus)

Review. *Variety,* September 10, 1990, 54.

Giddins, G. "Wild, Wild East." *Village Voice,* September 18, 1990, 66.

Kehr, D. "*State of Grace* Weds Scorsese Style, 30s Plot." *Chicago Tribune,* September 14, 1990.

Ebert, R. "Oldman's Crazed Criminal Sets off *State of Grace.*" *Chicago Sun-Times,* September 14, 1990.

Garner, J. "Twisting the Thriller." *USA Today,* September 18, 1990.

Kempley, R. "Grace Blood and Gruff." *Washington Post,* September 21, 1990.

Vadeboncoeur, J.E. "Gangster Film Falls Short." *Syracuse Herald-Journal,* October 5, 1990.

Cedrone, L. "State of Confusion Muddles *State of Grace.*" *The Baltimore Sun,* October 5, 1990.

Lyman, D. "Penn Adds Grace to Gritty Mob-flick." *Cincinnati Post,* October 6, 1990.

Grant, S. Review. *Time Out,* June 12, 1991, 60.

Cameron-Wilson, J. Review. *What's On in London,* June 12, 1991, 75.

Davenport, H. Review. *Daily Telegraph,* June 13, 1991, 16.

Walker, A. "Mafia versus Murhpia." *Evening Standard,* June 13, 1991, 37.

Usher, S. "Criminals with a Lot of Conviction." *Daily Mail,* June 14, 1991, 30.

Johnston, S. "Green Hoods and Black Berets." *Independent,* June 14, 1991, 18.

Hutchinson, T. "Baddie Penn Comes Good." *Mail on Sunday,* June 16, 1991, 38.

Johnstone, I. "Meditations on Crime That Pays." *Sunday Times,* June 16, 1991, 13.

Charity, T. Review. *Sight and Sound,* v. 1, n. 2 (1991): 64.

The Untouchables (1987, Paramount Pictures)

Kennedy, E. "Capone's Chicago Stirs Again." *New York Times*, January 4, 1987, 17.

Review. *Variety*, June 3, 1987, 14.

Ebert, R. Review. *Chicago Sun-Times*, June 3, 1987.

Schickel, R. "In the American Grain." *Time Magazine*, June 8, 1987, 40.

Hoberman, J. "Monument Valley." *Village Voice*, June 16, 1987, 53.

Corliss, R. Review. *Time*, June 25, 1987, 44–45.

"The Mob at the Movies." *Newsweek*, June 22, 1987, 62–64. (De Niro on cover as Al Capone.)

Gross, J. Review. *New York Times*, June 28, 1987, 31.

Kael, Review. *New Yorker*, June 29, 1987, 70–72.

Review. *Screen International*, n. 605/20 (June 1987): 8.

Bennetts, L. Review. *New York Times*, July 6, 1987, 13.

Sarris, A. Review. *Voice*, July 28, 1987, 57.

Heal, S. "Where's the Blood Cries the Ketchup King." *Today*, September 11, 1987, 26–27.

Brown, G. Review. *Times*, September 12, 1987, 22.

Walker, A. "The Clean Bunch." *Evening Standard*, September 17, 1987, 32–33.

Usher, S. "The Designer Mob Hijacks Al Capone." *Daily Mail*, September 18, 1987, 26.

Spencer, C. "When the Good Guys Have the Last Word." *Daily Telegraph*, September 18, 1987, 10.

Parente, W. "Another Fine Ness." *Scotsman*, September 19, 1987.

Hutchinson, T. "An Offer That Cannot Be Refused." *Mail on Sunday*, September 20, 1987, 38.

French, "De Niro's Touch of Evil." *Observer*, September 20, 1987, 25.

Johnstone, I. "Doing Justice to the Myth of Capone." *Sunday Times*, September 20, 1987, 55.

Driscoll, R. "Untouchable for Character, Beauty, Suspense and Style." *Western Mail*, September 26, 1987, 16.

Penman, I. Review. *The Face*, September 1987, 104–105.

Stanbrook, A. Review. *Films and Filming*, n. 396 (September 1987): 41.

Review. *Monthly Film Bulletin*, v. 54, n. 644 (September 1987): 284.

Cunliffe, S. "Back with a Bang." *Guardian*, October 1, 1987, 13.

Selected Web Forums and Fansites

http://boards.hbo.com/category/sopranos/2

http://forums.televisionwithoutpity.com/index.php?showforum=597

http://sopranos.yuku.com

http://thechaselounge.net

www.contractflicks.com

www.fanpop.com/spots/the-sopranos

www.flixster.com/movie/the-godfather

www.geocities.com/~mikemckiernon

www.imdb.com

www.jgeoff.com/godfather.html

www.mafiaflix.com

www.nj.com/sopranos

www.sopranoland.com

www.thesopranos.com

www.the-sopranos.com

Index